George Heriot

Postmaster-Painter of the Canadas

George Heriot (1759–1839), a Scot, is best known as a skilled landscape watercolourist and as the contentious deputy postmaster general of British North America from 1800 to 1816. He was also a travel writer (his *Travels through the Canadas* was published in 1807) and a poet.

In this volume, a combination of biography and art history, Gerald Finley presents, for the first time, a rounded picture of Heriot, revealing his motives and ideals while also illuminating the texture of life in Canada during the early years of settlement. In describing Heriot's several roles as artist, administrator, patriot, spy, Finley presents a portrait of an eighteenth-century gentleman whose superficial desires were for an active public life but whose deeper yearnings were for a life of contemplation.

As a member of the gentry it was natural that Heriot found his way into public service, for which he was suited both by education and by upbringing. Nevertheless, his public career did not always run smoothly and it ended in frustration and sadness. However, through his writing and especially his art Heriot found welcome relief from the tensions of his public duties.

Indeed, Heriot's chief importance lies in his art. Trained as a topographical artist, he was an important exponent of the picturesque landscape. As a mode of vision the Picturesque furnished him with a special way of looking at and recording the Canadian scene – to him Canada possessed the qualities of Arcadia. This viewpoint served both as aesthetic consolation and as stimulus to inspiration.

This volume serves to recognize Heriot's artistic achievement and to accord him the place he deserves in the history of Canadian art and of the country itself.

GERALD FINLEY is Professor of the History of Art at Queen's University, Kingston.

Self-portrait of George Heriot in silhouette (detail).
A photo-mechanical impression probably made from
a stencilled image in one of Heriot's sketch-books.
New Brunswick Museum, Saint John

GERALD FINLEY

George Heriot

Postmaster-Painter of the Canadas

UNIVERSITY OF TORONTO PRESS

Toronto Buffalo London

Toronto Buffalo London
Reprinted in paperback 2017

ISBN 978-0-8020-5584-2 (cloth)
ISBN 978-1-4875-9854-9 (paper)

Canadian Cataloguing in Publication Data

Finley, Gerald, 1931-
George Heriot: postmaster-painter of the Canadas

Bibliography: p.
'Check-list of the works of George Heriot': p.
Includes indexes.
ISBN 978-0-8020-5584-2 (bound). ISBN 978-1-4875-9854-9 (pbk).

1. Heriot, George, 1759-1839. 2. Painters - Canada - Biography. 3. Postal service - Canada - Postmasters - Biography. I. Title.

ND497.H45F553 759.11 082-095129-3

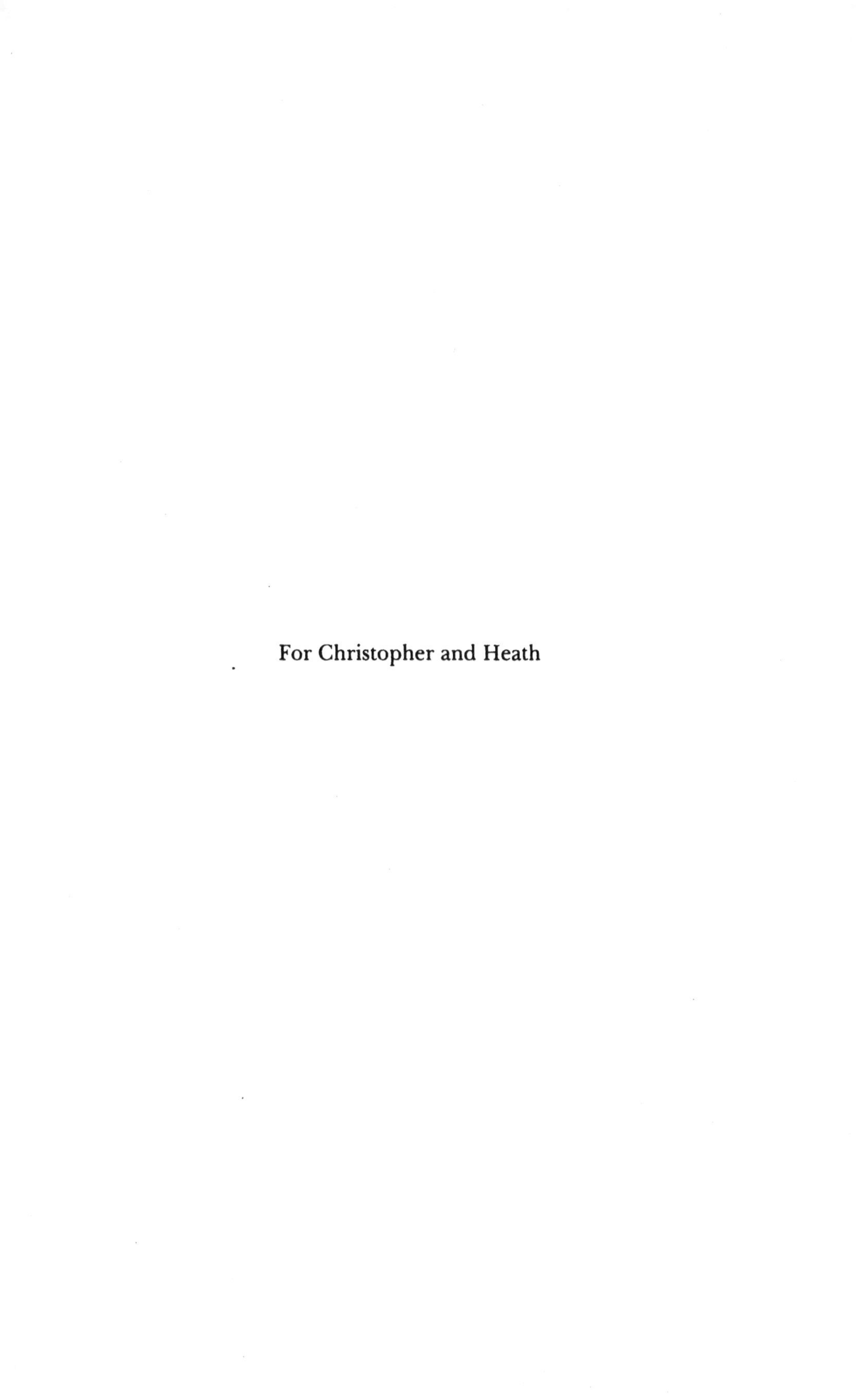

For Christopher and Heath

Contents

Illustrations

The works are by George Heriot unless otherwise specified.

PHOTOGRAPHIC CREDITS

Lloyd Bloom illustration 86
F. de L. Bois illustrations 11, 12, 13
Ken Brown illustration 34
Gladys Cada illustration 47
Courtauld Institute of Art illustration 21
John Freeman illustration 53
Jennifer Harper illustration 79
Kennedy Galleries illustrations 29, 33, 38, 41, 42, 43, 44, 48, 60, 83, 84
Robert Keziere/Vancouver Art Gallery illustration 28
Musée du Québec/Nueville Bazin illustration 90
Tom Scott illustration 1
Ron Vickers Ltd illustrations 15, 46, 51

Preface

George Heriot, one of those important early recorders of Canada, has left only the most elusive shadow behind him. There are few contemporary published references – none of them particularly illuminating, either for his life or for his art. The first comprehensive article on his life, which was published in 1910, has, until recently, also been the most authoritative publication; the author, J.C.A. Heriot, was a descendant (George Heriot was his great-uncle) who lived in Montreal and had a consuming interest in his family's past. This article provides a brief but useful summary of Heriot's Post Office career and some details of his ancestry. J.C.A. Heriot was the first writer to draw attention to the traditional confusion between the artist and his second cousin, 'Major General, the Honourable Frederick George Heriot, C.B., who served with distinction in Canada through the War of 1812.' The article, however, contains insufficient material to offer a clear picture either of Heriot's life and personality or of his art. Moreover, though we are given occasional glimpses of Heriot the painter, the value of the text is reduced by glaring errors, a few of them concerning the watercolours and their chronology – errors which have been repeated by most subsequent writers.

Recent intensive primary research has uncovered new information from which the modern writer on Heriot is able to profit. During the last fifty years significant cultural studies have appeared which illuminate certain relevant aspects of life in the period in which Heriot lived. For example, it is now possible to consider intelligently and fruitfully the concept and movement of the Picturesque (thanks to Christopher Hussey's pioneering study, *The Picturesque*, published in 1927), to discuss the education of an eighteenth-century gentleman (as a result of George C. Brauer Jr's *The Education of a Gentleman*, published in 1959), and to understand the poetic quest for happiness in pastoral retirement in the seventeenth and eighteenth centuries (because of M.S. Roestvig's *The Happy Man*, first published in 1954–8). Such studies as these provide the essential contexts within which to examine the lives of cultured men – and especially artists – such as Heriot, and to come to understand their art.

Very many have assisted me in my researches for this study and my earlier short essay on Heriot (*George Heriot, 1759–1839*, published in 1979). I am under a special obligation to the staffs of the Library of Congress, Washington, DC; the Glasgow Art Galleries; the Public Archives of Canada, Ottawa; the National Gallery of Canada, Ottawa; the Canadiana Department of the Royal Ontario Museum, Toronto; and the McCord Museum, Montreal. Mary Allodi of the Royal Ontario Museum and Conrad Graham of the McCord Museum have been especially helpful. I wish to acknowledge the assistance of the members and staff of La Société Jersiase, and also my debt to the staffs of the Witt Library in London and the Frick Library in New York, whose services have been much valued on more than one occasion, and to the proprietors of the Kennedy Galleries in New York and of the Laing Galleries and the Morris Galleries in Toronto, who have assisted me in various ways. Of those who initially encouraged me and gave me counsel, I owe a special debt to J. Russell Harper, Robert H. Hubbard, Dennis Reid, Kenneth Saltmarche, James John Talman, and the late W.P. Wolfe. During the later stages of preparation I received valued advice and assistance from J.H. Appleby, Roland J. Auger, the late R.G. Bartelot, J. Wallace Beaton, James Burant, Philip Malet de Carterer, Warda Drummond, W.E. Duggan Grey, Michael Ingram, David Irwin, Richard Ivor, George P. Kidd, Hughes Lapointe, Kenneth S. Mackenzie, Louis Melzack, Farquar Mackintosh, Duncan Macmillan, Willis Moogk, Gerald Paget, Matthew Pryor, Dudley Snelgrove, H.C. Torbock, Peter S. Winkworth, and Barbara de Veulle. For information concerning Heriot watercolours and/or the Heriot family I am indebted to W.L. Day, Richard Guy, Christopher Mackonochie, and Lillian Heriot Sternau. Mrs Sternau has been especially generous, providing me with unique documentary materials concerning George Heriot that have greatly assisted me in reconstructing aspects of the artist's final years. I am also grateful to P.T. van der Merwe of the Historical Section of the National Maritime Museum, London who has generously advised me on several occasions on a considerable number of points concerning the events leading up to the War of 1812. There are many who have assisted me in other specific ways and acknowledgment of their aid has been made in the notes to the text and in the check-list. One of the great benefits of my researches has been the personal kindness shown to me by so many, to whom full acknowledgment, unfortunately, cannot be made here. Undoubtedly the most deserving of mention are the private collectors and owners whose generosity, patience, and tolerance have made this undertaking not only eminently worthwhile but, indeed, possible.

For making the project feasible I am deeply indebted to the Queen's University Arts Research Committee, which funded the initial investigation and later provided me with an additional travel grant. I am yet again (as in the case of my recent studies *Landscapes of Memory: Turner as Illustrator to Scott* and *Turner and George IV in Edinburgh, 1822*) deeply indebted to the Social Sciences and Humanities Research Council of Canada. The amount of travelling necessary to complete this book has been considerable and the acquisition of photographs expensive: without the Council's aid I should not have accomplished what I have. The book has been published with the help of a grant from the Canadian Federation for the Humanities, using funds provided by the Social Sciences and Humanities Research Council of Canada, and with the assistance of the Publications Fund of the University of Toronto Press.

A further obligation is to my friends and colleagues who have aided me in special ways. William F.E. Morley, Curator of Special Collections, Douglas Library, Queen's University, and James Brennan of the National Postal Museum, Ottawa, have assisted me on numerous occasions in my quest for Heriot watercolours and for both published and unpublished documents relating to him. Jenny Hope Simpson and Ross Kilpatrick generously translated Heriot's Latin poetry. I am especially indebted to Ross Kilpatrick, who translated several particularly long poems. Pierre du Prey kindly examined the first draft of the short essay and pointed out parts that needed to be tightened. James Pritchard kindly read a draft of this book for its historical accuracy. To J. Douglas Stewart I owe a particular debt. In the late winter, when teaching pressures are at their greatest, he took time to read the final draft of this work, to make valuable suggestions, and to give me encouragement to complete it.

Last, but not least, I wish to thank my wife, Helen, for her counsel. She read without complaint many draft chapters. I am also indebted to the typist of the first draft, Thelma Hodgson, who not only successfully deciphered my rather poor handwriting but also discovered errors and inconsistencies in both text and check-list that I had overlooked.

Because of high production costs it has not been possible to illustrate in this book as broad a range of Heriot's works as I should have wished, nor to include colour plates, which would have furnished a valuable indication of the nature, diversity, and development of his colour. However, further information on Heriot's paintings, watercolours, and prints, and those prints made after his work can be found in the check-list of his works at the end of the book. (An asterisk preceding a check-list number or, in the case of a sketch-book, a folio number, indicates that the listed work or the folio is illustrated in the book.) This check-list, resulting from my wide search for Heriot's art during the investigations for and the preparation of this book, will provide the reader with a better understanding of the nature and variety of Heriot's artistic output.

GF Sommerville House, Kingston, May 1982

Chronology of George Heriot's Life

1759	Born at Haddington, East Lothian, Scotland
1769–74	Student at Royal High School, Edinburgh
1774–7	In Edinburgh; befriended by Sir James Grant of Grant; probably received initial training in art there
1777–81	In London; seeks career as an artist; leaves suddenly for West Indies, remaining there for four years; composes *A Descriptive Poem, written in the West Indies* (1781)
1781–92	Returns to England; becomes officer cadet at Royal Military Academy, Woolwich; studies topographical drawing under Paul Sandby; c 1783 appointed clerk at Arsenal, Woolwich, remaining in that position until departure for Quebec in 1792; travels to Channel Islands between c 1786 and 1787
1792–6	Settles in Quebec City, possibly at 6 Rampart Street; takes up position as clerk of cheque in Ordnance; visits Montreal
1796–7	Visits Britain; travels in England and Scotland; enrols at Edinburgh University; returns to London in early 1797; exhibits three watercolours at Royal Academy exhibition, spring 1797; returns to Canada
1798–1800	Visits La Malbaie; appointed assistant storekeeper, Ordnance; appointment suddenly withdrawn in 1799; takes up appointment as deputy postmaster general of British North America in 1800 and begins planning for the development of postal services, especially in Upper Canada
1801–2	Travels to Niagara and probably to York on postal business; attempts unsuccessfully to secure position of superintendent of *maîtres de poste* (provincial post-houses)

1804–5	Appointed clerk of survey, Ordnance Department, 12 March 1804; publishes first and only volume of *The History of Canada* (1804); visits Niagara probably in 1804, certainly in 1805
1806	Returns to Britain; travels through Scotland and possibly England
1807	Sails to Halifax from Britain; meets Judge Edward Winslow, who accompanies him on postal business, possibly around Nova Scotia and certainly through New Brunswick; publishes *Travels through the Canadas*
1808	Visits Niagara and probably York on postal business
1809	Attends special fête at Spencer Wood given by Sir James Craig, the lieutenant governor of Lower Canada, perhaps to celebrate fiftieth anniversary of Anglican services held at Quebec
1813	Attempt made to force Heriot to take Ordnance post at Kingston; Heriot refuses and is suspended from Ordnance
1815	Travels through eastern United States on postal affairs and intelligence mission; travels at least as far south as Washington, DC
1816	Travels to Niagara, Sandwich, and Amherstburg on postal business; resigns as deputy postmaster general; returns to Britain and settles in London; travels to Scotland; visits the south of England
1817–18	Continental tour; France, Italy (as far south as Sicily), Austria, Hungary, Germany (possibly)
1819	Visits Scotland
1820	Continental tour: France, Spain
1821	Travels in England
1822	Lives in Chelsea, London
1823	Visits Wales
1824	Lives in Dover Street, London; publishes *A Picturesque Tour … through the Pyrenean Mountains* (only two parts of which were published)
1828	Continental tour: France
1833	Death of brother John during cholera epidemic
1834	Lives at 7 Cadogan Place, London; sends many North American sketches to son of his brother Roger in South Carolina
1839	Dies at his residence at 32 Sloane Street, London, on 22 July

George Heriot
Postmaster-Painter of the Canadas

1

Topographical Landscape and the Picturesque

A Scottish painter who spent the central and most fruitful years of his life in Canada, George Heriot was a gifted member of that group of topographical artists who, during the late eighteenth and early nineteenth centuries, brought an imaginative interpretation of the picturesque idiom to bear on the depiction of landscape not only in Britain but also in Britain's colonies.

In Canada landscape painting really began with the conquest of Quebec by the British in 1759–60. For the ensuing hundred years British artists, working as administrators, clerks, or military officers in the service of the Empire, were to produce some of the finest pictorial records of colonial Canada's life and terrain that have come down to us. In order to understand what these men set out to achieve it will be helpful to consider briefly the origins of topographical art in Britain and its growth up to the late eighteenth century, and then to examine, in fuller detail, the influence which picturesque theory began to exercise on it from that time.

Of the artists who were working in Canada during the relevant period, three of the most significant, all born in the eighteenth century, were Thomas Davies (c 1739–1812), James Pattison Cockburn (1779–1847), and the subject of this study, George Heriot (1759–1839). All three received their training in topographical drawing at the Royal Military Academy at Woolwich, where they came under the influence of Paul Sandby (1725–1809), who was drawing master there from 1768 until 1799.

The training in topographical drawing which the gentleman cadet received was an essential and eminently practical part of his preparation for a career as an army officer. It equipped him to document terrain, structures, and troop deployment, to facilitate the planning of manœvres, and to provide historical records. However, the surviving drawings and watercolours executed by men who were trained in this way are mainly those painted during their leisure hours. These works are usually views of towns and countryside that were recorded because of their attractiveness or because they possessed personal associations for the artist. The styles and interests of Davies, Cockburn, and Heriot, as exhibited in their Canadian watercolours and drawings, are varied and distinctive. For subject-matter Cockburn seemed to enjoy the bustling urban scene, while both Heriot and Davies preferred the remoteness of the countryside and the outlying settlements or the grandeur of the Canadian rivers and forests. Their interests reflect those of most British topographical artists working in Canada during the colonial period and are part of a long-established tradition which had nothing to do with military draughtsmanship.

Topographical landscape drawings of English subjects dating at least as early as the first half of the sixteenth century were often commissioned by members of the court for either their strategic value or their descriptive content. By the end of the century documents indicate that topographical views were widely favoured and quite avidly collected for their purely artistic qualitites as well as for their descriptive value. The walls of Lord Burghley's house, Theobalds, were hung with a series of landscapes 'of the most important towns of Christendom.'[1] In another compartment of the house were pictures which 'depicted the kingdom of England, with all its cities, towns and villages, mountains and rivers.'[2] The frequent visits of Queen Elizabeth I, which prompted Burghley to enlarge Theobalds, may also have encouraged him to assemble this collection of views for her pleasure and entertainment. Such evidence suggests that topographical landscape representations were rising in esteem. Yet the depth and extent of interest in this genre in England during the first half of the seventeenth century is difficult to determine, since most topographical landscapes were engraved, and accounts of collections of engravings made at this time are rare.

We are better informed about the collecting of topographical landscape paintings during the second half of the seventeenth century. By that time increasing numbers of topographical artists from the Continent were visiting or settling in England, including several notable figures such as Wenceslaus Hollar from Bohemia, Jan Siberechts from Flanders, and

Leonard Knyff from Holland. The growing importance of topographical landscape painting did not lie simply in the strategic purposes for which it was to be employed for a long period to come or in the desire to record great cities. Topographical landscapes were increasingly being commissioned by the aristocracy and substantial gentry, who wanted their vast estates and great houses to be recorded in this way, not only as an index of their belongings, but as tangible symbols of social and political power and evidence of personal achievement. Knyff made a grand series of eighty drawings of country houses and royal residences, which were engraved by Johannes Kip and published by him in his *Britannia illustrata* (1707–8). It was mainly for proprietorial reasons that the volume of topographical landscape painting was maintained – and, indeed, expanded – during the prosperous years of the eighteenth century.

But in the eighteenth century topographical landscapes, considered purely as art, were seldom deemed worthy of particular attention. In his XIII Discourse of 1786 Sir Joshua Reynolds, then at the height of his fame as a portrait painter and president of the Royal Academy, noted that 'ordinary and common' views were vastly inferior to those produced by the 'poetical mind,' which did not require specific references in landscape. The basic distinctions between them, he suggested, were akin to the relationship existing between 'cold prosaick narration or description' and the poetry of Milton's 'L'Allegro' and 'Il Penseroso.' An imaginary scene, he believed, could 'make a more forcible impression on the mind than the real scenes, were they presented before us.'[3] Thomas Gainsborough, Reynolds's illustrious contemporary, shared his low opinion of specific views. In a letter to Lord Hardwicke, written about 1764 in response to a request for a topographical painting, Gainsborough wrote: 'Mr Gainsborough presents his humble respects to Lord Hardwicke, and shall always think it an honour to be employed in anything for his Lordship, but with respect to real views from Nature ... he has never seen any place that affords a subject equal to the poorest imitations of Gaspar or Claude.'[4]

Reynolds's and Gainsborough's reactions were typical of the prevalent academic distaste for topographical views, which were considered to be deficient in invention or in imaginative manipulation. In other words, to paint a topographical view was to indulge in a mechanical and uncreative activity. Yet well-born and propertied persons of the seventeenth and eighteenth centuries, neither connected with art academies nor formally acquainted with the society of artists, considered topographical views to be both familiar and eminently desirable commodities. They were to be found in folios of engravings, in printed books, and, even more readily to hand, on drawingroom walls. They were as much a part of the domestic setting as the family portrait.

Possibly because of this strong and widespread attachment in Britain to painted topographical landscapes, academies, while not approving of them, were not entirely, or too strongly, opposed to them. After all, the topographical artist Paul Sandby had become a founding member of the Royal Academy in 1768. When Gainsborough declined the commission for a topographical view from Lord Hardwicke, and observed that he had never seen 'any place that affords a subject equal to the poorest imitation of Gaspar or Claude,' he did add that 'Paul Sandby is the only man of genius ... who has employed his pencil that way.' Even Reynolds, who refused to consider topographical views to be within the realm of art, was prepared to accept the principle that such views could be raised to a higher level of aesthetic significance.

Reynolds proposed that to do this the topographical draughtsman should acquaint himself with the imaginary or ideal views of Italianate French painters of the seventeenth-century classical school, such as Claude Lorraine, Gaspard Dughet, and Nicolas Poussin. He believed that by wedding their generalized manner with a particular view a topographical painter could elevate a specific landscape to the realm of art.[5] However, by the time Reynolds publicly proclaimed the value of this union (1786) the idea was hardly novel: the 'elevation' of specific landscape views was by then widely familiar and generally practised.

By the beginning of the eighteenth century, when Englishmen were beginning to discover the beauties of wild nature, they were also beginning to seek an aesthetic system by which to evaluate scenery. They discovered it in the idealized landscapes of the French Italianate school, and also in those of the Italian Salvator Rosa; increasingly, too, the classicizing features of the Italianate Dutch landscapes, such as those of Jan Both and Nicolas Berchem, began to capture their attention. The superiority of idealized nature in paintings was espoused also in French and Italian theoretical works. Perhaps one of the most influential of these treatises was C.A. Dufresnoy's theoretical work, in Latin verse, *De arte graphica*, translated into French by Roger De Piles (published in 1668) and into English by John Dryden (whose translation was first published in 1695).

Concepts concerning the ideal expressed in these treatises influenced both the outlook and the writings of cultivated Englishmen such as Anthony Ashley Cooper (1671–1713), Third Earl of Shaftesbury, and Jonathan Richardson, the portrait painter. Shaftesbury's *Characteristicks*, first published in 1711, brought the discussion of the Ideal forcefully into English critical writing. In Richardson's *An Essay on the Theory of Painting* (1715), which was designed as much to inform the taste of gentlemen as to enlighten artists, the author draws attention to the link between the Ideal and landscape painting. Both Shaftesbury and Richardson were seeking rules by which they could judge works of art, and both certainly found these in the theory of the Ideal.

Shaftesbury advised the artist to employ idealization, because 'A PAINTER, if he has any Genius, understands the *Truth* and Unity of Design; and knows he is even then unnatural, when he follows nature too close, and strictly copies *Life*. For his Art allows him not to bring *All* Nature into his Piece, but *a Part* only.'[6] Richardson clarified the process of achieving the Ideal: 'a painter must raise his ideas beyond what he sees, and form a model of perfection in his own mind which is not to be found in reality, but yet such a one as is probable and rational.' In comparing Dutch, Flemish, and Italian masters of 'low subjects' Richardson considered the Italian painters superior, since 'they have not servilely followed common nature, but raised, and improved, or at least have always made the best choice of it. This gives a dignity to a low subject, and is the reason of the esteem we have for the landscapes of Salvator Rosa ... Claude Lorrain, the Poussins.'[7]

However, the theory of the Ideal soon hardened into a set of rules for the critic's guidance, and Shaftesbury emphasized the necessity of such rules in forming any judgments on works of art: 'I LIKE! I fancy! I admire! How? By accident: or *as I please*. No. But I *learn* to fancy, to admire, *to please*, as the Subjects themselves are deserving, and can bear me out. Otherwise, I like at this hour, but dislike the next. I shall be weary of my Pursuit, and, upon experience, find little *Pleasure* in the main, if my Choice and Judgment in it be from no other Rule than that single one, *because I please*.'[8]

It was against this background that Reynolds's theory of the Ideal evolved, and paintings of specific landscapes, such as those by Richard Wilson, were developed or modified to conform to principles determined largely by classical landscape. Topographical features essential to the identification of a view were retained but simplified, and subordinate elements, such as foreground and lighting, were manipulated according to classical tenets. In this way Wilson created the 'classicized' topographical view: one that evoked sentiment, or, as Reynolds would have put it (had he been more appreciative of Wilson's art), 'poetical' feeling.

While Reynolds's precepts and Wilson's canvases produced clear evidence of how topographical landscape could be fortified and elevated by elements of the classical style, there was perhaps a less focused yet none the less widely influential source of inspiration for the 'idealized' specific view. This was the theory and practice of the Picturesque. The picturesque movement owes its inception to the Reverend William Gilpin, an amateur artist and writer, who, during the 1760s and 1770s, devised the theory while considering ways of aesthetically examining landscapes. In his theoretical works and practical guides, most of which were published between 1782 and 1809, he provided step-by-step instructions by which to understand landscape in terms of art – for such was the basis of the Picturesque. Gilpin's theory, like Edmund Burke's *A Philosophical Enquiry into the Origins of Our Ideas of the Sublime and Beautiful* (1757), greatly enriched critical language and effectively broadened the aesthetic framework for the examination and appreciation of nature. By a thorough study of it Gilpin was able to 'evolve and formulate a general aesthetic attitude to landscape, which was to have considerable influence in determining English taste for fifty years or more.'[9]

During the last half-century much has been written on the theories of both the Picturesque and the Sublime. However, their practical importance for the art of landscape painting in the late eighteenth century had not been considered deeply until recently, and has never been adequately explained. Therefore it is essential that their relationships and practical importance be discussed, since their impact on the nature of topographical landscape painting was considerable.

Though Gilpin was a thinker of far fewer intellectual gifts than Burke, and with no special talents as an aesthetician, nevertheless he sought to devise an aesthetic system that was more practicable than Burke's – one that would assist the traveller and the artist in their appreciation of the natural scene. Despite Burke's assertion that the Sublime and the Beautiful could not be mixed, Gilpin believed that they were often conjoined in nature (although he admitted that, even when they were successfully combined, either one or the other principle should dominate). It was probably because he was convinced that the Sublime and the Beautiful could be blended that he devised his aesthetic system of the Picturesque, in which he could accommodate both.

Despite Gilpin's misleading assertion that the Picturesque was a 'species' of beauty, evidence provided in his tour guides supports the view that he did in fact believe it to be a separate aesthetic category. Perhaps when he stated that the Picturesque was a 'species' of beauty and assigned to it the quality of 'ruggedness' (Burke had referred to the 'rugged' and 'negligent' quality of the Sublime[10]), Gilpin was trying, in an awkward and illogical way, to illustrate the special character of the Picturesque, in which qualities of the Beautiful and the Sublime could be combined. (Such inconsistencies in Gilpin's theory resulted in those celebrated reassessments of it published by Uvedale Price and Richard Payne Knight.[11]) Still, it was because within a practical context Gilpin denied the validity of the totally separate and independent nature of Burke's categories that subsequent travel writers, tutored in the principles of the Picturesque, referred to the Sublime and the Beautiful in nature mainly in the Gilpinian sense. A picturesque view required ruggedness, which could be reinforced by other qualities, such as irregularity, variety, and light and shade. In addition, the picturesque landscape needed to possess 'the power to stimulate the imagination.'[12] Through his writings – which, as we have seen, include many travel guides – Gilpin not only described but critically analysed the landscape of Britain. Through them the traveller – or, indeed, the artist – could learn to appreciate new subjects and certain effects equivalent to those in art.

By the time Gilpin began publishing his theoretical works and tour guides, the habit of associating scenes in nature with landscape paintings of the classical school (such as those of the Italianate French painters Claude, Gaspard, and Poussin, as well as the Neapolitan Salvator Rosa) had already become well established. Writers of travel guides, therefore, readily accepted Gilpin's ideas, often referring to locations which they believed to be reminiscent of scenes found in paintings by these artists and sometimes remarking on their picturesque properties; they would even provide, in their published guides, special 'stations' or viewing-points that would present painterly scenes to the traveller's view.[13] To reinforce the picturesqueness of a landscape travellers sometimes carried a 'Claude glass,' which provided a reflection of nature that seemed like a painting. The 'glass' was a slightly convex mirror of black glass which reflected scenes of nature gathered by its convexity and which, by 'reducing the colours to a lower ratio,' described 'tonal values of the various planes, thus modifying a natural scene into a picturesque, idealized, "Claudian" view.'[14]

It is evident from journals that the tourist and painter alike 'saw' pictures in nature at almost every turn of the road. Charles Dibdin noted that 'Cumberland calls for the saucy touch of *Salvator Rosa*,'[15] while Arthur Young asserted that Lake Windermere presented scenes 'as elegant as ever fancied by *Claud* himself.'[16] James Denholm found that 'the rich vale of Leven had mountains reminiscent of the striking productions of Salvator Rosa,' while its lake had 'more of the character of the soft and pleasing pictures of Claude.'[17] Henry P. Wyndham found at Pont Aberglaslyn in Wales a tremendous cliff, much greater than could have been conceived by the 'eccentric and romantic imagination of Salvator Rosa.'[18]

Although Gilpin may not have made many references to works by specific painters of the classical school, the construction of their paintings provided him with the basic form of the picturesque view. Such a view would usually require framing 'side screens' or coulisses – usually of trees but sometimes of mountains or hills or even the banks of a river. In addition, there would be three spatial grounds, such as were present in the classical landscape. According to Gilpin, there should be a foreground of dark tonality, often silhouetted against a lighter middle ground and a still lighter distance or background. Of the three grounds, the forward ground was usually singled out by him for its especial significance. 'The foreground,' stated Gilpin, 'is a mere spot, compared with the extension of distance: in itself it is of trivial consequence; and cannot well be called a *feature of the scene*. And yet, tho so little essential in *giving a likeness*, it is more so than any other part in *forming a composition*.'[19]

Gilpin discovered that in a painting or a drawing 'broken ground' was suitably picturesque in the shadowed area of the nearest plane because of its 'accidental outlines and rough shapes.' The coulisses provided a silhouetted, fretted framework for the illuminated middle ground and background. In Gilpin's opinion such foreground framing elements would prevent the eye from wandering, and the picture from being turned into a 'map.'[20] The importance of the foreground was echoed by travel writers, such as Dibdin, who felt that the finest properties of a painted landscape would be destroyed 'where you have no foreground.'[21] Humphrey Repton, the landscape gardener, asserted that the painter's composition 'must have a foreground; and though it may only consist of a single tree, a rail, or a piece of broken road, it is absolutely necessary to the painter's landscape.' Repton summed up the importance of the foreground in Claude's paintings by comparing it to a window which 'would exclude all view from that adjoining.'[22]

The conceptual approach of the Picturesque might at first seem alien to the mode of specific landscape representation. And, indeed, Gilpin opposed the drawing of specific scenery. According to him, nature should be perceived initially in as non-particular a way as possible. A person who understood the principles of the Picturesque could modify the scene in his mind's eye, transform it, and make it approach perfection. The viewer's attitude to nature, according to Gilpin, must be 'creative and not imitative.'[23] Specific landscape might serve as inspiration but never as the final object of the painter's endeavours. Thus Gilpin, like Reynolds, believing in the idea of *general* nature, directed the aspiring artist to avoid 'painful exactness' and rather to 'concentrate on catching the *spirit* and *truth* of the original.'[24] What he proposed was similar to that which Wilson had practised years before: the creation of specific but elevated landscape in which the essential character of the topography was retained, with subordinate or inconsequential parts modified or redistributed to meet the compositional requirements of the classical landscape and thereby assisting in the generation of mood. Since Gilpin's Picturesque was a principle built largely on the general structure of classical landscape rather than on any specific conception of style, painted landscapes influenced by it are diverse. What they shared was a schematic type of composition, irregular surfaces and edges, and certain preferred landscape settings (often either mountainous or rural).

While in theory there was no limit to the variety of subjects suitable for picturesque landscapes, in practice Gilpin suggested those which seemed to him to possess the essential qualities of the Picturesque. It was perhaps for this reason that he often chose to describe the irregular and rough outlines associated with water scenery. What attracted him to water was its broken lights (caused by constantly changing surfaces), and also the irregularity of river banks and of the shorelines of lakes. In addition, waterfalls had a particular charm for Gilpin. The broken lines of small cascades undoubtedly possessed picturesque potential, though they were not perhaps as moving as the almost pure sublimity of the vast, uniform waterfall.[25]

But for the leading subject in a landscape Gilpin would invariably choose an ancient ruin. He found the ruin particularly picturesque, because of its crumbling, splintered, blotched surfaces, and because it stimulated associative ideas. 'The reigning ideas,' he believed, were '*solitude*, *neglect*, and *desolation*.'[26] Broken and irregular rock forms and bent, fractured, and gnarled trees were the equivalent, he considered, of decayed architecture, for he refers to them as 'natural ruins.'[27] Gilpin claimed that trees were appropriate adjuncts in Salvator Rosa's pictures because, in their bent and splintered majesty, they suited the character of Salvator's stormy landscapes. Indeed, Gilpin declared the 'blasted tree' to be a perfect subject and fully appropriate in a view where 'the dreary heath is spread before the eye and ideas of wildness and desolation are required.' 'What more suitable accompaniment can be imagined,' Gilpin asked, 'than the blasted oak ragged, scathed, and leafless; shooting its peeled, white branches athwart the gathering blackness of some rising storm?'[28] This tree evoked the same associations as did the ancient architectural ruin: these 'remnants of decaying grandeur speak to the imagination in a stile of eloquence, which the stripling cannot reach: they record the history of some storm, some blast of lightning or other great event which transfers its grand ideas to the landscape; and in the representation of elevated subjects assists the sublime.'[29]

No wonder that early visitors to Canada should have considered the landscape a suitable subject for the picturesque brush, with its abundant water and waterfalls, and its wilderness amply supplied with craggy rocks and 'blasted' trees. Indeed, since there were so few ancient ruined buildings in North America, such trees became accepted as excellent substitutes. As the blasted tree was also equated by Gilpin with wilderness landscape, it is not surprising that, in the early twentieth century, through the paintings of the Group of Seven, it was to become the chief symbol of Canada's northern frontier.

In the eighteenth century a knowledge of and practice of the principles of art (as espoused by Reynolds and put into effect by Wilson) and of the theory of the Picturesque were normally restricted to those who sought a career in art or to those interested laymen who enjoyed sufficient leisure to pursue the necessary studies. The latter belong largely to the upper strata of English society: they were young men of breeding, who, as future leaders of society, considered it a moral obligation to become widely informed on, and reasonably accomplished in, a variety of subjects. It was their responsibility, they believed, to learn at least a little about a good deal. The young gentleman was tutored in the fundamentals of the natural sciences and mathematics, in Latin, French, and possibly Italian, and was also given a solid grounding in history. Further, he was often instructed, formally or otherwise, in the 'polite accomplishments,' such as drawing, architecture, and music.[30]

Drawing was undoubtedly attractive to young men who would have the opportunity of making a Grand Tour of Europe, where such an 'accomplishment' would be useful. Proficiency rather than excellence was recommended. Too much attention to art might distract the young gentleman from those subjects which bore more directly on his future public duties. Lord Chesterfield believed that a gentleman should most certainly have a knowledge of painting and sculpture, yet only to a 'certain degree ... [for] they must only be the amusements, and not the business of a man of parts.'[31]

Despite the tendency in the seventeenth and eighteenth centuries to subordinate the 'polite accomplishments' to more 'serious' subjects, the importance of the former in the gentleman's education cannot be denied. Their significance is surely attested to by that conspicuous cultural phenomenon, the gentleman amateur, who emerged so strongly during the eighteenth century. 'Amateurs' they were, though the term then lacked the pejorative connotation with which it is burdened today. These were often quite knowledgeable men, whose contributions were sometimes notable. They might study architecture or art, and from their experience and reflection publish dissertations or gather together collections of *vertu*. As artists they made their contribution mainly in terms of landscape (in which subject, as landowners, they displayed considerable interest) and often in watercolour. This was their preferred medium in the late eighteenth century because it required little equipment and effects could be achieved relatively quickly. While amateurs may have been less significant as painters than as architects or collectors, none the less their contribution remains historically important. Indeed, it may be said that they, often as much as any other group of artists, provided the picturesque synthesis of the topographical view and the classical landscape.

As I have suggested, military academies, such as Woolwich, were influential in the training of those topographical artists who worked in Britain and the colonies. However, to see only a simple causal relationship here is to lose sight of the importance of the cultural background of those who attended the academies. These officers in training (such as George Heriot himself) were gentlemen cadets and thus mainly members of the gentry, or sometimes of noble families. In their recent youth they had had the benefit of a liberal education and often of the opportunity to practise in art. When these young gentlemen came to an academy like Woolwich (as Davies, Cockburn, and Heriot did), they arrived with already developed habits of perception and skills as draughtsmen that further tutelage under a superior artist or sensitive teacher, such as Paul Sandby, served to strengthen and refine. That their styles are so individual certainly speaks well of their teacher, yet it also suggests that the essential elements of these personal styles had been formed before they came to Woolwich.

2

The Formative Years

George Heriot was born in Haddington in 1759, the eldest son of John Heriot. His father was a convinced Tory and a member of Scotland's lesser gentry who had received the Crown appointment of sheriff clerk of Haddington, as had his father and grandfather before him. George's mother, Marjory Heriot, was a distant cousin of her husband, whose family lived at Ladykirk, Berwickshire, to the southeast of Haddington. George had a sister, Sophia (dates unknown), who married Melmoth Guy, nephew of Lord Saye and Sele. There were also two younger brothers. John (1760–1833), who was to become George's closest friend, served initially in the Marines, then began a literary career, and also became a newspaper editor; his final post, however, was as comptroller of the Royal Military Hospital at Chelsea. Roger (1769–1849) eventually settled in Charleston, South Carolina. Almost nothing is known about the first years of George's life – although he and John appear to have begun school in Berwickshire, first at Duns and subsequently at Coldstream. They were then sent to Edinburgh for further and more intensive education.

EDINBURGH

It was in 1769, when he was ten, that George arrived in Edinburgh to begin advanced studies at the Royal High School.[1] During his stay, which lasted until 1774, he was directed by two classical masters, Luke Fraser (1736–1821) and the rector, Dr Alexander Adam (1741–1809).[2] Fraser, under whom Heriot worked for four academic years, was considered to be 'a good Latin scholar and a very worthy man.' He prepared his pupils thoroughly in the fundamentals of the language by drilling them daily in vocabulary and by forcing them to memorize long passages from their grammatical textbooks. But his manner was dogmatic and his lessons were dull. 'Fraser took his pupils on to Corderius's uninspiring *Colloquia*,' readings from 'four or five lives from the *De viris illustribus* of Cornelius Nepos, and the first four books of Caesar's commentaries, *De bello gallico*.'[3]

Dr Alexander Adam, under whose tutelage Heriot spent his final year, was a man of seemingly limitless energies and devotion to his subject. His books, such as *Principles of Latin and English Grammar* (1772) and *Roman Antiquities* (1791), established for him a considerable reputation as a scholar, but, above all, Adam was known for his skills as a teacher. One illustrious former student described him as 'generally patient, though not, when intolerably provoked, without due fits of gentle wrath; inspiring to his boys, especially the timid and backward; enthusiastically delighted with every appearance of talent or goodness; a warm encourager by praise, play and kindness; and constantly under the strongest sense of duty.'[4] Attached to such a teacher, the young Heriot must have flourished. Adam placed much greater emphasis than Fraser on the content, rather than the form, of language. It must have been a relief for Heriot to be able to read with some enjoyment the prose of Sallust, Caesar, and Livy, the plays of Terence, and the poetry of Horace and Virgil. It was presumably under Adam that Heriot developed the enthusiasm for classical learning which later led to his studying Latin at the University of Edinburgh.

Heriot left the Royal High School in 1774. It was not until 1777 that he departed for London, but we know hardly anything of his life during the intervening years. This period, when he was between the ages of fifteen and eighteen, must have been crucial for him, and Edinburgh, which was then at the height of a cultural renaissance, would have been a highly stimulating environment for a youth at the most impressionable stage of his development. We can assume that it was probably during these years that Heriot discovered that he possessed a talent for writing, as well as an interest and a skill in art which were above the average.

In Edinburgh Heriot, as a result of his family's connections, probably had the opportunity to study landscape paintings in private collections: works by old masters as well as by well-known Edinburgh artists, such as members of the Norie family, whose classical compositions and views of Scottish scenery embellished the overdoors and overmantels of many of the better residences of Edinburgh and in its environs (see figure 68). However, the artist with whose landscapes Heriot is most likely to have become acquainted was Alexander Runciman (1736–85). On the occasion of his appointment as master to the Edinburgh Trustees' Academy in 1772 (almost immediately after his return from Italy, where he had been since 1767), Runciman was spoken of as an artist 'whose genius has been well known to the people of taste in this country' (figure 1). It is possible that Heriot attended the Trustees' Academy, where Runciman taught until 1785. Although the aims of the Academy had been to develop technical and industrial drawing skills, under Runciman's régime an emphasis on fine arts had been introduced, allowing the enrolment of increasing numbers of students who wished to 'make drawings merely as amusement.'[5] (Even though we cannot establish a recorded connection between Runciman and Heriot, we shall see that Heriot's earliest known watercolour seems to possess some stylistic qualities in common with drawings by Runciman.)

Whether or not Heriot studied with Runciman at the Trustees' Academy, it seems probable that he had some tutelage in landscape drawing during these years, for his developing abilities were soon noticed and sufficiently appreciated to assure him of their existence: letters prove that the young man was befriended and encouraged by the Scottish Maecenas, Sir James Grant of Grant (1738–1811). Heriot's family connections may have made possible the young man's initial contact with Grant, but it seems that Grant was soon attracted to Heriot by his seriousness of purpose and the potential of his talent.

LONDON

By about this time Heriot's father had encountered financial difficulties, with the result that his son John was forced to seek a career in the Marines. George, however, with Grant's encouragement, moved to London in 1777 in the hope either of attending classes at the Royal Academy or of finding an apprenticeship in an artist's studio. Grant provided the young man with a letter of introduction to his friend the great architect and Royal Academician Robert Adam, then at the peak of his fame, hoping that Adam could advise Heriot and also, with his influence and connections, ease him into the artistic profession.

Heriot's first meeting with Adam took place in August 1777, shortly after the aspiring artist had arrived in London, armed with his letter of introduction. Adam asked to see some of Heriot's work; unfortunately, Heriot had not brought any work with him and had to return the next day to remedy this omission. At the second meeting the young Heriot felt crushed, for, after examining his drawings, Adam seemed to imply that Heriot 'did not need to trouble to call for [sic] him again.' Upset, Heriot wrote to his patron, convinced that a further letter of introduction, to another of Grant's illustrious acquaintances, would now be necessary.[6]

But Heriot had misjudged Adam. Some time after posting his letter to Grant, Heriot received an invitation from Adam to meet him again, and on this occasion he was struck by what seemed to him Adam's complete change of manner. Adam now treated Heriot 'with the greatest kindness,' and furthermore, with a view to seeking an apprenticeship for him, 'made application in my favour to some of the most eminent Painters, particularly Sir Joshua Reynolds who is his intimate Friend, and President of the Royal Academy.' Heriot's misunderstanding of Adam's true intentions adumbrates his later inability to assess situations; but, even though Adam did his best for the young man, the results of his enquiries were not encouraging, and Heriot reported to his patron that 'few or none of the Artists take apprentices or journeymen.'

Heriot also considered the possibility of attending the Royal Academy Schools. He was optimistic about his chances of acceptance, believing that admission to that institution was 'very easy,' depending simply on his making a drawing from a plaster cast and showing it 'to a Gentleman [the Keeper] who is appointed for that purpose.' Because his family's financial difficulties forced him to practise a strict economy, he considered the free tuition a real advantage. However, he expressed regret that students were not granted an 'allowance or Salary as in France.'

But when Heriot proposed entering the Royal Academy it seems that he did not receive much family encouragement. Also, his associates advised him to seek a more practical vocation: 'Some Gentlemen who are my friends and welwishers advise me to lay aside the thoughts of following Painting, and endeavour to get into a Merchant or Banker's House.' Adam himself had encouraged this last course because of Heriot's situation, but he explained to the young man that finding a position in commerce would be difficult. Adam did, however, promise to assist him by giving him suitable recommendations.

Yet Heriot still nurtured a desire to pursue art. He realized the difficulties which confronted him, for there was keen competition. A large number of artists and art students in London found it impossible to earn a living at all, and even those endowed with considerable talent were 'complaining for want of employment.' Indeed, some were forced to leave their 'native Country, and seek [employment] ... in the most distant parts of the world.'[7] This was the dilemma that Heriot faced at the age of eighteen. It is not known whether Heriot took a Royal Academy drawing test. He certainly did not enrol as a student, for in 1777, in the very year of his arrival in London, he set sail for the West Indies.

THE WEST INDIES

Why Heriot suddenly left London is not known. There are several possibilities, which are not mutually exclusive. He may have failed the Academy test or he may have been unable to secure an apprenticeship. Also, his proposed career in art may have been opposed by his parents, who probably considered public service to be the most desirable occupation for someone of their class. Whatever the reasons, the West Indies must, in any case, have seemed to offer an attractive and exciting alternative to Heriot's existence in London; and the difficult circumstances of his family in Scotland would have done nothing to reconcile him to a life at home. One of his favourite poets, Edmund Waller (1606–87), had written a poem, *Battel of the Summer Islands*, in which he depicted the western hemisphere's Bermudas as a tropical Elysium.[8] Heriot's youthful imagination and enthusiasm were probably ignited by Waller's description, and he seemed to believe that in the West Indies he could both reassess his life and future and broaden his education.

In the eighteenth century foreign travel was considered an essential ingredient of a young gentleman's education, in many cases more essential than book learning. Lord Chesterfield remarked: 'No degree of learning will make a skilful minister: whereas a great deal of knowledge of the world, of the characters, passions, and habits of mankind, has, without one grain of learning, made a thousand. Military men have seldom much knowledge of books; their education does not allow it; but what makes great amends for that want is, that they generally know a great deal of the world; they are thrown into it young.'[9] That Heriot regarded his visit to the West Indies as educational is confirmed by his *A Descriptive Poem, written in the West Indies* (1781), which is largely modelled on Waller's *Battel of the Summer Islands*. Heriot makes it clear in this poem that his purpose was to learn both 'science and virtue' in the West Indies.

Heriot remained in the islands for four years, at a time when he had little, if any, financial support from home, and thus it is likely that he found employment there, perhaps in a minor civil service position connected with the military establishment. However, if he had employment, it did not interfere with the cultivation of those artistic and literary interests in which his creativity was to find at least partial fulfilment. On his return to England in 1781 he wrote to Sir James Grant:

> During my residences in the tropical Climates, I employed myself chiefly in the study of Natural History, for which in the West India Islands this is a large field. I travelled on this pursuit from one island to another, making curious drawings from Nature, and taking some views of those different places. I have likewise wrote [of] the present state of those Islands, particularly where the seat of war is.[10] By this means I have had the Honour to recommend myself to the notice and regard of the Royal Society, and to procure their leave and indulgence, to inscribe to them a small Poetical work of mine, written in the West Indies, A Copy of which, I shall take the first convenient opportunity of transmitting to you. I sailed from Saint Eustatius on the third of May last, and arrived at Portsmouth on the 26th of June.[11]

It was perhaps coincidental that Heriot's brother John, who by now had joined the Marines, was in the West Indies during the same period. John, a subaltern on the frigate HMS *Brune*, had experienced the destructive hurricane that struck the coast of Barbados in October 1780. He recorded that the storm 'so fearfully devastated ... [the island that it] nearly reduced [it] to ruin,' and believed that he was fortunate to have escaped death there. Indeed, he was so relieved that he 'ever after commemorated the return of that day as one of solemn festival and devout gratitude.'[12] George may also have witnessed the storm while there, for in his poem he alludes to the hurricane: 'Horrors like these, of late *Jamaica* felt, / And most the Carribean isles. – But thou / *Barbadoes* chiefly.'[13]

While we may speculate about whether or not the young Heriot visited Barbados, there is little doubt that he travelled to Jamaica. There exists a watercolour (the earliest of all his watercolours to come to light) dating from these West Indian years which depicts the White River, St Mary's Jamaica (figure 2). Probably executed when Heriot was between eighteen and twenty-two, it is of special interest. Ambitious in size and composition (though clumsy in execution), this finished watercolour appears to reflect the stylistic influence of the drawings of Runciman, the drawing master at the Edinburgh Trustees' Academy. For instance, the umbrella forms of distant trees, the shapes of leaf clusters, and the brushwork of Heriot's watercolour seem to echo characteristics of Runciman's drawings, for example, of *La Sedia del Diavolo on the Via Nomentano, Rome* (see figure 1). Further, although the subject of Heriot's watercolour was probably taken from his on-the-spot sketches, it is unlikely that its forms were entirely drawn from these studies or that the composition of these forms was Heriot's invention. There are many elements of this drawing that he may have derived from landscape illustrations in books. The lush moist background foliage and the great palm trees of the middle distance provide a leafy framework for the waterfalls: a typically classical arrangement of elements that adumbrates his later compositions influenced by the Picturesque. In addition, the dark, flat foreground area and silhouetted figures all suggest that the young artist had been making a close study of engraved views. His figures especially are like those found in engravings of the time: one figure is pointing to the beauty of the cascades and the expanse of river, while another, a seated artist, records the natural scene before him.

We know from the letter to Grant that, in addition to Jamaica, Heriot also visited Saint Eustatius. A watercolour of Grenada (figure 3), executed in later years and undoubtedly based on sketches, suggests that he also went there between 1777 and early 1779.[14] No further information, however, concerning Heriot's West Indian years has yet come to light.

WOOLWICH

Back in London in June 1781, Heriot decided to further his artistic ambitions. Before he had left for the West Indies, his youthful dream of becoming an artist had seemed to come to nothing. Yet his broadening experience of life endowed him with fresh confidence to chart for himself a career in art. It is possible that, before reaching this decision, he once more turned to Robert Adam. Adam – acquainted with most, if not all, of the Academicians – knew quite well one of the Royal Academy's founding members, the famed topographical artist Paul Sandby, then drawing master at the Royal Military Academy, Woolwich, down river from London. It may well have been on Adam's advice that Heriot, already a draughtsman of 'views,' entered the Royal Military Academy to take advantage of Sandby's presence there.

As we have seen, officer cadets were required to complete a course of instruction in topographical landscape drawing, and many of them possessed the background and the skills to become superior practitioners in this art. A syllabus of Sandby's advanced course at Woolwich indicates the drawing master's aims: 'Putting Perspective in Practice by copying from Drawings, which qualifies them [the students] for Drawing from nature; teaches them the effect of Light and Shade; and makes them acquainted also with Aerial Perspective. Then to proceed to take views about Woolwich and other places; which teaches them at the same time to break ground, and forms the eye to the knowledge of it.'[15] It was Sandby's task to direct the cadets' artistic studies and to refine their skills. While studying under the sympathetic direction of this artist, Heriot would have been acquiring at the same time the training necessary for a career soldier.

When Heriot entered the Royal Military Academy at Woolwich is not known. He seems not to have taken a commission, and non-commissioned officers were not recorded. However, he may have entered late in 1781 and perhaps remained at the Academy for two years. As Heriot became acquainted with Sandby, the master would not only have encouraged him to develop his drawing skills, but perhaps would also have introduced him to the reproductive processes of etching, especially that of aquatint, a medium in which Sandby had by then become both interested and highly proficient.

In the late eighteenth century the landscape of the Thames at Woolwich was still rural and undisturbed by urbanization; it possessed a pastoral serenity and charm that young Heriot probably enjoyed. Yet he found the nearby town of Greenwich, with its quaint shops and old houses and the imposing towers of Wren's Greenwich Hospital, equally inviting. The earliest watercolours associated with Heriot's return to Britain (determined on the basis of the style of his Jamaican view) must be two landscape watercolours of Greenwich, which probably date from about 1783 (figures 4, 5). One of these displays the linear columns of foliage, the relatively large uninflected patches of wash, and the overlapping and contrasting planes of light and shade characteristic of the Jamaican view. Yet one is more struck by the differences between the Greenwich landscapes and the Jamaican view than by the similarities. The Greenwich watercolours display a tonal articulation and spatial cohesion that are much more skilled and consequently evoke a decidedly more tangible 'mood.' There is another aspect in which these British views differ from the Jamaican landscape: they are far more consciously topographical. That is to say, they are strongly horizontal landscapes in which salient topographical features are carefully related one to another. The towers of Greenwich Hospital, which dominate one watercolour, are related to the distant dome of St Paul's, and in the other watercolour even the barely perceptible twin towers of Westminister Abbey are emphasized by being framed by the domes of the hospital. These Greenwich watercolours represent so marked an advance on the style of the Jamaican view in the direction of topographical accuracy that they must reflect Sandby's influence.

From about 1783 Heriot was no longer formally associated with the Royal Military Academy but he continued to live at Woolwich. In this year, perhaps as a result of his association with the Academy, he appears to have succeeded Henry Forman as a civilian clerk at the army's Ordnance Establishment, Woolwich, attached to the Royal Laboratory at the Arsenal, a position for which he was paid a salary of £100 a year.[16] We do not know his precise duties there, but the Ordnance staff were responsible for ordering, stocking, and dispensing military supplies, equipment, and the tools and materials necessary to maintain this equipment. While at Woolwich Heriot seems to have sustained his relations with Sandby: they appear to have become much closer during the remaining years of this decade. At this time Heriot was still working at the Ordnance Establishment, where he remained in his clerical post until 1792.

What must be one of the earliest watercolours executed by Heriot while he was a clerk in Ordnance is his *View of the Town of Greenwich* (figure 6). The date inscribed on it is '178-,' the last digit having, annoyingly, been obscured. The slight mark remaining suggests that this digit might have been a '5.' Composed of two pages from a sketch-book, this watercolour is basically a pen drawing, enlivened by colour washes. It is tighter and more restrained than the two earlier Greenwich views. Its essential architectural features are wrought from a taut, yet fragile network of lines that carefully and neutrally trace the topographical character of the town. The twin towers of the hospital and the noble spire of St Alphège are prominently displayed. This delicate, linear landscape is enhanced by planes of transparent colour washes that provide cosmetic embellishment and also suggest space. Though primarily topographical, the landscape is more than merely documentary: it is a watercolour in the tradition of aesthetically attractive records of which Sandby's own work is a splendid example.

The mid- to later 1780s represents a critical period in Heriot's artistic development. By about 1786 his style appears to have undergone a gradual but perceptible change. The panoramic, narrow band of landscape becomes somewhat less frequent in his work. The tight linear structure of his *View of the Town of Greenwich* seems to give way to a style such as is found in *Greenwich Park and the River*, c 1786 (figure 7), a style which approximates in some respects to that of the two views of Greenwich of about 1783, where loose strokes of pen and brush describe form without strain. Here, however, they do so with more freedom and obvious skill.

THE PICTURESQUE

As the act of creation demanded from Heriot a progressively more profound and aesthetically more demanding unity, he began to discover himself as a painter of landscape. In *Greenwich Park and the River* Heriot has captured something of the multifarious forms of nature and their tonal richness and diversity; the landscape forms, especially those of trees, are richly varied, and the tonal possibilities of nature seem to have been more strenuously explored. It was also at this time that Heriot, under Sandby's tutelage, became aware of the pictorial possibilities of the Picturesque; indeed, Sandby may have introduced Heriot to Gilpin's tour guides, especially his recently published *Observations relative to Picturesque Beauty . . . On Several Parts of England; particularly the Mountains and Lakes of Cumberland and Westmoreland* (1786). The influence of the Picturesque on Heriot's style manifests itself in some sensitive but strong pen and wash studies in his sketch-books, in which he records objects of irregular form and silhouette; decrepit barns, old inns, and trees with shaggy foliage and gnarled and twisted trunks and branches (figures 8, 9). However, Heriot was not to be preoccupied entirely by the practice of the Picturesque.

By about 1788 Heriot's watercolours began to reveal a tonal structure even further developed, increasingly favouring implication rather than overt statement, mood rather than fact. *Path through a forest*, c 1788 (figure 10), is a watercolour which, even through simply massed tone and wiry lines, illustrates Heriot's devotion to natural appearances and, to some extent, mood, expressed in a study of the basic structure of trees and of the essential qualities of light and shade. It is this more acute examination and the understanding which results from it that are the essential features of this watershed of his style. Nature in his art is now more than something to record, albeit with an aesthetic approach: it is a living, breathing phenomenon. *Path through a forest* reinforces this particular quality of his work by suggesting light filtering through branches and the action of breezes. Although Heriot might have considered both his *View of the Town of Greenwich* and *Path through a forest* as documenting the reality of nature, nevertheless he would have admitted that they show different realities. In *Path through a forest,* while he has captured the facts and mood of nature, he has also presented, with equal fidelity, his own vision of it: that is, the work projects the ideal world of which he was becoming increasingly aware.

This new approach is evidence of Heriot's wider search for truth – for an equilibrium between what he saw and what he felt. In this pursuit he was aided by the ideas of the Picturesque: the associative ideas generated by a landscape, the ordering of nature's forms so as to make them conform to picturesque compositional requirements, the simplification of landscape elements, and the use of irregularity as both a decorative and an expressive device. By employing the ideas of the Picturesque Heriot was able to imbue his landscapes of fact with an added, more conscious aesthetic dimension and, in consequence, to furnish them with an expanded capacity for meaning.

This period was important for Heriot in another way. As a result of his growing sensitivity to nature and its aesthetic potential, and to his own rapidly developing skills as an artist, he began to gain confidence in himself and his art. Perhaps on the advice of or in emulation of Sandby, Heriot prepared a large series of etched picturesque views in the Channel Islands, 1789–90 (figures 11–13), probably based on watercolours which he had made on the spot in about 1786–7.[17]

Heriot's characteristic wiry pen line was easily and accurately approximated by the etching needle, and so the linear framework of these prints probably reflects something of his drawing style of the years 1786–7. In these prints (which he coloured by hand, in order to make them appear like watercolour drawings) the foliage masses of trees show a typical picturesque irregularity, and tree trunks (like those in Sandby's own watercolours and prints of this time) are picturesquely gnarled and twisted, as for example in his *View near the Town Mills, Jersey* (see figure 12) and also in *S.W. View of Mont Orgueil Castle* (see figure 11). If Heriot believed that he was following Sandby's example as a print-maker (figure 14), he was wrong: his own prints are simply etched outlines. Nor did he achieve Sandby's success, for it seems that very few impressions of Heriot's prints were actually made. Still, these views are interesting and significant as apparently unique examples of Heriot's earliest printmaking. In addition, they provide evidence of his broadening artistic skills and interests. Prints and print-making were to attract him in later years, especially when he decided to have his watercolours translated into prints with which to illustrate his travel books.

Heriot's sojourn at Woolwich lasted about ten years. The earliest intimation we have that it had come to an end is an announcement which appeared in an issue of the *Quebec Gazette* dated 27 September 1792, which reveals that Heriot was working as a civilian clerk of cheque in the army's Ordnance Department at Quebec.[18]

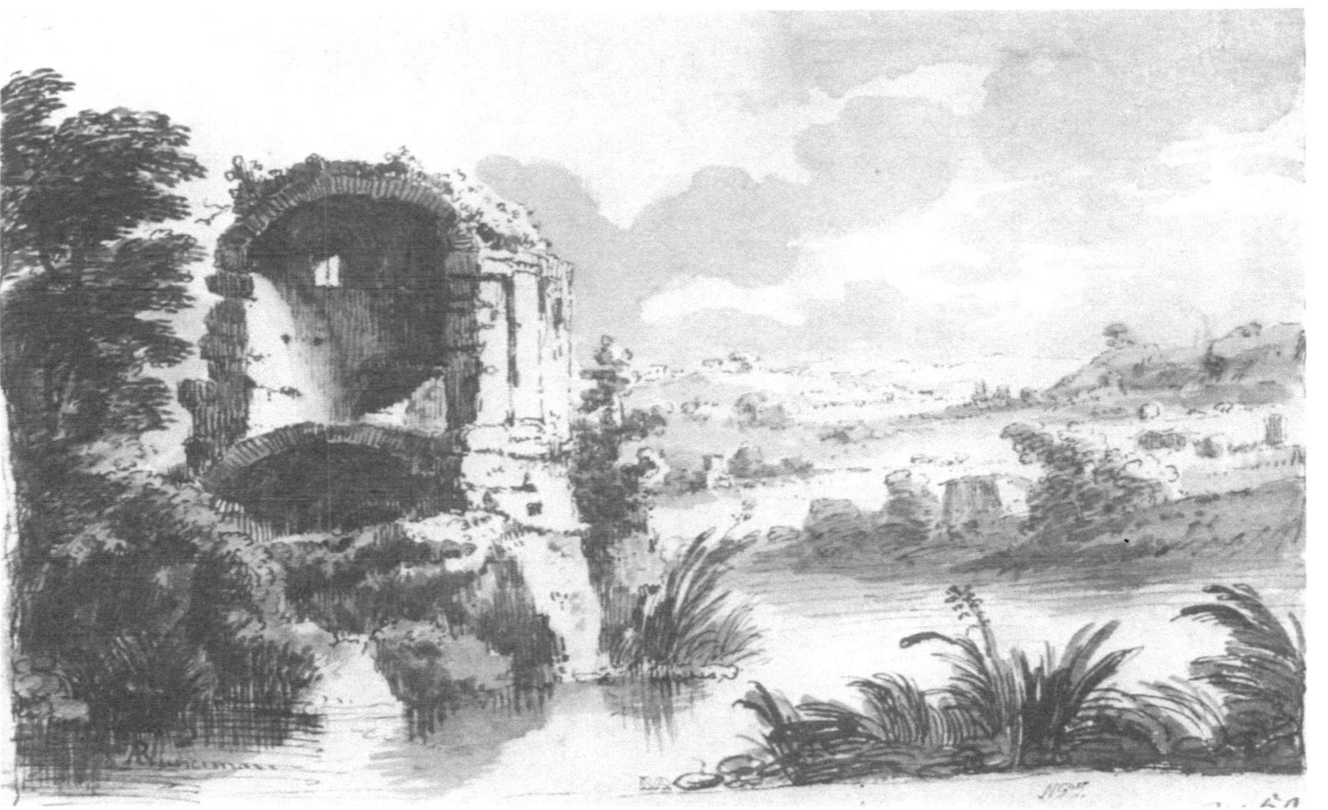

1 / Alexander Runciman, *La Sedia del Diavolo on the Via Nomentano, Rome*, n.d. Pen, ink, and wash, 219 × 330 mm.

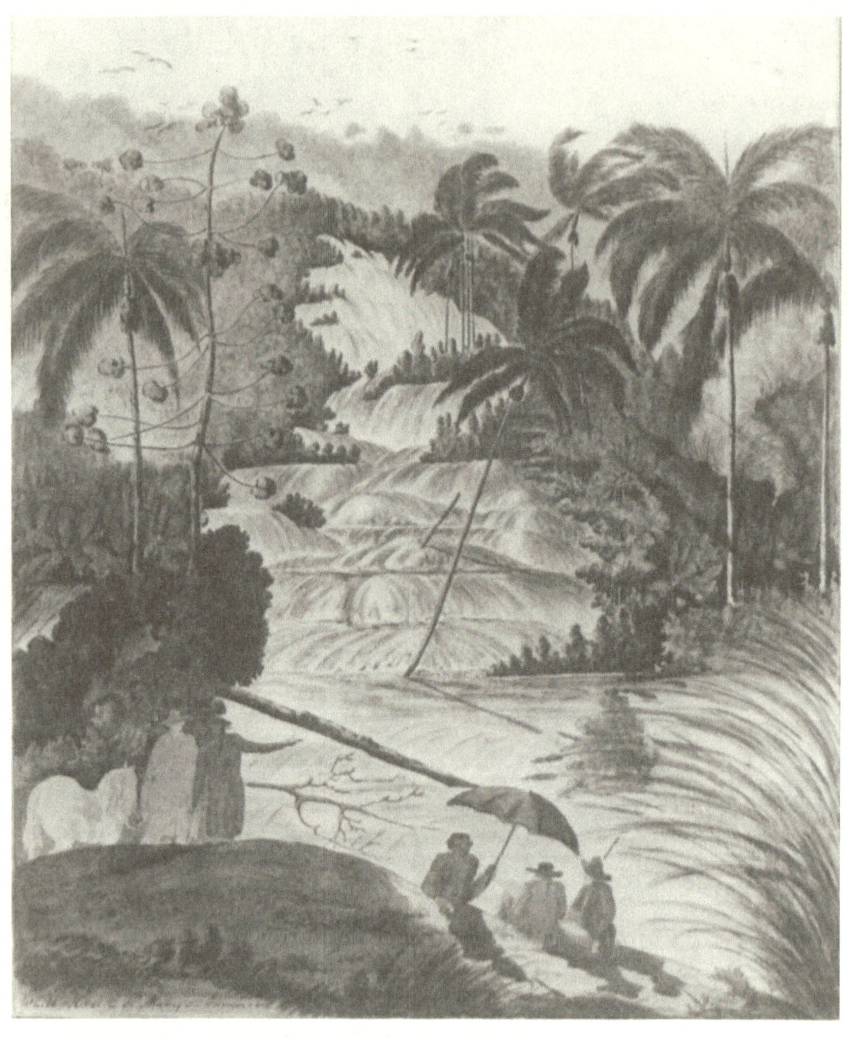

2 / *White River, St Mary's, Jamaica*, c 1780. Pen, ink, and watercolour, 387 × 324 mm. (check-list 4)

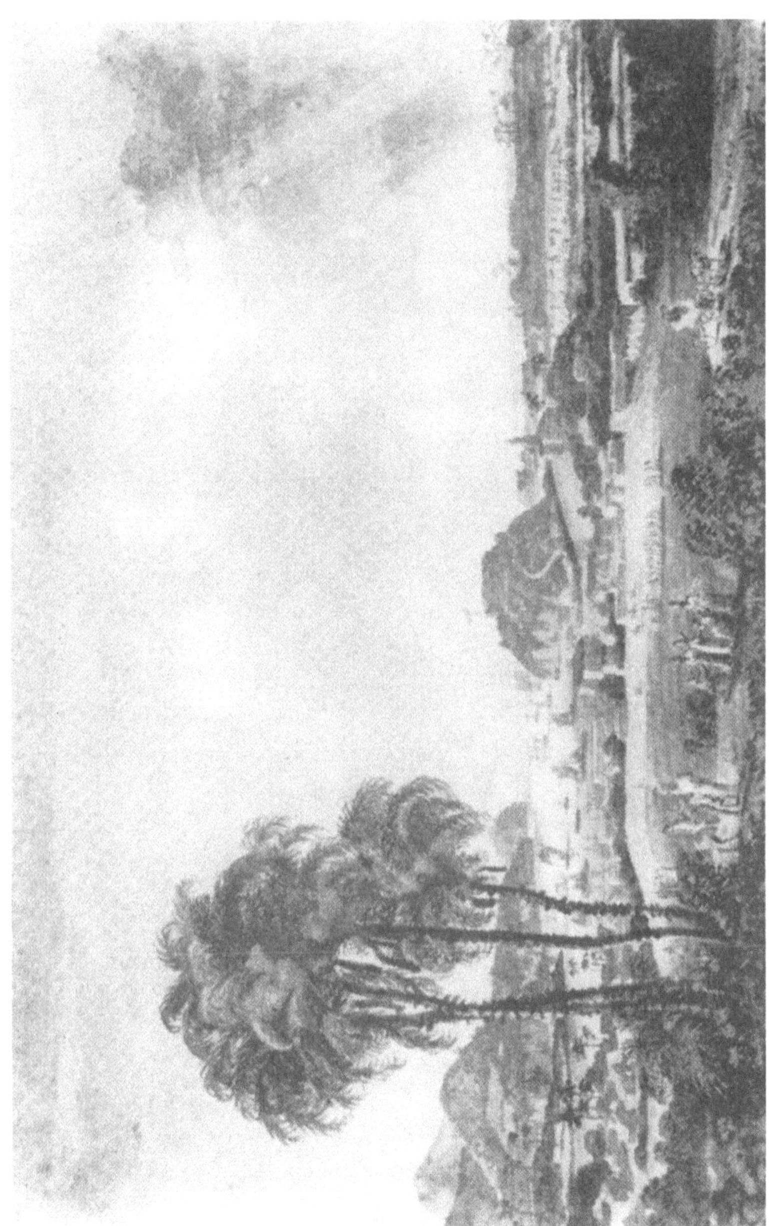

3 / *Grenada, Harbour of St George*, c 1820. Watercolour, 191 × 298 mm. (check-list 267)

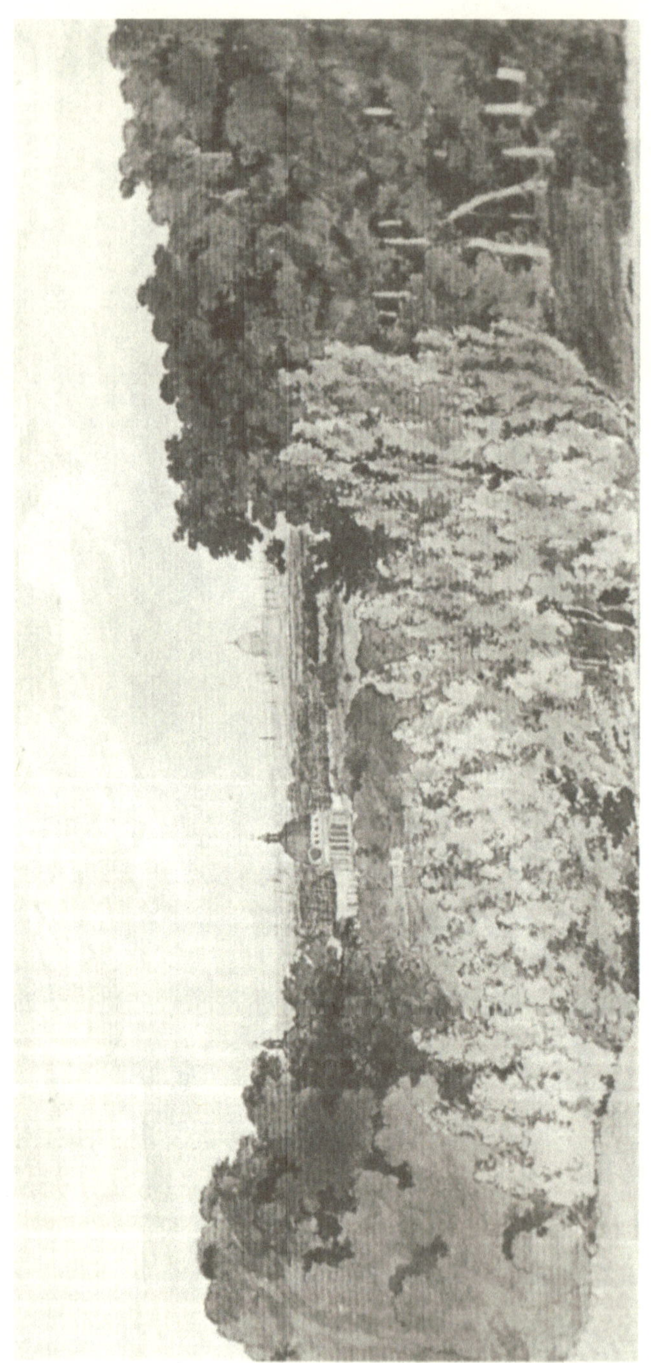

4 / *Greenwich with tower of the Hospital*, c 1783. Pen, ink, and watercolour, 125 × 279 mm. (check-list 5)

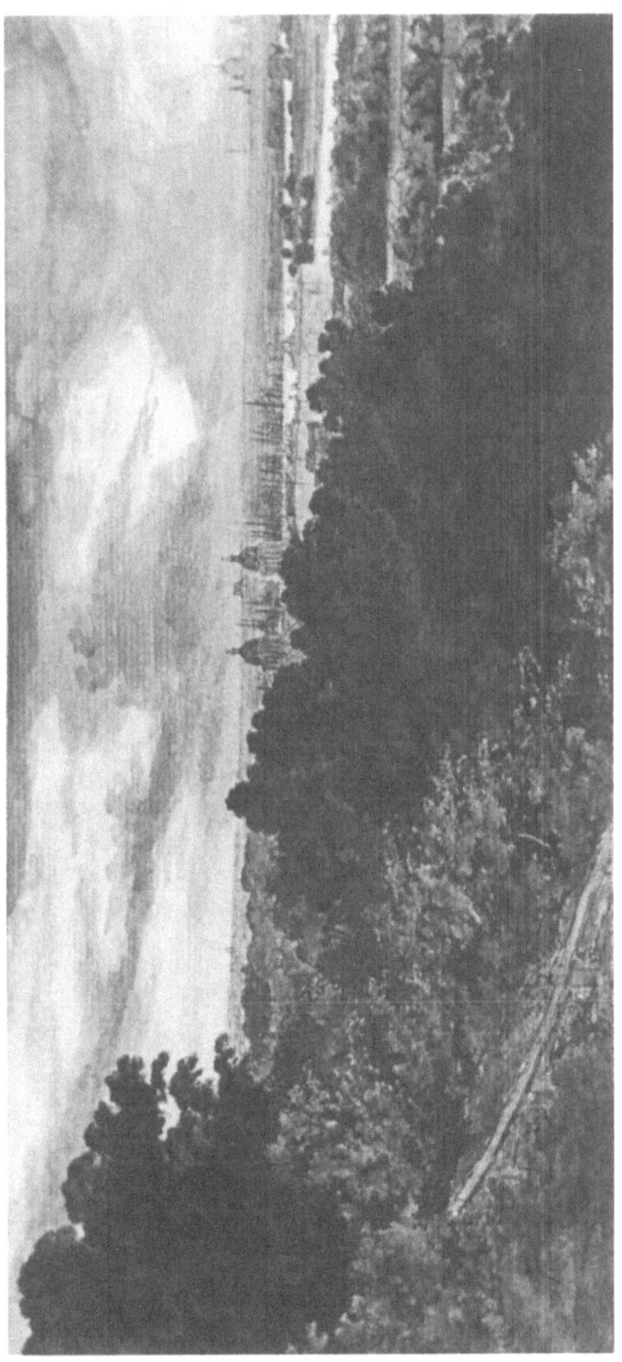

5 / *Greenwich with Hospital towers*, c 1783. Pen, ink, and watercolour, 125 × 275 mm. (check-list 6)

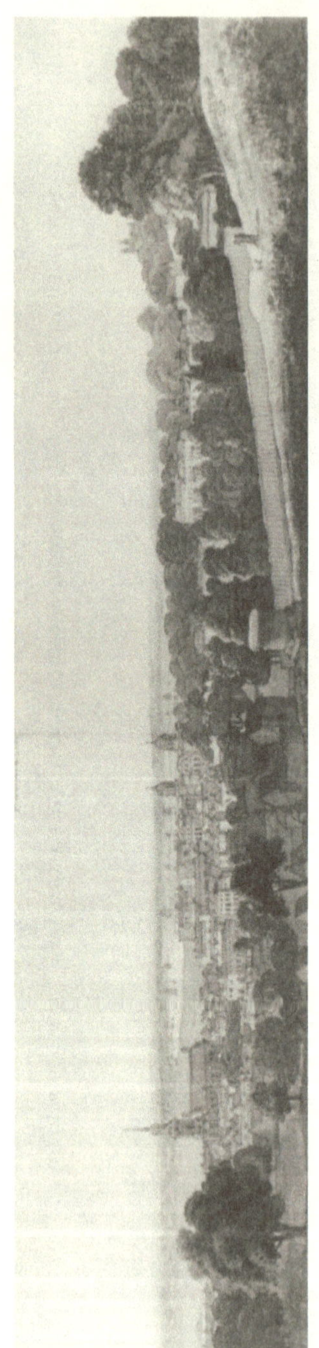

6 / *View of the Town of Greenwich*, c 1785. Pen, ink, and coloured washes, 108 × 521 mm. (check-list 7)

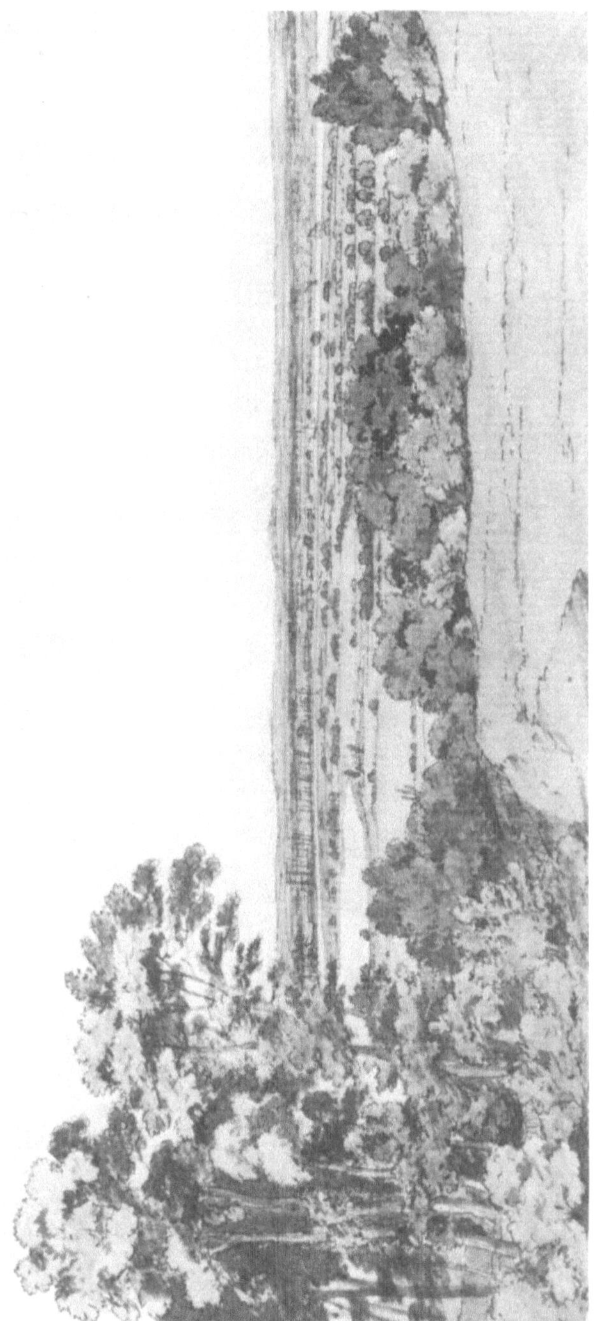

7 / *Greenwich Park and the River*, c 1786. Pen, ink, and watercolour, 91 × 192 mm. (check-list 9)

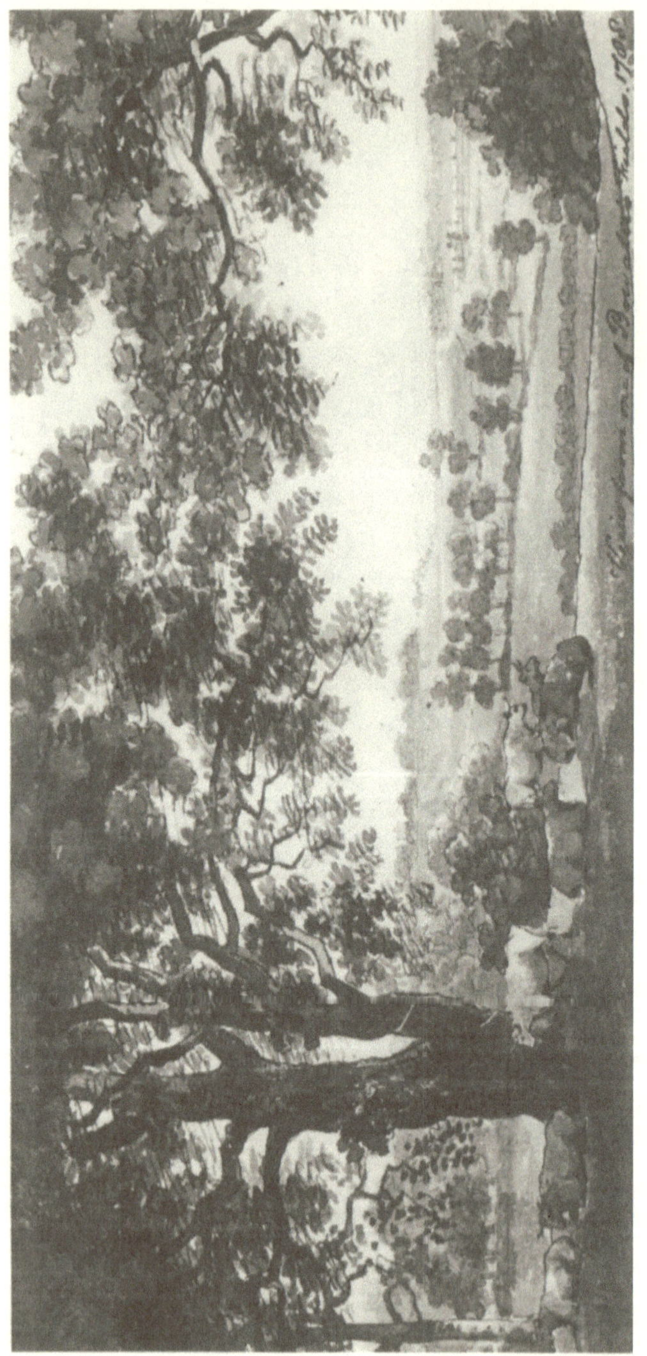

8 / *View from one of Bowater's Fields*, 1788. Watercolour (detail), 114 × 255 mm. (check-list 333, 32v)

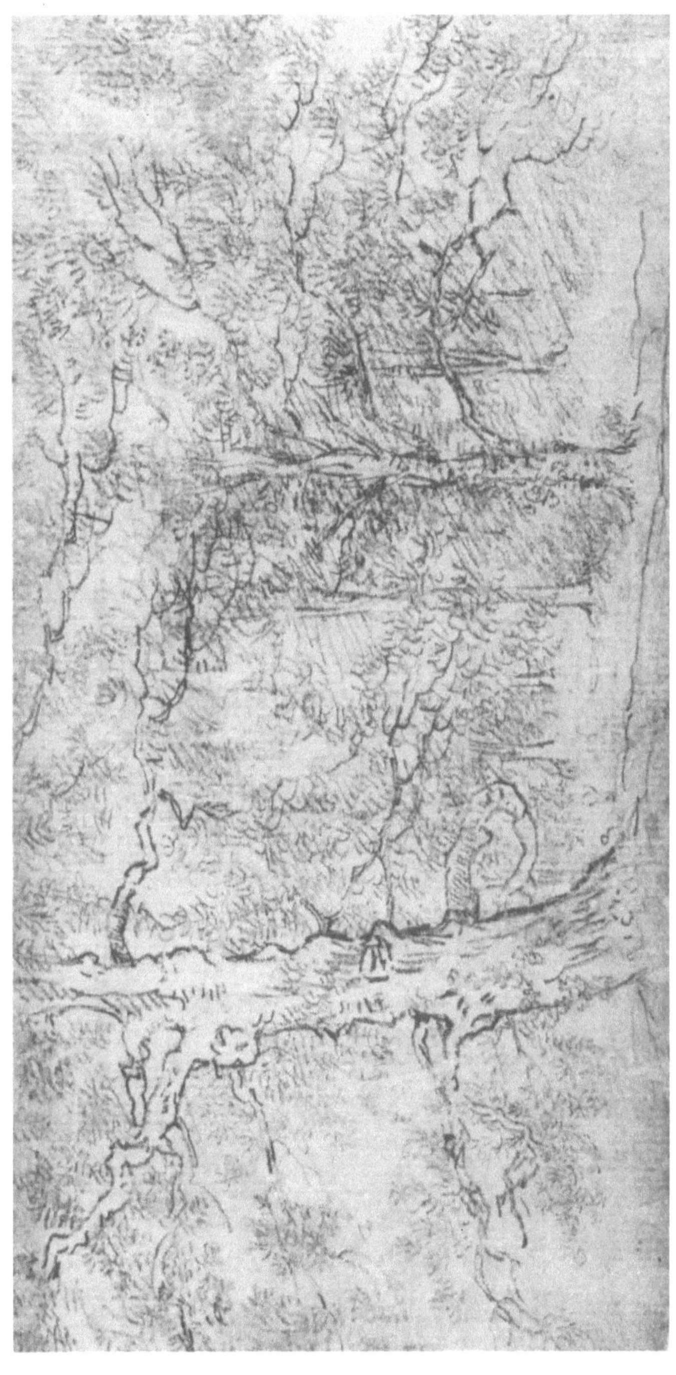

9 / *Study of trees*, c 1787–c 1789. Pencil, 114 × 255 mm. (check-list 333, 2v)

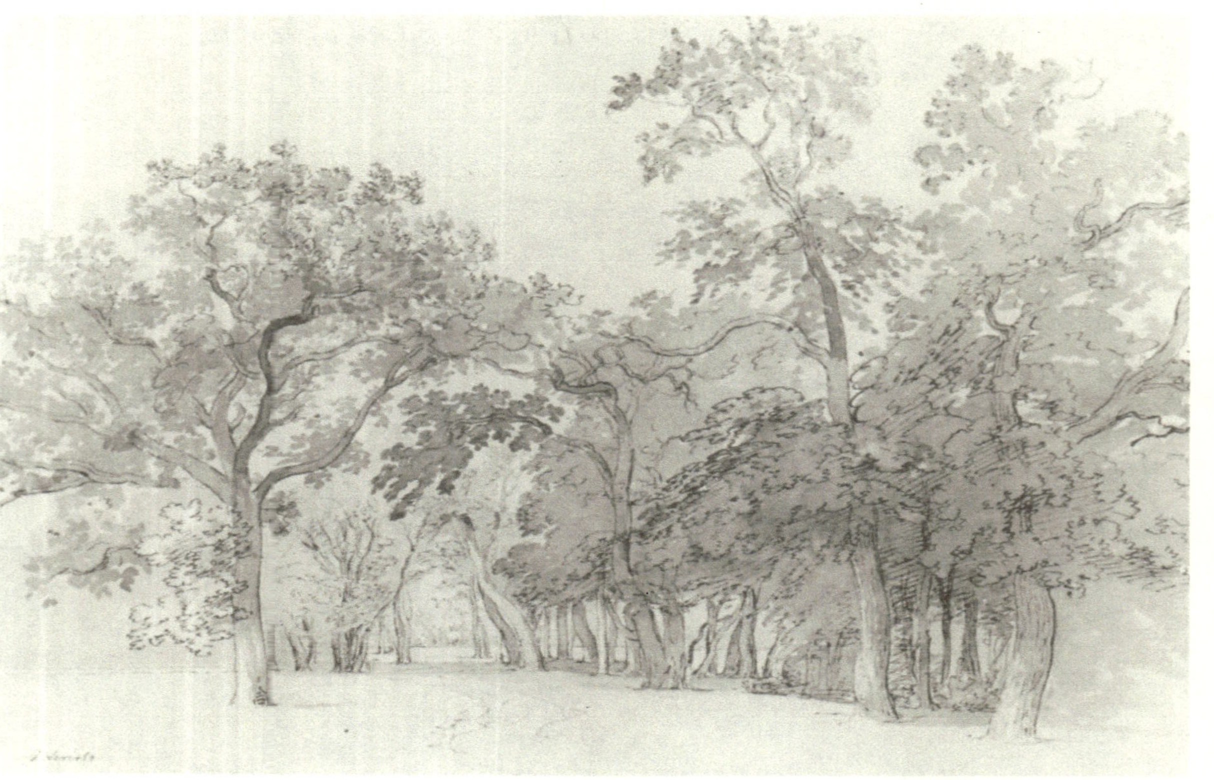

10 / *Path through a forest*, c 1788. Pen, black ink with grey wash, 276 × 430 mm. (check-list 11)

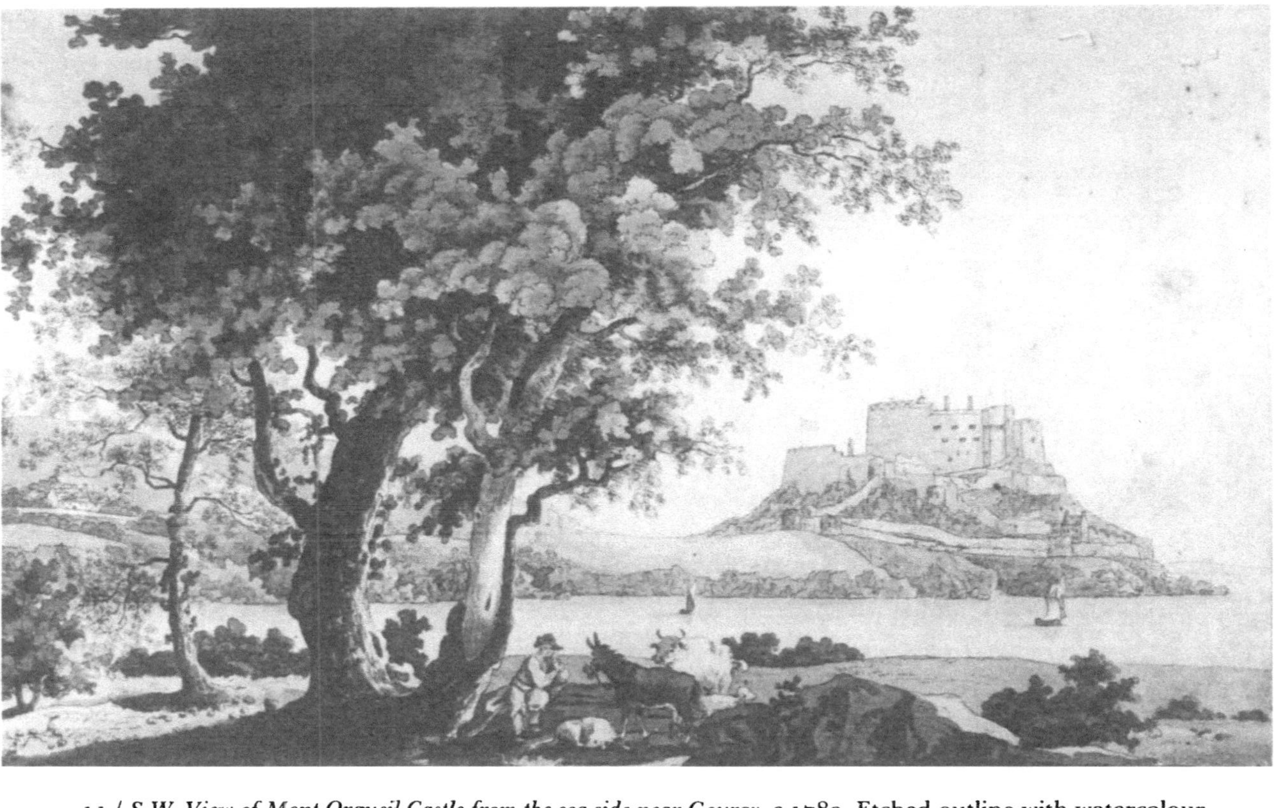

11 / *S.W. View of Mont Orgueil Castle from the sea side near Gouray*, c 1789. Etched outline with watercolour, 176 × 252 mm. (image) (check-list 350A)

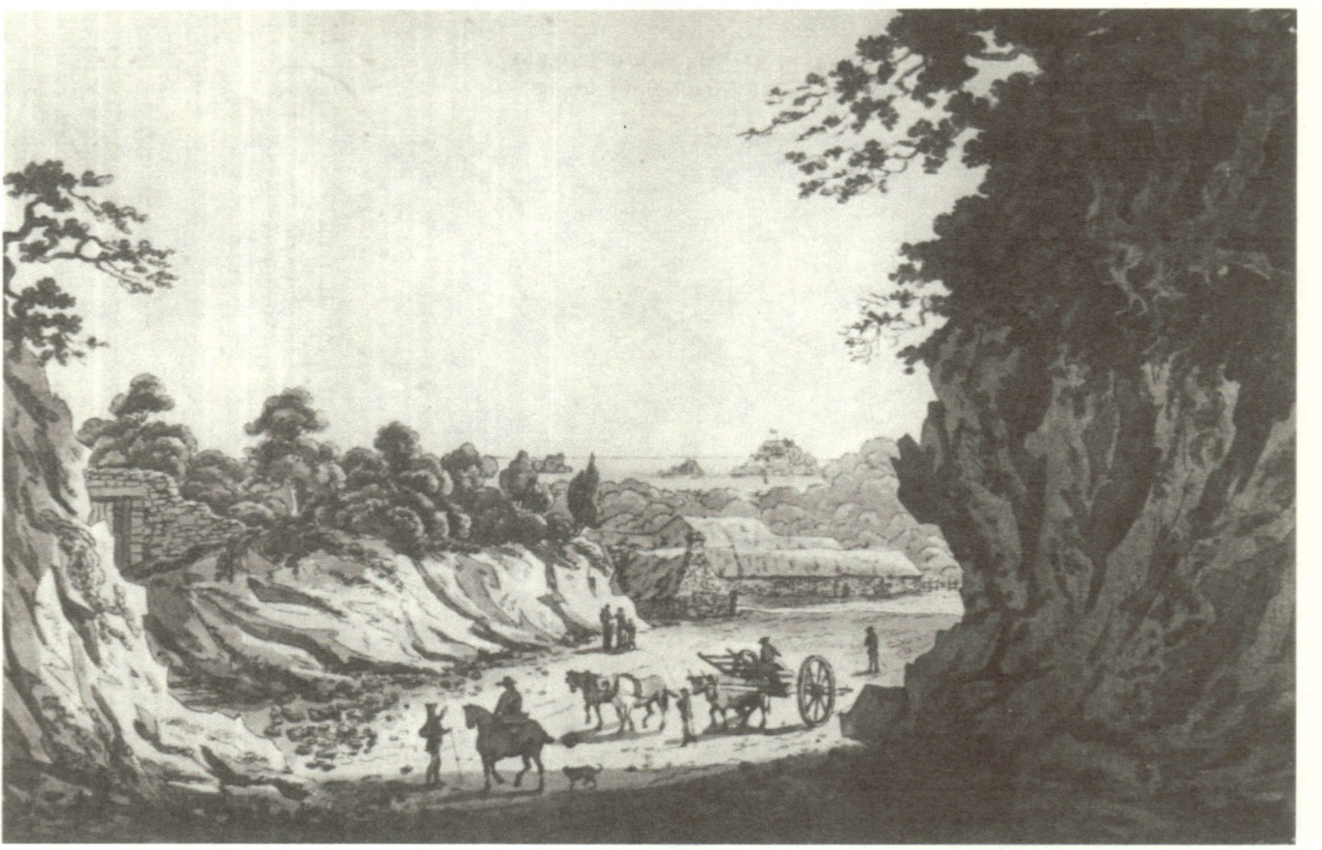

12 / *View near the Town Mills, Jersey*, c 1790. Etched outline with watercolour, 179 × 260 mm. (image) (check-list 343A)

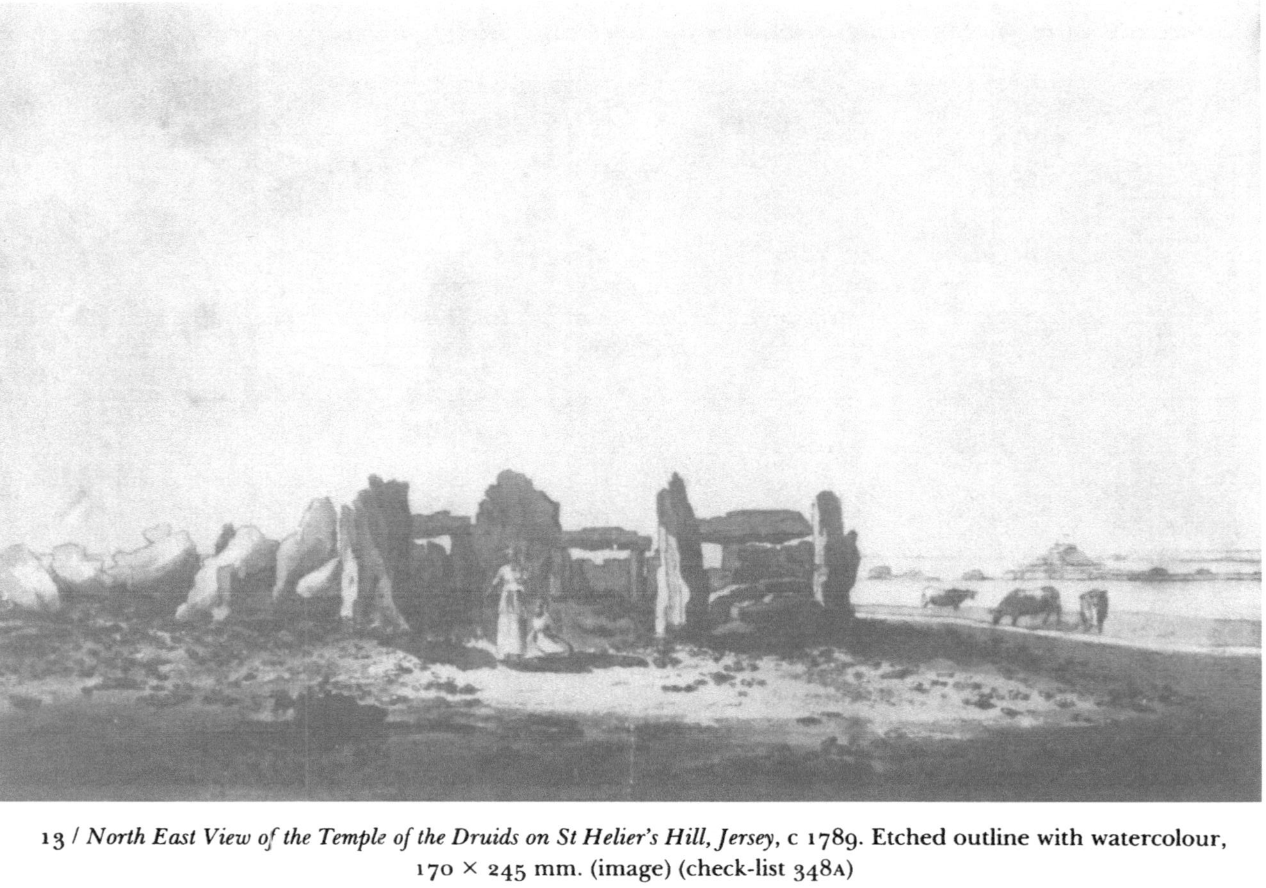

13 / *North East View of the Temple of the Druids on St Helier's Hill, Jersey*, c 1789. Etched outline with watercolour, 170 × 245 mm. (image) (check-list 348A)

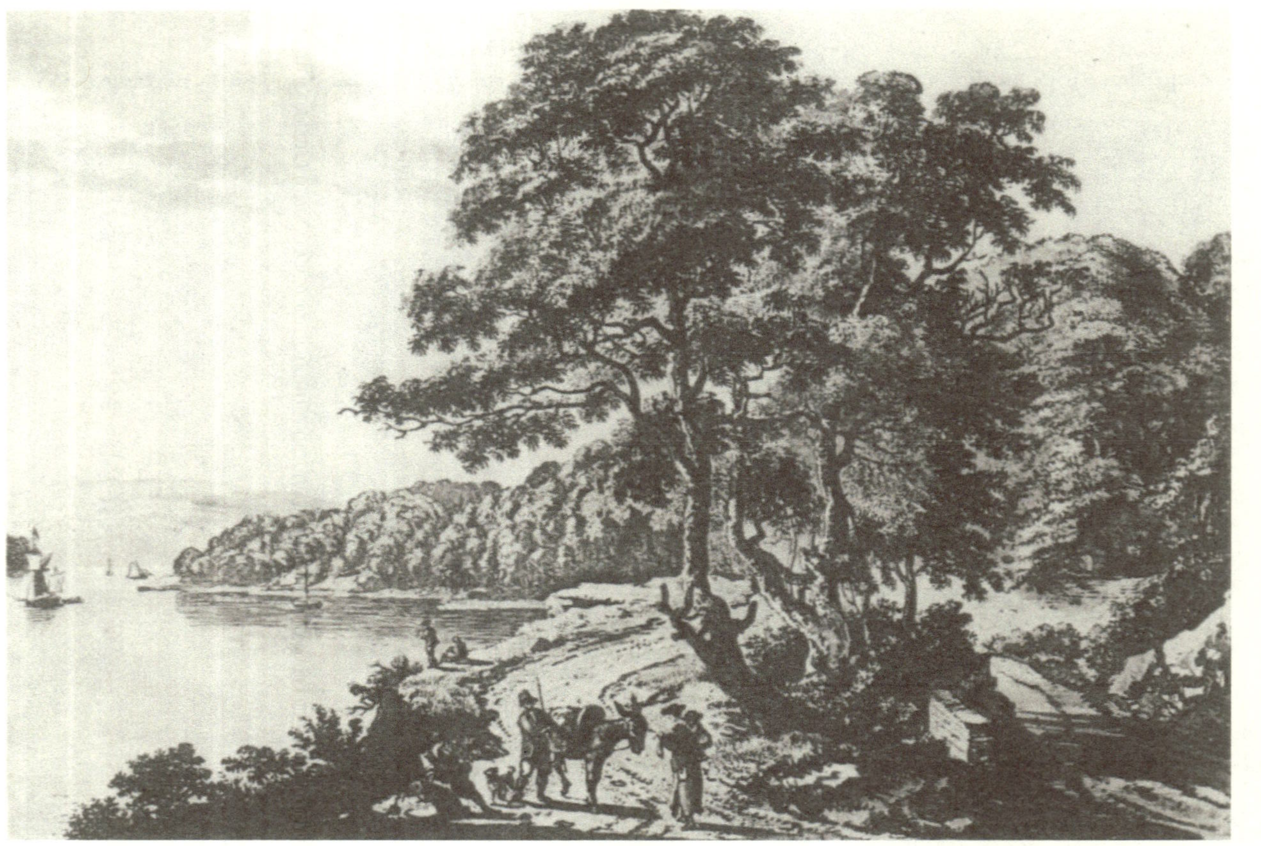

14 / Paul Sandby, *View up Neath River from the House at Briton Ferry in Glamorganshire*, 1775. Aquatint, 229 × 330 mm. (image)

3

The Canadian Experience 1792–1800

What persuaded George Heriot to take a position in Canada we do not know. But the Heriots were born travellers, and George was evidently conforming to a family tradition. John, the brother to whom he was so deeply devoted, had already seen service in several parts of the Empire. And the youngest brother, Roger, had emigrated to the United States. George had already lived in the West Indies and may have considered Canada an equally fascinating outpost of civilization. Also, he probably believed that greater opportunities for advancement existed in the colonies than in England. In Ordnance at Woolwich he had proved to be a capable worker, and, since he was ambitious, he may have decided that a few years in the colonial service would provide him with the basis for a career. Heriot's progress in the Quebec Ordnance Department was equally successful but in no way startling. He won a reputation for dependability, and his methodical habits, careful accounting, and shrewd grasp of detail soon earned for him the respect of his fellow-workers and his superiors.

Heriot was typical of those many-sided individuals that eighteenth-century Britain bred and from whom the British colonial service so greatly benefited. He was a man of intelligence and dedication who had the capacity to seize opportunities and took care to acquire the political influence with which he could exploit them. Unfortunately, however, he was, as we shall see, far from being an ideal candidate for a career at the senior levels of the public service, for he lacked the tact and diplomatic skills that are the mark of a truly successful administrator. These personal shortcomings were to fetter him and prevent him from attaining the status that he believed should in due course have been his. In the event the senior positions went to lesser men, intellectually far less gifted than he and in some cases with fewer connections. Yet, since they possessed the capacity to adapt themselves to circumstances and the flair for human relations that Heriot seemed to lack, they succeeded where he failed. In Quebec society, with its complex network of patronage and power, Heriot might survive, but he could never flourish; his personality militated against his professional progress.

When Heriot first arrived in Quebec, the provinces of Upper and Lower Canada had already been created (in 1791) by an order in council. After the French had ceded Canada to the British in 1763 by the Treaty of Paris, Quebec became the capital of the new British colony of Quebec. Then, on the creation of the province of Lower Canada, it became the capital of the province. But the importance of Quebec as a capital did not diminish, for essential government functions continued to be exercised from there. Still, in the 1790s Lower Canada was emerging from a decade of depression and, according to many inhabitants, Quebec left much to be desired. Many people considered it dour and forbidding in appearance, with its precipitously steep streets. Also, Quebec's winters were bitter. In the city's often commodious and austerely impressive stone houses fireplaces were insufficient protection against the elements, and the owners had to install stoves or *poêles*, 'with pipes ... conveyed through every room.' Even so, in severe weather wine would freeze and brandy 'exposed to air will thicken to the consistency of oil.'[1]

Quebec may not have been either a Paris or a London, but during the short, fiercely cold days of winter public entertainment was not wanting. There were warm coffee-houses to be frequented where the most recent news from abroad and the current local gossip could comfortably be exchanged. And, in the evenings, more formal *divertissements* could be experienced: against a snowy background the grey, looming form of the Château St Louis provided the setting for many a lively ball, where, under the warm glow of heated stoves and flickering chandeliers, the 'Money Musk' and the 'Jupon rouge' were the fashionable dances (figure 15). There was also entertainment in the houses of the titled, the gentry, and the well-to-do merchants: sparkling dinner parties and colourful dances were often held and regular *soirées* of card-playing lent an additional rhythm to the winter's social whirl. Not all the local pastimes were pursued indoors however. As one contemporary writer noted: 'the gay scene [of

Quebec] is at its height when the great river freezes over, and it sometimes does from side to side. The island of Orleans is then accessible, and every body turning out upon the "pont" as they call it, on skates, or else in sleds and carrioles [figure 16], "the then gay land is maddened all to joy."'[2]

No doubt, after settling in, Heriot began to participate in the leisure activities of Quebec's polite society and soon, through his military connections, he became friendly with the garrison officers and members of the merchant class: his good humour, his sharp wit, and his clever manner of recounting a story would have made him an attractive companion. We know that he joined at least one club and that he enjoyed entertaining at home in a two-storey stone house, 'pleasantly situated' at no. 6 Rampart Street, near Hope Gate.[3] When spring burst forth and its days were warmed and extended by the returning sun, he made fishing trips to the many rivers and streams, then teeming with trout and salmon, which were within easy reach of the city. Moreover, his fluency in French enabled him to mix with the élite of Quebec's Canadian society. He also attended their cathedral, to enjoy either the high-flown rhetoric or the down-to-earth bluntness of a visiting priest.

Heriot was equally responsive to other diversions, though these were of a kind very different from those that attracted the majority of the Quebec population. He may have hoped that life in the colonies would offer him the opportunity to pursue his literary and artistic interests; certainly the evidence suggests that he resumed them almost as soon as he arrived in the city. In November 1792 he published one of his etched Jersey views, *Temple of the Druids* (check-list 348D), in the *Quebec Magazine*. In order to give substance to the forms of this landscape – as we have seen, these prints are simply etched outlines – Heriot re-etched his plate, enriching some areas with a dense mesh of lines and others with a light, modulated aquatint tone. (This aquatint technique he had also probably learned from Sandby at Woolwich.) Although not very successful, the resulting impression was proudly proclaimed by the *Quebec Magazine* as 'an elegant and correct representation, taken upon the spot by a Gentleman at present in this City.' It was probably in 1793 that Heriot etched his first Canadian view, a panorama of the city of Quebec, seen from Pointe Lévis, to which he added aquatint in order to strengthen his pictorial image.[4] This is a much more accomplished work than the reworked *Temple of the Druids*. Perhaps intended for publication in the *Quebec Magazine*, Heriot's etched view of Quebec provides us with the means of dating some of his earliest Canadian watercolours, for its source seems to have been the watercolor *City of Quebec from Point Levi* (figure 17), which probably dates from 1792, the year of Heriot's arrival in the city. Another watercolour which is stylistically related to this one, and which therefore must date from the same time, is the *West View of the Chateau Riché* (figure 18).

These two delicately linear landscape watercolours (whose forms display a certain picturesque irregularity which, to some degree, relates the designs to Heriot's watercolours and prints of the late 1780s) do not prepare us for the on-the-spot sketches of Quebec and Montreal which Heriot made during the next year (see figure 19). These 1793 sketches offer a vision which is at once stronger and purer than that embodied in *City of Quebec from Point Levi* and *West View of the Chateau Riché*. Broad patterns now dominate detail, though without excluding it, and the sketches possess a tonal articulation that is far more structural than that of the watercolour compositions. Moreover, light irradiates the leading edges of form and provides the topography with a conspicuous, luminous order that endows it with a distinctive and palpable mood.

It is evident from the nature of these on-the-spot studies that Heriot regarded them as being distinct in style from his composed landscape views. This is confirmed by his *Fall of Montmorenci in Winter*, c 1794 (figure 20), and his *North View of Lake St Charles, Quebec*, painted in 1795 (figure 21), which are more closely related to the two watercolours of 1792 than to the on-the-spot watercolour sketches of 1793. Like the 1792 watercolours, *North View of Lake St Charles* possesses a delicate structure and atmosphere and embodies some attributes of the Picturesque: not only the irregularity of the landscape forms, but also the dark foreground, the light middle ground, and the still lighter background. Yet these watercolours lack vigorous chiaroscuro – the expressive massing of light and shade which usually characterizes picturesque landscapes – a quality which would have made these views more dramatic and hence, particularly in the case of *North View of Lake St Charles*, more convincingly rugged, and thus Canadian, in character.

It seems paradoxical that this artist, who in Britain could sometimes represent its serene and civilized landscape in watercolours of great energy and dramatic chiaroscuro, should choose to paint in Canada in a style that, in its fragility, seems essentially foreign to the nature of such a wild terrain. Yet it may be that Heriot's early Canadian composed landscapes contain evidence of a cautious attempt to discover an appropriate pictorial idiom in which to represent Canada – to which, after all, he had only recently been introduced. Still, in *North View of Lake*

St Charles Heriot has presented a particular aspect of the country that attracted him: the lake is envisaged as an oasis of tranquillity and undisturbed natural beauty – an impression which is reinforced by the presence in the scene of Indians, two men and a mother and child, who seem perfectly at ease in these surroundings. Heriot seems to be depicting a Canadian idyll.

In the early summer of 1796, a year after Heriot painted *North View of Lake St Charles*, he left Quebec to spend a twelve-month leave in England. During the four years which he had so far passed in Canada the country seems to have provided him with an opportunity to reassess the Picturesque as a principle, but its theory did not at that time help him to discover a suitable idiom in which to represent pictorially Canada's topography. During his spell in Britain, however, Heriot was to become acquainted with certain recent artistic developments and some newly published prints which were to illuminate and bring into focus for him the picturesque potential of the Canadian landscape.

While he was on leave in Britain, Heriot, with the perspective that physical and emotional distance can bring, consciously began to explore his feelings towards Canada. There can be no doubt that this British visit proved vital to his artistic development. Heriot first travelled to London, where his sister Sophia, who had married well, lived in some splendour. John, too, lived there: he was now a highly successful and influential Tory newspaper editor. While he was in London, Heriot may have renewed his association with Sandby; however, he stayed in the capital for only a few months, leaving several times to make sketching trips, including one to Wales. He then moved north to Edinburgh, where he lived for the remainder of the year. This northern visit seems to have been necessitated by family business, though this did not demand his full time and attention.

Always eager for knowledge, Heriot, now aged thirty-seven, enrolled at Edinburgh University in August. One of his classes was supervised by John Hill, professor of Latin.[5] Heriot matriculated at Christmas, then packed his baggage and returned to London, where he lived in a house off the Strand.[6]

Although no artistic records of this Scottish stay seem to exist, several finished watercolours from Heriot's Welsh tour survive. From these the extent of his ambitions as an artist and the real strength of his achievement at this time can readily be measured. While these watercolours confirm his renewed allegiance to the Picturesque and to the style of Sandby, especially the latter's published views of Welsh landscape, dating from the 1770s (see figure 14), they also display, more significantly, a marked difference in style from the immediately preceding Canadian drawings. They chart clearly a course of development that is distinctive, but one that was to come to an abrupt end. They are highly wrought, strong compositions, which have been invested with a richness and variety of form, especially in the deployment and handling of figures, that have little affinity with the same features in the Canadian landscapes of 1794–5. They demonstrate also Heriot's profound understanding of what Sandby had to teach him, being in many respects both a summary and a revision of his former master's style.

Two of these watercolours, *Neath Abbey, Glamorganshire*, 1796 (figure 22), and *Penrith Castle, Glamorganshire*, c 1796 (figure 23), both of them picturesque landscapes, display the distinctive three grounds and balancing coulisses of trees, through which mouldering ruins can be seen. Figures in Welsh dress are in groups in the foreground; a few of them are dancing, some are seated, and many are standing. In *Neath Abbey* there is a harpist. In these unusual watercolours, which may have been intended for public exhibition (they were probably stylistically similar to a Welsh landscape which Heriot exhibited at the Royal Academy in the spring of 1797,[7] but which has apparently not survived), Heriot skilfully served the public's taste for topographical views, for their picturesqueness is enhanced by a well-developed classical style and by the introduction of both local custom and local costume. It was doubtless his London visit which prompted Heriot to execute such imposing views, and which was to help him to paint even grander landscapes after his return to Canada. In conception many of these watercolours show Heriot to be increasingly ambitious, but they mirror also the artistic attitudes which were dominant in London during the 1790s, attitudes of which he must have been aware.

In 1783 the Free Society of Artists (1760–83) had collapsed; eight years later the Society of Artists (1760–91) had also ceased to exist. Both institutions had organized exhibitions in which watercolours were welcome. With their demise only one official body remained which would admit watercolours to its annual exhibitions: the Royal Academy of Arts. Yet the Royal Academicians were never enamoured of watercolours or watercolourists; they considered watercolours mere drawings. In the Academy exhibitions watercolours were at a disadvantage; they did not compete well with the larger, stronger designs of oil paintings. Moreover, watercolours were often hung high on the Academy walls in ill-lit galleries where, under these conditions, they were usually difficult to see. Watercolour artists believed that watercolours should have the same status as oil paintings, or a comparable one, and should be accorded equal attention and acclaim. Perhaps partly as a result, by the 1790s at the earliest some watercolours hung at the Royal Academy were stronger in design than examples shown in previous exhibitions. Stronger designs are likewise a feature of Heriot's ambitious Welsh watercolours, and also of a number of important watercolours which he painted after his return to Quebec.

But recognition of his artistic talents was apparently not, for Heriot, the chief yardstick with which to measure success, for never again were his watercolours exhibited either at the Royal Academy or at any other gallery. Presumably he no longer possessed the ambition to be a professional painter, and he therefore ceased to submit works for exhibition. Painting was a 'polite accomplishment' for a gentleman: it was associated with the contemplative life, not with a career. For this reason Heriot decided that his future lay in the public service – in administration, where he had already displayed some talent. Yet, despite this decision, he continued to paint, and later he profited from the experience he had gained by exhibiting at the Academy. For he was to reassess his Welsh watercolours and, in subsequent landscapes, give new form and vigour to some of the ideas which they embody.

Probably in the spring of 1797 Heriot sailed again from London. His return to Canada was to mark the beginning of a new response to this land. He was determined to learn more about the country and to contribute to, as well as share in, its development. On his return voyage Heriot took careful notes and made sketches of the things he saw and the places he visited. He made his first series of sketches while his ship was still in the English Channel. He sketched the Isle of Wight, Dartmouth, and finally Plymouth. From there his ship sailed on a southwesterly course to the Azores, 'nearly at an equal distance from Europe and America.' There it temporarily dropped anchor, and Heriot had the opportunity of surveying and sketching these volcanic islands. He visited St Michael, whose 'aromatic herbs, trees, and fruits, perfume the atmosphere with their sweets; and the breeze thus impregnated, becomes, when blowing from the land, highly grateful to the traveller in sailing along the shore.' Indeed, after having been on board ship for almost three weeks, Heriot was 'sensibly impressed by its enlivening influence,' which recalled to him the following lines from the poem 'Ode to May' by his illustrious ancestor George Buchanan (see appendix): 'Talis beatis incubit insulis, / Aurae felicis perpetuus tepor, / Et nesciis campis senectae / Difficilis, quaerulique morbi' ('Such is the everlasting gentle warmth of the happy breeze, that lies upon the blessed isles and the fields that know not crabbed age and complaining disease').[8]

From the Azores Heriot's ship proceeded northwestward. The first shore sighted was that of Newfoundland. As the ship entered the Gulf of St Lawrence, Heriot again took up his sketch-book. He made topographical outlines of the shore at Cape Gaspé and then at Cape Rosier, which he referred to as 'the place which limits the farthest extent of this gigantic river [St Lawrence]; and [where] ... the breadth of its mouth, which is ninety miles, must be estimated.' On entering the river he drew Cap Chat, which 'exhibits a bold appearance.' From there the ship sailed past Saint Barnaby's Island, of which he also made a pictorial notation and remarked that it was 'near the south shore ... upon the banks of which is a settlement called Rimouski.' His ship then approached Cap à l'Orignal, which he also drew: 'a promontory of a rugged and singular form ... in whose vicinity is the Isle of Bique, well known to navigators for its excellent harbour, and as being the place at which pilots are landed from vessels proceeding down the river.'[9] Heriot noted that in 'ascending the Saint Lawrence, the country on either side affords pleasure and amusement to the traveller, by the exhibition of a profusion of grand objects. Amid the combination of islands, promontories, and hills cloathed with forests, some scenes, more striking than others, attract the attention.'[10]

For example, on the north bank of the river he discovered and sketched a view that he considered highly picturesque: 'a bold and interesting scene [which] is formed, by the huge masses of rock, interspersed with shrubs, and by the east side of the hills called *les Eboulements*, which with majestic elevation project into the river.'[11] 'On their side are several cultivated spots, and the settlements appear one above another, at different stages of height. The houses, corn-fields and woods, irregularly scattered over the brow of the hills, produce an effect, luxuriant and novel.'[12] As he approached the island of Orleans, he found the scene before him worth recording, both pictorially and in words. 'On approaching the island ... a rich and interesting view displays itself; it is composed by the eastern extremity of that island, cloathed with trees, the Isle *de Madame*, the Cape [Tourment], and the mountains which recede from it towards the west and north, with the cultivated meadows which spread themselves under its rocky basis.'[13] From that point onwards Heriot found nothing but picturesqueness:

... a number of objects combine to produce a lively and interesting prospect. The foaming clouds of the Montmorenci, pouring over a gloomy precipice, suddenly open on the eye. The rocks of Point Levi, and the elevated promontory, on whose sides the city of Quebec is placed, seem to bound the channel of the great river. The north side of the town is terminated by the Saint Charles. The settlement of Beauport, in extent about seven miles, intervenes between the Montmorenci and Quebec, and is situated on a declivity, extending from the hills to the Saint Lawrence, whose banks gradually slope towards the little river of Beauport, from whose western borders the land becomes level. A chain of mountains towards the north intercepts the view.[14]

Heriot accumulated many sketches on his return voyage from England to Canada in 1797, but these were only topographical references and not finished compositions. The lessons that he had recently learned in London had no application here. Even after his return to Quebec he gave no hint in his finished watercolours of the 'muscular' classicism of the Welsh views of 1796. He seems to have reverted to some extent to the brittleness of his previous Canadian manner, as exemplified by *North View of Lake St Charles*, 1795 (see figure 21). Elements of this style persisted until about 1800. However, there is, in fact, a significant difference between the style of the watercolours executed before his English trip and that of those painted after it. This change is most graphically illustrated by a comparison of *Fall of Montmorenci in Winter*, c 1794 (see figure 20), with *View of Quebec taken from the Pont near Point Levi*, 1798 (figure 24). The latter watercolour displays a remarkable new strength in light and shade effects, in brush work, in spatial control, and in the rich variety of its incident. Also, figures and movement are more natural and the grouping of forms is more successful.

Almost certainly the change in Heriot's style can be largely attributed to his acquaintance with a set of six aquatint plates of picturesque North American scenery generally known as the 'Edy-Fisher prints.' These prints, published in London in 1795–6, appear to have influenced Heriot's work profoundly. They present a view on the North or Hudson River in the northeastern United States and five Canadian views: *Cape Diamond, Plains of Abraham, and Part of the Town of Quebec* (figure 25); *The Falls of Chaudière*; *A Bold and Romantic Scene on the St Ann's or Grand River* (figure 26); *A Near and Full View of the Fall of Montmorenci from below*; and *A*

View Descriptive of the Scenery and Banks of the River St Lawrence, in which is a Distant Representation of the Fall of Montmorenci from the Island of Orleans. The five prints of Canada have been described as 'probably the most beautiful aquatint prints of Canada ever produced.' All six prints were etched by J.M. Edy from landscape drawings by Lieutenant George Bulteel Fisher (1766–1834) of the Royal Artillery. It seems hardly possible that Heriot would not have known of these almost as soon as they were published, and thus he probably saw them in London. If not, then he would certainly have seen them after he returned to Quebec. Their influence appears in watercolours which Heriot painted soon after his return to Canada: for example in *Oystermouth Castle* (figure 27) and *Neath Abbey with Gnoll Castle* (check-list 50), both of which were developed from sketches made on the 1796 Welsh tour and date probably from late 1797 or early 1798. They are different from the Welsh watercolours of 1796 in that they possess the brittle qualities of the early Canadian style; but, if they possess elements of this manner, they also reveal a new expressiveness and a new, more intricate style of design. Also, forms are now enhanced by reinforcing chiaroscuro, and foreground areas are typically picturesque, since they are more prominent and the forms (especially the figures) which they contain are presented in strong silhouette.

The importance of the Edy-Fisher prints to Heriot was not only that they offered him a new vision of Canada but that they seemed to sum up and present in concentrated form a picturesqueness that had already been evolving in his Canadian watercolours of about 1795. But if these prints provided confirmation that a picturesque viewpoint was indeed suitable for the presentation of the Canadian landscape, then they also demonstrated that the effectiveness of such a viewpoint depended on the exploitation of the more rugged and grandly dramatic contours of this landscape. This was a lesson from which Heriot began to profit as soon as he returned from England to Canada.

There was another aspect of picturesqueness in the Edy-Fisher prints that attracted Heriot: their emphasis on water. By the late eighteenth century the importance of water for communication and commerce was well understood by the British public, but it required the cult of the Picturesque to focus attention upon its aesthetic qualities. In 1782 Gilpin published his *Observations on the River Wye, and Several Parts of South Wales &c. relative chiefly to Picturesque Beauty*, and in 1786 his *Observations relative chiefly to Picturesque Beauty ... on several parts of England; particularly the Mountains and Lakes of Cumberland and Westmoreland*, both containing extended discussions of the picturesque attributes of water. In the wake of these books by Gilpin there followed a new wave of tour guides and journals, primarily dedicated to the beauties of lake and river scenery. River views, in particular, caught the imagination of the tourist and as a consequence they came to be regarded as among the most admired locations of the Picturesque.[15]

As we have seen, each of the six Edy-Fisher prints centres on water – all of them are river views. Undoubtedly Fisher's choice of subject for the prints had largely been determined by their pictorial potential; but it must be remembered, too, that at this time a traveller's experience of the Canadian landscape was to a considerable extent limited and influenced by the fact of accessibility: much of Canada could be reached only by water, for roads were few and those that did exist were little better than tracks.

It was for the same aesthetic and practical reasons that Heriot in so many of his watercolours represented Canada as the domain of lakes and rivers.[16] One very attractive watercolour inspired by the style of the Edy-Fisher prints is *Colonel Nairne's Settlement at Mal Bay*, 1798 (figure 28), with its sparkling water, irregular leafy foreground, and small figures in silhouette. The disposition of foreground figures in relation to landscape and water is reminiscent of the placing and handling of the Indians in the Edy-Fisher *Fall of Montmorenci from below*.

Two of the grandest and most handsome of Heriot's Canadian views executed under the influence of the Edy-Fisher prints were of the falls of La Puce, not far from Quebec (figures 29, 30). These watercolours, painted in about 1799, may have been commissioned, or perhaps they were made for presentation. However they were prompted, both their theme and its treatment suggest that for Heriot they possessed a special importance. His choice of the waterfalls of La Puce as a subject was undoubtedly dictated by their well-known picturesqueness. Heriot described the falls in the following account:

> The river *la Puce* ... invites the attention of the traveller; it rolls its current, broken into a refulgent whiteness equalling that of snow, from the summit of a lofty hill, and afterwards conceals itself midway, behind an intervening eminence of inferior altitude, cloathed with trees. The motion of its water is perceptible, and the reflexion of light arising from the fall, glistening with the rays of the sun, produces a powerful contrast with the deep verdure of the forests by which it is environed ... The environs of this river display, in

> miniature, a succession of romantic views ... In vain would the labours of art, endeavour to produce in the gardens of palaces, beauties, which the hand of nature scatters in the midst of unfrequented wilds.[17]

In these attractive, decorative drawings Heriot has dramatized the topographical setting, capturing through his own picturesque idiom the exalted grandeur and nobility of this untamed river scenery in a way comparable with the most eloquent of the Edy-Fisher views of Canadian landscape.

The interior views of the remains of the Intendant's Palace (figure 31) in Quebec, dating from 1798 and 1799, show that the stylistic impact of the Edy-Fisher prints had begun to fade (though their majestic vision of Canada remained unimpaired and continued to be essential to Heriot's artistic development). Heriot conceived of these views as a decorative group, for the subject of ruined buildings, with their irregular outlines and associative ideas, was close to the heart of the Picturesque. The ragged outlines and texturally enriched surfaces of the ruin, together with the relatively low viewpoint from which it is surveyed, also suggest Canaletto, whose style of drawing had been attractive to those in search of a mode of vision sympathetic to the ideals of the Picturesque. Indeed, Canaletto's style became extremely popular with some draughtsmen of topographical subjects who lived and exhibited in London during the 1790s. While Heriot was in London in 1796, he would no doubt have seen works painted under Canaletto's influence. Joseph Farington, for instance, a former pupil of Paul Sandby and virtual 'dictator' of the Royal Academy, was certainly influenced by Canaletto. Heriot may well have been acquainted with him – Heriot's brother John knew him – and have seen his drawings. It is also possible that Heriot saw the work of younger artists, such as J.M.W. Turner or Thomas Girtin, both of whom were exploring the Canalettesque idiom in their watercolours at that time. A comparison of, for example, Girtin's *Ruins of the Chapel in the Savoy Palace, London*, c 1795–6 (figure 32), with Heriot's *Ruins of the Intendant's Palace* reveals similar characteristics in both works.

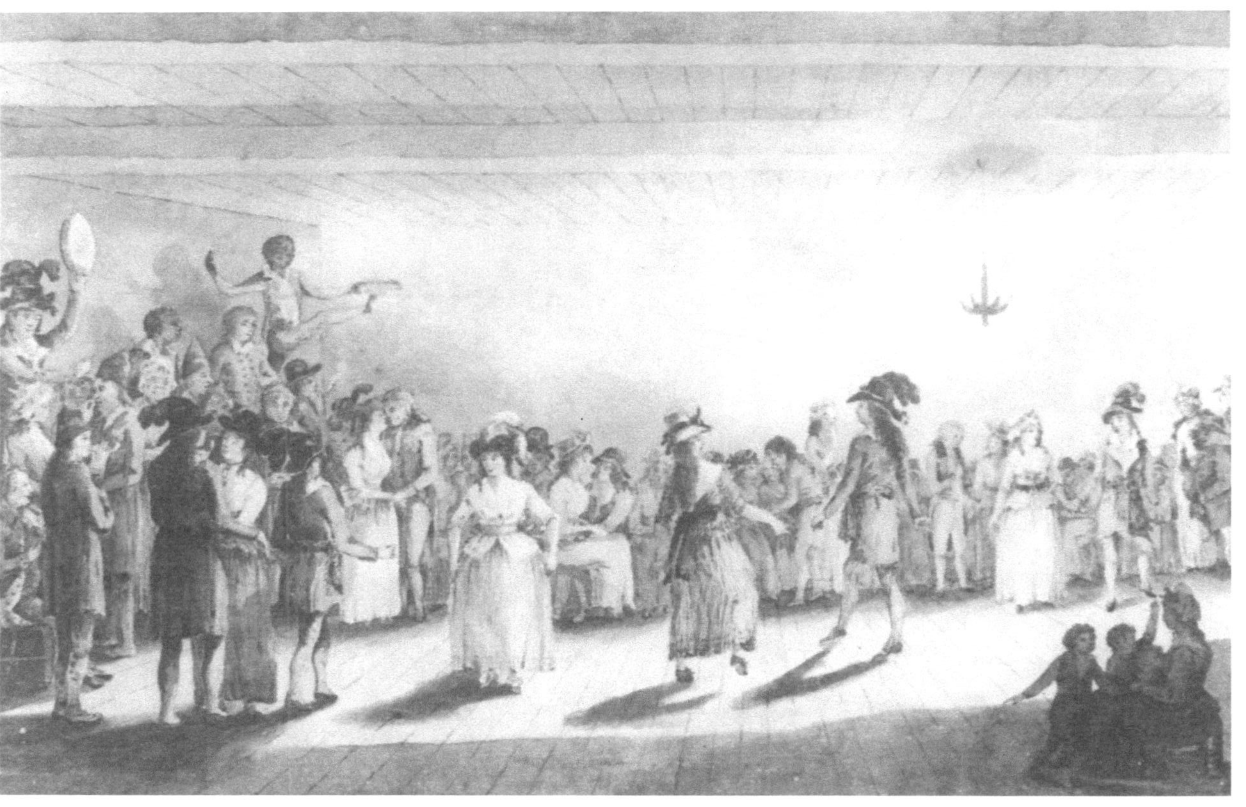

15 / *Minuets des Canadiens*, c 1801. Watercolour, 214 × 328 mm. (check-list 97)

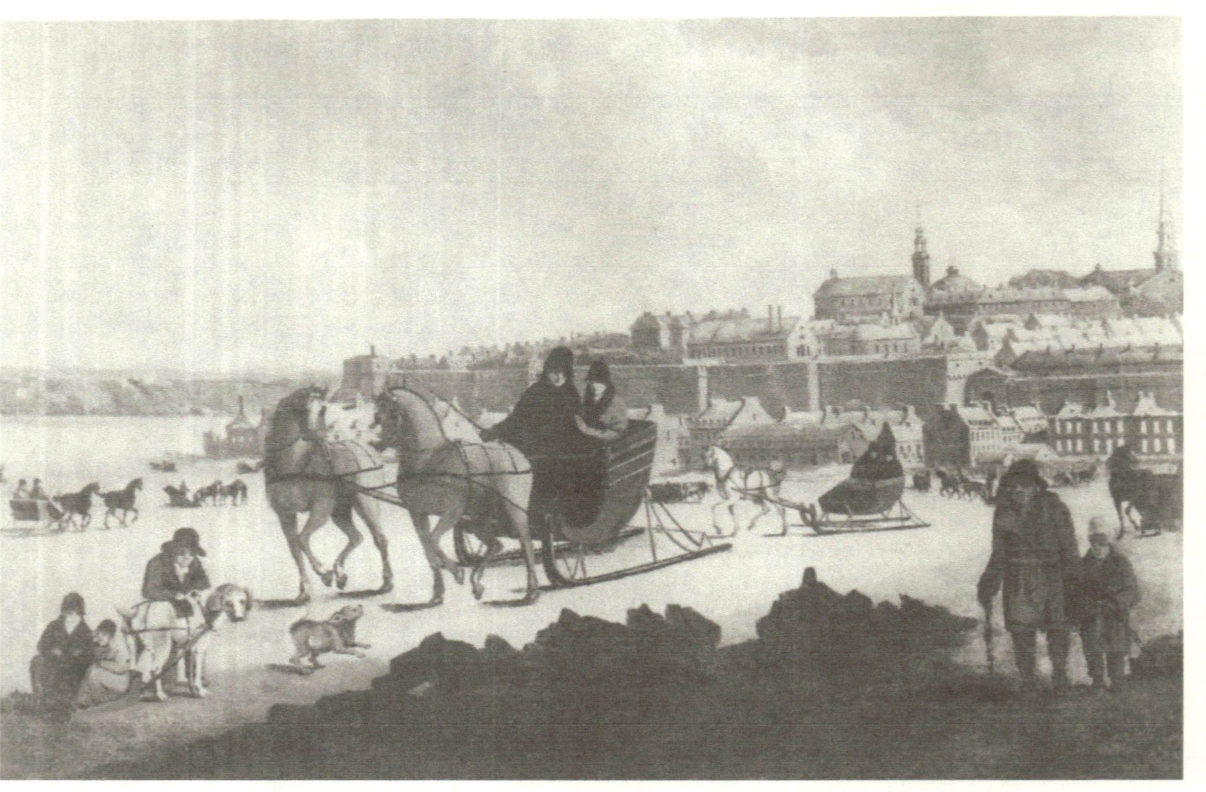

16 / *The North West Part of the City of Quebec taken from the St Charles River*, c 1804–c 1810.
Oil on canvas, 737 × 1105 mm. (check-list 1)

17 / *City of Quebec from Point Levi*, c 1792. Watercolour and brown ink, 214 × 324 mm. (check-list 17)

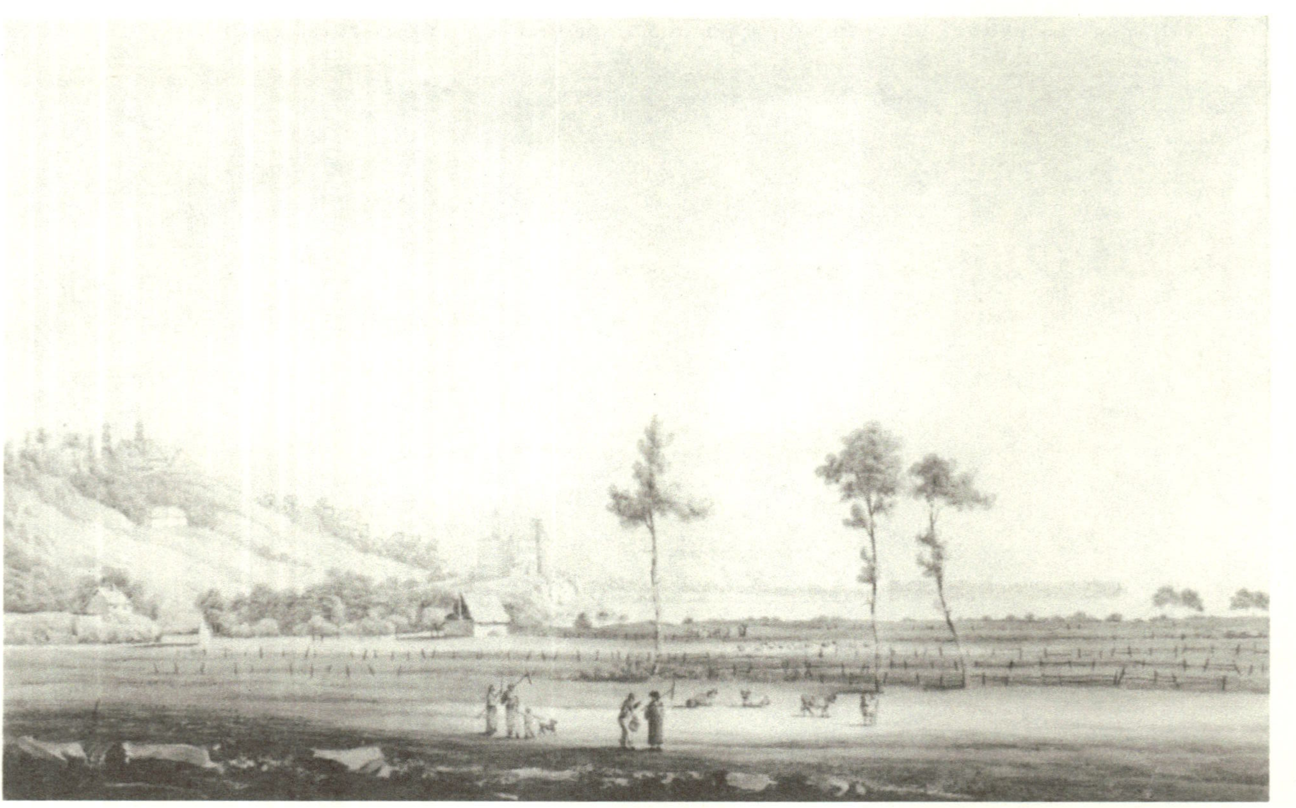

18 / *West View of Chateau Riché*, c 1792. Watercolour and brown ink, 214 × 324 mm. (check-list 15)

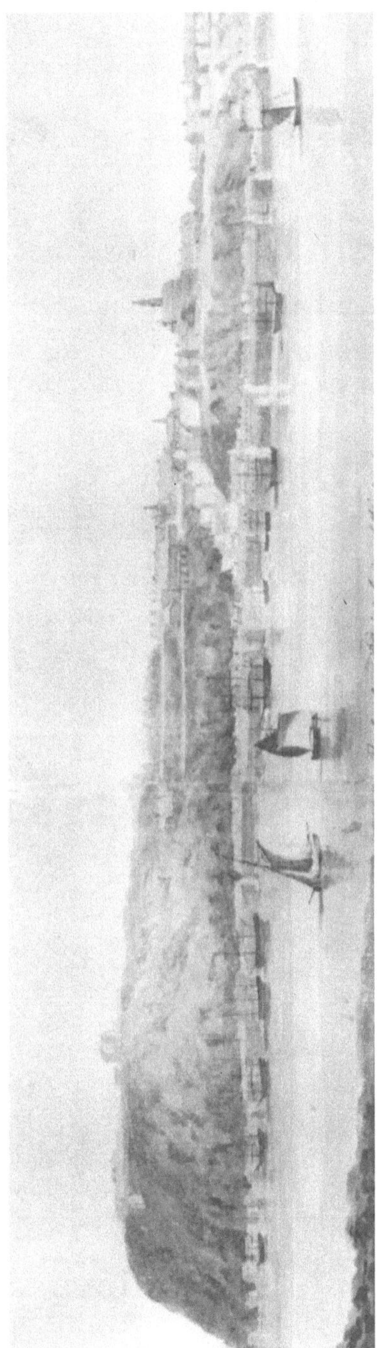

19 / *Quebec from Point Levi*, 1793. Watercolour, 113 × 407 mm. (check-list 21)

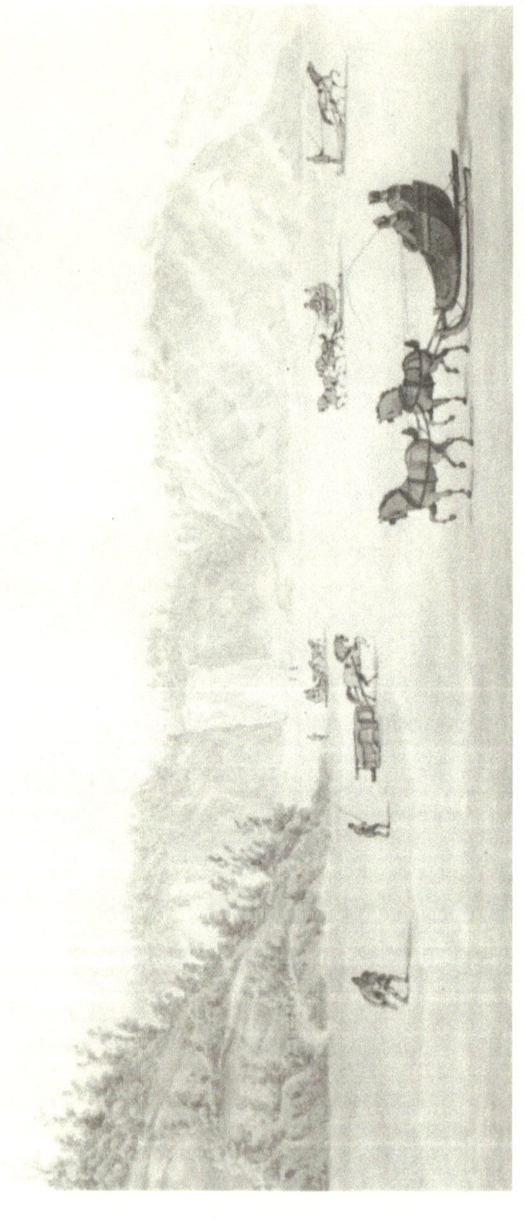

20 / *Fall of Montmorenci in Winter*, c 1794. Pen, ink, and watercolour, 216 × 325 mm. (check-list 41)

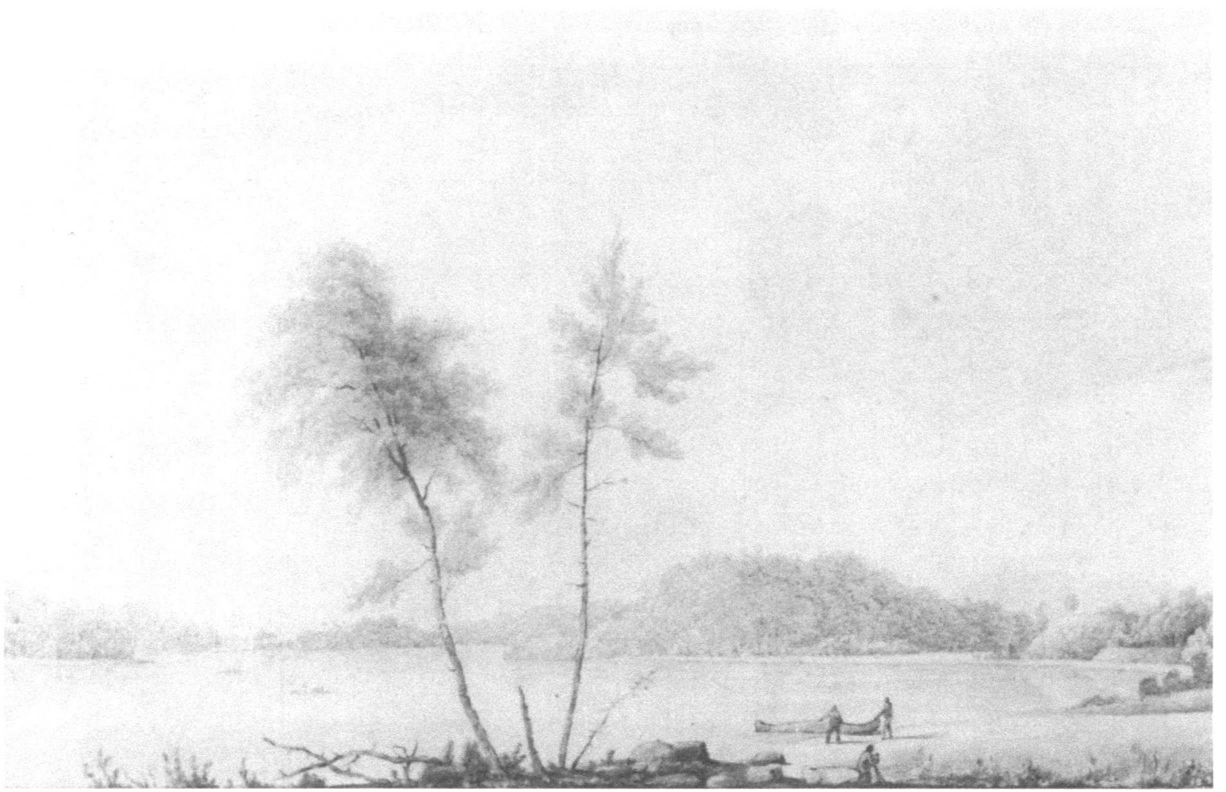

21 / *North View of Lake St Charles, Quebec*, 1795. Watercolour, 216 × 324 mm. (check-list 42)

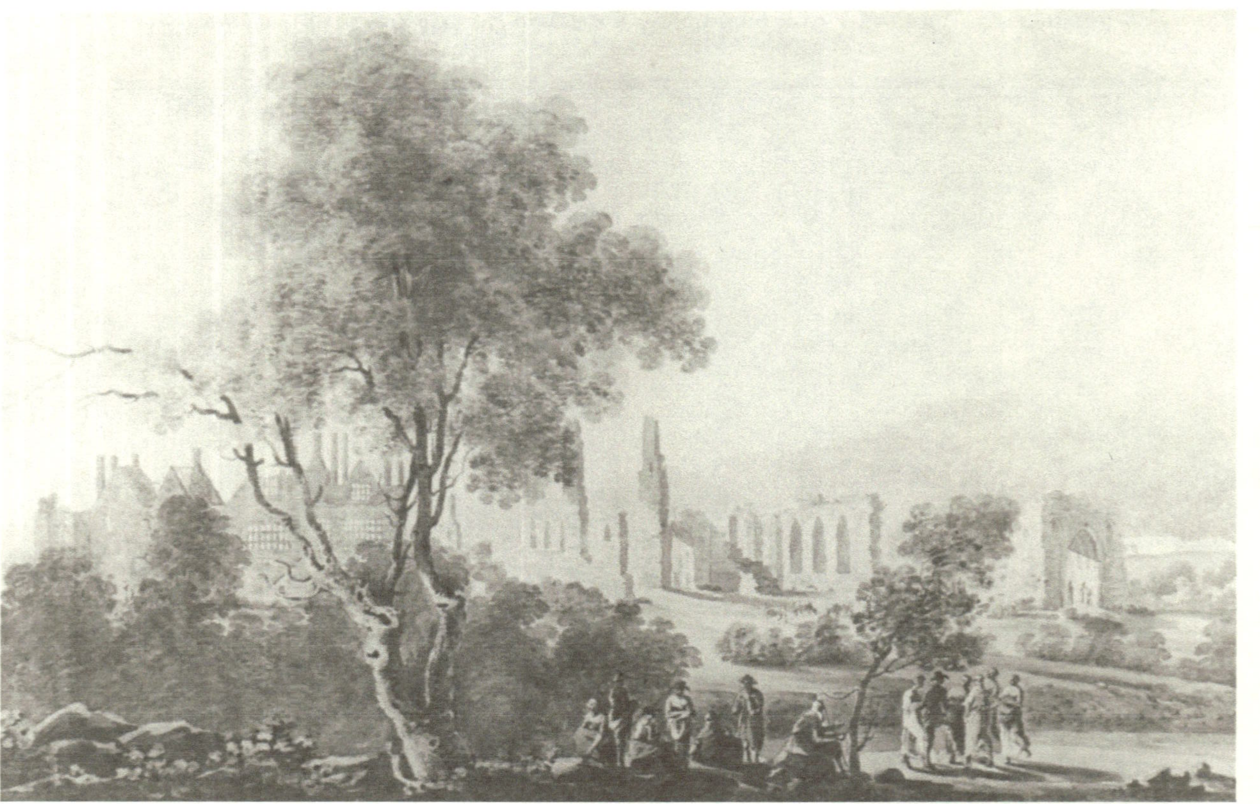

22 / *Neath Abbey, Glamorganshire*, 1796. Watercolour, 267 × 368 mm. (check-list 43)

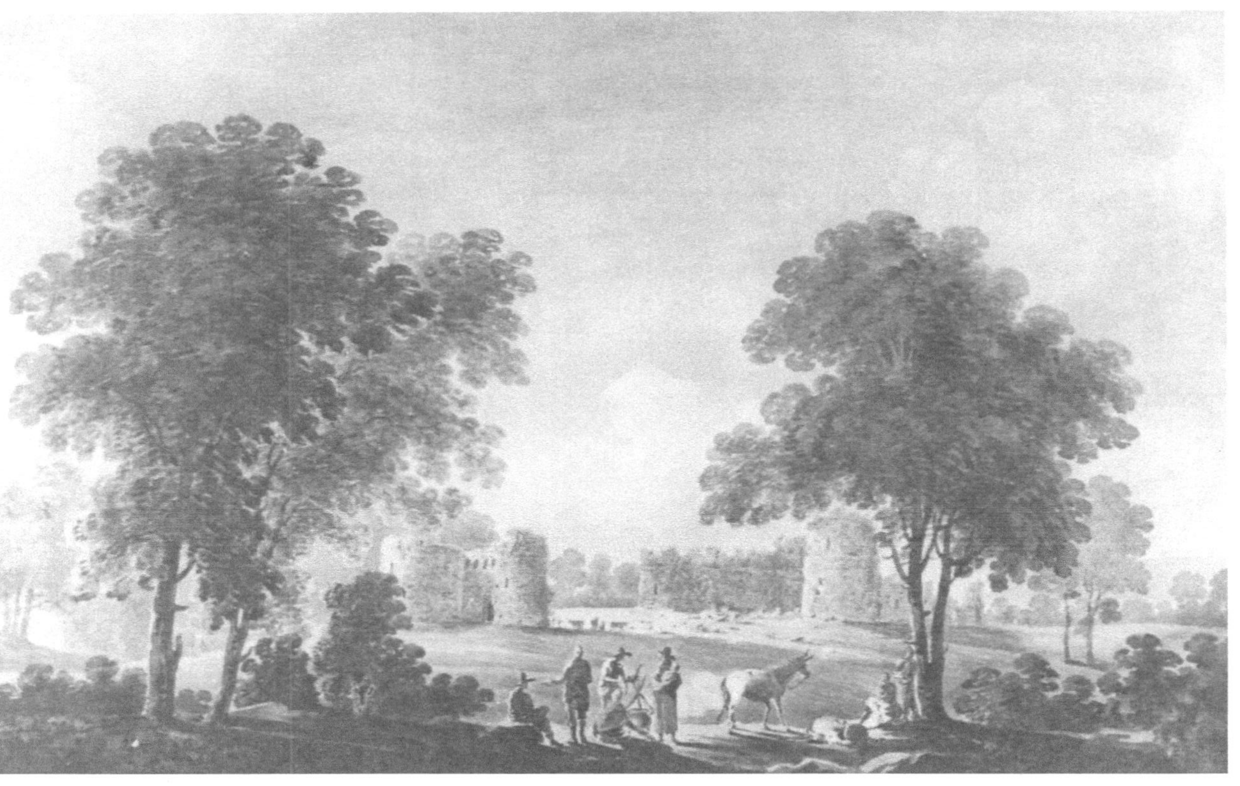

23 / *Penrice Castle, Glamorganshire*, c 1796. Watercolour, 241 × 381 mm. (check-list 46)

24 / *View of Quebec taken from the Pont near Point Levi*, 1798. Pen, ink, and watercolour, 254 × 356 mm. (check-list 53)

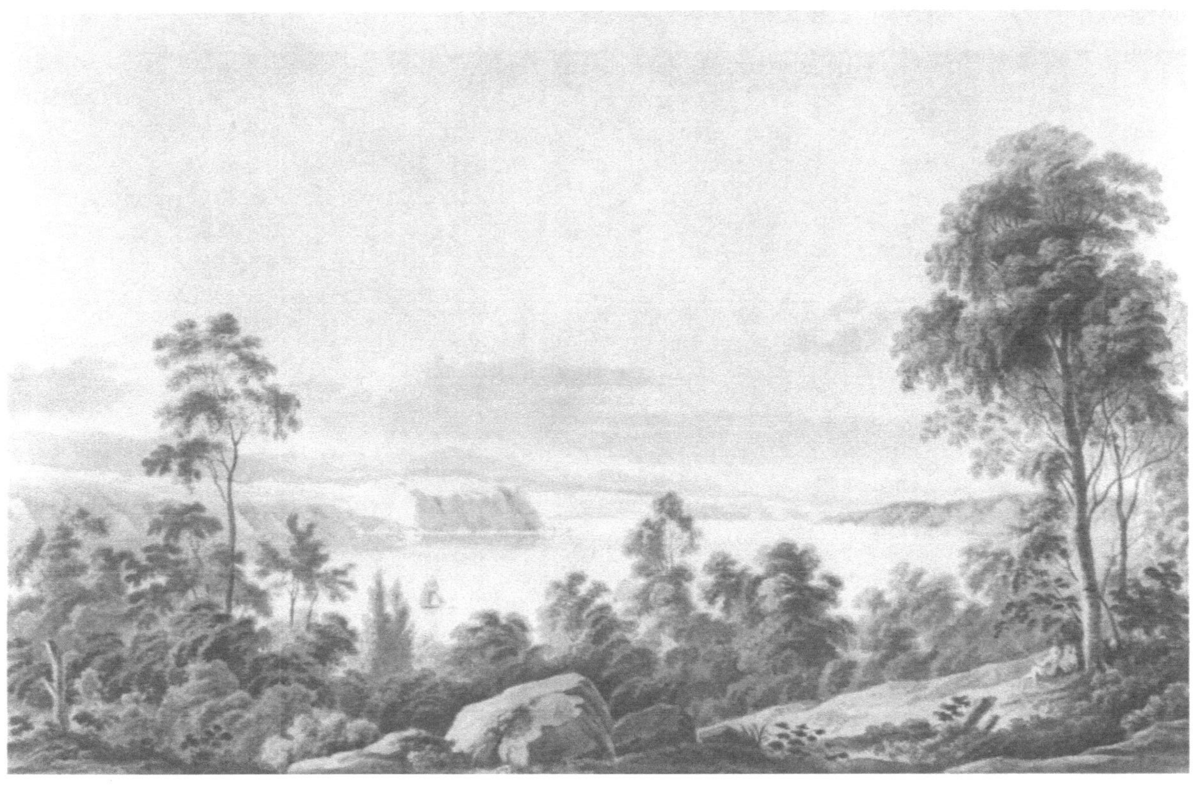

25 / J.W. Edy, *View of Cape Diamond, Plains of Abraham, and Part of the Town of Quebec*, 1795/6. Aquatint after G.B. Fisher, 418 × 613 mm. (image)

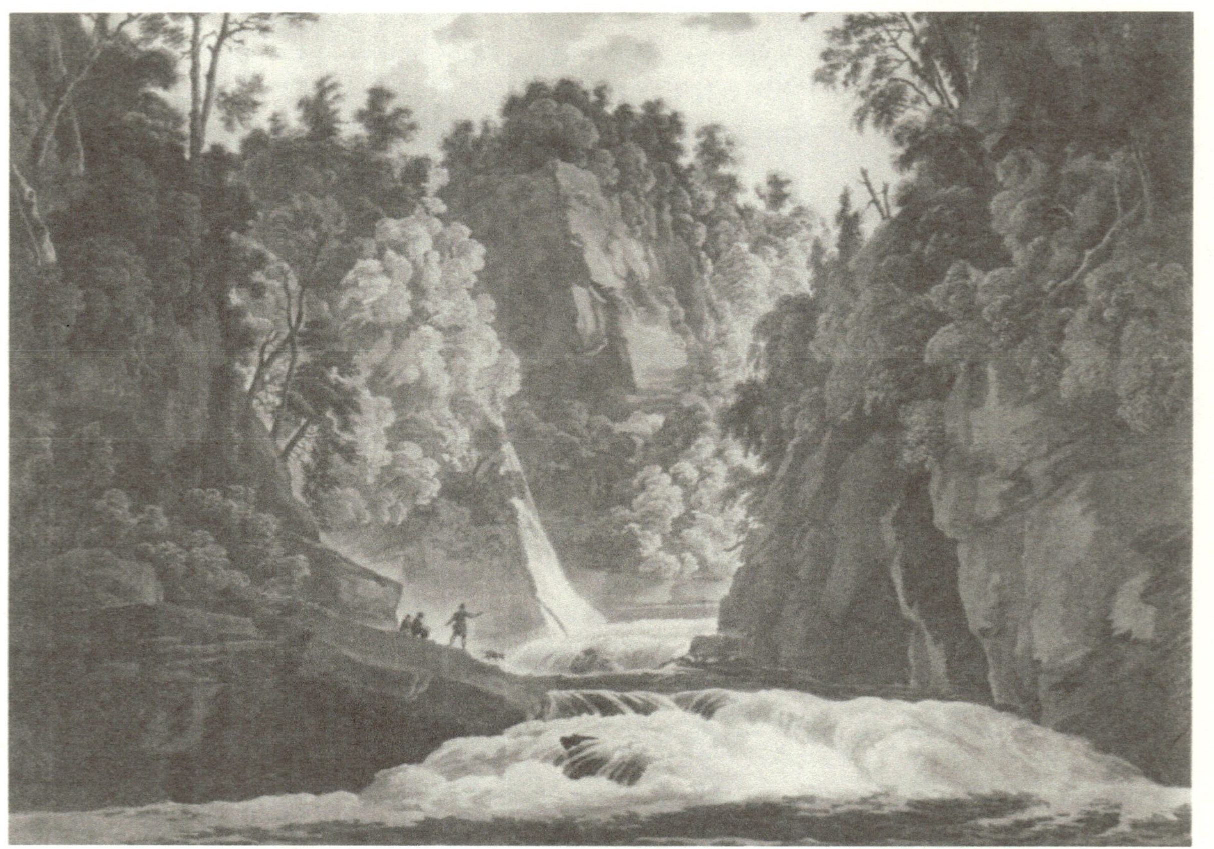

26 / J.W. Edy, *View of the St Ann's or Grand River*, 1795/6. Aquatint after G.B. Fisher, 450 × 625 mm. (image)

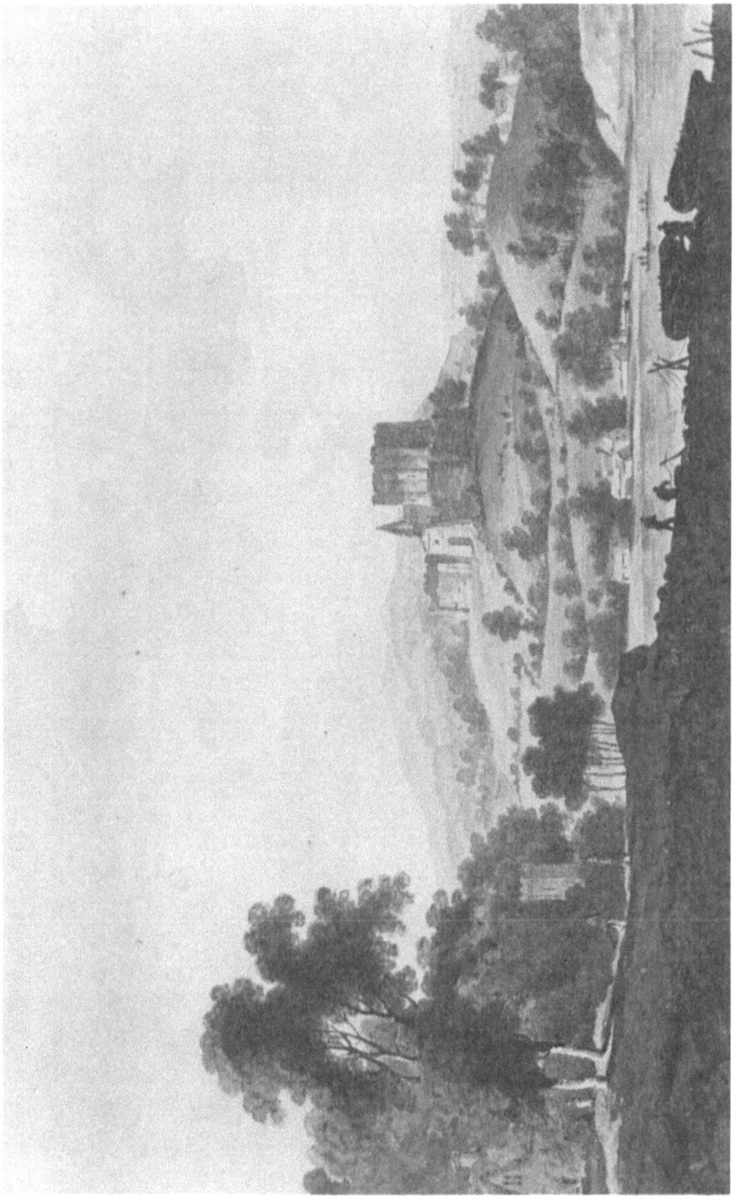

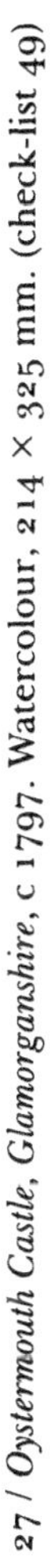

27 / *Oystermouth Castle, Glamorganshire*, c 1797. Watercolour, 214 × 325 mm. (check-list 49)

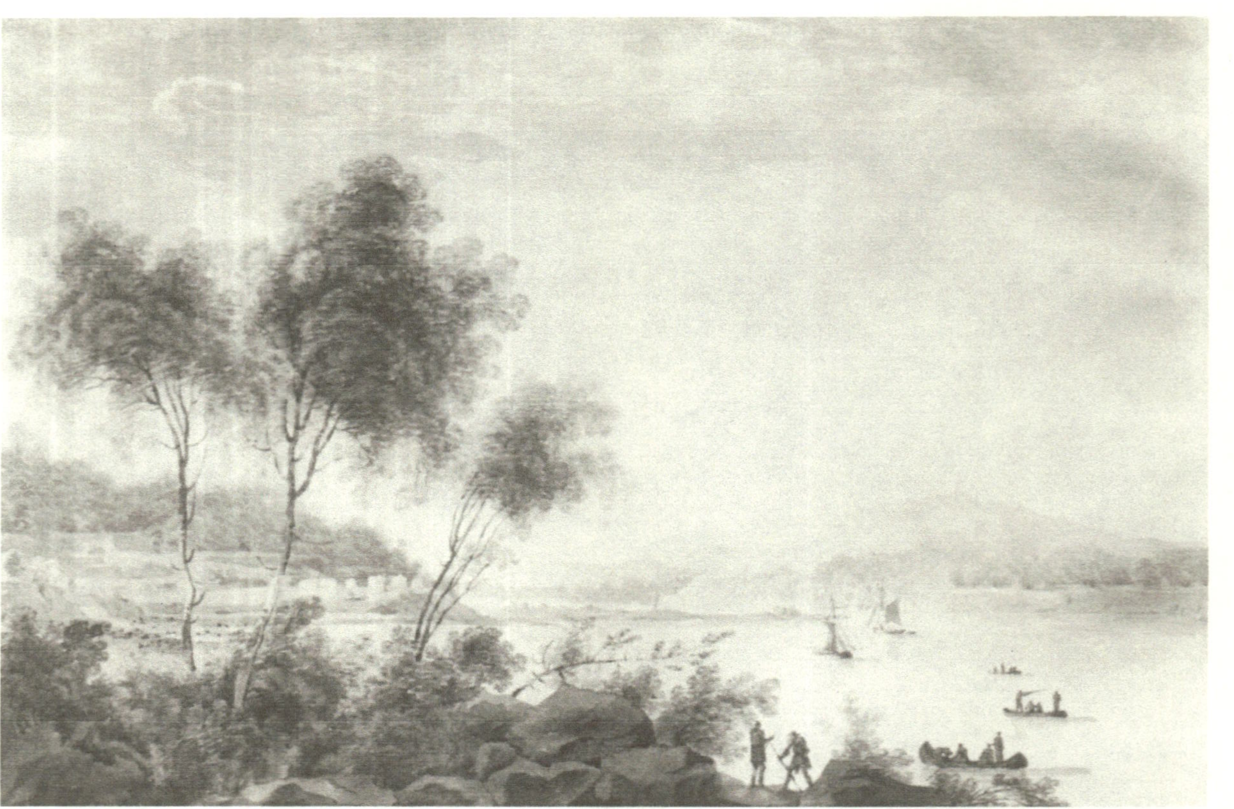

28 / *Colonel Nairne's Settlement at Mal Bay*, 1798. Watercolour, 264 × 378 mm. (check-list 54)

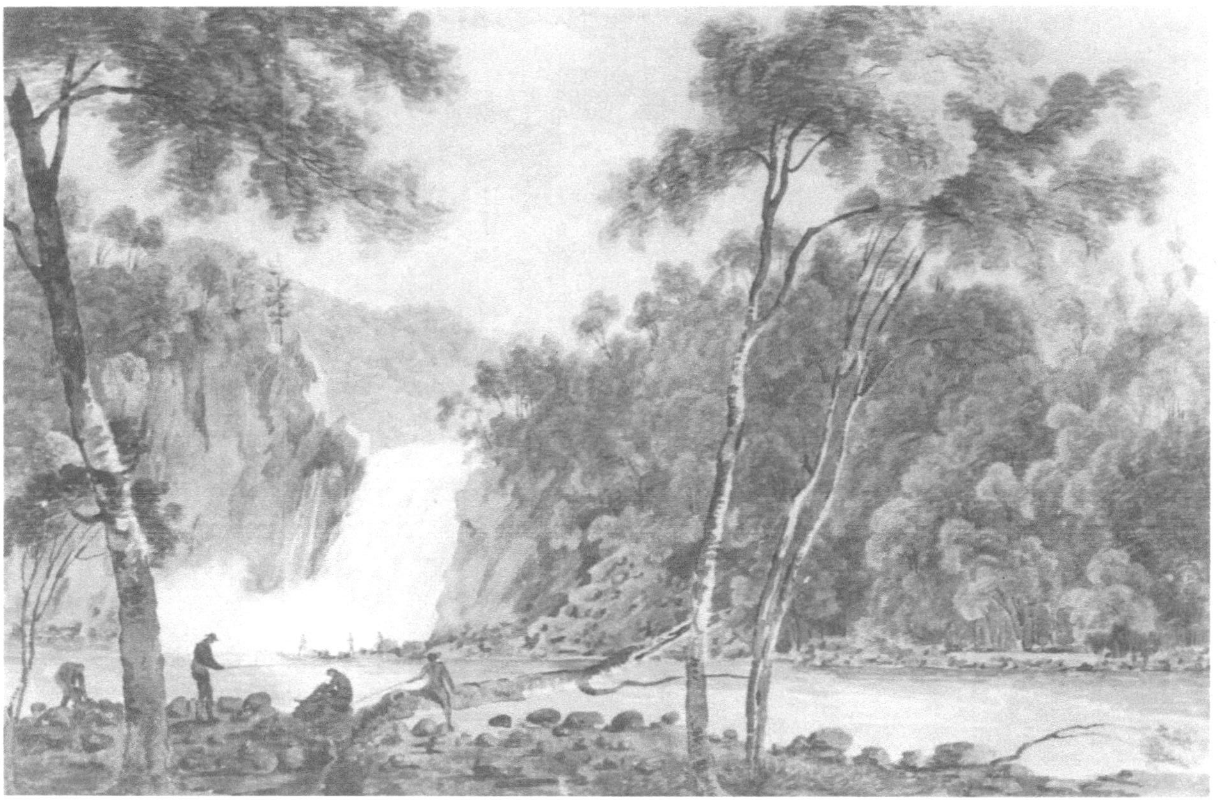

29 / *Cataract of the River La Puce, Canada*, c 1799. Watercolour, 213 × 318 mm. (check-list 67)

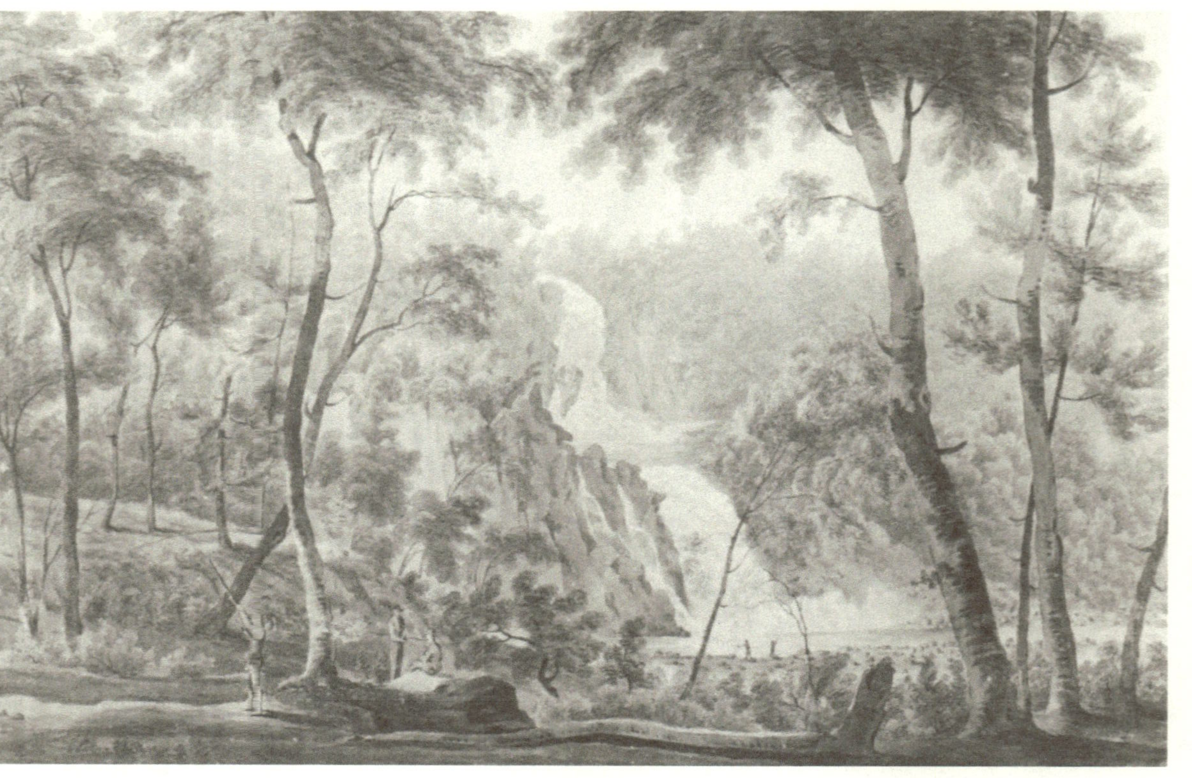

30 / *Double Fall of the River La Puce*, c 1799. Watercolour, 216 × 324 mm. (check-list 66)

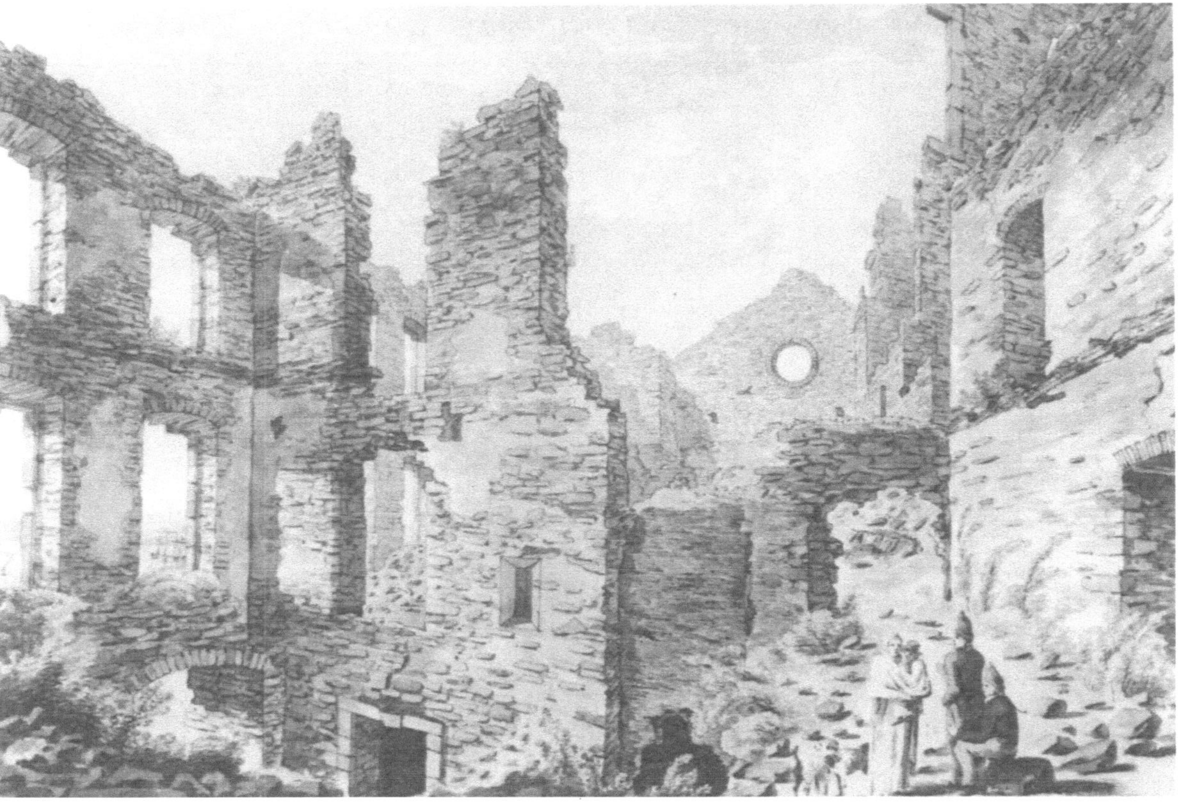

31 / *Ruins of the Intendant's Palace, Quebec*, 1799. Watercolour, pen, and ink, 268 × 379 mm. (check-list 60)

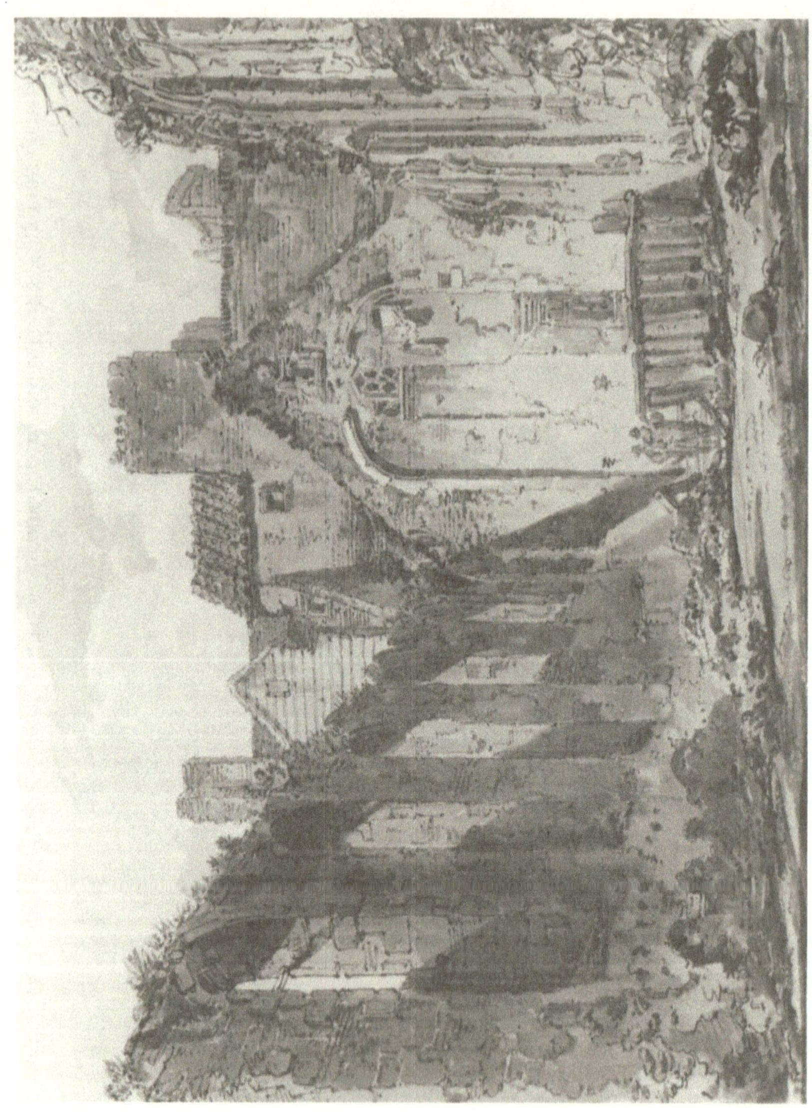

32 / Thomas Girtin, *Ruins of the Chapel in the Savoy Palace, London*, 1795/6. Watercolour with pen and ink, 228 × 288 mm.

4

First Years as Postal Administrator

In 1800, three years after Heriot returned to Canada, he began his career as the head of the Canadian Post Office. Before going to England on leave Heriot had been content with his position in the Ordnance Department, but his year in England wrought a change in him. There he had made personal decisions about his attitude to Canada and had given much thought to the advancement of his career as one of His Majesty's colonial servants. With this in mind he had spoken to his brother John, who may have pointed out the opportunities which, if he made the necessary effort, would be within his grasp. So powerful were John's connections that, when Heriot returned to Quebec in 1797, he was not only appointed to a much more senior position on the Board of Ordnance (that of assistant storekeeper), but was allowed to retain his previous post as clerk of cheque in the same department. The senior position did not come to him through the normal channels; it was likely because of pressure from London that the governor of Lower Canada, General Robert Prescott, reluctantly appointed this unknown, minor civil officer to a more lucrative post.

The appointment was certain to create more difficulties than it would solve, since not only was it made in an irregular manner, but it involved the awarding of two posts, and two salaries, to one man. Not that the seeking or obtaining of a sinecure was illegal: it was a practice that was generally tolerated, if not widely advertised. However, Heriot's rapid promotion and accumulated salaries seem to have aroused hostility, and it was not long before the Duke of Kent, the commander-in-chief of His Majesty's forces, was made aware of Heriot's twin posts.

The duke responded swiftly and decisively. Writing in October 1799 to the commander of the forces of Upper and Lower Canada, General Peter Hunter, he brought to his attention what he considered to be an untenable situation: 'I perceive that Mr Herriot, who holds a situation under the Board of Ordnance at Quebec, is also Deputy Storekeeper General, and I understand, he holds it only under an order from General Prescott, not by a Commission from His Majesty. As I entirely disapprove of my Servants under the Board of Ordnance holding a Post in the Contingent Department, you will acquaint that Gentleman that I am under the disagreeable necessity of superceding him.'[1] Heriot was accordingly deprived of his appointment as assistant storekeeper but was able to retain the post of clerk of cheque.

This was but a minor episode in a larger drama that was beginning to unfold with Heriot and his superiors on the Board of Ordnance as protagonists. The next episode was Heriot's appointment, in April 1800, to the post of deputy postmaster general of the 'Provinces of Upper and Lower Canada, Nova Scotia and New Brunswick in North America, and their Dependencies,' with an annual salary of £400.[2] That Heriot received this appointment was once more because of his brother's considerable influence. While Heriot was in London in 1796, he apparently met, through John, a number of ministers of the Crown, among them the prime minister, William Pitt. As a dedicated Tory and newspaper editor, John had faithfully supported Pitt's policies in print. When the post of deputy postmaster general of British North America became vacant on the dismissal of Hugh Finlay in 1799,[3] the prime minister, very much aware of John Heriot's allegiance, seems to have acted on the latter's recommendation that George Heriot should be nominated by him for the position.[4] Not unexpectedly, Heriot was appointed.[5]

The position of deputy postmaster general at first seemed well suited to Heriot's skills and aspirations, combining as it did material advantage with considerable prestige, not to mention everything else that constituted the patronage and bounty of a government appointment. Shortly after taking up his duties Heriot made recommendations for the reform of the postal service which were both sound and relatively wide-ranging. The main problems of the Post Office were the state of the communications between Montreal and the whole of Upper Canada and the conveyance of mails from Quebec to Halifax: in both areas Heriot saw a need for improvement.

He was pleased to find that Hugh Finlay had placed postal deliveries between Quebec and Montreal on a fairly sound footing; even though the road linking these towns was badly rutted and boggy in places and its bridges were not always secure, twice-weekly posts were operating. East of Quebec, however, the picture was different. The eastern service was poorer and less regular because the terrain was more sparsely settled and less hospitable. The maintenance of the difficult land route between Quebec and Halifax during the winter months (when navigation on the St Lawrence was closed and vessels could no longer reach Quebec) had been dictated by historical circumstances. Before the American War of Independence the traditional route from the east coast had been from New York to Montreal. Old and well-established, this route used some tolerable roads and accessible waterways; but after the war and the recognition of the United States' independence, the old North American postal system was dissolved, and Canada and the United States established their own separate services. The Americans then demanded what the British regarded as excessive toll for conveying mails across their territory and so the British were compelled to consider developing the extremely arduous land route to the sea from Quebec to Halifax. But it was soon discovered that, among other difficulties, the cost of establishing a regular, frequent land service between these towns would be too great: there was not yet a sufficient volume of mail to justify the necessary financial outlay. It was believed that, for the moment, most mails between Canada and England should continue to be sent by way of New York, despite, apparently, the Americans' exorbitant charges for doing so.

In 1792, after this land route to the sea had been investigated and the recommendation for its eventual development transmitted to England, a postal convention was concluded between Canada and the United States whereby the United States Post Office agreed to act as an intermediary for mails passing between Britain and Canada and to charge reasonable rates for this service. When post from Britain for Canada reached New York by packet boat, the resident British packet agent sorted this mail and then placed it in sealed bags and forwarded it through the United States postal service to Burlington, Vermont, not far from the Canadian border. There, mails were collected by couriers from Canada and transported to Montreal.

However, the Quebec-Halifax land route was maintained throughout the year. In winter, for example, monthly deliveries were made between Quebec and Fredericton; between Fredericton and Saint John, and Saint John and Halifax, there was a weekly service. Regular deliveries on this route were made not only for the benefit of the local people, but also in order to provide the relative security of a route through British territory in the event of war with the United States. Heriot, at the outbreak of the War of 1812, proposed to improve the condition of this route in order to make it less treacherous and to reduce the travelling time between Quebec and Halifax.

The postal service west of Montreal to Kingston, York (Toronto), and Niagara was even less well developed than that east of Quebec, again because of the sparseness of the population, for Upper Canada's settlements stretched thinly along the exposed shores of the lakes. In 1799, during the navigable months, the king's vessels regularly carried mails to the several widely separated posts along Lake Ontario, but during the winter there was only a single delivery by courier from Monreal to Niagara; a round trip took from about 20 January until 24 March. The delivery consisted of post that had accumulated from November (when navigation on the lakes closed) until January (when the round trip began).[6]

Heriot, determined to improve Upper Canada's mails by increasing the number of regular deliveries, was in touch with General Peter Hunter, the lieutenant governor of the upper province at York (the capital since 1796), by 1800.[7] Hunter was equally anxious to improve the province's communications, especially during the winter months. He had begun to construct a road from York to Kingston, which, from the Bay of Quinte to York, 'was sufficiently good to allow any of the common conveyances of the Country to pass along without difficulty.'[8] Many responsible people, he had discovered, lived on this route, on whom the Post Office could rely to provide shelter for couriers and collecting and dropping points for the mails.[9]

Heriot was as convinced as Hunter that the establishment of this mail route was vital. He arranged with the postmaster at York that excess revenue received from the western part of the province should be kept aside to be used to improve this service. But he first required official permission from the Post Office in London to do so. He accordingly wrote a letter to the joint postmaster general asking for approval to develop the service. The importance of the route, he wrote, lay in 'the rapid increase of late years in the population of that Country, from the extent of Territory now settled, from the salubrity of its Climate, and the fertility of its Soil, it has the fairest prospect of soon becoming one of the first of the British Settlements in North America, and I have reason to flatter myself that from the proposed intercourse by land, the revenue of the Post Office here, will in a short time be considerably augmented.'[10] The postmaster general's reply was cautious: Heriot was advised not to create or extend services unless such an action would yield revenue adequate to cover the costs.[11]

Heriot was astonished. The Post Office regulations, he now discovered, presented all kinds of obstacles and the postal authorities in London displayed a profound lack of understanding of the needs of the colonial society among whom he worked. Even if a well-populated part of the country could produce sufficient revenue to underwrite the losses incurred by the service in a more meagrely settled region, this was not allowed; all revenues not required for the operation of the service in the area which yielded them had to be returned to Britain. Thus, if General Hunter had not agreed to underwrite for a limited period any deficit that the Upper Canada postal route might incur, Heriot could not have proceeded with his plans.[12] But by the winter of 1800 a monthly service was begun between Kingston and Niagara.[13]

In 1801 Heriot undertook what appears to have been his first trip to the western frontiers of Upper Canada to develop this new service. (He had another, private mission: to observe, make notes, and sketch, for he was collecting material for a book, *Travels through the Canadas,* on which he was then engaged.) He travelled from Montreal to Kingston in a flat-bottom government boat, 'narrow at each extremity, and constructed of fir planks.'[14] In dock at Kingston there were several large lake-going vessels in the king's service, 'two of which are appropriated for the military, and one for the civil department.'[15] Heriot seems to have sailed on one of these to York, where he probably conferred with the postmaster, William Willcocks – and perhaps also with General Hunter, if the latter's new position as commander-in-chief of the forces did not at this time require him to be elsewhere.

From York Heriot would have sailed to Niagara. There he met this district's associate postmaster, Joseph Edwards, in order to discuss with him the development of the service and the extension of mail deliveries from the small settlement at Amherstburg, on Lake Erie, to Niagara, in order to provide a fuller and more effective communication between these far-flung settlements of Upper Canada. For the same reason he also wanted to establish post offices at Queenstown (Queenston) and Chippawa.

Heriot was especially impressed by his visit to Niagara – by its natural beauties and its settlement. Of the town of Niagara he observed: 'The houses are in general composed of wood, and have a neat and clean appearance; their present number may amount to near two hundred. The streets are spacious, and laid out at right angles to each other, so that the town when completed will be healthful and airy.'[16] There was a degree of 'neatness and taste' about the architecture of the town that Heriot found especially attractive and for which, he observed, 'we in vain might look among the more ancient settlements of the lower province.'[17]

Queenstown, which he also visited, he found to be 'a neat and flourishing place, distinguished by the beauty and grandeur of its situation.' Here 'all the merchandise and stores for the upper part of the province are landed from the vessels in which they have been conveyed from Kingston, and transported in waggons to Chippawa, a distance of ten miles, the falls and the rapid and broken course of the river, rendering the navigation impracticable for that space.'[18]

He also saw Chippawa and made a sketch of it as it appeared in 1801 (figure 33), commenting on its appearance: 'A wooden bridge is thrown across this stream, over which is the road leading to Fort Erie. The former fort consists only of a large blockhouse near the bridge, on the northern bank, surrounded by lofty pickets; it is usually the station of a subaltern officer and twenty-five men ... There are in the village some mercantile store-houses, and two or three taverns.'[19]

Although Heriot probably made another visit to Niagara and its environs in 1804 (and certainly did so in 1805) in an attempt to maintain a frequent courier service from Montreal to Niagara, the programme that he and Lieutenant Governor Hunter had originally envisaged had to be abandoned, since the population along the shores of Lake Ontario was too small to yield enough revenue to support such a service.[20] However, Heriot did manage to increase the service in Upper Canada; instead of the single winter delivery that used to take place when Heriot first became deputy postmaster general, by 1805 four services had been established. Two couriers were supplied for the route between Montreal and Kingston and another courier for the route between Kingston and Niagara. The first of the winter mails was forwarded in December, the second in January, the third in February, and the fourth and final delivery in March.[21]

Heriot gained respect for his early efforts to improve Upper Canada's post, though initially he had been hampered by the intransigence of the joint postmaster general in London. Certainly the fact that, under

Heriot's administration, the colonial Post Office did not substantially expand can be largely, though not entirely, explained by Post Office policies. As I have suggested, Heriot's personality and the privilege of his position tended to militate against him. He was never able to learn lessons in tactics or diplomacy. Although cultured and cosmopolitan, he was also strong-willed and fiercely independent. Moreover, he adopted a defiant attitude towards the British administration of the colonial government which eventually generated deep dislike. His prejudice and pride were bitterly resented, and many of his associates secretly longed for him to be recalled from the colony. However, he was protected by a certain patrician toughness, as also by the citadel of privilege, which seemed no easier to storm than that of Quebec.

Heriot's defiance of the colonial government was possible only because, as deputy postmaster general, he was independent of it, his responsibilities as an official in the colonial service being solely to the postmaster general's office in London. Though he pursued power, his haughty attitude towards the colonial administration in fact caused him to be denied opportunities that would otherwise have been his, and his chances of further promotion became increasingly remote.

Finlay, Heriot's predecessor as deputy postmaster general at Quebec, had held a seat in the lower province's Legislative Council. He had also managed to have himself appointed to the post of superintendent of *maîtres de poste* (superintendent of provincial post houses), though in seeking this appointment he had initially encountered vigorous opposition from the then-governor, Frederick Haldimand. The important duty of the holder of this post was to supervise the local *maîtres de poste*, who transported passengers and operated the post houses placed at regular intervals on the road between Montreal and Quebec (these were Canadian property-owners who, though they were not wealthy men, were independent and took pride in their service to the government). Earlier in his Post Office career Finlay, aided by the government, had been able to gain the close co-operation of the *maîtres de poste*, who furnished his mail couriers with transportation at a cost lower than that normally charged to the public. To ensure the continuance of this valuable association Finlay eventually sought formal control over the *maîtres de poste* through the position of superintendent of *maîtres de poste*, a position which, as I have noted, was ultimately granted to him. Thus the position of superintendent and the seat in the Legislative Council gave Finlay the means by which to facilitate the operation of the postal service and reduce the tensions which its short-comings had caused to arise between the Post Office and the colonial government. When Finlay, already superseded by Heriot in the post of deputy postmaster general, died in late 1801, Heriot was confident that Finlay's two positions would now fall to him. In December 1801 he accordingly wrote to the lieutenant governor of the lower province, Sir Robert Milnes, suggesting that he should now be appointed to the position of superintendent of *maîtres de poste* and to membership of the Legislative Council of the government as his predecessor had been.[22] Heriot knew that Finlay had made special arrangements with the *maîtres de poste*, and that he had been empowered to appoint them and to exact an agreement from them to carry 'Mail couriers for 6d. per league,' which, as Heriot knew, was 'less than half the Fare paid by ordinary travellers.' He also knew that Finlay had been able to keep them to these terms during his entire period in office. Therefore, while awaiting the outcome of his application, Heriot wrote to the joint postmaster general in London, warning them that 'unless the Controul [sic] over the Maitres de Poste is given to Me it will not be in my Power to prevail on them to act agreeably to the terms of their former Contract. Should that take place, I must necessarily have Recourse to new Contracts with Persons in different Situations on the Road which could be attended with more Expense.'[23]

There is no doubt that Heriot's sense of public duty, instilled in him in early life, led him to believe, quite sincerely, that the allocation to him of the position of superintendent of *maîtres de poste* was necessary for the effective and economical operation of his department and, therefore, would be in 'the interests of His Majesty's Service.' But he also believed that on account of his status and prestige the appointment was no more than his due. He was even willing to forgo most of the salary, if necessary, and to present it to Finlay's family, who, since Finlay's death, had been experiencing difficult times: 'I shall be happy if any Part of the Salary could be of Service to the family whom Mr Finlay has left. I should receive nothing more than may be deemed reasonable Compensation for expenses incurred in visiting the Post Houses.'[24]

We may reasonably assume that Heriot and the lieutenant governor were initially on good terms. Milnes had almost certainly met Heriot before on official business and at government functions. A watercolour by Heriot dated 1802, but perhaps painted as early as 1800 (figure 34), suggests that he had been invited by Milnes to attend a function at Powell Place. This house, which was used as the setting for the government social functions over which the lieutenant governor presided, had the dual advantages of being attractive (with spacious grounds overlooking the St Lawrence River) and of being only two miles from Quebec. On this particular occasion Heriot sketched the house, in front of which he represented the lieutenant governor, Mrs Milnes, their children, and the Anglican Bishop of Quebec, Dr Jacob Mountain. It seems probable that Heriot presented this watercolour to the lieutenant governor, since it remained in the possession of the Milnes family for many years. However informal the relation between the two men at this time, it did not continue. For the lieutenant governor's subsequent association with the deputy postmaster general made him increasingly wary. He became conscious of Heriot's deeply ingrained ambition, and although Heriot was no more anxious to gain material advantage and prestige than were other men, Milnes came to the conclusion that he lacked those qualities which the successful candidate for the post of superintendent of *maîtres de poste* should possess. Heriot was therefore passed over, and a formal announcement was made on 9 January 1802 that one M. Gabriel-Elzéar Tachereau, a Canadian property-owner who enjoyed local political power, had been appointed superintendent of *maîtres de poste*.

Although Heriot was furious at this rejection, he seems to have contained his anger and hid most of his frustration for more than a year. Early in 1803 he wrote to Milnes, stating that the new incumbent 'cannot with efficacy execute his duty but through the medium of His Majesty's Couriers who are under my Command; nor can I effectually serve His Majesty while destitute of the influence and authority, which are vested in Mr Taschereau.'[25] Heriot also expressed his disquiet at the news, which he had recently received, that the postal couriers should pay to the *maîtres de poste* 'the same fare as that allowed ... for ordinary Travellers.' For, 'in order to maintain the communication between the parent State and the Provinces in America, the General Post Office incurs an Expenditure of more than ten times the produce arising from the Postage of Letters throughout all the Provinces and their dependencies.'[26] Heriot believed that the only solution to what he considered an intolerable state of affairs would be to 'nominate Mr Taschereau to some better situation than that of Provincial Superintendent as a reward for those merits which every candid person cannot fail to acknowledge.'[27] In a subsequent letter to Milnes Heriot wrote: 'I hope your Excellency, for the welfare of the Service, will be pleased to vest that situation in me,' for, he declared, 'I cannot preserve the chain of communication for the conveyance of His

Majesty's Mails, whilst I have not the power of appointing the Maitres de Poste.'[28]

Time was to prove Heriot correct. But Robert Milnes had his own ideas and as the lieutenant governor was all-powerful. It was he, and he alone, who was responsible for appointing members of the Legislative Council and for selecting the superintendent of *maîtres de poste*. When eventually he was asked by the home government why Heriot had not been appointed both to the position of superintendent and to membership of the Legislative Council, Milnes wrote to the secretary of state in London, Lord Hobart, saying that he did not 'consider Mr Heriots Qualifications sufficient to entitle him to expect such an appointment [as superintendent of *maîtres de poste*] or that of a Legislative Councillor.' Another reason which he gave for passing over Heriot was that Heriot still retained 'the appointment of Clerk of Check in the Ordnance Department worth about £150 p[er] annum, from which he was raised to his situation under the Post Office, to which a net salary of £400, p[er] annum is, I understand, annexed, so that his situation is now equal to some of the first in this Province.'[29]

In this letter, which was marked 'secret,' Milnes confided to the secretary of state some underlying reasons why he could not, and would not, appoint Heriot. Heriot, Milnes declared, was not always candid; he displayed an objectionable self-importance, as well as 'inconsistency and a want of Judgment'; he also bragged and would remark on how business in Britain required his personal supervision. Furthermore, wrote Milnes, Heriot's disposition in general was such that it precluded 'all possibility' of consultation with him. Milnes wrote that he was now obliged to avoid all correspondence with the deputy postmaster general, 'except when absolutely necessary.' He concluded by saying that, in view of these faults in Heriot's character, he would 'stand justified with Your Lordship in the conduct I have held toward him.'[30]

Milnes gave yet another and sounder reason for not appointing Heriot superintendent of *maîtres de poste*. The association between the postal administration and the *maîtres de poste* had not always been amicable. Milnes knew that Finlay in his capacity as superintendent had had some difficulty in his later years in maintaining the agreed low rates of passage. After Finlay's death the *maîtres de poste*, as Heriot discovered, had refused to continue to abide by their former agreement, demanding from the Post Office a higher rate of payment than they had received hitherto. Because of the independence of the *maîtres de poste* and these new circumstances

Milnes was of the opinion that it would be impolitic for the Post Office to insist on maintaining its former privileged relationship with them, and therefore unrealistic to expect from them the favourable rates which that relationship had involved. Thus Milnes was determined that the supervision of the *maîtres de poste* should be in the hands of a responsible person, one not associated with the Post Office, preferably a Canadian, and someone who possessed local political power. Taschereau seemed a sound candidate for the appointment.

The home government was more sympathetic to the deputy postmaster general's view than to the lieutenant governor's but because of Milnes's determination to appoint someone other than Heriot, it voiced no objection when Taschereau was appointed. However, Lord Hobart, probably knowing of Heriot's powerful connections in London, and learning of his disappointment and displeasure, wrote to Milnes recommending that, 'in consideration of the expectations he [Heriot] may have entertained of succeeding to both the appointments which were vested in the late Deputy Postmaster General Mr Finlay, an opportunity may be afforded to you of nominating him to some situation in addition to his present office, of equal emolument with that of Superintendent of Maitres de Poste.'[31] Milnes, however, did not offer Heriot any compensating position, and even if he had done so, it is difficult to assess how Heriot would have reacted to such a 'sop to Cerberus.' He had set his mind on these particular positions; both on the post of superintendent and on a seat on the Legislative Council: the former would have given him control of the *maîtres de poste* (which would certainly have eased the difficulty of administering his department); the latter would have secured him power within the colonial government. Milnes was only too conscious of Heriot's hunger for power, and had already suffered from his high-handed, independent methods and manner. He was determined to prevent such a man (who, as a member of the Legislative Council, would not be under his government's direct jurisdiction) from gaining a voice in provincial matters.

Heriot's disillusionment with the colonial authorities – and especially with the lieutenant governor – soon degenerated into spite. In time he saw an opportunity for revenge and grasped it. One night in August 1805, after the close of the mails, a man employed as a waiter arrived at Heriot's house bearing despatches from Lieutenant Governor Milnes which were to be taken on board the *Uranie*, then at anchor in the river, but about to depart for England. Since Heriot had received no written request from the lieutenant governor, he believed that, technically, he was not obliged to accept these despatches. He also knew that the lieutenant governor would be travelling on the ship himself and so could easily take the papers with him. Heriot therefore decided not to accept the despatches. On receiving a protest from Milnes, Heriot immediately replied: 'I consider the sending [of] papers to me without any written request, seven hours after the Mails were closed, as highly disrespectful, and that I am by no means officially obliged to cause any Letters or dispatches to be sent on board of Vessels. When I make up these Mails at the office, this part of [my] duty must therefore be considered as a matter of favor only.'[32] Stung by the deputy postmaster general's belligerence, Milnes immediately sent off a letter to the secretary of state in London, complaining of the treatment he had received at Heriot's hands: 'Feeling as I do, that the line of Conduct which is adopted by this Gentleman may be of essential detriment to His Majesty's Service, I cannot avoid laying this matter before your Lordship that, in case you should judge proper, it may be submitted to their Lordships the Postmaster General.'[33]

The home government was concerned about Heriot's behaviour and probably advised the joint postmaster general to issue a reprimand, but Heriot did not believe that he had done anything wrong. He had been given the guardianship of the Canadian postal service and he considered it to be his duty to protect it from government interference. The action he had taken was intended merely to demonstrate the extent of his power and the strength of his convictions. But he was to act in this way on many occasions in the future, thus building up among the colonial officials a swell of resentment against him that was to increase in volume and violence as the years passed.

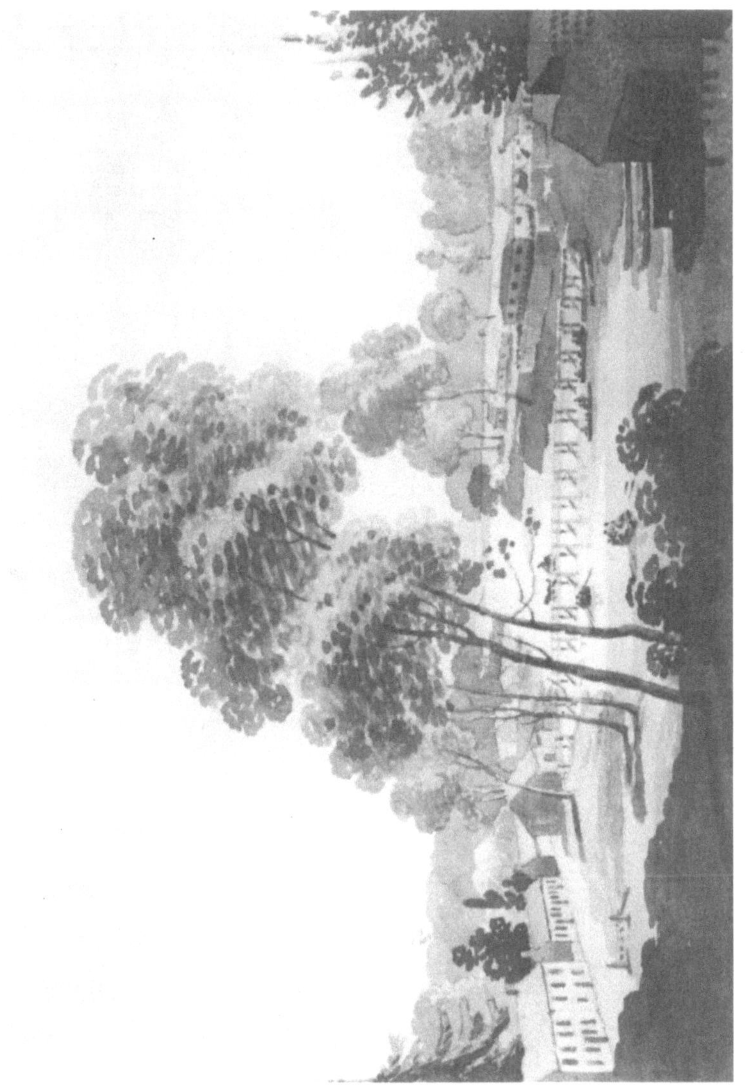

33 / *Village of Chippawa near the Falls of Niagara*, c 1801. Watercolour, 140 × 181 mm. (check-list 92)

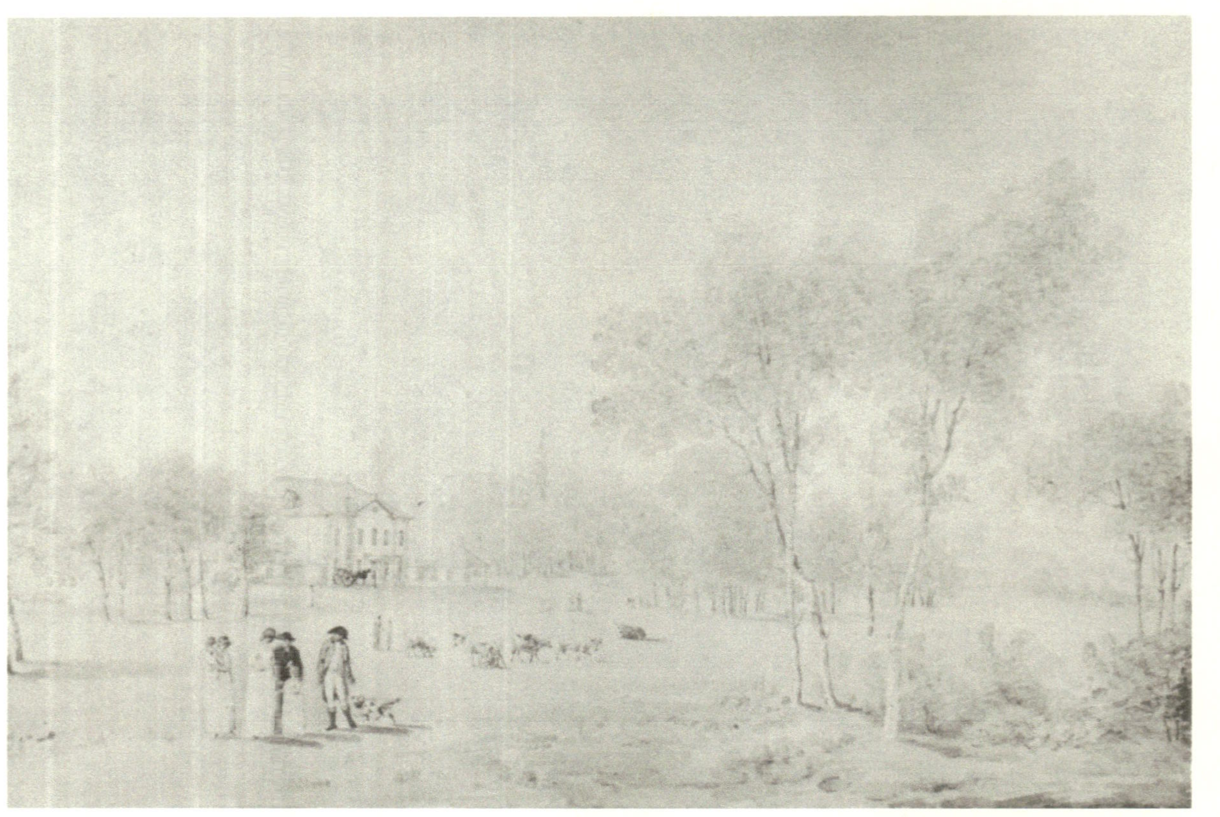

34 / *Powell Place*, c 1800. Watercolour, 260 × 368 mm. (check-list 74)

5

The Maturing Vision 1800–6

Heriot's early years as deputy postmaster general caused him much anxiety; but if he found little cause for satisfaction in the administration of this office, there was room for some degree of contentment in the regulation of his private life. As pressures on him mounted, he found a refuge in writing – he wrote *The History of Canada from its first discovery* (published in London by T.N. Longman and O. Rees in 1804), a work that he based on the published writings of various missionaries and travellers (which he may have found in the Jesuit library at Quebec), particularly on *Histoire et description generale de la Nouvelle France* (1744) by the early eighteenth-century Jesuit traveller, historian, and missionary Pierre François Xavier de Charlevoix. Heriot took his history of Canada up to the year 1731; he had proposed to publish at least one further volume – presumably to bring the history up to the time of his writing – but, unfortunately, this volume never materialized.

Heriot devised other escapes from his administrative anxieties. Sometimes he found excuses to travel, to leave the close and confining society of Quebec. On these solitary journeys (ostensibly made on postal business) Heriot's spare moments were chiefly devoted to making notes for a proposed Canadian travel book, and to sketching; each of these activities, he found, was an effective palliative for his troubled mind.

Heriot had been encouraged to write a travel book based on his Canadian experiences by his English friends (this must have occurred before his departure from England in 1797). This book was to be the embodiment of his firmly established interests: writing, sketching, and travelling. Although he had already travelled extensively in Canada, his knowledge of the country and its cultures was wider than his first-hand experiences of them. Probably his research for *The History of Canada* aided him; but he also studied many other published and manuscript sources in order to provide himself with an adequate context for his own more limited, first-hand impressions. Heriot's selection of material (both borrowed and personal) for his proposed book was highly subjective: it bore the strong imprint of both his prejudices and his taste.

Travels through the Canadas was published by Richard Phillips in London in 1807, the year when Heriot returned to Canada after a brief visit to Britain. The *Travels* is a substantial book, over six-hundred pages in length, and containing a map and twenty-seven plates after Heriot's own drawings and watercolours. In outward form the book followed an established pattern for travel books on the subject of North America. The first of its two parts is largely devoted to descriptions of the immigrant society (its culture and its commerce) and of the topography (Heriot describes the landscape from east to west – from Newfoundland to Lake Superior); the second part is devoted to the wider subject of the indigenous tribes of the Americas.

Heriot observed that in preparing this second part he drew heavily on documentary materials in the Jesuit library at Quebec and supplemented them with memoirs, travel literature, and other works, 'which ... [were] published at different periods.' Among these writings were Joseph François Lafitau's *Mœurs des sauvages americains*, William Robertson's *History of America*, and the accounts of voyages of several travellers, including that of Count Louis Antoine de Bougainville.[1] However, Heriot did not accept indiscriminately all the information which he gathered from such books. As a resident of Canada 'for a series of years,' he noted that he had had opportunities 'of witnessing the modes of life pursued by several of the Indian nations,' and was thus able 'to adduce what he has himself observed, as well as to reject what he deemed improbable in the writings he consulted.'[2] Heriot's own experience also enabled him to examine critically and include in his book information derived from 'living observation, communicated by men on whose veracity a reliance could be placed.'[3]

A contemporary British critic, writing in the *Edinburgh Review*, attacked the excessive length and detailed descriptions of the *Travels*. It 'could only have been filled,' he remarked, 'by inserting every thing, whether dull or interesting, which now appears for the first time ... We have a detail of the lakes, rivers, and cataracts, the villages, farm-houses ...

considerably more minute (need we say how much less interesting?) than we possess of the county of Northumberland ... The enumeration of different townships, or districts nominally settled and only begun to be cultivated and cleared, are in the highest degree uninteresting to all but persons having estates in those parts.'[4] As J.J. Talman has recently pointed out, the amount of detail in the *Travels*, of which this early reviewer complains, is of great value and interest to us today, since the character of the country has been so radically altered since the book was published.[5] Heriot's written descriptions (like his watercolours) are important to us as social documents, aiding us in our reconstruction of Canada's past. For instance, Heriot provides us with a remarkably precise and interesting (if limited) descriptive catalogue of important buildings in Quebec City, and he also includes personal observations (in a book which only very rarely reveals the author's character) on the city's town-planning. Heriot describes the Protestant cathedral and the court-house, both of which had recently been built on the site of the Place d'armes; although he admired them (they were 'constructed with the best materials ... and executed in a neat and handsome stile'), he felt that their siting was unfortunate: '[although] considered as ornaments to the city of Quebec, it is to be regretted, that separate situations have not been allotted for them, and that in a country where public buildings capable of attracting notice are rarely to be met with, two edifices of such consequence should have been placed so near to each other.'[6]

In the first part of the book Heriot's discussions of the peoples of Canada are equally interesting. He divides the population into four classes: 'those belonging to the church and to religious orders, the *noblesse* or *seigneurs*, the mercantile body, and the landholders, stiled *habitants*.'[7] While indigenous people seem not to be included in these categories, recent settlers are. Heriot provides striking and historically valuable impressions of the immigrants from the United States who were settling in Canada: 'Families ... are daily coming ... bringing with them their stock and utensils of husbandry, in order to establish themselves on new lands, invited by the exuberance of the soil, the mildness of the government, and an almost total exemption from taxes.' He notes that these immigrants 'either purchase lands from the British subjects, to whom they have been granted, or take them upon lease, paying the rent by a certain proportion of the produce.' Heriot considers the most desirable of them to be 'men born and educated in the northern states ... [who] are of the greatest utility in the settlement of a new country, as they are endowed with a spirit for adventure, activity, industry, and perseverance, rarely to be equalled. Nor are they deficient in the power of inventive faculty, particularly when applied to mechanical objects.'[8]

The life and institutions, the towns and villages of Canada do not absorb all of Heriot's attention; in this first part of the *Travels* he takes pleasure in describing the country's natural beauty. Since Canada was so young, it could yield 'few objects which ... [could] occupy the enquiries of an antiquarian,'[9] but its landscape furnished a subject which would captivate the attention of those who enjoyed scenery. Heriot had been struck by the beauty of Canada's broad, shining lakes, its impetuous rivers, its awesome cliffs, and its vast, wooded distances – all of which, in the *Travels* he describes and discusses within the context of the Picturesque. It is Heriot's picturesque viewpoint in the *Travels* that makes this book different from many other contemporary published accounts of North America; indeed it must be one of the earliest books to examine the North American landscape almost entirely from a picturesque point of view. For Heriot the most notable picturesque feature of Canada was its lakes and rivers, which he considered 'vast and principal objects ... calculated to inspire wonder and gratification': 'The immense volumes, the irresistible weight and velocity of the ... [rivers], tearing through and overpowering the obstacles opposed to their course, by the rugged and unequal territories amid which they roll, produce falls and cataracts of singular sublimity, and of commanding beauty; these, although in some degree similar in effect, are, notwithstanding, inexhaustible in variety.'[10]

If the Picturesque registering itself in Heriot's *Travels* added to the attractiveness of his descriptive text, it seems also to have contributed a remarkable new simplicity and structural quality to his watercolours after about 1800, both those used to illustrate the *Travels* and others. Gilpin's theory of the Picturesque and the prints (chiefly in aquatint) which illustrate it in his tour books furnished Heriot with the basic ingredient of his classical watercolour style in its new phase, which began about 1800 (when he effectively took up his duties as deputy postmaster general) and continued until 1806 (when he left for Britain on what appears to have been family business). His earliest, strongest, 'classical' watercolours are the Welsh views painted in Britain (contemporary with the one exhibited at the Royal Academy in 1797); in these watercolours forms have been compositionally integrated and expressive individuality is limited – although the same characteristics can be found in the earliest of Heriot's known picturesque landscape watercolours (c 1787), for 'picturesque' and 'classical,' as we have seen (see chapter 1), are not mutually exclusive aesthetic and artistic terms.

If Heriot knew of Gilpin's published tours as early as the 1780s when he was at Woolwich, we may reasonably assume that by the 1790s he must have read at least some of them. Possibly he also studied Gilpin's theoretical work on the Picturesque, *Three Essays: – on Picturesque Beauty; – on Picturesque Travel; – and, on Landscape Painting. (Notes on the Poem – Explanation of the prints)*, which was published in London in 1792, the year in which Heriot left England for Canada. All Gilpin's books would have interested Heriot, with their many references both to the practice and to the theory of the Picturesque.

But by 1800 it was surely the strength and simplicity of the landscape prints with which Gilpin's guides were illustrated, with their compact forms and clearly defined spatial planes, that would chiefly have impressed Heriot (figure 35); these refreshingly spare, mainly aquatint compositions have a restrained charm which he would have found most attractive. Gilpin's designs would have presented a sharp contrast to the more festive and more decoratively picturesque Edy-Fisher prints which Heriot had so recently admired and emulated. Gilpin's more austere, classical picturesqueness was remarkably well suited to Heriot's sensibilities, since it projected a conception of nature that he admired for its timeless and therefore dependable and secure quality. It was Gilpin's restrained classicism, then – as expressed in his plates – that seems to have inspired Heriot and modified his landscapes.[11] Gilpin's theoretical disquisitions would have been less influential in helping to establish the character of Heriot's art, since the extent of Heriot's adherence to the Picturesque was apparently determined more by motifs borrowed than by precepts understood.

Heriot's new classicism can particularly be observed in the watercolours which he executed on his trip in 1801 to southwestern Upper Canada, when he was negotiating with government officials concerning the establishment of a regular mail route to the province's western limits. The luminous, unifying quality of the atmosphere found in watercolours of this time and earlier is combined with a new formal clarity and simplicity, as can be seen in *Niagara River* (check-list 89) and *Whirlpool, Niagara River* (figure 36). But these landscapes, though they indicate a stylistic change, are not the most striking examples of Heriot's new style. Perhaps the transformation is most evident in a strong, large finished watercolour, the almost Claudean *Lake St Charles near Quebec*, c 1801 (figure 37), which brings together the most expressive ingredients of Heriot's newly developed classicism.

The differences between the watercolour *Lake St Charles* painted in 1795 (see figure 21) and the later view of the same subject reflect a fundamental change in Heriot's interpretation of Canada. The pale hues and fragile linearity of the earlier style is replaced by dense colour and a dramatic chiaroscuro. The scene appears to be transformed; it is much grander. The hills are higher and more varied in contour and the trees now blossom forth in thick, more luxuriant foliage. In aesthetic terms the view evokes a sense of classical calm and equilibrium like that found in Gilpin's plates. Certainly, in the later *Lake St Charles* the lake itself has become a picturesque location as Gilpin would have understood it. A year or so later Heriot was to write this description of the lake:

> On arriving at the vicinity of the lake, the spectator is delighted by the beauty and picturesque wildness of its banks. It is, around small collections of water like this, that nature is displayed to the highest advantage ... Trees grow immediately on the borders of the water, which is indented by several points advancing into it, and forming little bays. The lofty hills which suddenly rise towards the north, in shapes, singular and diversified, are overlooked by mountains which exalt beyond them, their most distant summits. The effect produced by clouds, is here solemn and sublime, particularly during thunder storms, when they float in rugged masses, around the tops of the hills, whose caverns, and defiles, re-echo to the trembling forests, the hoarse and awful roar.[12]

The classicism that Heriot had developed was consolidated in the watercolours painted during the next few years – especially those of figures, a subject which increasingly absorbed him.

By 1804 Heriot's classical style had been modified in several important respects. While the light and shade effects (which served to articulate his landscape compositions more forcefully than hitherto) were continued and enhanced, there was also a renewed emphasis on textural enrichment and an innovative use of line. A landscape such as *View at Cape Rouge* (1804) (figure 38) is remarkable less for its stylistic affinity with the 1801 *Lake St Charles* than for its obvious innovations. We notice especially a revival and development of the textural enrichment discoverable in the watercolours of about 1799 and a new-found relationship between tonality and line. There is an abstract compactness of tree forms, and also a stress on diagonal hatching – a device introduced to create and reinforce shadow, as well as to function as a separate decorative adjunct, modulating surfaces and enriching them texturally. By incorporating linear elements Heriot provided a fresh dialectic between the powerful, structural capacity of light and shade and the delicate, decorative and whimsical freedom of line.

The substantial vision of Canada which Heriot achieved in the watercolours of 1804, such as *View at Cape Rouge* and *Falls of Niagara* (check-list 104), was largely the outcome of his effective reconciliation of light and line. It was this reconciliation that provided the basic configuration of his mature Canadian manner – a manner derived from his evolution as a topographical artist under the influence of the Picturesque, but united now with his renewed understanding of nature as a source of fundamental nourishment and as the material of a personal mode of expression. What Heriot achieved in his works of 1804, in terms of stylistic equilibrium, was to provide the basis of his Canadian watercolours for many years to come;[13] this is immediately evident in the works – still more highly wrought, decorative, and monumental – that Heriot painted in the following year. If the tree forms in *View at Cape Rouge* and *Falls of Niagara* are notable for their abundant foliage, enriched by a network of short diagonal strokes, then the tree forms in works dating from 1805 are even more decorative. To textural richness is added a new and notable emphasis on plump, rounded leaf clusters, such as occur in a view entitled *River Landscape* (check-list 123). Here individual trees, as well as clumps, display a new formal complexity. Rock forms, too, are now more distinctive as a decorative device. A large drawing, *River Landscape*, is also striking for the spontaneity of its brushwork and the subtlety of its colouring. It reinforces the image that most people have of the grandeur of Canada's scenery – an image, however, that is discoverable anywhere, and not only in those places which have been traditionally regarded as aesthetically pleasing.

This is not to say that Heriot avoided the famous locations. In 1805, for example, he seems to have undertaken a series of sketches of Niagara Falls. He had first seen the falls in 1801, and had subsequently painted them several times, as well as describing them in his book *Travels through the Canadas*. But his visit to Niagara in 1805 must have given him a new sense of the overwhelming grandeur of the river and falls and filled him with an urge to record this quality as he had never recorded it before – first, capturing it in his original sketches, so that he could later amplify it pictorially and refine it in a larger format. In his finished watercolours he did succeed in conveying the dramatic power and scale of the river and falls, both by taking a panoramic view of the subject through a screen of trees (figure 39) and by examining it at close range (check-list 359 [21]).

For Heriot Niagara epitomized the true sublimity of nature, as defined by Burke and as described by Gilpin in his travel books. During his first visit in 1801 Heriot put on paper his thoughts on the falls, which, he declared,

> surpass in sublimity every description which the powers of language can afford of that celebrated scene, the most wonderful and awful which the habitable world presents. Nor can any drawing convey an adequate idea of the magnitude and depth of the precipitating waters. By the interposition of two islands, the river is separated into three falls ... The lofty banks and immense woods which environ this stupendous scene, the irresistible force, the rapidity of motion displayed by the rolling clouds of foam, the uncommon brilliancy and variety of colours and of shades, the ceaseless intumessence [sic], and swift agitation of the dashing waves below, the solemn and tremendous noise, with the volumes of vapour darting upwards into the air, which the simultaneous report and smoke of a thousand cannon could scarcely equal, irresistibly tend to impress the imagination with such a train of sublime sensations, as few other combinations of natural objects are capable of producing, and which terror lest the treacherous rock crumble beneath the feet by no means contributes to diminish.[14]

It was in the period between 1799 and 1805 that subjects in Canada other than landscape began to command Heriot's artistic attention. As we have seen, his view of nature and of Canada had been widened by his reading, but he was always augmenting his first-hand knowledge of the country – its scenery, peoples, and fauna – during the travel which his Post Office duties frequently enjoined on him. Over the years he frequently sketched scenery of Canadian life, noting the national customs and pastimes, and he also documented the country's animals and insects.

Heriot's watercolours and drawings of Indians and Canadians, though broad in treatment, are none the less pictorially probing and in some cases reminiscent of similar studies executed by his former mentor Paul Sandby. Sometimes Heriot sought to represent custom and costume; at other times he seems to have been more interested in capturing character. Whatever his final purpose, in these works, as in his landscapes, he invests the scene which he has recorded with an imaginative element that transcends mere literal representation.

Though Heriot's interest in Canada and its peoples was not fully aroused until after he had returned from his visit to Britain in 1797, his fascination with different cultures had been established long before. While he was in the West Indies (1777–81) he recorded local ceremonies (check-list 268), and in his Welsh views of 1796, such as *Neath Abbey* (see figure 22), both Welsh costume and Welsh dance are celebrated. It was, indeed, the motif of dancing figures that Heriot was to introduce into his Canadian drawings.

Soon after he first arrived in Canada, Heriot depicted landscapes with Indians; but both Indians and Canadians became a more frequent and more important subject for his brush after his return from leave in Britain in 1797. His *Island of Orleans* (c 1797) (figure 40) must be one of the first watercolours painted after his return which represents Canadian Indians. Their presence in this picture may have been inspired by the print *View of Cape Diamond* (see figure 25) in the Edy-Fisher set: Heriot's landscape displays a similar compositional character, with Indians in the foreground and Quebec in the distance, viewed over the broad expanse of the St Lawrence. But there are also some striking differences. The Indians in the Edy-Fisher view are distinctive, both in stance and gesture; they are languid and relaxed, like misplaced Arcadian shepherds. The Indians in *Island of Orleans*, on the other hand, display an almost uncomfortable stiffness and angularity.

But it is not in landscapes with figures that Heriot chiefly shows his interest in Canada's inhabitants: it is in several series of watercolours, painted between about 1799 and about 1805 (or later), of which the most important record the Indians' ceremonies.

Almost as soon as Heriot returned to Quebec in 1797, he began to read accounts of the North American Indians and visit the Huron village Jeune Lorette, which was between eight and nine miles from Quebec. He was fully aware of the disasters which the coming of the white man had wrought among the Indians: the disease, the undermining of the Indians' culture, and the invasion of their lands. At Jeune Lorette, however, he found a community of Indians who appeared to have preserved some of their old values and to be living in proximity to Canadians 'in a state of almost uninterrupted harmony and tranquillity.'[15]

It was the habit of Quebec gentry, administrators, and officers to visit Jeune Lorette as a diversion, and to ask the Indian residents to perform some of their traditional dances for them. Heriot and his friends fell in with this practice, and on such visits the artist made notes that he was later to use in the preparation of both *Travels through the Canadas* and a number of watercolours. In the *Travels* he mentions that on one occasion he and his friends assembled 'a number of males and females of the village, who repeatedly performed their several dances, descriptive of their manner of going to war, of watching to ensnare the enemy, and of returning with the captives they were supposed to have surprised.' Their dances he considered unattractive, for they 'move their limbs but a little way from the ground, which they beat with violence.' Indeed, their dancing and their music 'are uniformly rude and disgusting.' Heriot concludes his description of the dances with the observation that 'the only circumstance which can recompense a civilized spectator, for the penance sustained by his ear, amid this boisterous roar, and clash of discordant sounds, is, that to each dance is annexed the representation of some action, peculiar to the habits of savage life, and, that by seeing their dances performed, some idea may be acquired, of the mode of conducting their unimproved system of warfare.'[16]

The earliest of the watercolours depicting Indian dances appears to be *Calumet Dance* (figure 41), with its emphasis on harsh angularity and confusion of detail and forms; it dates from about 1799 and illustrates the gracelessness and violence of which Heriot writes. It appears to have been painted immediately before Heriot's classical period and lacks the serenity and order which characterize the watercolours painted after 1799. In the earliest of the post-1799 watercolours on this theme, *Ceremonial Scalp Dance*, c 1801 (check-list 95), Heriot represents a group of Indians performing dances watched by visitors (probably from Quebec). The Indians' gestures are now more restrained, the movements more graceful. Moreover, the forms of the figures are more clearly defined; they are also more carefully arranged, parallel to the picture plane, almost as if they were part of a classical sculptured frieze. In one of these watercolours of Indian subjects, the luminous *Dance of Indian Women*, c 1802 (figure 42), the classical ingredient of the composition is still more pronounced. Heriot has employed his resilient controlled line, which is here more palpably associated with the drawings of neoclassical artists: he was probably inspired by drawing styles which he had either encountered in Britain or seen in engravings.

After about 1799 but before 1805 Heriot's watercolours of Indian subjects seem to adhere to the classical mode; but in those from 1805 the openness of the groupings of forms, which characterizes the drawings made slightly earlier, now decreases: Heriot adopts a more compact arrangement, with the resulting complexities. Figures, which are now smaller, appear to be increasingly agitated and disordered, as the watercolours reflect Heriot's renewed interest in more complex patterns and textures; two examples of works in this style are *Dance for recovery of the Sick* (figure 43) and *Dance on the reception of Strangers* (figure 44).

The watercolours dating from 1805 may be the last which Heriot painted of Indian subjects. It is possible that he planned to publish them as illustrations to his *Travels through the Canadas*, which was, at that time, close to completion; but, when it was published, the book contained very few illustrations of Indian subjects and none of Indian dances.[17] The surprising feature of these watercolours is that, though they show a measure of historical accuracy, they do contain glaring errors. For example, at the time Heriot executed them, nowhere in eastern North America could he have seen near-nude Indians with roached hair and body painting. Recently some sources which Heriot may have seen and on which he may have based the Indians' coiffure, attitudes, and costumes have come to light: he often looked to old engravings for inspiration. For example, the source of the design for and the attitudes of the Indians in his *Dance on the reception of Strangers* is an engraved plate from Lafitau's *Mœurs des sauvages ameriquains ...* (1724) (figure 45). Again, a figure from Heriot's *Dance for recovery of the Sick* may have been based directly on 'The Conjurer,' an engraving which appears in Thomas Harriot's *A briefe and true report of the new found land of Virginia* (1590).[18]

While Heriot may have romaticized the Indians, he was more accurate when he depicted Canadians, with whom he had had continuous social contact. Because he spoke French fluently, he had access to a culture from which many members of the British community were excluded, since relatively few of them had even a barely adequate command of the language. Thus privileged, Heriot met many members of Canadian polite society and probably attended their fêtes, balls, and other functions. We know that he attended services at the French cathedral, for he has put on record an occasion when he went to hear the brother of a former French financier who was a celebrated preacher. Heriot describes the priest's delivery:

> His manner is violent and boisterous, and calculated to make an impression on the lower orders, to whom he chiefly addresses himself. His sermons

> are extemporaneous and he plainly appears to be in earnest in his address. The extravagance of his action, violates as Doctor Johnson remarks the propriety of language, but it is better to use violence of action and loud vociferation than lose the opportunity of converting souls. The preacher is about eighty-four years of age. There was one poetical flight in the course of his sermon which I thought rather pretty: – Mes freres, vous ne regardez pas la Croix – vous n'avez point d'amour pour la Croix – vous avez le cœur froid comme la glace de ces regions Hyperboréales ou vous demeurez – Vous avez le cœur dur comme les roches que le fleuve St Laurent lave avec ses ondes.[19]

Heriot found the 'lower orders' of the Canadian community picturesque and fascinating, and it may be that this is why he illustrated aspects of their cultural life in the plates in his *Travels through the Canadas*. Both his interest and his attitudes are at once apparent in a description of them which he included in the *Travels*: He considered them to be:

> honest ... religious, inoffensive, uninformed, possessing much simplicity, modesty and civility. Indolent, attached to ancient prejudices, and limiting their exertions to an acquisition of the necessaries of life, they neglect the conveniences. Their propensity to a state of inaction, retains many of them in poverty; but as their wants are circumscribed, they are happy. Contentment of mind, and mildness of disposition, seem to be the leading features in their character ... The whole of the Canadian inhabitants are remarkably fond of dancing, and frequently amuse themselves at all seasons with that agreeable exercise.[20]

One of Heriot's earliest pictures of Canadian people is *La Danse Ronde* (figure 46), which seems to date from about the time (c 1799) of his first Indian watercolours, though in this case the composition, while complex, is less confused. It is a delightful, light-filled watercolour, showing happy people out of doors, tripping lightly in a large open circle to the strains of a single violin. The motif of dancing people with seated figures, and children in the foreground, appears in watercolours on the theme of the *danse ronde*, such as an interior scene of about 1801 (figure 47). Here the rich pattern and complexities of the arrangement of the figures seen in the first watercolour on this subject are simplified, and the figures are shown in a more frieze-like fashion. Even the foreground figures have been coalesced in order to make them function as a classical coulisse device – contributing to the definition and separation from each other of foreground and middle-ground spaces.

There also survive a number of character and attitude studies which Heriot made in Canada – possibly at this time. In these watercolours we see individuals, and sometimes groups, who illustrate by their expressions and sedentary poses what Heriot referred to as the Canadians' 'propensity to ... inaction' as well as their happy dispositions. Heriot had probably been inspired by Paul Sandby's studies of soldiers, gentlemen, women, tradesmen, and travellers. For example, Heriot's *Old Woman* (figure 50), which dates from some time between about 1800 and about 1816, shares qualities, both in the subject's attitude and in style, with Sandby's *London Pieman (*figure 51). Also, both drawings emphasize the character of their subjects as well as their costumes.[21] Delightfully fresh, Heriot's studies, like Sandby's, have a directness, a spontaneity, and a remarkable simplicity and strength of design. Because they have the stylistic unity of a series, it is possible that, like the watercolours of Indian dances, these studies may have been intended for publication.

Although the sketches and watercolours of Indian and Canadian subjects reflect Heriot's general interest in Canada, they hardly prepare us for his pictorial forays into the world of insects (figure 49) which date from the same years. Nevertheless, this facet of Heriot's creative personality strikingly exemplifies the continuing expansion of his geographical and intellectual horizons, for his eager curiosity about Canada obviously developed as a result of what it fed upon. Remarkable and exquisite as they are, Heriot's watercolours of insects are, ultimately, the fruit of an interest in entomology which dates from at least as far back as his years in the West Indies. At that time he wrote:

> My Muse, in strains minuter still, descends
> Down to the class of Insects; which in swarms,
> And numbers almost infinite, pervade
> The face of Nature.

Heriot was attracted by the insects' aesthetic charm:

> How pleasing, and how gaily, Nature decks
> The painted wings of *Butterflies*! She deals
> Even to the humble *Beetles*, from her store,
> Bright, beauteous colours, variegated, mix'd.[22]

He was also conscious that insects live in a separate world, a microcosm that could be revealed by the 'new science,' and whose pattern and processes were like those of the macrocosm and therefore evidence of God's power. Heriot's was a typical eighteenth-century response: he believed in the implicit harmony of the universe, a belief that provided him simultaneously with a sense of awe and contentment:

> Even in these objects of minutest size,
> The wisdom of *Creative power* is seen
> Conspicuous. For, if we shou'd survey,
> By help of microscopic glass, those beasts
> Bred in the purest water, there we find
> Their frame and structure every way compleat:
> ...
> Thus life extends
> Through infinite gradations.[23]

Paradoxically, Heriot made these detailed drawings of insects at a time when, in his landscapes, he was working towards a broader and more distilled abstraction. But to find such variety rather than consistency in his work during one period must surely enhance our interest in him and his art. Moreover, while recording these insects in a style and technique so different from those which he employed in his other work, he reveals to us an acuity of vision and an accuracy of observation which must also lie behind the more simplified landscapes. Perhaps it was partly his belief in the implicit harmony of the universe that led him to reduce the complexities of topography to those unified, simplified, dynamically ordered compositions that we have come to regard as typical of Heriot's mature Canadian style.

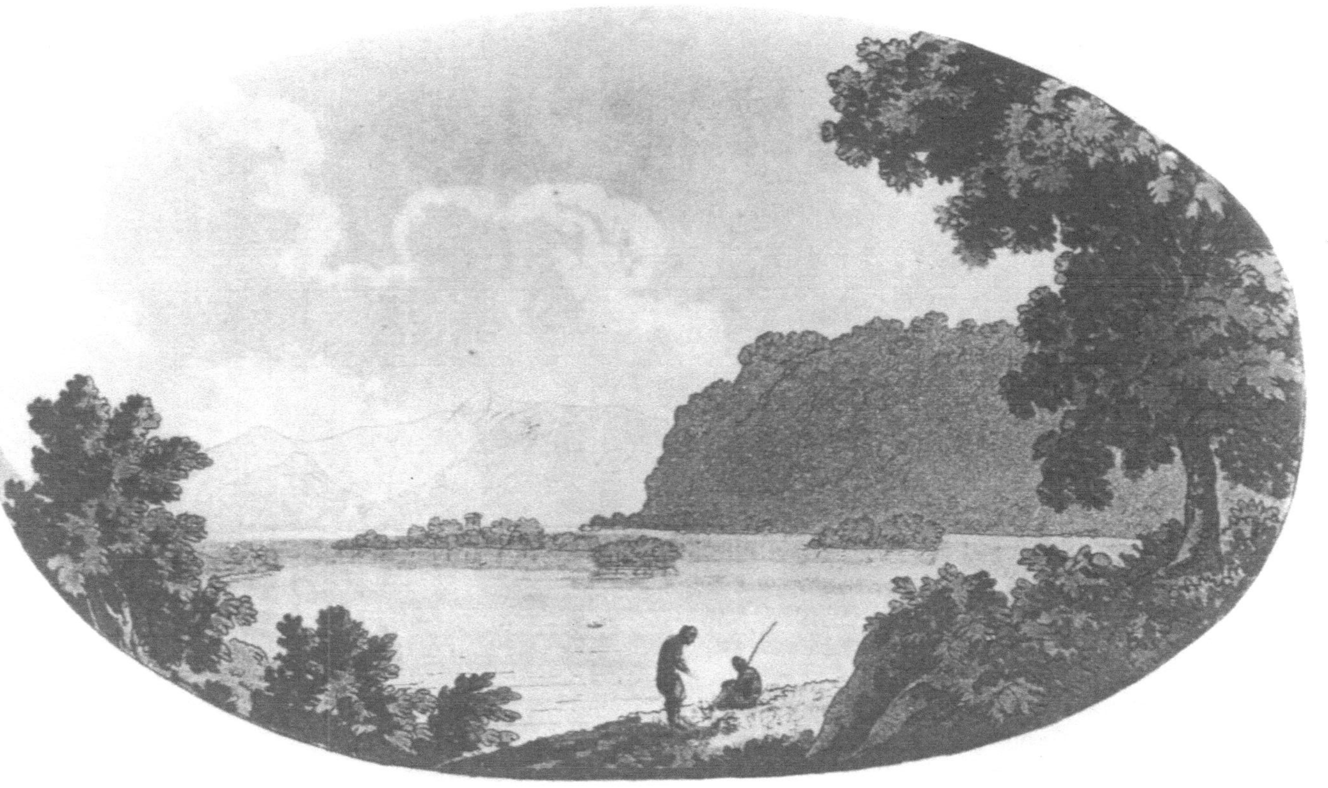

35 / Unidentified etcher, *Windermere*, c 1786. Aquatint after William Gilpin, (oval) 100 × 165 mm. (image)

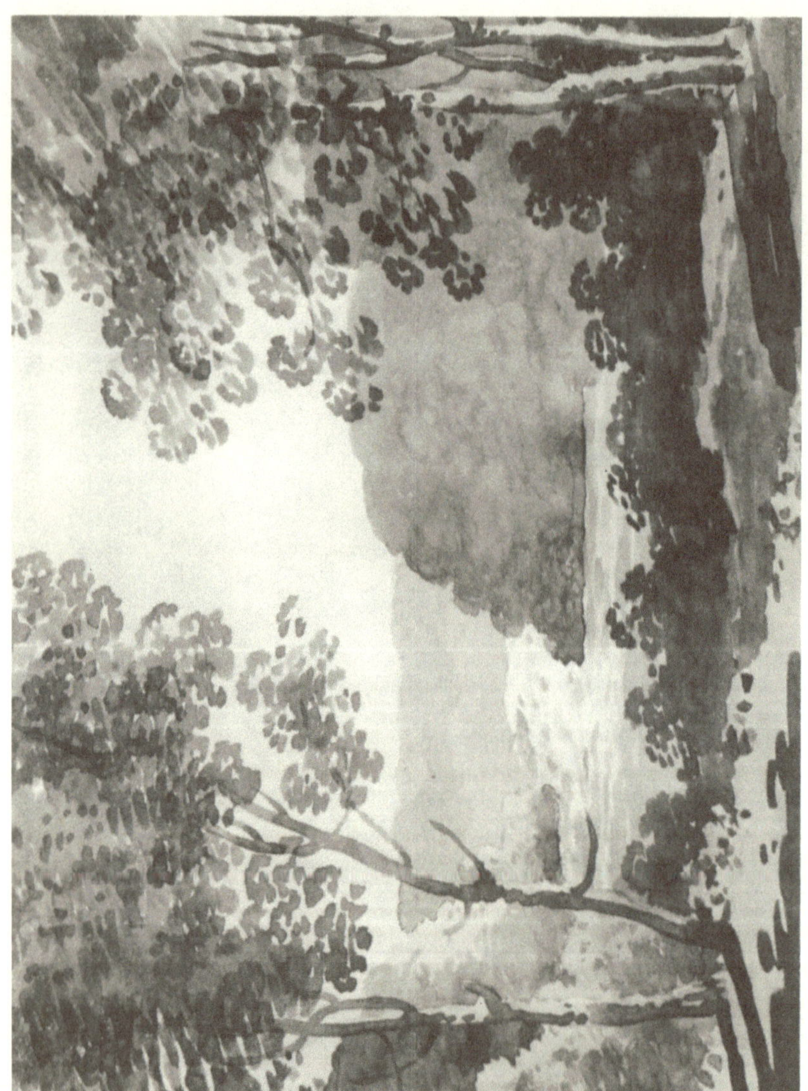

36 / *Whirlpool, Niagara River*, 1801. Watercolour, 143 × 187 mm. (check-list 90)

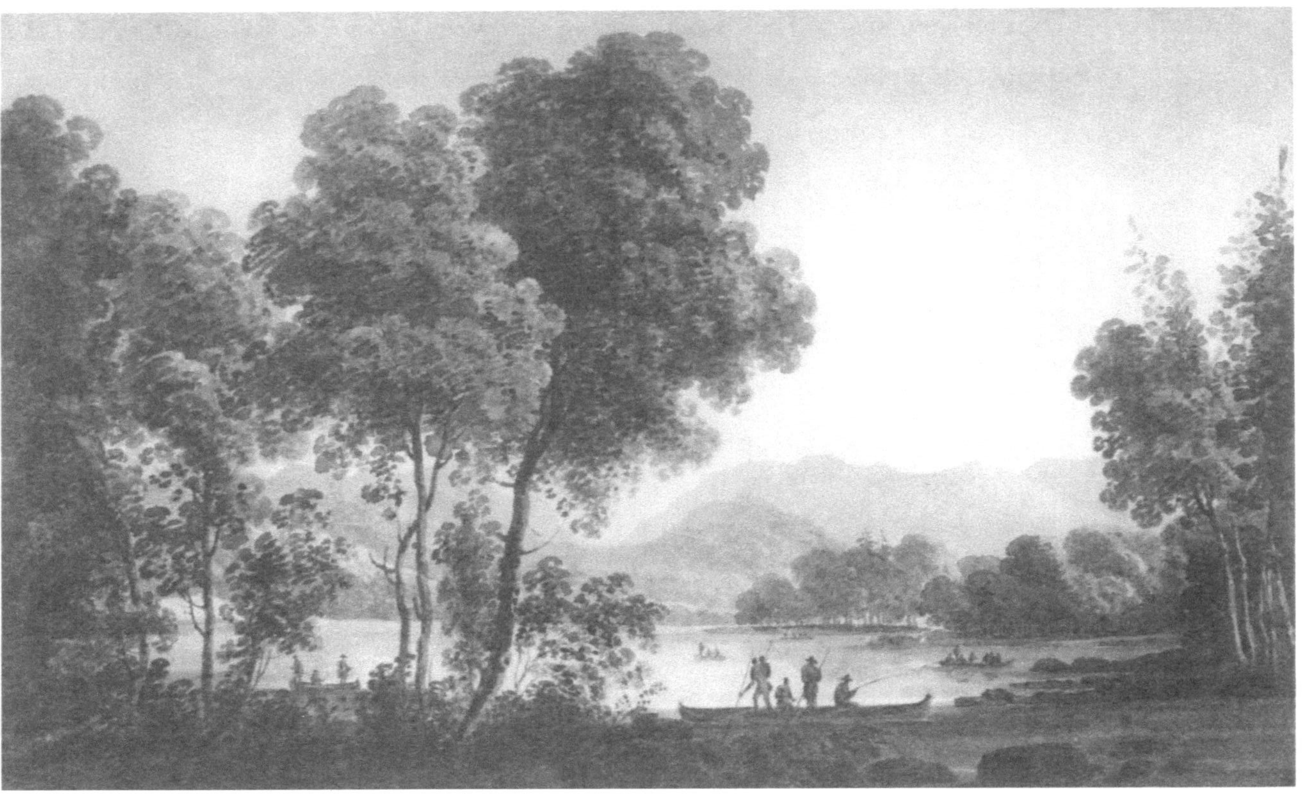

37 / *Lake St Charles near Quebec*, c 1801. Watercolour, 271 × 445 mm. (check-list 93)

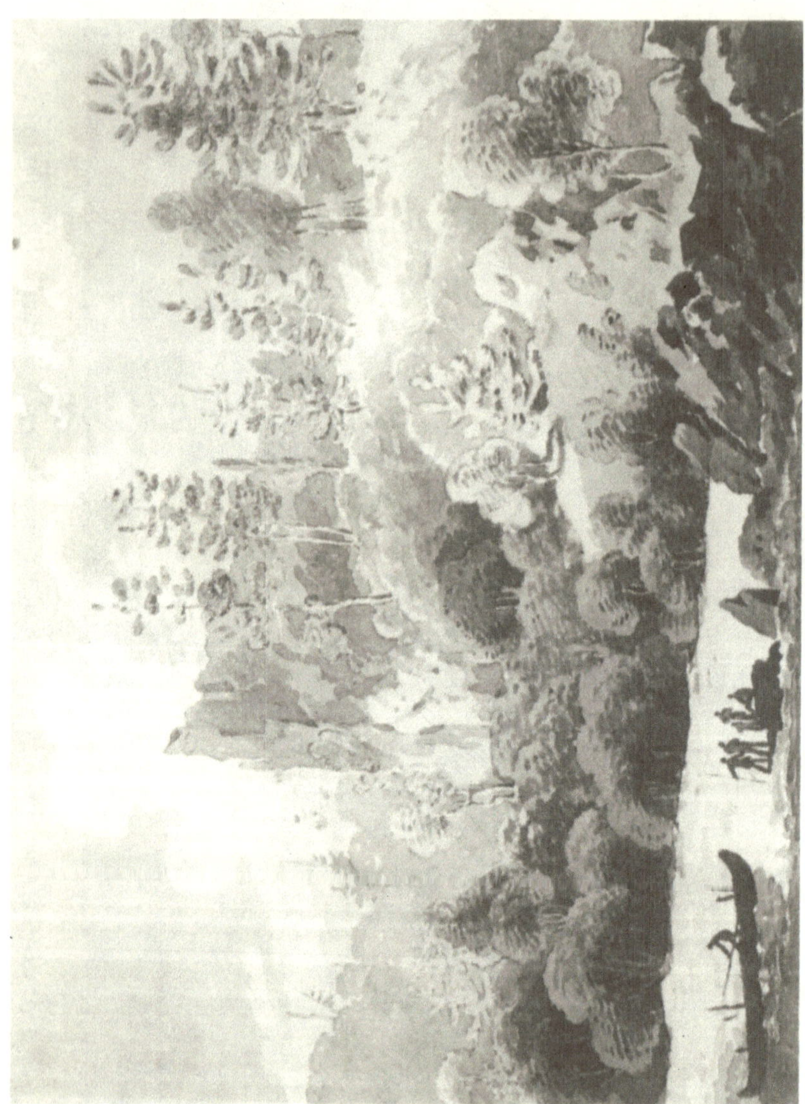

38 / *View at Cape Rouge*, 1804. Watercolour, 133 × 181 mm. (check-list 103)

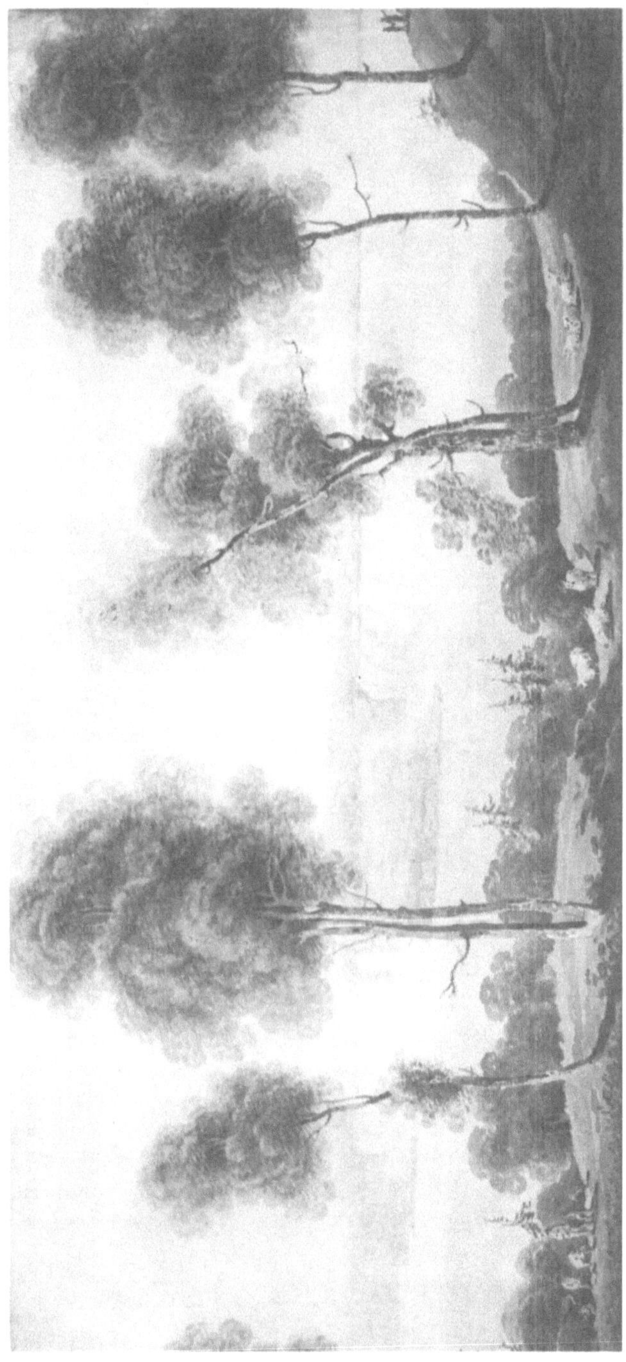

39 / *Falls of Niagara*, 1805. Watercolour, 311 × 705 mm. (check-list 117)

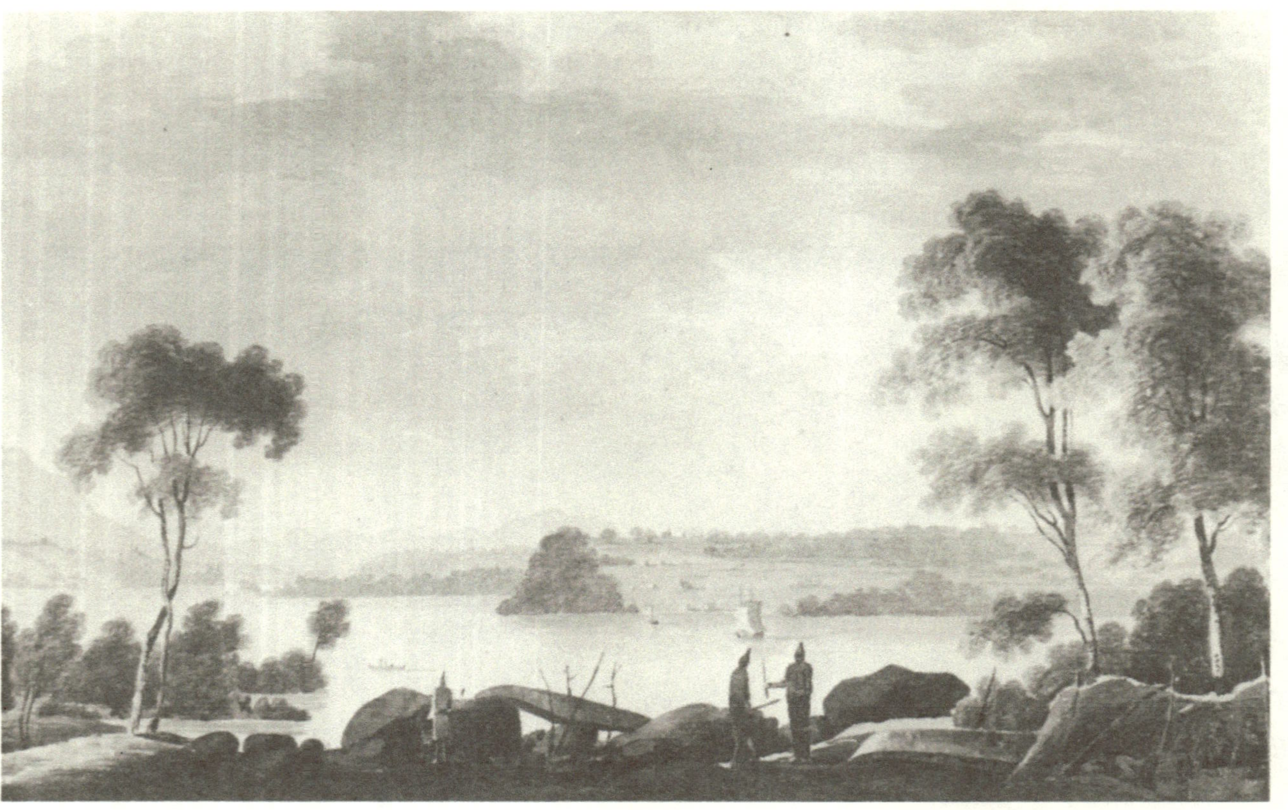

40 / *Island of Orleans with Quebec in the distance*, c 1797. Watercolour, 214 × 322 mm. (check-list 48)

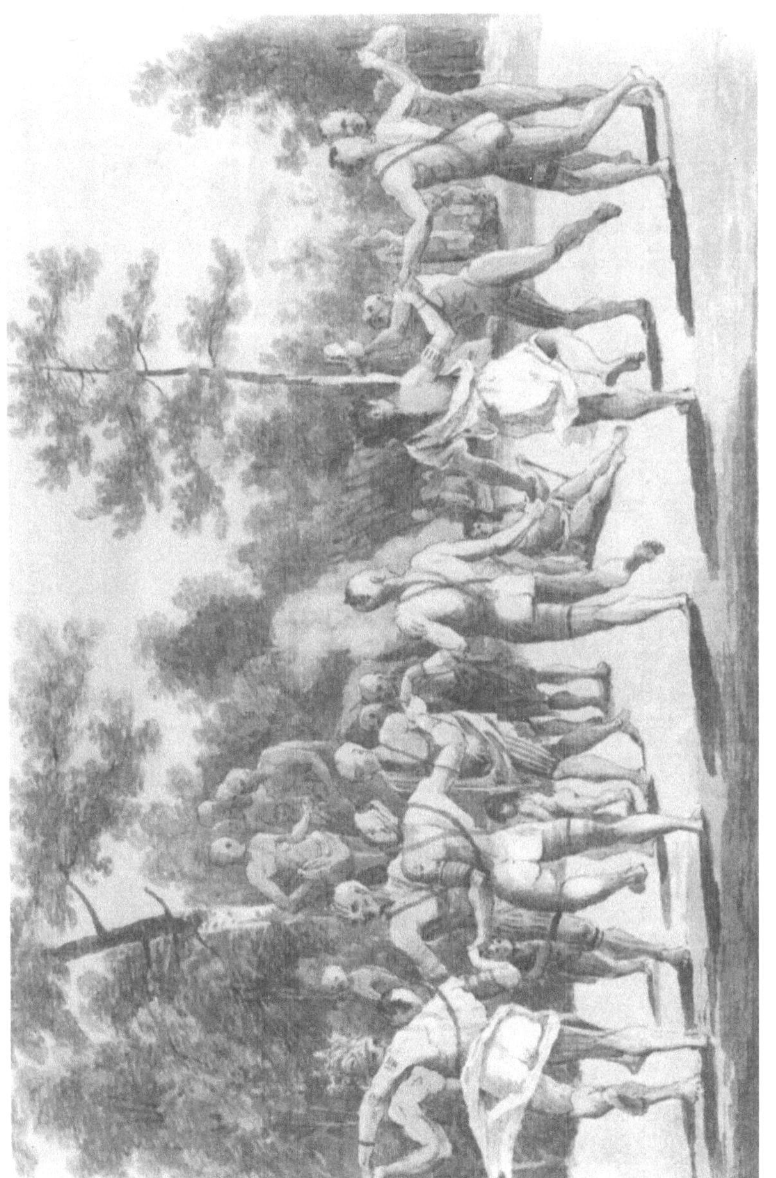

41 / *Calumet Dance*, c 1799. Pen, ink, and watercolour, 213 × 330 mm. (check-list 63)

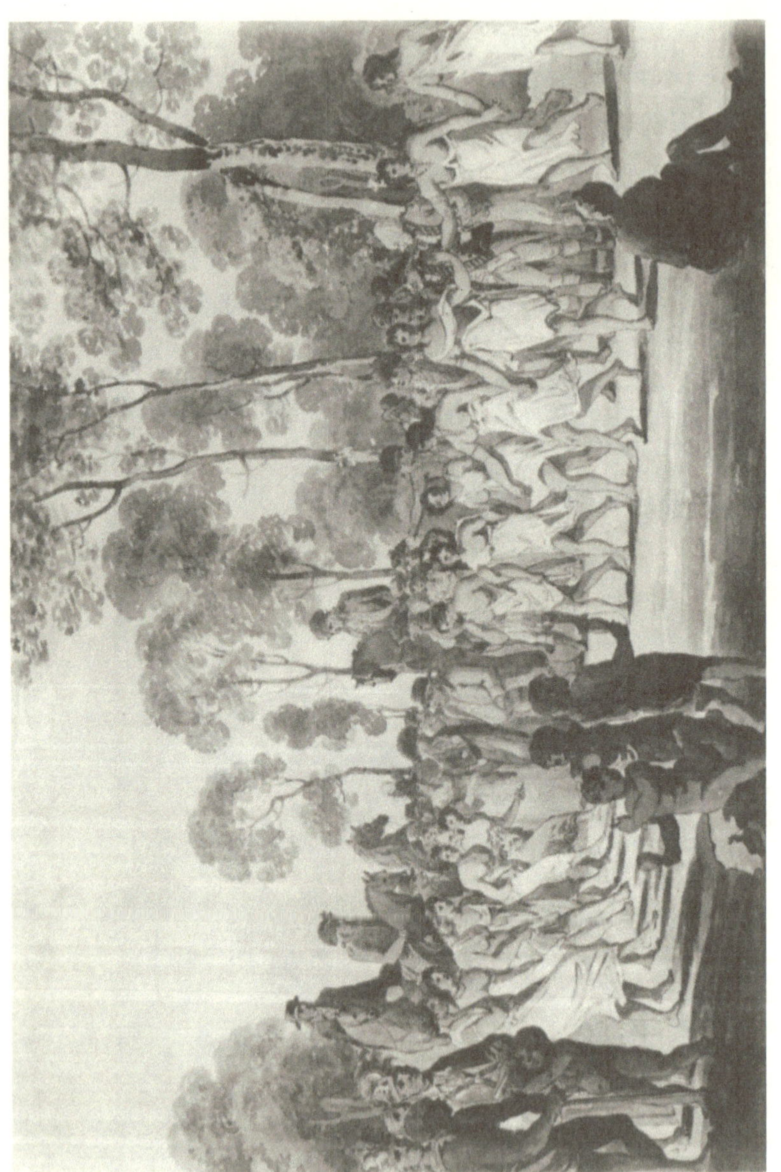

42 / *Dance of Indian Women*, c 1802. Pen, ink, and watercolour, 219 × 324 mm. (check-list 99)

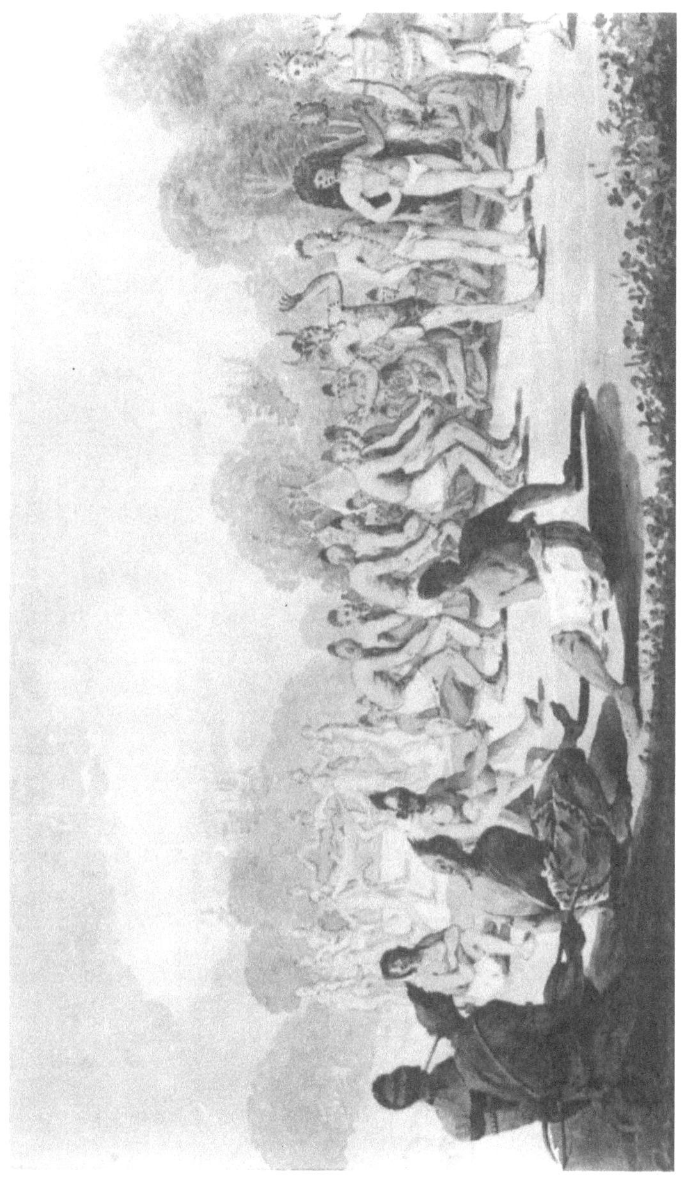

43 / *Dance for recovery of the Sick*, 1805. Watercolour, 175 × 298 mm. (check-list 111)

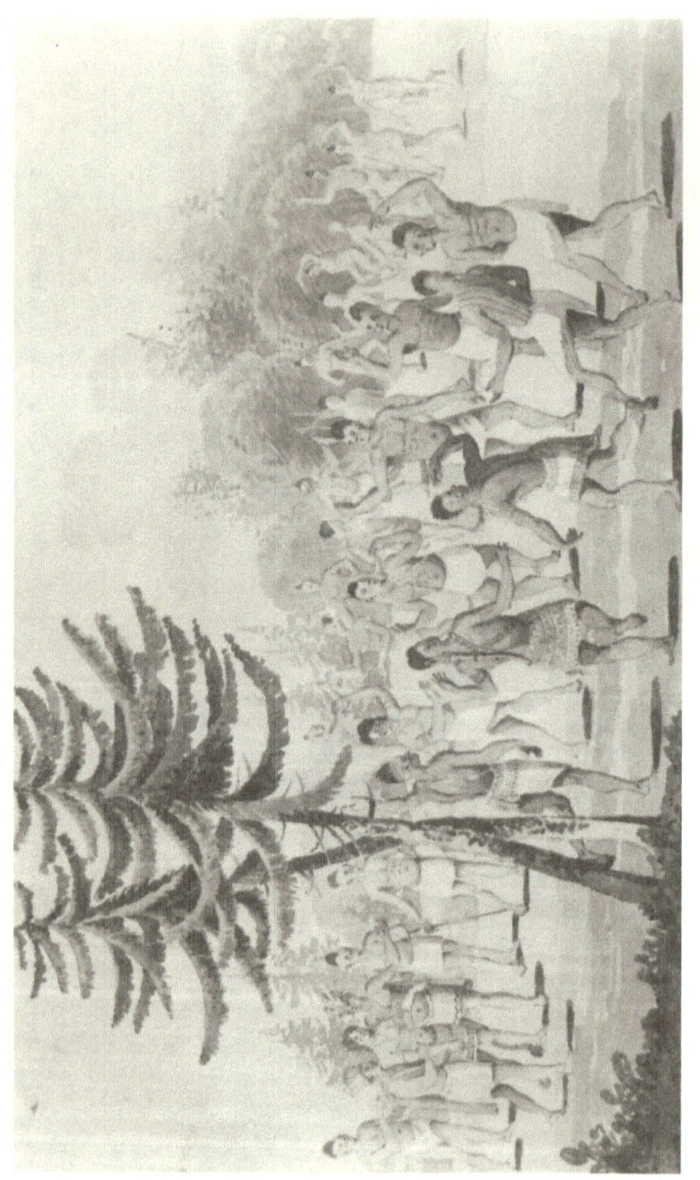

44 / *Dance on the reception of Strangers previous to their introduction into the Village*, c 1805. Watercolour, 175 × 298 mm. (check-list 120)

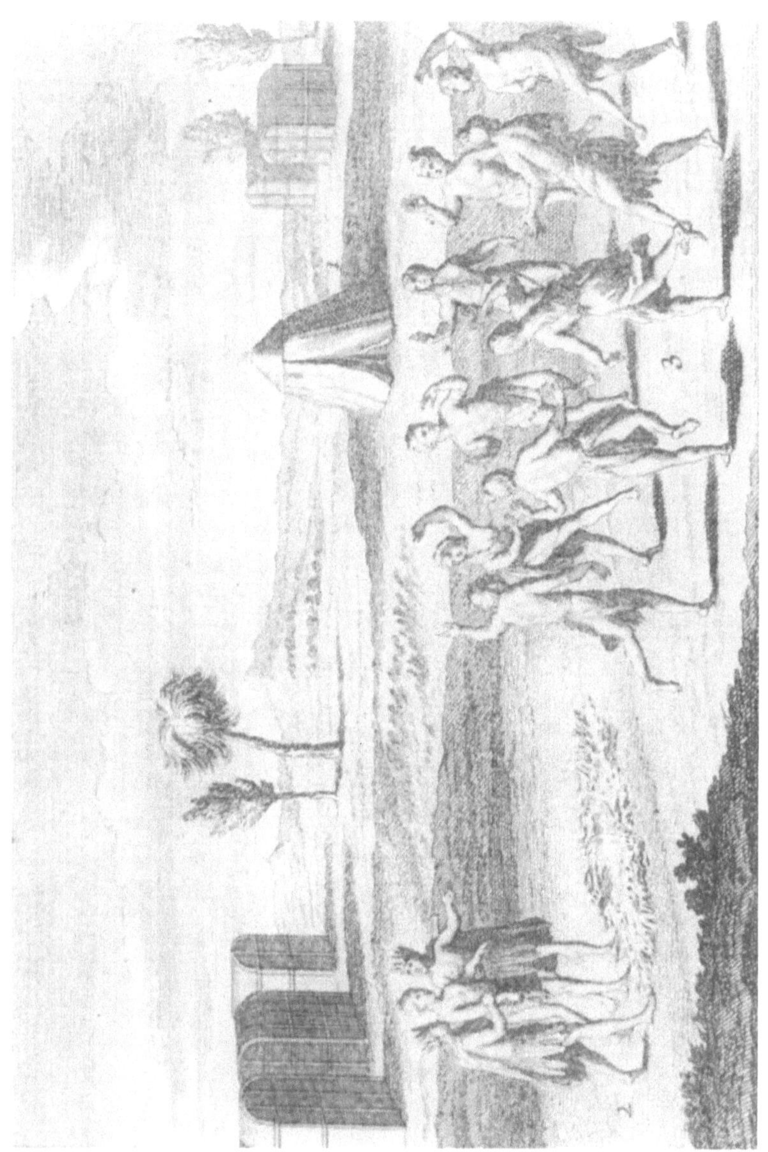

45 / Unidentified engraver and unknown artist, design depicting an Indian dance, from P. Lafitau's *Mœurs des Sauvages Ameriquains* (1724)

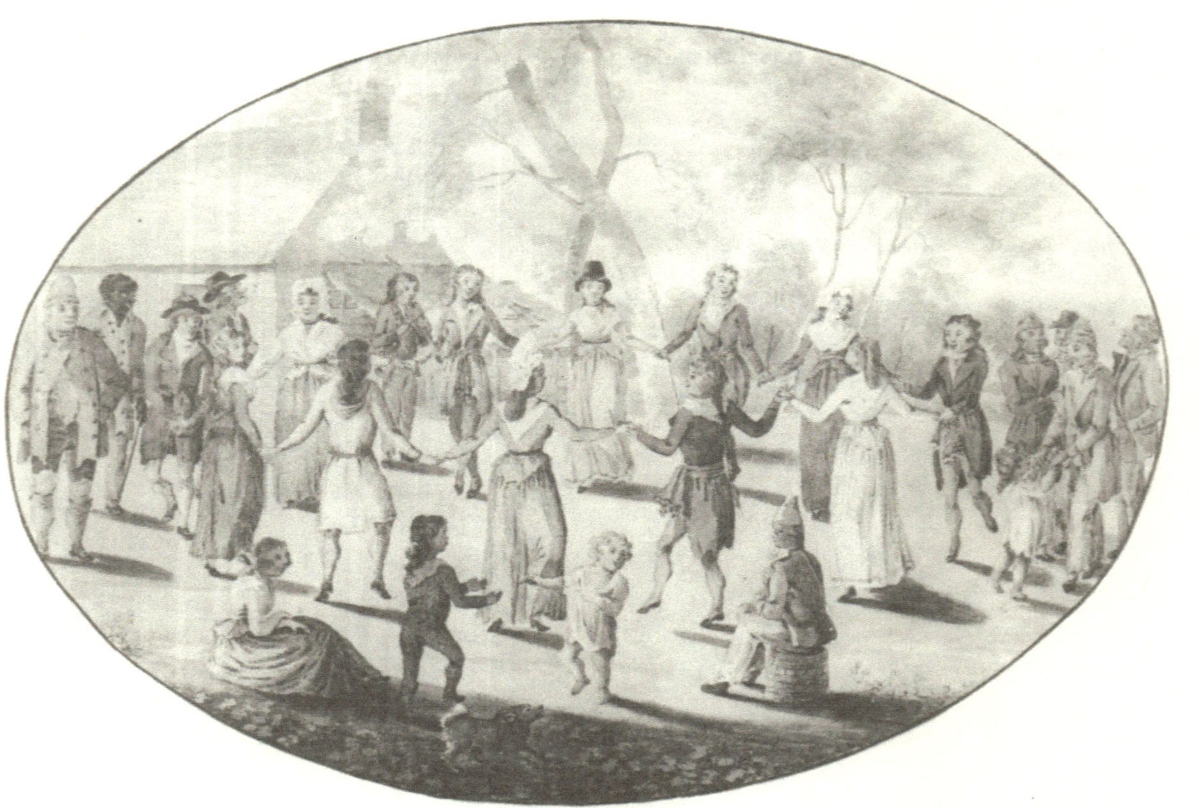

46 / *La Danse Ronde*, c 1799. Watercolour, 216 × 298 mm. (check-list 65)

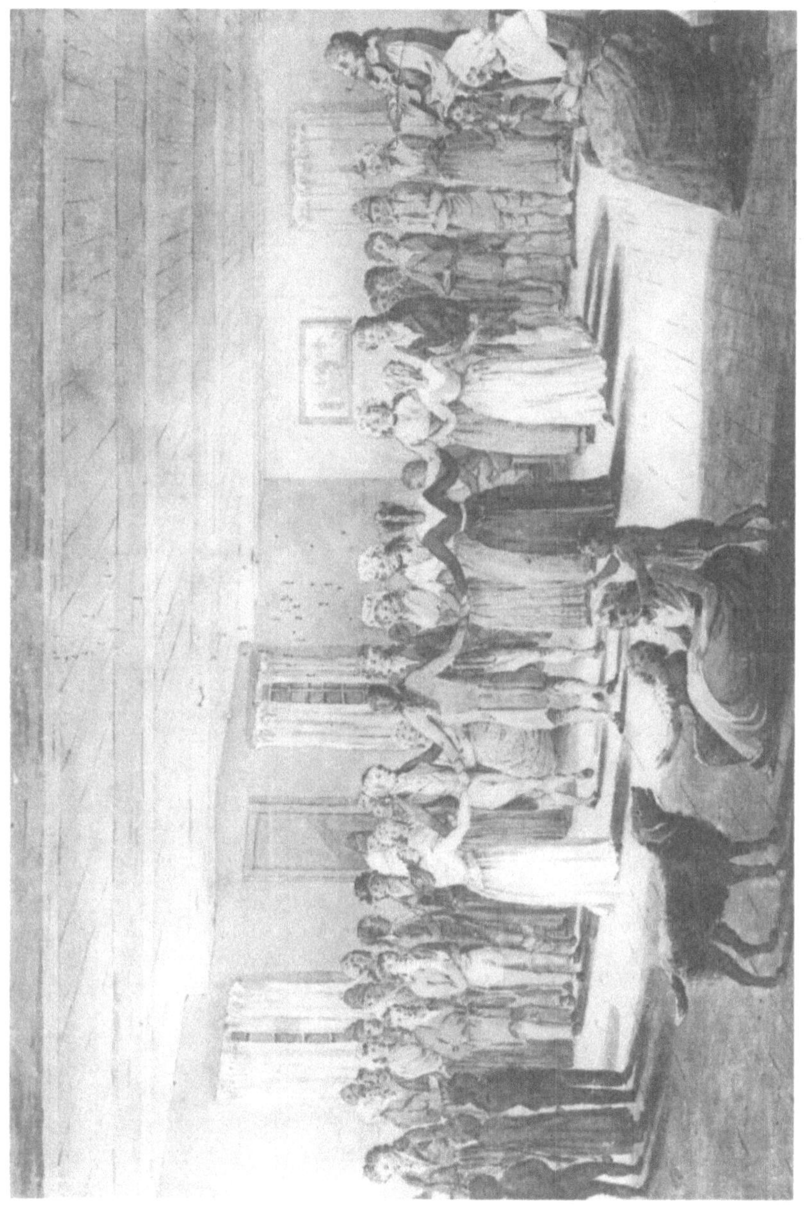

47 / *La danse ronde a l'Intérieur*, c 1801. Watercolour, 214 × 321 mm. (check-list 96)

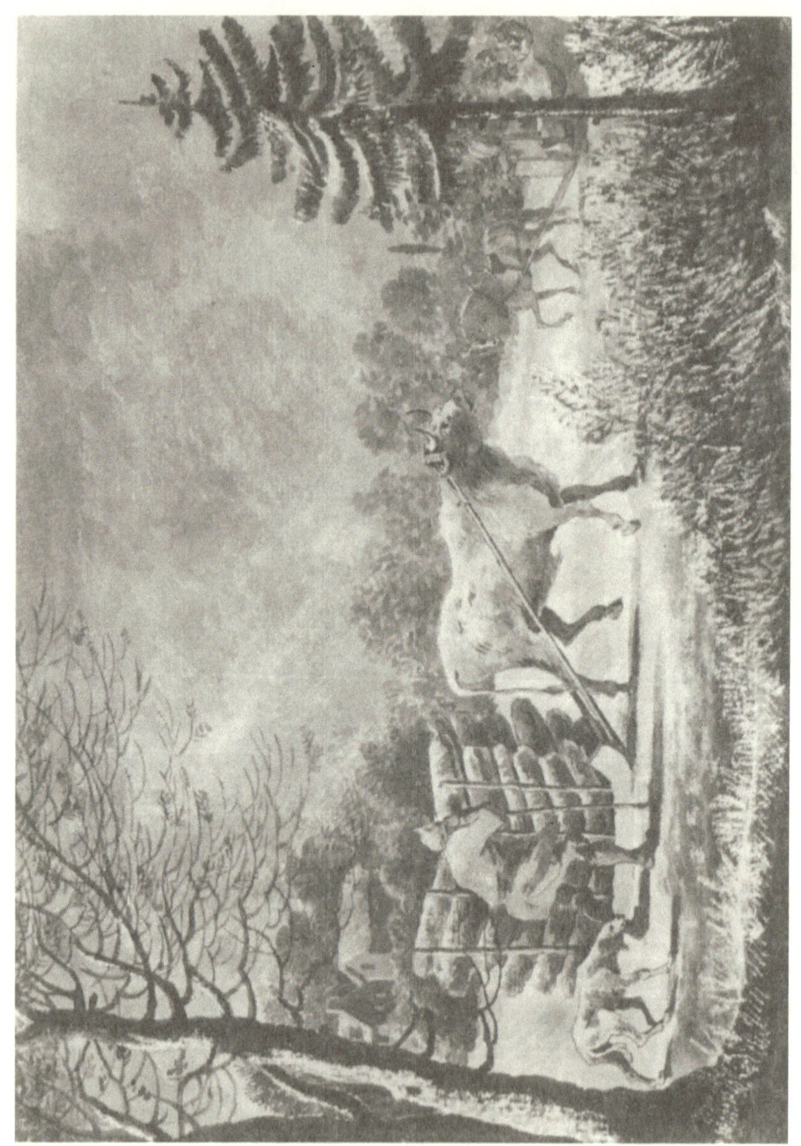

48 / *An Encounter, Canada*, c 1799. Watercolour with scraping, 203 × 292 mm. (check-list 64)

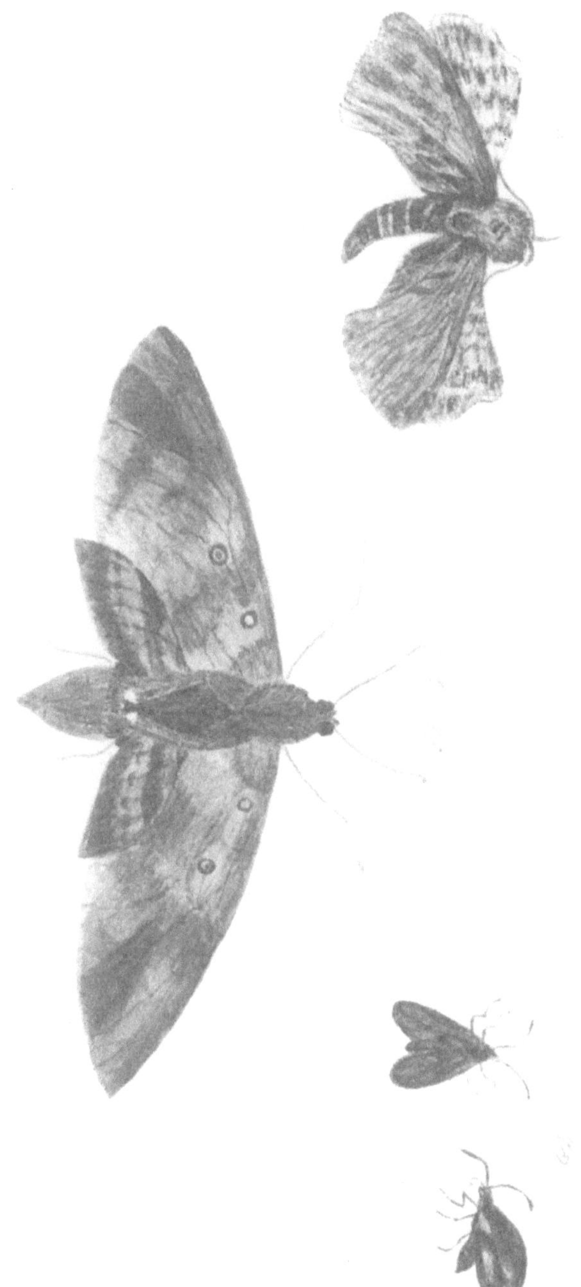

49 / *Insects*, c 1800–c 1805. Watercolour, 137 × 255 mm. (sight) (check-list 83)

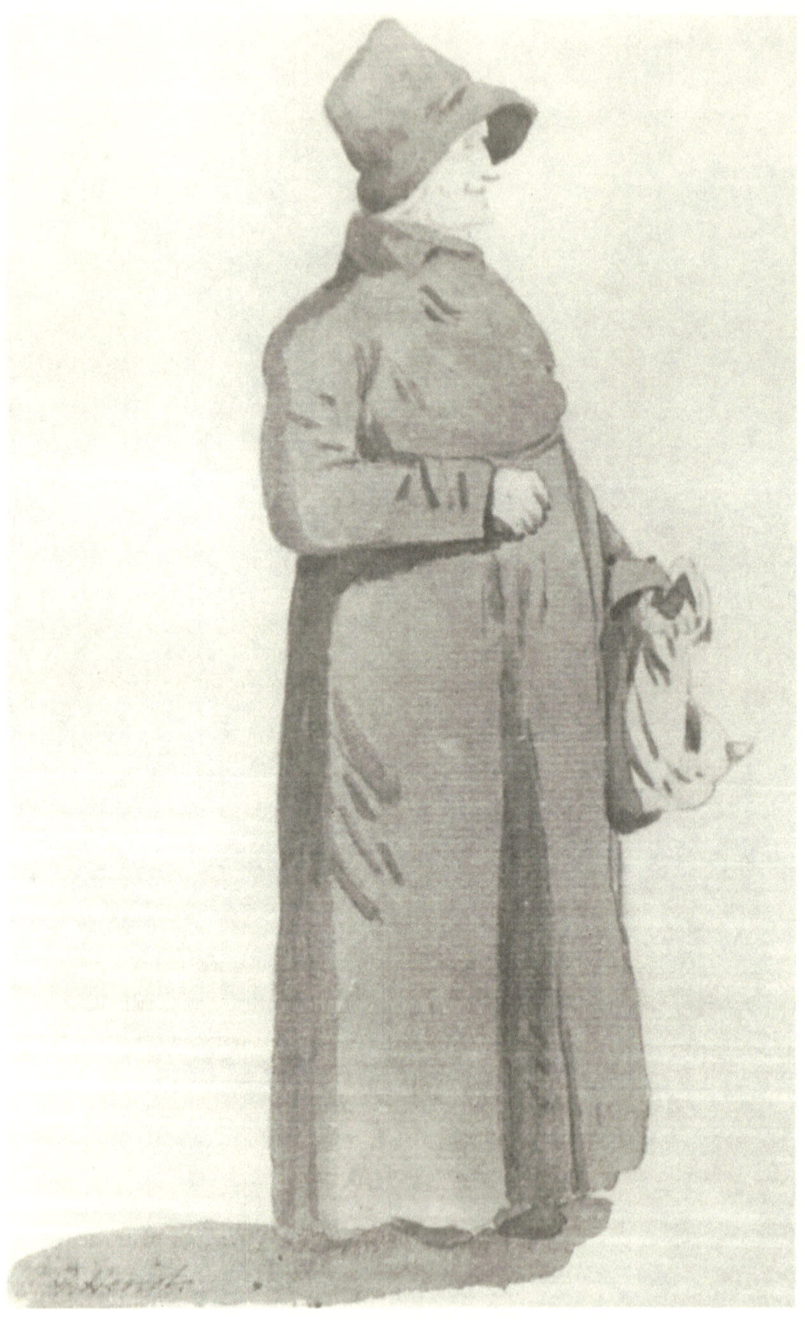

50 / *Old Woman*, c 1800–c 1816. Watercolour, 241 × 152 mm. (check-list 81)

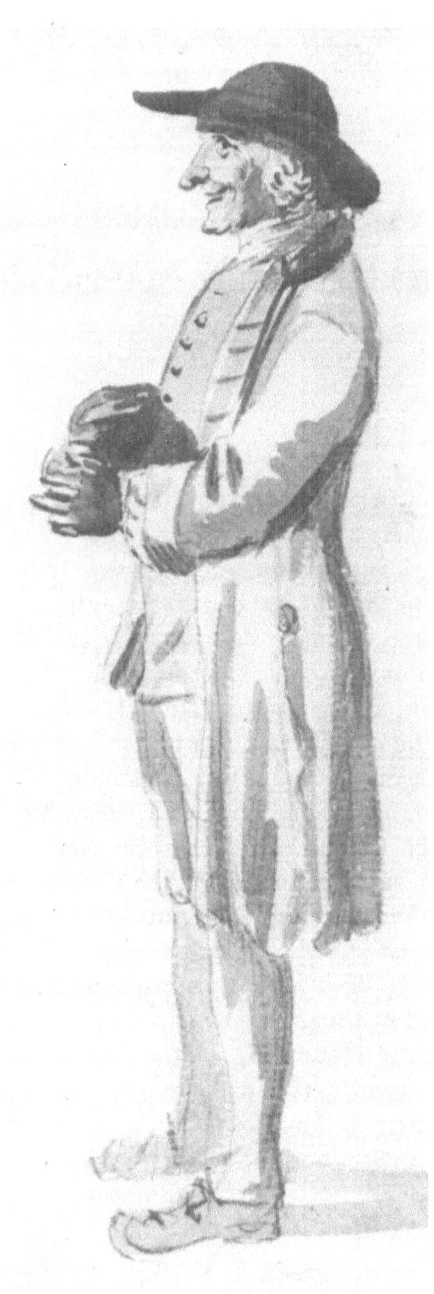

51 / Paul Sandby, *A London Pieman*, n.d. Watercolour, 173 × 60 mm.

6

A Scottish Interlude and Colonial Friendships

It was probably in September 1806 that Heriot paid a second visit to Britain. He had taken a leave absence from the Post Office – life, for the moment would be less stressful. Since he seems to have sailed directly to Scotland, the journey may have been on family business. Nevertheless, he took the opportunity to make sketches. It is certain that he visited the district where his family lived, for at least one watercolour was painted on the eastern border, not far from Ladykirk – his cousins' home town, where as a youth he himself had spent many happy days.

Though Heriot may have toured England on this visit, he seems to have spent more of his time in Scotland. He travelled to the mouth of the Clyde, visited Loch Lomond and Loch Tay, and also went to Perth. A study such as the watercolour *South View of Perth* (figure 52), with the knotted foliage of the trees and the tightly knit tapestry of topographical forms, bears witness to the continuation – and, indeed, the further development – of the decorative picturesque treatment of landscape that Heriot had revived in 1804.

Whatever the reason for his trip, Heriot did not stay in Britain for long: he left for Canada early in the spring of 1807. He did not sail directly to Quebec, but landed at Halifax, so that he might confer with the postmasters of Nova Scotia and New Brunswick, in the hope of improving the maritime service. He was also planning to make a short sketching foray into the United States before returning to Quebec. It was fortunate that he decided to disembark at Halifax, for there he met and was befriended by Judge Edward Winslow – a kindly man, many years Heriot's senior, who was to make his remaining time in Canada much pleasanter than it had been.

We know lamentably little of Heriot's friendships. With his lively mind he hungered for people to talk to, and his sensitive spirit craved congenial companionship. Fortunately he found both in Quebec; but of his particular associations there are only tantalizing glimpses and hints in his correspondence and in his pictures. During his early years at Quebec he had been closely associated with the military and had acquaintances among them. We know that he occasionally met Colonel Roger Hale Shaeffe and his wife socially. Colonel Shaeffe was stationed in Canada 1787–97, 1802–11, and 1812–13. In 1810 he married Margaret Coffin of Quebec. When Major-General Sir Isaac Brock was killed at Queenston Heights in the first year of the War of 1812–14, Shaeffe, then a major-general, succeeded him, not only as commander-in-chief of the British forces, but also as president and administrator of Upper Canada. But Heriot was not on as close terms with the Shaeffes as he was with his second cousin, Major-General Frederick George Heriot (1786–1843) of the 49th Regiment, who was stationed at Quebec during at least part of the period of George Heriot's residence there. Unfortunately we have hardly any detailed information about these relationships.

There is, however, ample evidence that, as a frequent guest at government functions, the deputy postmaster general had the opportunity to meet Lower Canada's administrative élite. A rare and revealing glimpse of one such occasion is furnished by a watercolour by Heriot which depicts a special fête given in 1809 by the then lieutenant governor of Lower Canada, Sir James Craig, at Spencer Wood (previously known as Powell Place) (figure 53). The occasion may have been the celebration of the fiftieth anniversary of the holding of Anglican services in Quebec City. The watercolour makes it clear that this fête, held on a sunny, summery day in the tree-shaded grounds of the residence, was a splendid affair. Refreshments were served from marquees set among the trees, and the spritely rhythms of martial music, provided by the band of the 100th Foot Regiment, served as counterpoint to the easy ebb and flow of chatting guests. In addition to the host, Sir James Craig (who is represented in the right foreground with his family), the guests included General Isaac Brock, Dr Mountain, the Anglican bishop, whom Heriot had already met; and Chief Justice Sewell, who in this year had been made Lower Canada's speaker of the Legislative Council.

Heriot also made other acquaintances and friends among Quebec's titled people, its gentry, and its well-to-do merchants, partly through his membership in the exclusive Beef Steak Club or Barons' Club, which was largely composed of influential administrators and 'barons' of commerce and high finance. The Barons met regularly during the winter season. Club entertainment began 'soon after the River Navigation is shut' and concluded with the 'arrival of the First European vessels in the Spring.' At least by 1807 meetings of the club were being held regularly at the Union Hotel.

On 4 February of that year the club laid on a lavish dinner and a splendid ball, at which associate members, or 'knights,' of the club were to be admitted to full membership.[1] This great festivity was reported to be of 'that degree of splendour appropriate to the occasion.' After dinner the Barons received their badges of rank. Staunch Tories all, they did not need to be reminded by the 'general' of their club of 'that loyalty which you owe to the best of Kings, our Sovereign, and the inviolable attachment due to his Government; those principles I know are deeply rooted in your hearts.'[2] After the presentation of medals the Barons entered the glittering hotel ball room, where 'the Ladies and Gentlemen invited ... had met. Shortly after the Honorable Thomas Dunn, President of the Province was announced.'[3] All the Barons duly gathered at the grand curving staircase to greet him; then 'they conducted him to a Canopy raised under the Portrait of His Majesty, where His Honor seated himself with several other persons for whom the Canopy was intended. The music struck up *God Save the King* and shortly afterwards, a trumpet sounded the opening of the Ball.'[4]

Several prominent men were present at this function, including Sir John Caldwell (a solicitor and member of the Executive Council of the government of Lower Canada) and Herman Ryland (who was clerk of the council and possessed considerable political influence within the government). There were also such colourful characters as Angus Shaw, who began his career as a fur trader, who between 1795 and 1799 was a partner in the North West Company, and who in 1802 had been appointed agent in charge of the King's Posts, headquartered at Quebec. Though Heriot as a member of the club must have enjoyed the comradeship of such men, we have no evidence of his acquaintanceship with any one of them. We know of only two of Heriot's friendships: one (established by tradition) with Colonel John Nairne, the other with Edward Winslow.

Colonel John Nairne (1728–1802) was a member of the seigneurial gentry, who lived at La Malbaie, some eighty miles down river from Quebec. Although the association between the two men rests on tradition, this tradition is reinforced by persuasive pictorial evidence. Nairne, like

Heriot, was both Scottish and well born, and the two men also shared the same Tory sympathies. When they first met is not known, but Heriot may have encountered Nairne either at Quebec or at his seigneury or estate at La Malbaie. As seigneur Nairne made annual visits to Quebec, where, on the periodical changes of governor, he was required to appear to 'render fealty and homage' to the new incumbent.[5] At Quebec Nairne would take part in the round of social occasions attended by the gentry and the scions of nobility, at which functions Heriot also would probably appear. The two men may have met on one of these occasions.

If Heriot did not meet Nairne in Quebec, then he probably met him at La Malbaie. As an officer in the Ordnance Heriot may have visited Nairne because the latter was colonel of the local militia of one hundred men. Heriot was certainly at the seigneury in 1798, and possibly earlier. Tradition has it that a watercolour of La Malbaie which Heriot painted in 1798 was given by him to the seigneur as a token of their friendship (see figure 28).

Far removed from Quebec, the seigneury of La Malbaie was largely self-sufficient. Hunting and fishing were activities of crucial importance to the Canadian inhabitants of the seigneury. Nairne, like other British seigneurs, attempted to impose his interpretation of the French seigneurial system on his tenants, overlooking Canadian laws and traditions which guaranteed certain rights to them. For example, in 1797 Nairne, wishing to protect the salmon in the Malbaie River, forbade the practice of fishing for them at night with lanterns and torches. His Canadian tenants duly rebelled against this injunction. Nairne suffered many such upheavals as a result of the tenants' refusal to recognize his authority, and he wrote to a friend: 'I had rather have no power at all and no seigneurie at all [than] not to be able to keep up the rights of it.'[6] Heriot's watercolour certainly suggests not only the artist's familiarity with the topography of the place but also a knowledge of the seigneury's hunting and fishing industries.

Although Nairne may not have been especially happy about some aspects of life at La Malbaie, he was otherwise content with the country existence that he had established for himself and his family. He considered his domain a virtual Elysium. Heriot, when he first arrived, was certainly struck by the physical beauty of the setting: it was 'a rich and romantic valley, through which a river [the Malbaie], abounding in salmon and trout, winds its course into the bay. The soil, which consists of a black mould upon sand, is fertile; and the inhabitants, whose communication with other settled parts of the country is not frequent, possess within their own limits, an abundance of the necessities of life ... The entrance to this bay, presents to the eye, a landscape, at once singularly romantic and beautiful, being terminated by mountains, whose varied and elevated summits, sharpen into cones of different magnitudes.'[7] Heriot's watercolour of La Malbaie also bears eloquent witness to his response to the place.

Although we can only speculate about Heriot's relationship with Nairne, there are actual records of his friendship with Judge Edward Winslow (c 1746–1815), who lived at his country estate, Kingsclear, near Fredericton, New Brunswick, and whom Heriot met at Halifax in the spring of 1807. Winslow had been muster master of provincial forces from 1776 until 1783, and both at that time and since took an interest in the militia – which suggests that he and Heriot may have met through the latter's connection with the Ordnance.[8]

It is possible that Heriot persuaded his newly found comrade (whom he discovered to be both cultured and charming) to accompany him on horseback around Nova Scotia, while he visited the postmasters, for there is evidence that the two men may have been together for at least part of Heriot's tour. In order to relieve the monotony and fatigue of the journey Heriot visited the houses of at least two of Winslow's acquaintances. This was in mid-June, when he seems to have travelled the dusty forty-six miles to Windsor for a meeting with the local postmaster. After his business was concluded, Heriot (and possibly Winslow too) travelled to the villa of the judge's friend Chief Justice Blowers, where he (or they) may have passed the night. Heriot, who was attracted by the beauty of the house and its location, took time to sketch it (check-list 139). He also limned the nearby Minas Basin and undertook a series of sketches possibly from Partridge Island, and certainly of it as seen from Parresboro – vistas which seemed to him particularly picturesque.

It was possibly on the return journey to Halifax that Heriot visited the villa of another friend of Winslow's, Sir John Wentworth. (We do not know whether Winslow suggested this visit, but we do know that he was with Heriot when it took place.) Set back from the road and separated from it by a fence, Wentworth's villa, originally called the 'Friar's Cell,' was enhanced by a magnificent eighteenth-century garden, complete with follies and statues.[9] Heriot found the place quite delightful and with his usual enthusiasm sketched it. Winslow recorded that Heriot 'afterwards touched off [the sketch] and gave [it] to me and I sent it to Lady Wentworth, supposing it would afford her ladyship a moment's amusement.'[10]

Heriot must have enjoyed Winslow's cheerful sociability and found his candidness refreshing. It seems that after Heriot's tour of Nova Scotia the two men made plans to travel together to New Brunswick, where Heriot also needed to consult with his postmasters. The voyage from Halifax to Saint John furnished the opportunity for their acquaintance to develop and they arrived at Saint John firm friends.[11]

At Saint John Heriot conferred with the postmaster and then set out with Winslow for Fredericton. After completing his business at Fredericton, Heriot went on, at Winslow's invitation, to his host's residence at Kingsclear. While staying there Heriot sketched the surrounding countryside; he also drew 'Spring Hill,' the magnificent country seat of Winslow's friend and neighbour Chief Justice Ludlow, to whom Heriot may have been introduced by his host. After his return to Quebec Heriot painted an elaborate watercolour of Ludlow's house, showing it decoratively framed by the foliage of the surrounding trees (figure 54). However, enraptured as he was by the countryside around Kingsclear, and much as he had enjoyed Winslow's companionship, Heriot was becoming increasingly restless and, despite his host's protestations, anxious to return to Saint John, from where he intended to take a ship, probably bound for Boston, in order 'to pursue his route thro' America,' to make a pictorial record of its landscape.[12] This was not to be, however, for fate intervened in the form of a flare-up of hostilities between Britain and the United States in the early summer of 1807.

Relations between the two countries had been deteriorating ever since Britain's close blockade of French-held Europe in 1806, and Napoleon's counter-blockade – the 'Continental System' (1806–12) – had forced the maritime trade of the beleaguered Europeans into neutral vessels. Of the neutrals, the Americans above all expanded their shipping and made enormous profits, but not without risk from privateers and warships of both sides. In particular, the Royal Navy, with its overall grip on the European seas, stopped American vessels and confiscated goods suspected as being 'contraband' bound for Europe. American displeasure at this practice was exacerbated by the Royal Navy's practice of stopping American merchant ships and of impressing those members of their crews who were believed to be British subjects. The fires of hostility were further fanned when, on 22 June 1807, the British frigate HMS *Leopard* shot at and boarded the American warship USS *Chesapeake* and removed four sailors, only one of whom subsequently proved to be a subject of the British Crown. Americans were enraged, deeply resenting this insult to their country. For political reasons the American president, Thomas

Jefferson, chose to avoid an open conflict at this time; but while the threat of war subsided, relations between the two countries remained strained. In a letter to a friend, Winslow refers to the encounter between the *Leopard* and the *Chesapeake* as the 'noise of a rupture' which alarmed Heriot, who, he added, was 'now on his way to Canada through the woods. I fear the flies of New Brunswick will interrupt his sketches on this tour.'[13]

Winslow underrated the determination of the Scottish artist to record pictorially this part of the country, whose beauties had come as a revelation to him. Unperturbed by 'the flies of New Brunswick,' Heriot returned to Quebec with a harvest of sketches. Fortunately an itinerary of what appears to be his return journey (which began in late July and which reveals Heriot's interest in tracing the mail routes) has survived. It was planned by Winslow himself, who included in it detailed instructions, as from one gentleman to another, on how the well-bred and moneyed visitor should equip himself to travel by water through the Canadian wilds:

> The Baggage in a Birch canoe should be fitted to it; that is each article should have its proper place. The canteen should be between the two forward bars, with the lock towards you, so that you can take a cut or a drink without disturbing anything else. Your portmanteau, men's provisions, etc, will go between the foremost bar and the bow. Your fusee will lie at your left side; your umbrella on the right. If you don't take a mattrass your great coat just over the bar behind you makes a good seat, and by drawing one end up you preserve your back from the hard bar. When your arrangements are once made, directions should be given to the Boatman and servant, when you come to your ground in the evening, that the baggage be so placed as that the articles may be returned to their proper stations in the morning.[14]

Winslow wrote that on the Saint John River, between Fredericton (Heriot's point of departure) and Great Falls, his friend would have 'plain sailing.' By the third night of his journey he would be at Presque Isle. Two nights later Heriot would be at Grand Falls. On the morning of his sixth day he would have time 'to view the Falls, the Post etc' before proceeding to the French settlement of Madawaska. From there it would be a 'good days work to get to the mouth of Timisquata Lake.'[15] Eight or ten more miles of travelling would bring Heriot to the St Lawrence, and to the beginning of the final stretch of his journey back to Quebec.

We do not know whether Heriot and Winslow had the opportunity to see each other again, but the warmth of their ensuing correspondence (which seems to have lasted from about 1807 until at least 1813 – three years before Heriot left Canada for good) suggests that they may have met on a subsequent occasion. Heriot's letters to Winslow document the deepening attachment between the two friends and furnish insights into the artist's character of a kind which his voluminous official correspondence could never yield. The letters are witty, gossipy, and voluble, revealing that Heriot was continuing to enjoy life in Canada, despite the difficulties that his management of the Post Office had created for him. He still took pleasure in society and could discover humour in almost any situation – if he so wished. When Winslow writes of his difficulty in finding a cure for gout, Heriot observes that the climate of Quebec is not 'particularly favourable to Gouty constitutions,' adding: 'I do not know of any person afflicted with that disorder except Pontifex Maximus, alias the [Anglican] Bishop [Jacob Mountain], who has long been confined to his house. This however, you will say is not much to be wondered at in a Man of his Rank in the Church.'

In this letter to Winslow Heriot discloses that, having reached the age of fifty-three, he is seriously contemplating marriage. He lived in an austerely handsome, commodious stone house, whose rooms were full of fine furniture and books and whose walls were hung with paintings and prints. In the easy tones of friendship he tells Winslow that an 'old maiden lady' had recently visited him at his house (with a view, it seems, to buying one of his paintings, since he writes of how he guided her 'through the rooms to look at pictures'). This lady took the opportunity of telling him that he 'wanted nothing but a wife – but she qualified her remark,' he writes, 'by adding that she advised me not to take an American Lady, for she would only *derange my place*. Whether she meant my pictures or my plans of life, I cannot say but I had the assurance to repeat the story to several Ladies at my own table, who did me the honour of dining with me.'[16]

There is no doubt that Heriot enjoyed female companionship. Already, he writes, he had 'flirted with a great number of favourites.' Although he now felt 'a disposition for a settled life – that is a married one,' he was not certain that he could find the type of marriage partner he wanted in Quebec, for 'the countenances of the Ladies at Quebec are become too familiar, and none of them exactly correspond with my ideas either of beauty or the manners likely to be productive of mutual & domestic enjoyment.'[17] Heriot had become too selective in his middle age:

'A dash ... of the spirit of ancient Chivalry would dispose me to migrate from home in search of a wife.' He desired a 'young woman,' and especially one 'reared in the calm tranquility of retirement – who possesses some taste for the fine arts – who is a stranger to gadding, racketting cards and late hours. But Solomon wisely remarks "who can find a virtuous woman; her price is far above rubies!" Pray have you many fine girls in New Brunswick?'[18] Despite his declared wish to find a wife Heriot did not ultimately marry.

Heriot's correspondence with Winslow is important, not only because of what it tells us about the artist's personality, but also because it provides the context for the period during which he produced some of his most decorative and evocative landscapes. The most exuberant of these were painted on his tour of Nova Scotia and New Brunswick in June and July of 1807. Winslow notes that Heriot had been enthralled by the countryside, and especially by its water scenery. The year after his visit Heriot wrote to Winslow: 'I very often reflect with pleasure on the agreeable days I passed in New Brunswick, and on the beautiful and picturesque Scenery exhibited by the banks of the St John which I think is the most romantic river I ever viewed, and of whose bold and varied Landscapes I have made a great number of sketches.'[19]

The sketches, and the finished watercolours developed from them, provide a remarkably complete record of the countryside through which Heriot travelled. They are highly ornamental in style and soaked in light. The irregular compactness of the tree foliage, the sometimes jewel-like colour and conscious convexity of the landscape forms extend the patterned images that Heriot had created in his recent Scottish drawings. His decorative picturesqueness (which is most apparent in the drawings of scenes which include water) powerfully conveys Heriot's strong feeling for this maritime country. The hillsides – thick with grasses, brilliant with wild flowers, and studded with full, rounded trees – furnished a rich backdrop for the Saint John River by which he was so enchanted. In a view such as *Belle Isle Bay, St John's River* (figure 55) we see the increased roundness and ripeness of the vegetation which is typical of Heriot's mature Canadian landscapes, as well as his power to capture the abstract shapes of trees against the light of river, hills, and sky. There is also a new liquidity of brushwork which demonstrates a growing assurance in the handling of the medium. The picturesqueness of these maritime scenes perhaps achieves its apogee in *View from Partridge Island* (figure 56), with its foliage-bordered rock cleft through which a distant landscape is framed, and in *West View of Partridge Island from Parsborough* (figure 57).

Yet, for Heriot, the significance of this maritime topography went deeper than its picturesque attractiveness. This part of British North America symbolized for him a particular, ineffable quality of life. 'You seem to possess,' he wrote to Winslow, a 'great abundance of every article for the support of life, and to enjoy the most perfectly undisturbed state ... your society is composed of reasonable people who have learnt to set a value on the tranquillity of retirement.'[20] Heriot himself yearned for such a life, in which he could cultivate more fully the pleasures of the mind and the senses. In his view New Brunswick possessed the essentials of Arcadia: its inhabitants lived in a land of natural abundance which his watercolours celebrate and whose spirit his style was fashioned to convey. Had it not been that he was now constantly harried by demands for an improved postal service and by threats to his position in the colony, Heriot might have realized his dream: to publish these drawings and present his own impressions, in pictures and in prose, of this maritime paradise.[21]

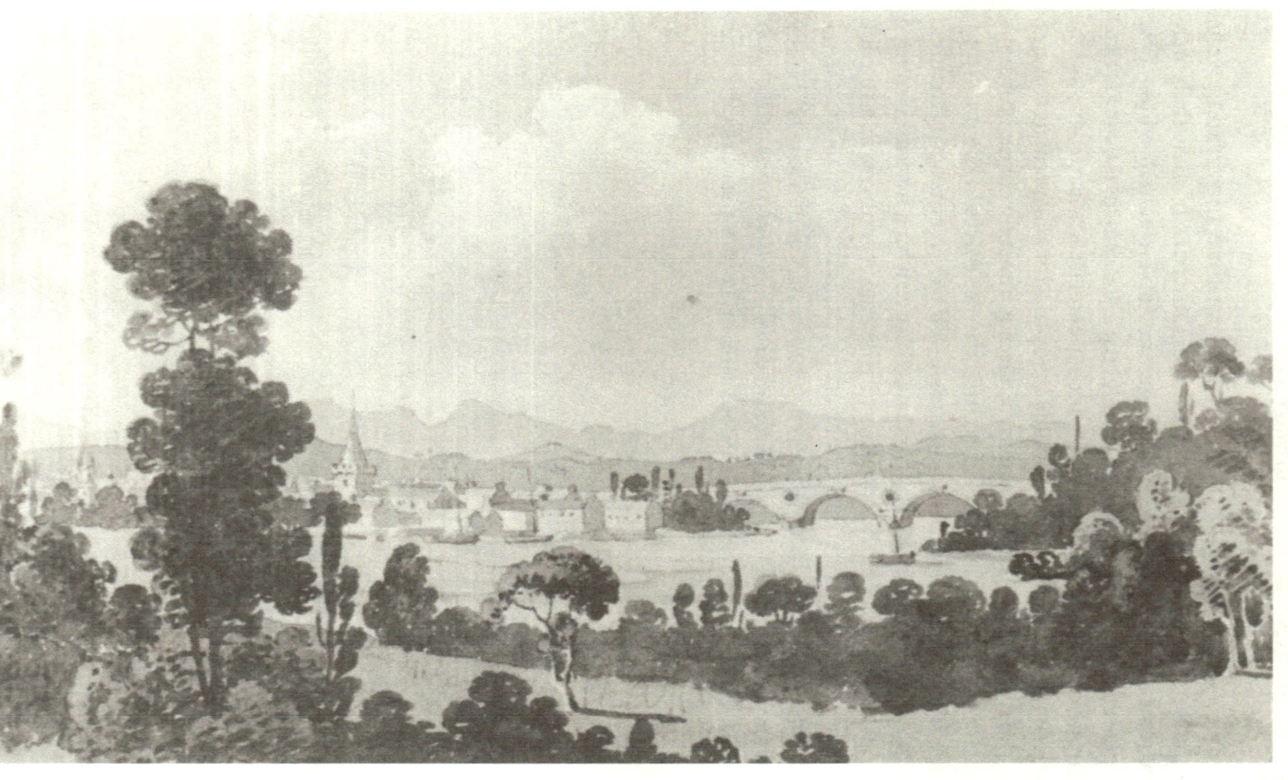

52 / *South View of Perth*, c 1806. Watercolour, 119 × 189 mm. (check-list 138)

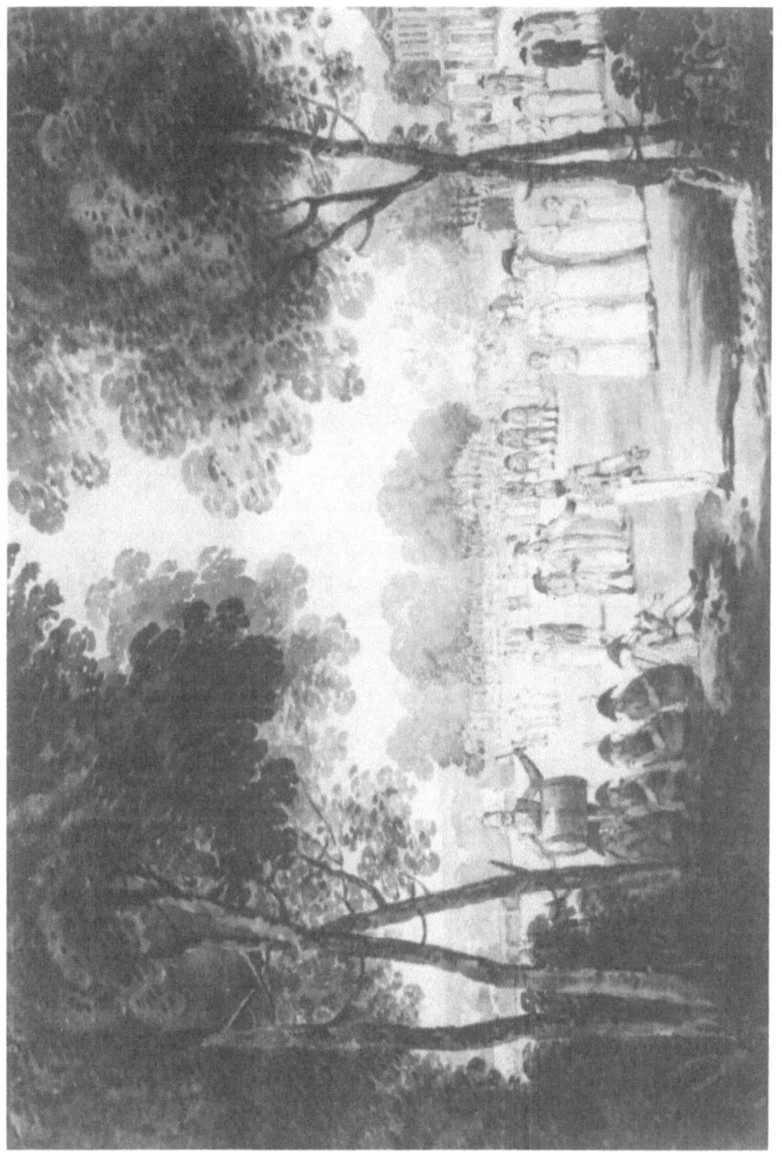

53 / *Fête given by Sir James Craig at Spencer Wood*, 1809. Watercolour, 247 × 365 mm. (check-list 166)

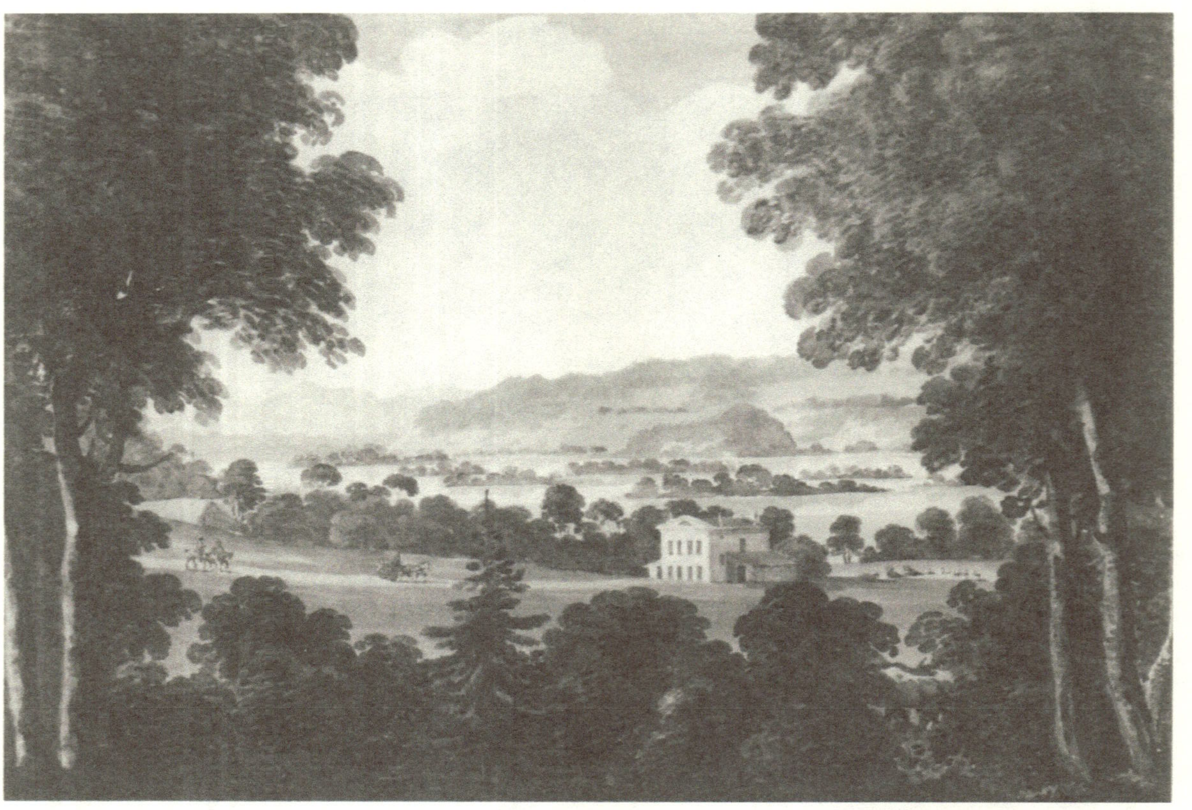

54 / *Chief Justice Ludlow's on the River St John, New Brunswick*, 1807. Watercolour, 336 × 489 mm. (check-list 147)

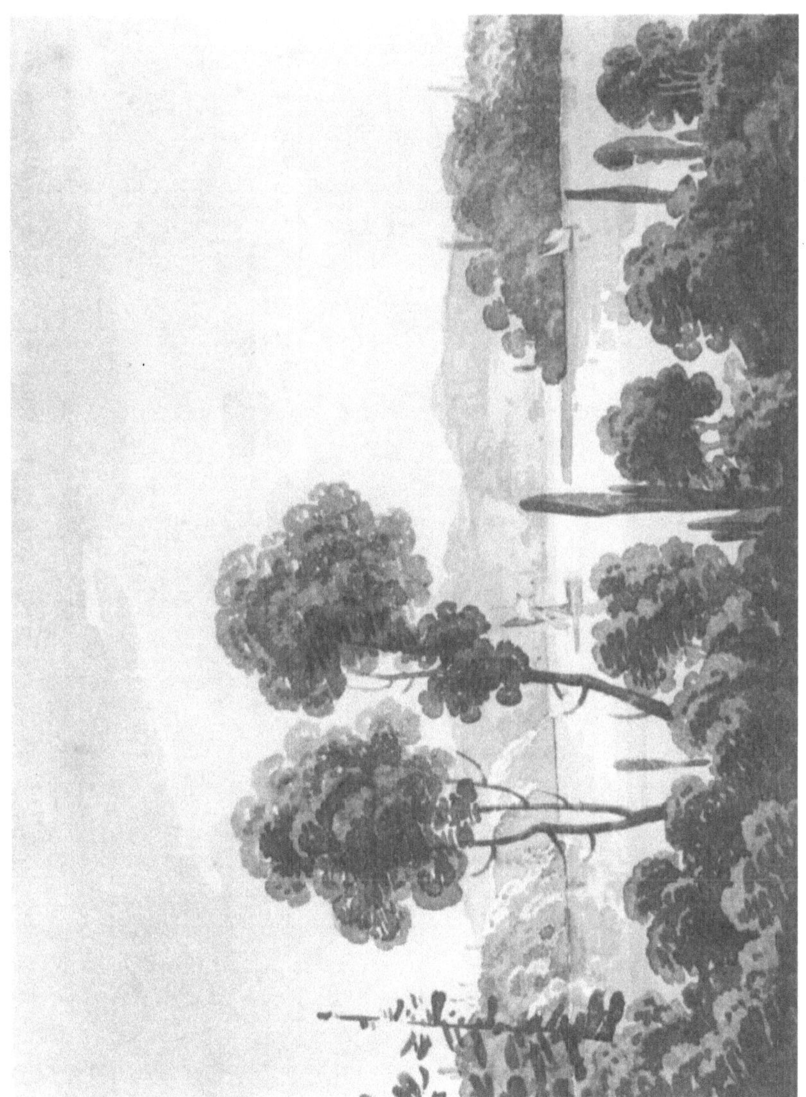

55 / *Belle Isle Bay, St John's River*, 1807. Watercolour, 133 × 184 mm. (check-list 148)

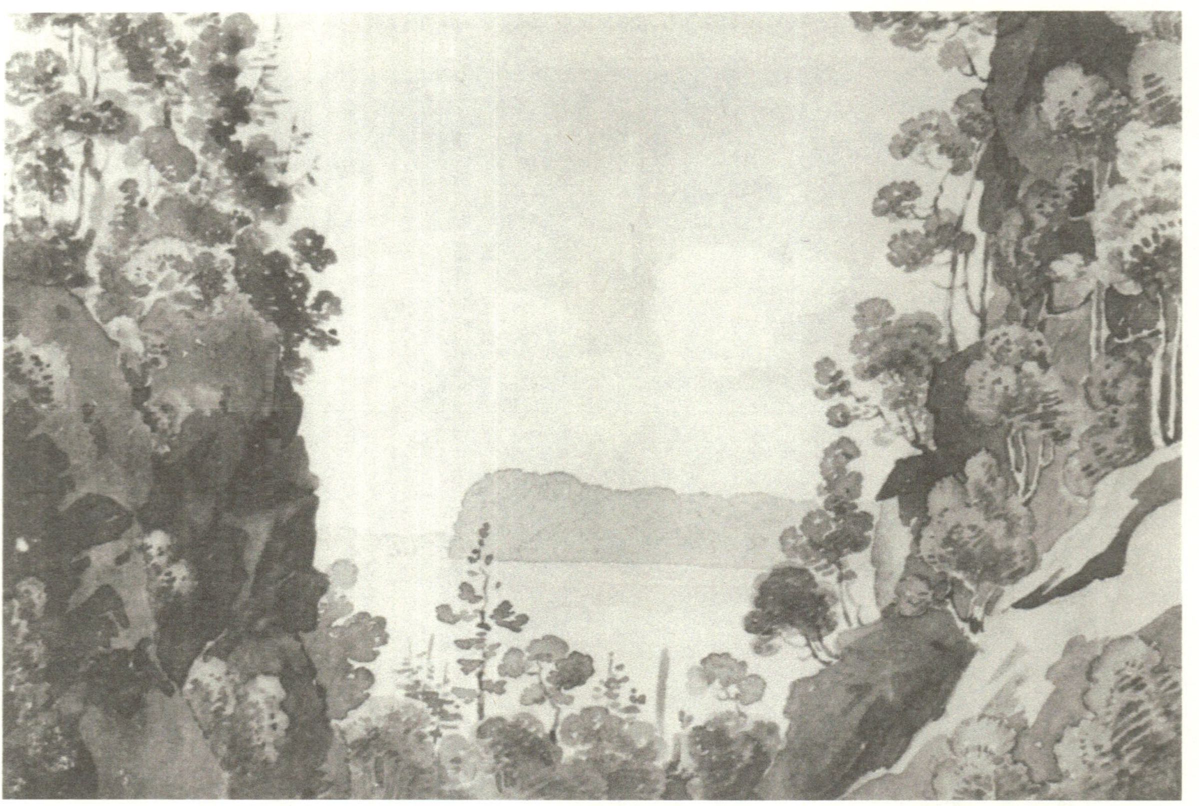

56 / *View from Partridge Island in the Bay of Fundy*, 1807. Watercolour, 124 × 184 mm. (check-list 143)

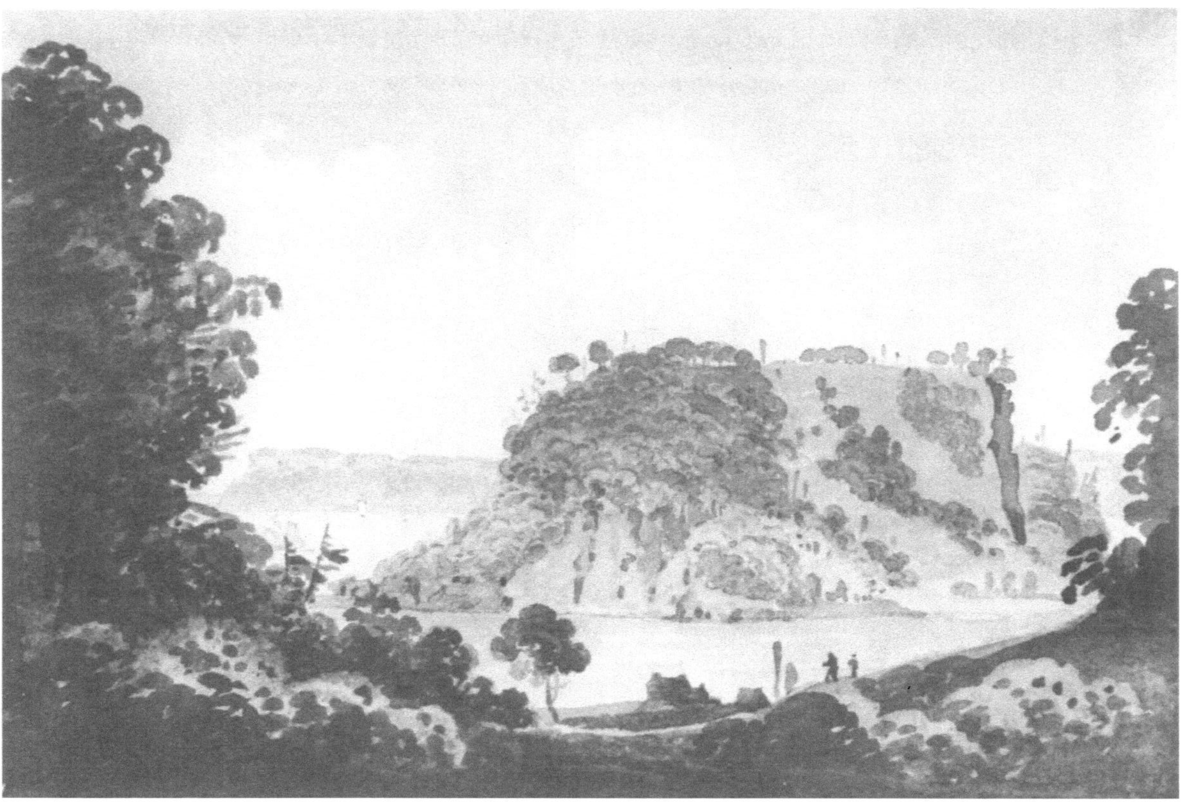

57 / *West View of Partridge Island from Parsborough*, 1807. Watercolour, 135 × 186 mm. (check-list 145)

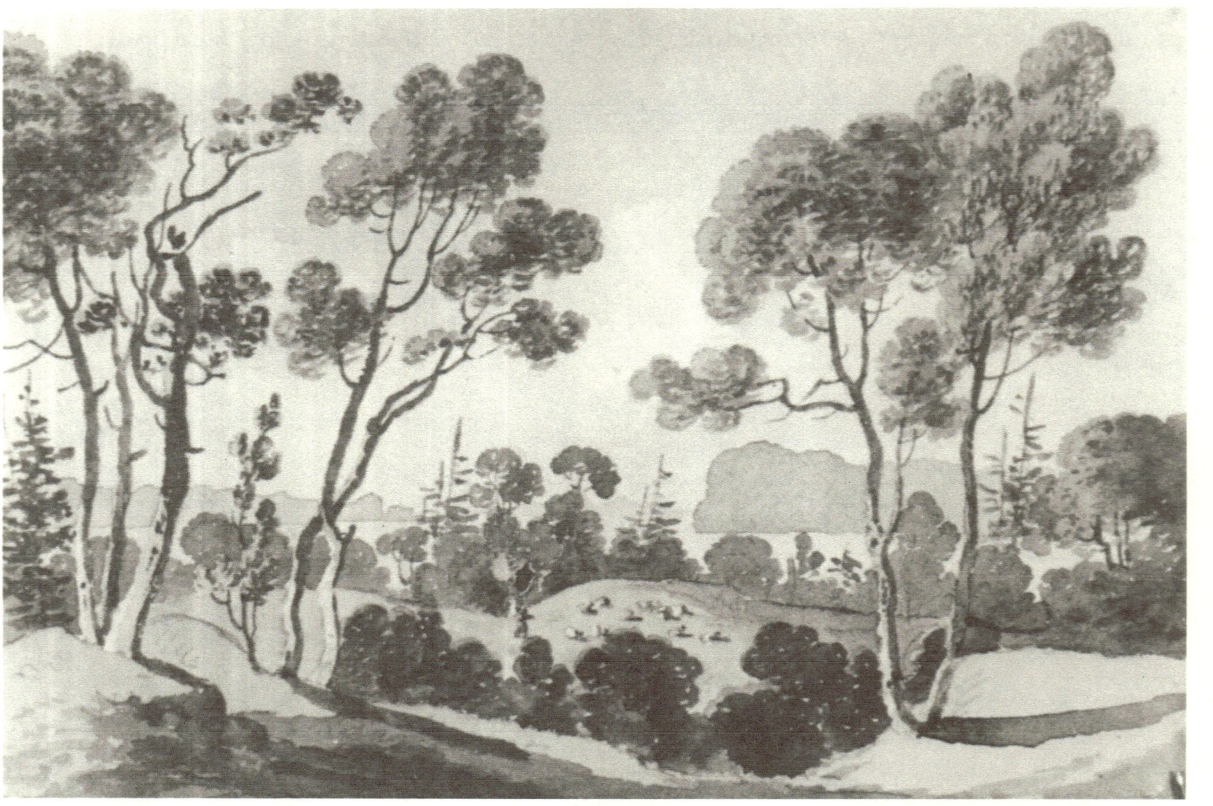

58 / *View on Partridge Island, Bay of Fundy,* 1807. Watercolour, 127 × 184 mm. (check-list 146)

7

Gathering Clouds

Heriot had only a few more years to spend in Canada, and these were to be marred by tension and growing disenchantment. Opportunities for travel, which he had previously taken for granted as a perquisite of his position as deputy postmaster general, became ever fewer as the problems of his administrative life engulfed him. By 1808, only a year after his return from Britain, reports had reached London concerning the lack of development and inadequacy of the postal service in Upper Canada and the shortcomings of the service between Montreal, Quebec, and Halifax. In reply to criticisms from London, Heriot argued that the difficulties with the service between Montreal and Quebec largely resulted from the fact that he had not been appointed superintendent of *maîtres de poste* (see chapter 4) and that he was therefore, as he had stated in 1802, unable to 'exercise the functions of that situation [the Post Office] in a manner the most conducive to His Majesty's Interests and to the public advantage.' Through being denied this post he had repeatedly experienced serious inconvenience in the discharge of his duties.[1]

In 1810 and 1811 the complaints at Heriot's management of the postal system became even shriller and more insistent than before.[2] British merchants, both in Canada and in Britain, severely criticized the tardiness of the mails which was adversely affecting their business and prosperity.[3] Once again, criticism often, though by no means exclusively, centred on the delays between Quebec and Montreal and Quebec and Halifax. Complaints were again directed to the Post Office in London, so that Heriot was eventually forced to give a detailed account of his administration and to advance reasons for the slowness of the service.[4]

With regard to the route between Montreal and Quebec, Heriot again maintained that his real problem was his lack of control over the *maîtres de poste*:

> As the Office of Superintendent of Provincial Post Houses has been given by the Governors of this Colony to Canadians, it has become almost a Sinecure, as no Person can execute that Duty with Effect, but the Officer at the Head of the Post Office Department. – the Maitres de Poste have therefore been accustomed, for some time past, to act agreeably to the Impulse of their Inclinations – they have fallen into habits of negligence and even Insolence, and Travelling has become wretched and uncomfortable.[5]

There were other difficulties too. Although three postal towns had been established between Montreal and Quebec (Berthier, Trois-Rivières, and, recently, L'Assomption), not only the road but its connecting bridges were in poor condition. Furthermore, Heriot noted, the mode of transport was primitive and slow: passengers and mails were being carried by *calèches*, which were 'small vehicles with two wheels of a homely and rude construction hung upon Bands of Leather, or Thongs of unmanufactured Bull Hides, by way of Springs.'

The merchants also complained about the tardiness of postal communication between Quebec and Halifax. They argued that, in favourable conditions, the route between these centres could be covered in six days instead of the month that was then required. Heriot's reply to this charge was that any such journey made in six days 'must indeed be considered as a very extraordinary and rapid March, as the Distance is 633 Miles, during three hundred & Sixty eight of which, neither Horses nor Carriages are to be found, and the nature of the Road is such, that it can be travelled with safety in Day time only – The Traveller must therefore stop during Night, as the Rapids of the Rivers are too dangerous to be passed even by Moonlight.' While the passage between Quebec and Halifax was fairly expeditious, since the courier's canoe was travelling with the current, the return journey was extremely slow and laborious. The courier had to ascend the Saint John River 'in a Birch Canoe, which for a considerable part of the way must be impelled by the use of a long Pole.' Even in the best of conditions, Heriot believed, the Quebec to Halifax route was a difficult one, particularly during the winter months, and were it not for the need to sustain regular communications between the military and civil establishments, 'it would be unnecessary to have regular Couriers on that Road,' as mails could be forwarded more quickly and at less expense by specially despatched couriers.[6]

Heriot was also attacked for the slowness of the mails through the United States. He believed that the responsibility for this was to be placed on the shoulders of the American postmaster general. Long before, he explained, he had written to Washington, to the American postmaster general in Washington, to the postmaster at New York, and to the British packet agent at New York (a Mr Thomas Moore)[7] with a proposal to have postal couriers from Canada carry the post between Montreal and New York, yet to pay the United States Post Office as though their couriers had carried it between these centres. Heriot also proposed that 'the four winter English mails which come by Packet [should be] forwarded by way of Boston instead of through New York to Albany and then north'; this, Heriot maintained, would be the most 'expeditious mode of conveyance.'[8] However, he had not succeeded in persuading the Americans to agree with these proposals, and it was for this reason, he pointed out, that postal communication between Canada and the United States had not yet been improved.[9] (In 1815 he was to visit the United States in the hope of improving the American route and hastening the delivery of mails to and from Britain.)

If Heriot had to admit to certain failures in the Post Office, he could, nevertheless, boast of some successes, such as the recent (1810) establishment of the regular service between Montreal and Kingston on a fortnightly basis throughout the year. He excused the lack of further development on the route between Kingston and York on the grounds of the poor state of the road and the small population residing in and between these settlements, quoting the recommendations of 'judicious Persons' who lived in this district, who believed that communication by land once a fortnight, for the six months during the period of closure of navigation, was fully adequate 'for the purpose of commerce.'[10]

Heriot had always considered the development of the postal service in Upper Canada a special responsibility, though by 1805 he had not made any major improvements. Three years later, however, after many unfavourable reports on the mails in the upper province had been sent to London, Heriot set out for Niagara, and probably also York, on a tour of inspection, as a result of which he made further efforts to increase the number of deliveries.[11] By 1812 even the administrator of Upper Canada at York, Major-General Isaac Brock, was to testify to the positive results of Heriot's actions: 'The Post, under the able management of Mr Heriot has

[been] provided during the whole of the winter with admirable regularity. I now receive, through his kind interference, my English letters and news papers immediately from New York, which we esteem a great luxury in this retirement.'[12]

While the joint postmaster general in London accepted Heriot's explanations of the state of the Canadian mails, the home government, anxious to improve and develop the commercial potential of its provinces, brought the matter to the attention of the then-administrator of Lower Canada, who was soon to become governor-in-chief of the Canadas; Sir George Prevost (1767–1816). Prevost immediately consulted with Heriot, who persuaded him that a better road system would serve to expedite the postal service, especially between Halifax and Quebec. Prevost then proposed certain changes in procedures to Heriot[13] and in March 1812 recommended to the secretary of state, Lord Liverpool, that it was absolutely necessary that 'a road should be opened through the unsettled Country between this place [Quebec] & Fredericton, so as not to depend altogether upon the winter communication by the Rivers & Lakes, which is often precarious & hazardous.'[14] The crucial point, Prevost believed – and Heriot agreed – was that there was a 'necessity of a ready and sure communication at all seasons between Quebec and Halifax that is becoming ever day more obvious from the state of American Politicks, & from the risk and delay to which public as well as private letters must be subject whilst passing through the American territories.'[15]

Prevost also reported to the home government that the deputy postmaster general was now proposing measures such as 'will eventually remove all the former grounds of Complaint against that Establishment [the Post Office] and essentially promote the interests of Commerce as those of the Public in general.'[16] He added: 'I am happy to be enabled to inform your Lordship that the Deputy Postmaster General has either adopted or is about to adopt such regulations as appear to me will fully meet the wishes expressed by the Merchants trading to British North America.'[17]

Although Prevost wanted to give the impression to the home government that he and Heriot were in accord over the proposed operation of the Post Office, in fact they were not, and news of their disagreement very soon reached London. Heriot, who had taken an instant dislike to Prevost, had been plagued by Prevost's interference almost as soon as the latter came to Quebec in September 1811. However, Heriot had no wish to antagonize him: he had suffered enough under previous administrators to desire nothing more, at this stage, than to live out the term of his professional career with as little incident as possible. In 1812, however, the American declaration of war on Britain was to prevent Heriot from achieving the more tranquil way of life of which he had dreamed.

The depression and worry which outspoken criticisms of the postal service had brought to Heriot from 1810 onwards forced him to remain at Quebec and to devote himself almost entirely to business affairs. He had methodically arranged the different elements of his life – his administrative career, his social activities, and his artistic pursuits – in a balanced equilibrium, but this was now being upset. Nevertheless, Heriot by no means forsook his painting during the difficult years from 1810 onwards: he still had the will to create, and the stresses which his duties placed on him found, indeed, a release in his art. He seems to have converted one of the rooms in his house into a studio, where as late as 1810 he had begun to paint in oils (figure 59). That year he had written to his friend Winslow: 'I now employ my leisure time in painting with oil colours, and am now finishing a naked Venus and two Cupids with which I am tolerably pleased.'[18] At this stage he was able to spend more time in sketching and in painting watercolours – and, simultaneously, in enjoying the variety and beauty of the Canadian landscape – than would be possible a few years later.

Also in 1810 Heriot was able to escape the tedium of his duties to go with some friends on a fishing trip to the Jacques Cartier River, some thirty miles from Quebec on the upper road to Montreal. He had visited and sketched the river before; he was once again enthralled by its appearance, which inspired him to compose a Horatian tribute to it. He wrote to Winslow,

> It is particularly beautiful and romantic and is of considerable magnitude . . . I composed a small ode in Latin addressed to the River, of which the following verses descriptive of the scenery which it exhibits are a part:
>
> AD FLUVIUM IACARTINUM
> Angustos inter scopulos repressus
> Rivum vexatas fundit per asperum
> Undas, et atras fluctibus proruptis
>   Lambit speluncas.
> Per Saxa, per agros, strepitu fremente
> Tortilem agit cursum, et umbrosa
> Nemora sonant, dum Laurentem petit
>   Ore spumante.[19]

The enthusiasm which Heriot expresses here for Canadian scenery is matched by the increasingly spirited brushwork of his watercolours. We see the beginnings of his late style in a watercolour, *Terrebonne*, which he painted in 1810 (figure 60). Terrebonne is a small settlement to which Heriot was summoned in that year by Post Office business. He was much struck by its appearance. The village, he noted, 'is certainly the loveliest place in all America. The beautiful islands, the foaming rapids of the Grand or Outaouais river ... together with the white stone houses of a superior construction for America, and the sloping banks on which they are placed, forms a singular combination of objects which convey an agreeable impression to the mind.'[20] He wrote this description immediately after his return to Quebec and its accuracy was ensured by the on-the-spot sketches which he had made and from which he developed the finished watercolour. The work shows not only picturesque qualities but also the liquid washes which begin to appear more frequently in his watercolours at this time.

By 1812 this stylistic breadth had become even more evident in Heriot's watercolours. He assaulted the paper with a brush even more heavily loaded, with the consequence that liquid patterns of light and shade begin to articulate the composition in a way that they had never done before, reinforcing, in certain respects, the two-dimensional structure and simplifying landscape forms. The small, mobile figures that had earlier animated his landscapes have become, by this time, noticeably sculptural, and if their movement is not stilled, it is certainly slow and laboured.

While the activity of the figures within the landscape is curtailed by Heriot's more liquid style, that of the topography is not. The discovery that the brush, even when fully charged, could still describe form adequately is one thing, but that it could also in some respects provide an equivalent vitality to that of nature itself was quite another. In the *Falls of the Chaudiere, Quebec* (figure 61), which must date between 1811 and 1812, the artist has painted a landscape in which the style serves to emphasize the fluid nature of the river, and particularly the character of water in motion. The waterfall itself is nobly represented: Heriot captures in paint the force of the descent, as well as the screen of mist, flung up from the collision of waters, which serves to soften the harsher tones and lines of the background forms.

Heriot's increasingly free brushwork furnished his watercolours of about 1812 with a greater expressiveness than we find in his earlier work. Such brushwork was promoted by his more immediate and instinctive response to nature, and for this reason many of these later watercolours seem to be richer repositories of feeling than his earlier drawings.

This liquidity of brushwork, and the emotional responsiveness which it suggests, enabled Heriot to discover something else. With the beginning of his classical phase around 1800, he had understood more fully than before that, while his landscapes could be faithful to the external world, they could also embody an inherent permanent order of their own. A landscape such as *Distillery at Beauport near Quebec*, painted in 1812 (figure 62), is a later, more highly developed expression of this understanding. It is a landscape whose forms have been greatly simplified and ordered according to the principles of the Picturesque (for example, in its balanced composition and patterns of irregularity), but which, neverthe-less, possess the essential qualities of a portrait.

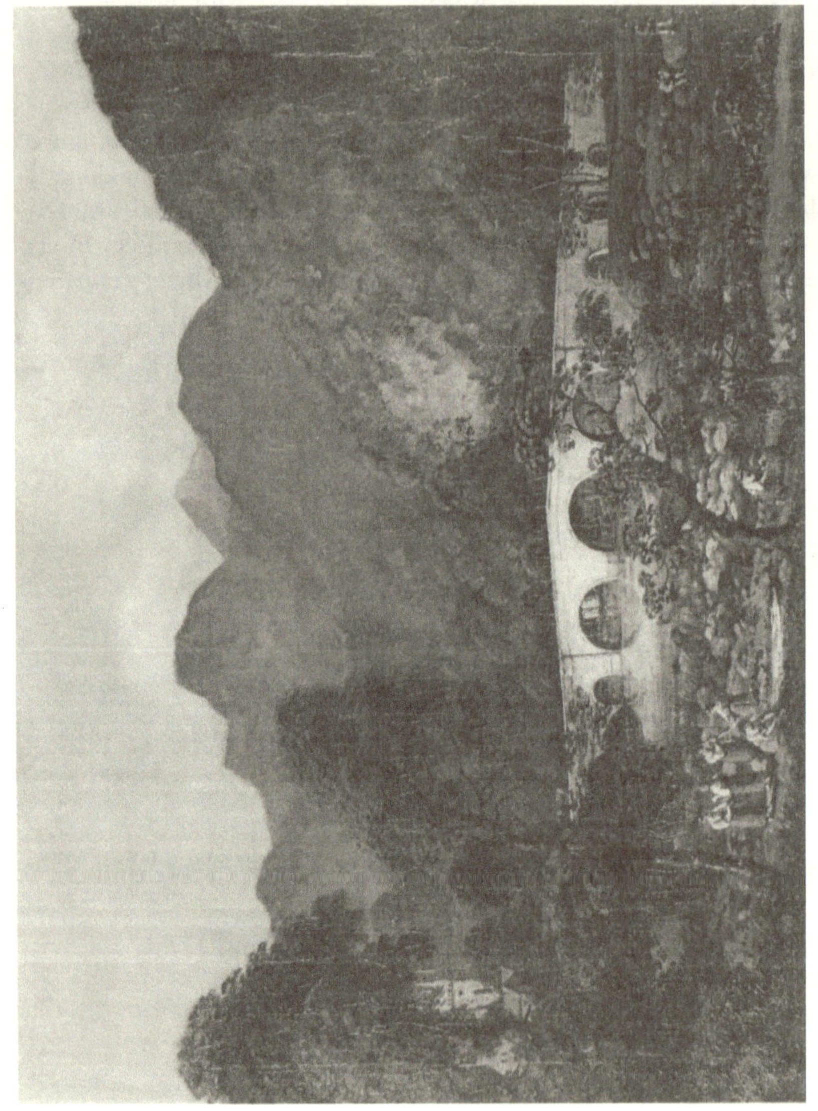

59 / *View of Taymouth or Kenmore Bridge, Perthshire,* c 1812. Oil on canvas, 640 × 822 mm. (check-list 3)

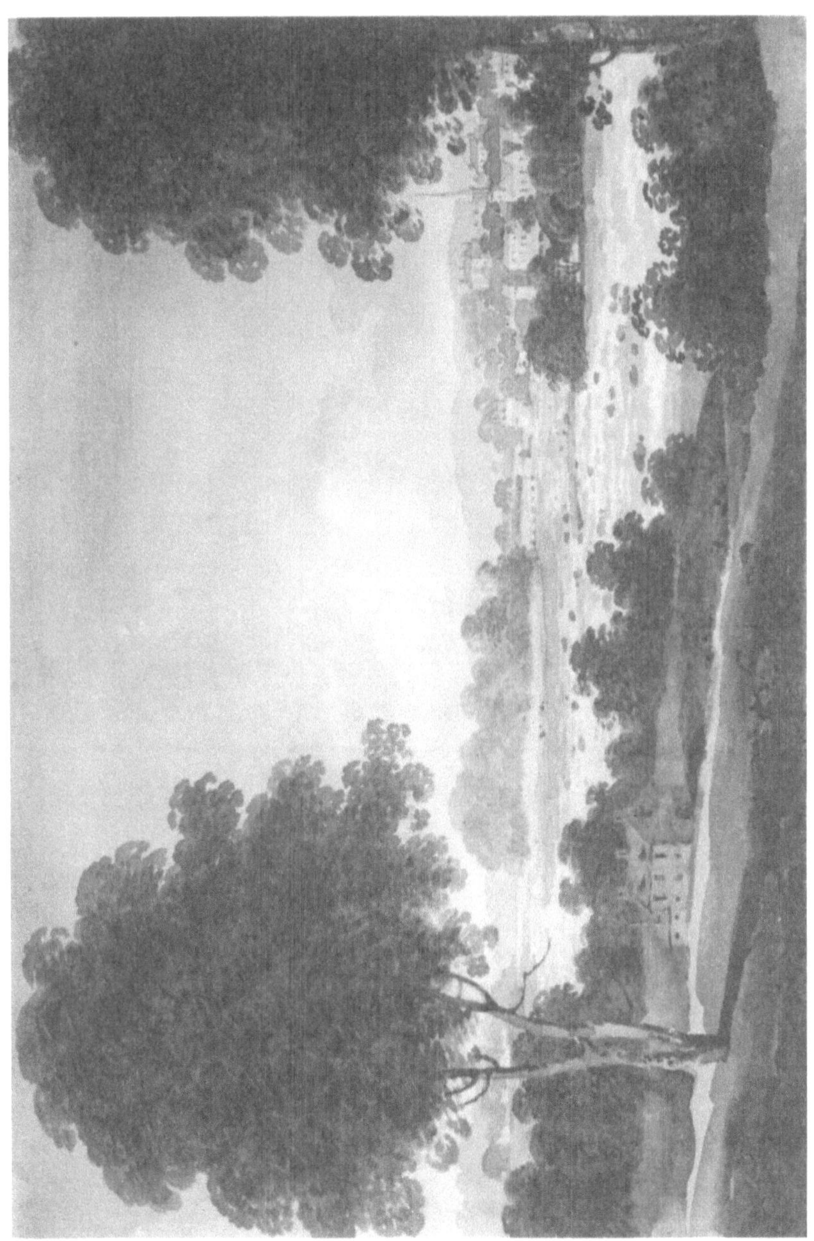

60 / *Terrebonne*, 1810. Watercolour, 192 × 292 mm. (check-list 171)

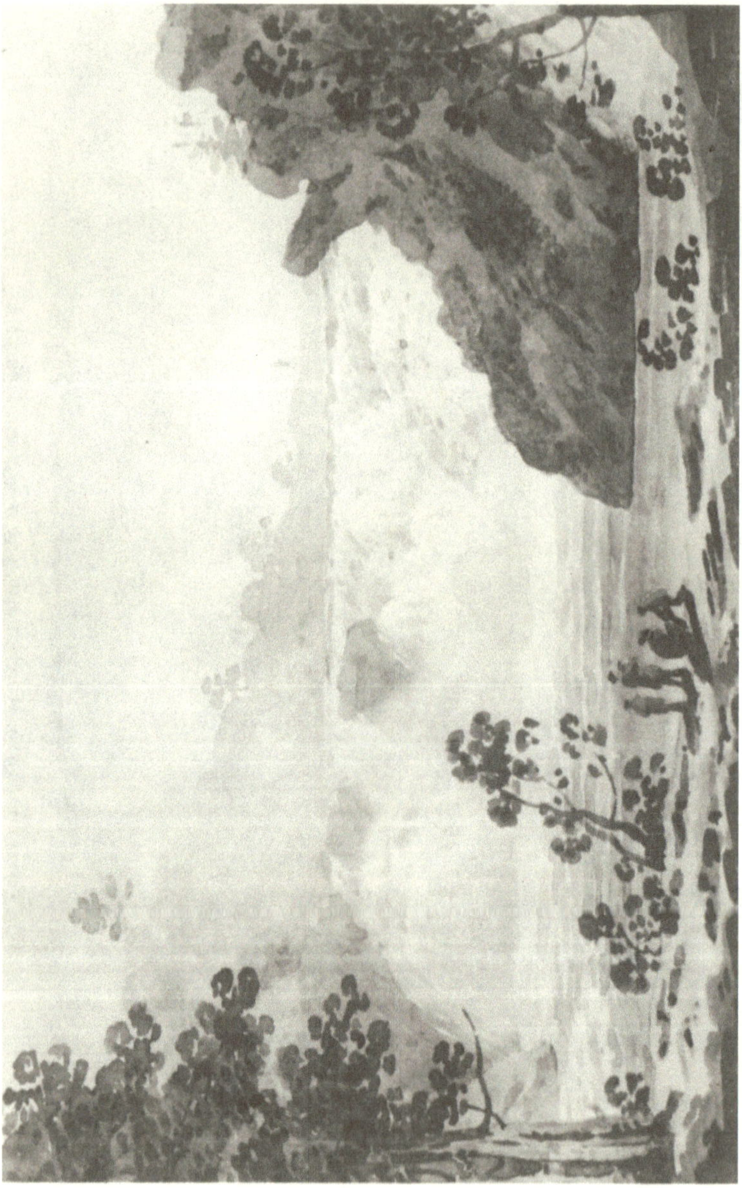

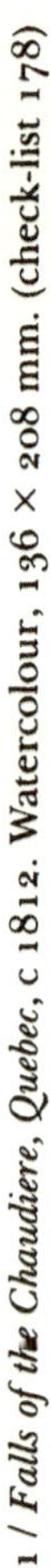

61 / *Falls of the Chaudiere, Quebec*, c 1812. Watercolour, 136 × 208 mm. (check-list 178)

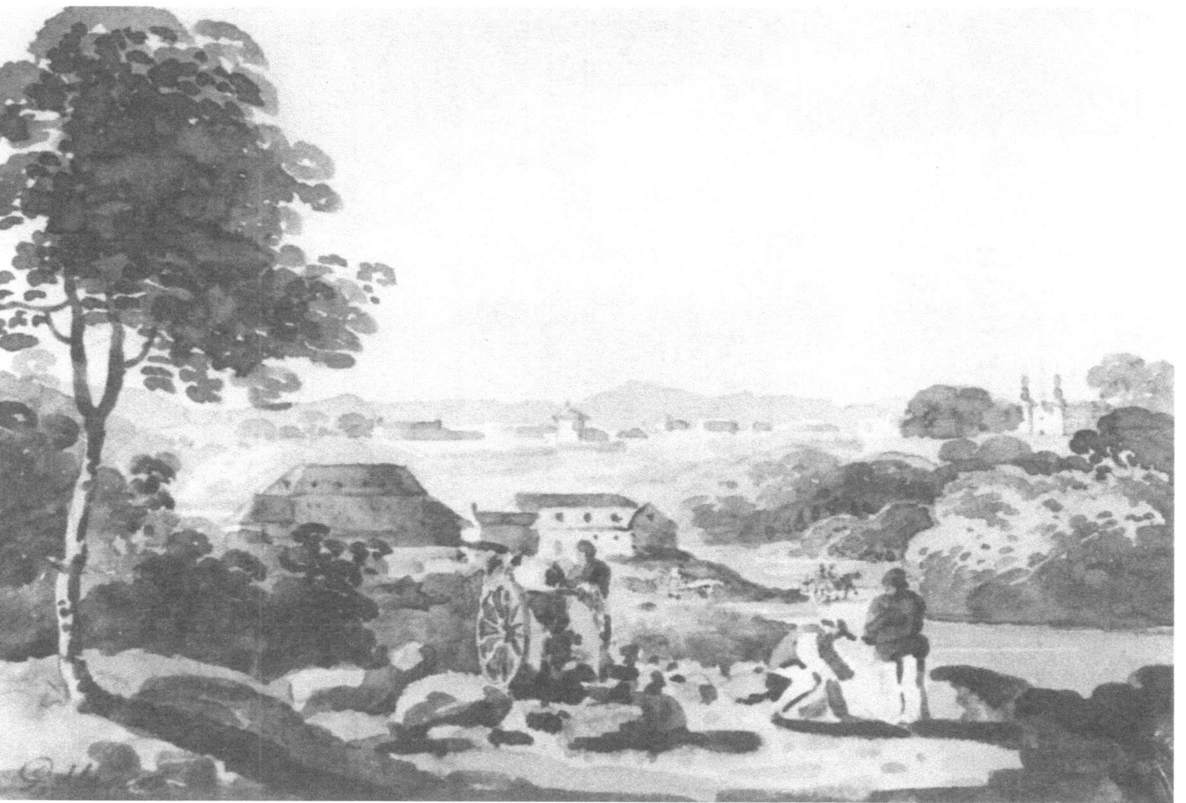

62 / *Distillery at Beauport near Quebec*, 1812. Watercolour, 121 × 174 mm. (check-list 177)

8

The War of 1812 and Its Aftermath

The War of 1812 shook Heriot into a state of deep concern for the welfare of his adopted country. At least as early as 1807, when there had seemed to be the possibility of hostilities with the United States, he had expressed his fear of the consequences. He was hopeful that 'negotiations with America will terminate amicably, and that these provinces will continue to enjoy the blessings and advantages of tranquillity.'[1] By 1811 his hopes for a continued peace were less sanguine. 'War with the United States,' he wrote, 'appears to me inevitable,' though 'it is my opinion the Americans will not attempt a regular invasion of Canada ... Were Canada to be conquered ... the States would not long hang together. We must expect ... frequent irruptions and predatory expeditions.'[2]

Heriot believed that, if the Americans were to carry out a successful invasion of Canada, the commander of the forces would become a virtual dictator and would find the means to maintain his army there. Yet Heriot felt reasonably confident that, even if an invasion did take place, there would be no real threat of defeat: Britain's might would be wholly adequate to repulse the invaders, those 'undisciplined Yankies,'[3] and, if it found itself in combat with the British navy, the American fleet would suffer and 'soon disappear.' Still, he did regret the hardship that innocent settlers on both sides of the border would suffer as the result of a war:

> An American war must, from the nature of the country, be productive of more instances of inhumanity, and barbarity, than any other, as the savages will not remain idle spectators, but exercise their native ferocity on the families of inoffensive and remote settlers. Warfare has ever been the

principal occupation of mankind. Peace is only a breathing time, and a great portion of the civilized world is occupied in that interval, in multiplying, inventing and improving the instruments of destruction.[4]

The causes of the war were linked to the continuing strife between Britain and Napoleonic France, which had provided the occasion for American expansion westward into areas still technically controlled by the European combatants, the Louisiana Purchase of 1803 (from France) and the related annexation of West Florida in 1801 being major examples. In the north, American pioneers came into conflict with Indian tribes which received support from Canada, and anti-British feeling increased to the extent that the American expansionists demanded that Canada be annexed.

At sea matters were equally serious. As we have seen in chapter 6, Britain's close blockade of French-controlled Europe and Napoleon's counter-blockade had forced European trade to operate through neutral vessels – to the advantage of American interests, whose activities prompted reprisals from the Royal Navy in turn. American shipowners, however, had preoccupations well beyond Europe. By 1812 retaliatory American legislation was beginning to be modified in favour of a diplomatic accommodation with Britain; they and the British had no desire for war. But the American extremists did; at their instigation the United States declared war on Britain on 8 June 1812. This proved a mistake, for though American feelings were relieved by a series of bitter sea-fights and minor actions on the American mainland, the end of the European conflict in 1814 not only allowed Britain to bring massive forces to bear on the Americans but also undermined the causes for which the War of 1812 had been declared. The Treaty of Ghent, signed on 24 December 1814, closed the North American affair with little gain to the Americans beyond the assertion of their independence. The legacy of bad feeling was exacerbated by the six weeks that it took for the treaty to reach the United States for ratification and by the poor communications which, as late as 23 March 1815 (when the USS *Hornet* captured HMS *Penguin* in the south Atlantic), allowed hostilities at sea to continue into the peace.

The War of 1812 had broken out on 8 June. The American declaration of war on Britain immediately affected Heriot's life, increasing his responsibilities. He had to organize special postal services and was required to justify the exemption of couriers from military service.[5] In addition, the war increased the difficulties which Sir George Prevost's earlier interference in the Post Office's business had already caused Heriot. Ironically fresh conflicts erupted between the two men only months after Prevost had despatched his letter to the secretary of state in London in which he assured him that the Canadian postal service was beginning to function efficiently. In July 1812, only a month after the declaration of war, Prevost was proclaimed governor-in-chief. As administrator he had been able to do no more than recommend to Heriot certain postal reforms, but now he believed that he had the power to insist on them. Heriot's responsibilities, already considerable, were thus enlarged by Prevost's demands for an improved service; these demands had the additional effect, however, of undermining the deputy postmaster general's authority.

Heriot withstood Governor Prevost's meddling for almost a year. When in 1813 Prevost imperiously commanded Heriot to establish a daily mail service between Quebec and Montreal, he obeyed, but he did so reluctantly. He had always refused to act on such a proposal; the current delays, he maintained, should be blamed on the government (which had not remedied the poor state of the roads) and on the *maîtres de poste* (over whom he had no control). Moreover, the costs of launching and running such a service, he claimed, would be prohibitive. But the governor was determined that the service should be established and, knowing Heriot well enough, was able to forestall further excuses by observing that he (Prevost) had 'less hesitation in urging the Adoption of it on Account of the very considerable income which must have taken place in the Revenue of the Post Office, arising out of the War.'[6] In May Heriot accordingly (and with a heavy heart) took a *calèche* to Montreal to complete the arrangements.[7]

However Heriot could no longer tolerate Prevost's interference. Two months later, in July 1813, he wrote a blistering attack on the governor and sent it to the joint postmaster general in London:

> Ever since the arrival of that Governor he has made it a practice to interfere with the Post Office, as if that Department were solely under his Controul ... [his] Conduct ... is so unlike anything I have ever before experienced, that I find it a very unpleasant Circumstance to remain longer here whilst he has direction of Affairs, and unless he can be told by the Secretary of State that he has no Controul over the Post Office, I regret to think the business of that Department in this Country will not go on as it has hitherto been conducted.

So deeply had Heriot come to detest Prevost that he could not resist making, in addition, an observation on the governor's direction of colonial affairs: 'A want of Experience joined to Incapacity strongly characterize every measure of the present Administration of the Colonial government. I am doubtful whether such chicane & Intrigue is not practised to support a System so feeble and inefficient.'[8] Heriot's dislike and distrust of Prevost were not to be assuaged, and were now displayed more openly. His feelings were observed, keenly resented, and reciprocated by the governor, who eventually wrote to the secretary of state that he did not 'at all times find in Mr Heriot, the D.^{y} Postmaster Genl of America, that promptitude & zeal for promoting H.M. Service by a due attention to my wishes respecting this Depart[ment] which I had [the] right to expect from him.'[9] But Heriot was determined to offer Prevost as little assistance as possible, and he carried his attacks on Prevost into other areas as well.

If Heriot found Prevost's interference in postal affairs upsetting, he was equally distressed by Britain's direction of the war. Because of the intimate and necessary connection between the Post Office and the military during war, Heriot had access to current information concerning the progress of the war. It was probably for this reason that, in April 1813, he expressed strong concern over the inaction of the Royal Navy on the eastern coast of America. Only gradually had British ships begun to establish an effective commercial blockade of American ports which, however, did not initially include the ports of New England. 'Our fleet,' Heriot wrote to Winslow, 'seems to be extremely indolent, for although now three times superior to the whole navy of the Yankies, Stores ships richly laden from China, have been suffered to gain the port of Boston unmolested. I am afraid our worthy Admiral [Sir John Borlase Warren] has forgot his fighting days and has become too much the *Drawing Room Gentleman*, as the Diplomatic character is not very consistent with the authority and energy of a naval Commander.'[10] Heriot also anticipated the more decisive British strategy that was soon to be implemented: 'Let the Ministry order the blocade of the port of Boston &c; the inhabitants will feel the effects of the war and take immediate measures to arrest its further progress.'[11] Indeed, by 1814, the last year of the war, the Royal Navy did effectively blockade the American eastern seaboard.

During the last months of hostilities there had been a swell of discontentment among both British civilians and troops living in Canada who considered their nation's military performance during the war to have been shameful. Heriot certainly felt thus, and in October 1814 he wrote a letter to the colonial administration at Quebec, expressing candid views on the incompetence shown by the British command. It is perhaps not surprising that he should have chosen to mention, and to focus on, the particular incapacities of his long-standing foe, Sir George Prevost, who, as the commander of a powerful British force of regular troops, had failed to capture the American naval base at Sackett's Harbour on Lake Ontario on 29 May 1813. Conveyed to the harbour by British ships under the command of Sir James Yeo, Prevost's soldiers had met strong resistance from the American defenders. Still, the British advanced until the American militia, which had fallen back, rallied; then Prevost, never one to tempt fortune, ordered his troops to retreat and, complained Heriot, 'neglected to attain the object of the expedition when it was in his powers.'[12]

Heriot also mentioned the recent 'inglorious' expedition to Plattsburg in New York State in September 1814, which also had been led by Prevost.[13] Entering New York State at the foot of Lake Champlain, Prevost's force had advanced to Plattsburg. But when the British naval squadron which was protecting Prevost's flank was destroyed by an American fleet, Prevost, unnerved, retreated, as he had at Sackett's Harbour. Heriot, reflecting on Prevost's action, observed that the 'whole army felt themselves disgraced, and Officers as well as men could not refrain from giving vent to their feelings of disappointment and indignation.' Such occurrences depressed Heriot, who reported that 'many General Officers as well as others of subordinate rank are said to have applied for leave to return to England.'[14] Indeed, Heriot admitted that, at the time he was writing, he himself was so shaken that he felt ready to return to England. He felt 'disgusted with the country' and anxious to clear the memory of the experience from his mind.[15]

His difficulties with Governor Prevost were not the only ones that Heriot experienced during these war years. Enmities established long ago with other administrators were still plaguing him, and at least one of these was to prove a serious threat to his career. George Glasgow, formerly lieutenant-colonel and a member of the Board of Ordnance,[16] had quarrelled bitterly with Heriot (possibly in 1805, a year after Heriot had been promoted from clerk of cheque to clerk of survey to the Board).[17] By 1813 Glasgow held the rank of major-general in the Royal Artillery and was second in command to Sir George Prevost. He therefore found himself at last in a position to settle an old score. Knowing that the deputy postmaster general still held his post as clerk of survey, Glasgow decided to engineer his removal from it. As director of posts Heriot had to remain based at Quebec. When the commander of the forces at Kingston ordered Glasgow to send a 'Civil Officer' to take charge of the Kingston stores immediately, Glasgow seized his opportunity and saw to it that Heriot was selected for the post. On Heriot's refusal to take up the position in Kingston because of his responsibilities at Quebec, Glasgow signed and issued a general order, suspending him from his post as clerk of survey.

Glasgow's personal grudge against Heriot is plainly expressed in a letter which he wrote to his military superior, the commander of the forces, about his general order: he could not refrain from noting that 'on this subject I have to observe that when Mr Heriot's private concerns took him to England some years back [in 1806] he found no difficulty in leaving his Post Office concerns to the management of a Substitute.'[18] In an attempt to defend himself against Glasgow's attack Heriot forwarded correspondence concerning the affair to the office of Glasgow's military superior, observing that 'General Glasgow has repeatedly told me, that he had recommended to Sir George Prevost that I should be sent to Kingston, and I have as often assured him of the impossibility of my compliance.' He added: 'I regret to find that differences which did exist several years ago at the Board of Respective Officers, should be so long retained in remembrance.'[19] Despite Heriot's protestations and his efforts to arouse sympathy and support, his suspension from the clerkship was never revoked, nor was his salary ever restored.

The distress that Heriot must have experienced when he learned of his suspension from the clerkship was intensified by the growing burden of his Post Office duties. Indeed, so onerous had Heriot's administrative tasks become that by early 1815 he felt obliged to inform the postmaster general in London of his plight. His duties, he maintained, had become 'too great and accumulated to sustain under the pressure of circumstances'; his responsibility filled 'nearly the whole' of his time, and deprived him of the 'opportunity of cultivating society.'[20] It was almost certainly because of these pressures that by this time Heriot was able to devote less time to his sketching.

But an opportunity to escape briefly from under the weight of these increased responsibilities occurred a few months later – about six months after the war ended. At that time Heriot made a trip to the United States to investigate the possibility of re-establishing a regular passage for

British mail through that country. At first he believed that Boston should be the port of entry, although later he decided on New York.[21] However, this was not his only mission in the United States. He seems to have been drafted to undertake intelligence work, and one of his primary objects during this visit to the United States was to obtain information about American harbour and shipping in the event of a fresh outbreak of hostilities with the United States.[22] British interest in the eastern American ports had arisen as a result of the blockade by the Royal Navy especially during 1814, the last year of the war. This efficient blockade – whose desirability Heriot had foreseen – proved highly successful: soon 'grass grew in the streets of Boston.'

When Heriot left for the United States he started out by following the regular postal route through Vermont and along the shores of Lake Champlain. He then made a detour to the coast and to Boston, where perhaps he discussed with the postal authorities the possibility of routing all British mails through New York. Then, in apparent innocence, he made sketches of a number of American coastal ports on his way to New York, where he held discussions with the New York postmaster and the British agent for His Majesty's packets, Thomas Moore, and also examined the port facilities. From New York he continued south through Philadelphia to Washington for deliberations with the American postmaster general.

Fortunately two sketch-books survive (New York Historical Society; see check-list 335, 336) which provide a record – almost daily, apart from one gap – of Heriot's progress to the south and his return trip. Through them we can trace his movements in detail. He may have left Quebec on 1 June, travelling by coach (a coach service had by then been established on the route) to Montreal. After spending a few days there, he probably rode to Chambly on 6 June. By the 8th he was at Lake Champlain. On his route south he took time to sketch the Vermont landscape, including a dramatic, liquid study of Sutherland's Falls and its mill, where he stopped on 10 June (figure 63). On the 11th he drew a waterfall at Rutland. For the period from the 12th until the 22nd, when he began making sketches in New York City, there is no record in the first sketch-book. However, two important topographical watercolours, both highly finished, have come to light. Each documents one of the days in this intervening period. One of the watercolours is a detailed, elaborate, and very large panorama (almost nine feet in width) of Salem Neck and Salem, from Beverly to Marblehead, a location which Heriot originally sketched on 17 June (check-list

184). The other watercolour – less detailed and less elaborate and smaller – is a panorama of Providence, Rhode Island, which he sketched on the following day (figure 64). Both watercolours were created by a careful enlargement of numerous detailed studies made on the spot and presumably included in a sketch-book which has not survived; their significance is perhaps primarily military rather than artistic.

While Heriot was investigating and sketching the port of New York and its activities, it appears that, as the Americans had little concern for security, he freely carried out an examination of the shipyards. These were housed in a large wooden compound, probably covered, and Heriot notes that here 'hulls ... intended for the service of the American Government' were being constructed. He remarks that 'progress of the work suffers no interference from the State of the Weather.'[23] These observations come from a document that Heriot submitted to the military at Quebec on his return later that year; it is clearly an intelligence report, for most of it is devoted to a description of a new type of warship which Heriot may have seen anchored off Long Island. This was the steam frigate *Fulton the First,* which had been built at New York and was launched there on 29 October 1814. If Heriot did see the ship, he may have had the opportunity to sketch it, but no pictorial evidence has yet come to light. He expresses the view that *Fulton the First*'s 'immense and singular structure is perfectly new in Naval Architecture,' and notes that the keel 'throughout the whole length is double,' and also that the engine, which could develop a power 'equal to that of one Hundred and Twenty ... Horses,' was placed in the centre of the ship. Clearly impressed by the frigate's capabilities, Heriot remarks that she was 'one of the most powerful efforts for Defence which the Ingenuity of Man has yet produced ... and well calculated for the protection of a Harbour or Dock Yard from any attack which might be attempted by Water.'[24]

Heriot's intelligence work at New York must have been completed in a few days, for he was heading south on 25 June. He stopped briefly at Philadelphia, which he sketched on 27 June, taking at least eight views of the city's harbour. From Philadelphia he coached directly to Washington, which he reached at least as early as 30 June. There he discussed the New York-Montreal route with postal officials, but he also found time to make detailed drawings of public buildings which had been burned by the British troops during the late war in retaliation for the sack of York in 1813. For example, on 30 June he carefully sketched the partially restored Capitol, making a note of its length and width. On the following day he sketched the refurbished Palace of the President (figure 65), whose dimensions he also recorded. After completing his pictorial inventory of Washington's public buildings he began his return journey north.

Heriot's return trip through the hot, radiant days of July was more discursive and leisurely and, because he had probably completed his intelligence work, was accomplished with less strain. He again paid a brief visit to New York, where he arrived on 14 July. While staying there, he undertook a special trip on 16 July to see the famous Passaic Falls in New Jersey. Enthralled by the sight, Heriot drew several views of the river and falls, one of which he later completed in full colour. He also composed a poem, perhaps on the spot, inspired by the picturesque beauty of the scene:

O'er rugged cliffs his rapid current pours,
Throwing through gloomy chasms his silver showers;
Like a coy fair, whose beauties, half conceal'd
Impart a lustre to the charms reveal'd.[25]

After returning from the Passaic Falls to New York, Heriot seems to have boarded a ship sailing on the Hudson River. The journey offered him ample opportunity to record the topography of the river banks, and it was at this time that he began to fill his second sketch-book. Though he drew such well-known features of the river scenery as the imposing Palisades and Anthony's Nose, he also sketched places of military significance, such as Fort Montgomery, West Point (figure 66), and Fort Clinton. On 19 July he was at Poughkeepsie and by the next day had landed at the picturesque town of Hudson. There he seems to have bought a horse, on which he may have ridden to the Cohoe Falls, which he reached and sketched on the 21st. Three days later he was at Ballston, near Albany; there he possibly stayed overnight at a large 150-bedroom hotel. On the following day, 25 July, Heriot was at Saratoga Springs; on the same day he sketched Glens Falls.

Picturesque Lake George's shining surfaces, leafy borders and lakeside mountains occupy many pages of Heriot's sketch-book (see figure 67). He arrived at the lake on 26 July; the last of the many sketches which he made as he travelled round it dates from the 27th. From Lake George he set out for Lake Champlain and Ticonderoga, which he reached the next day. The last views of Lake Champlain are dated 29 July. Heriot was probably back in Quebec with his collection of sketches before the end of the first week in August.

So enchanted was Heriot by the beauty of the scenery which he had discovered on his American trip that he resolved to act upon his earlier proposal to write a guide to the eastern United States. He had wanted to travel to the United States in 1807, but then the skirmish between the *Leopard* and the *Chesapeake* and its threat of war had prevented him. Later, in 1811, he wrote: 'I have it in contemplation to make a Tour to Boston New York and Philadelphia ... and take some of the most striking of the Views, which I might perhaps publish in a Tour through that Country, as I have not yet seen any work of the kind that pleases me.'[26] However, no opportunity to make the journey presented itself, and the next year the outbreak of war forced Heriot to shelve the plan.

Even after his trip in 1815 Heriot's proposal to write an illustrated picturesque guide to the eastern United States came to nought. We do not know why, although Heriot was certainly under increasing pressure from his Post Office duties and would therefore have had little time for such an undertaking. And we know, too, that he was never anxious to establish a literary reputation: 'I hate ... to be thought an author, it is not creditable for a Gentleman – people are shy of him – When the late Mr Gibbon the Historian of the Roman Empire, went one evening to the [residence?] of Her R. Highness the Dutchess of Cumberland in Pall Mall, the late Duke addressed him in the following stile – Eh! Mr Gibbon, still continue to scribble – scribble – scribble, eh!'[27]

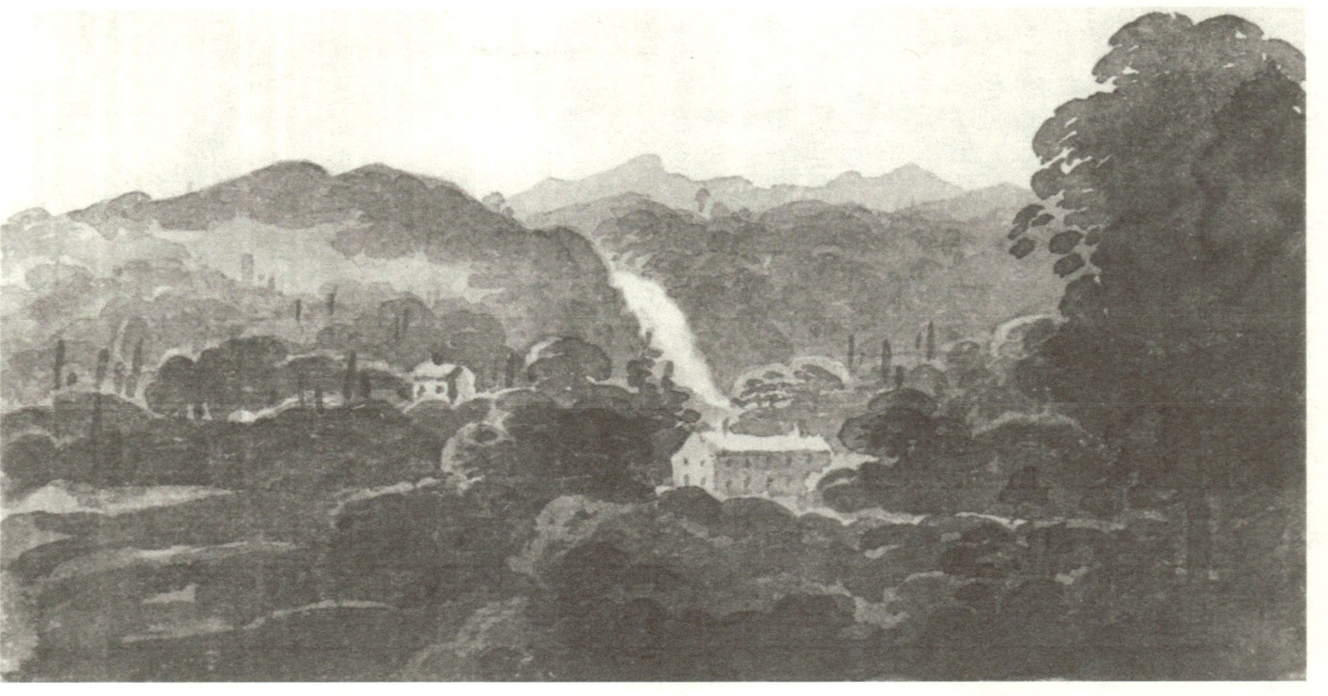

63 / *Sutherland's Falls, Vermont*, 1815. Watercolour, 105 × 201 mm. (check-list 335, 10r)

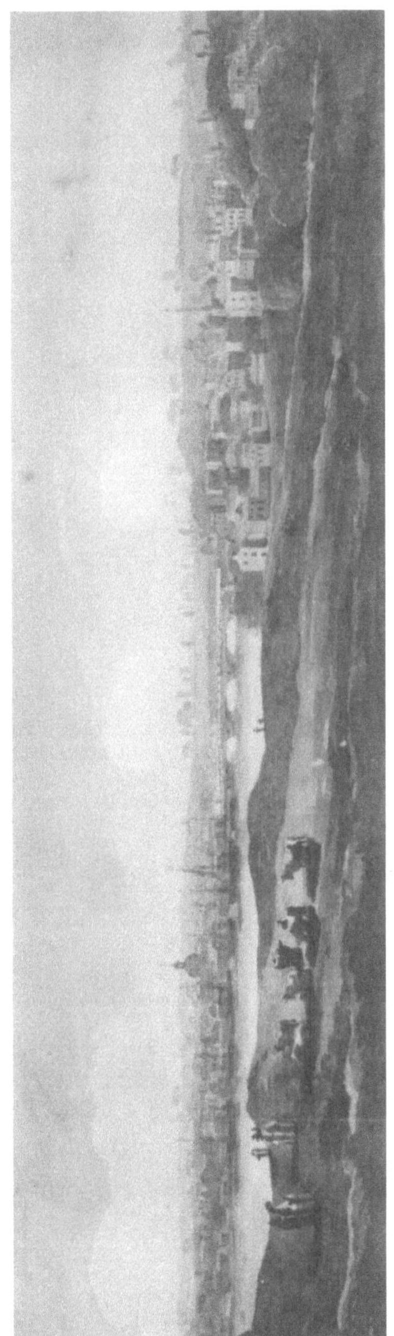

64 / *Providence, Rhode Island*, 1815. Watercolour, 154 × 584 mm. (check-list 181)

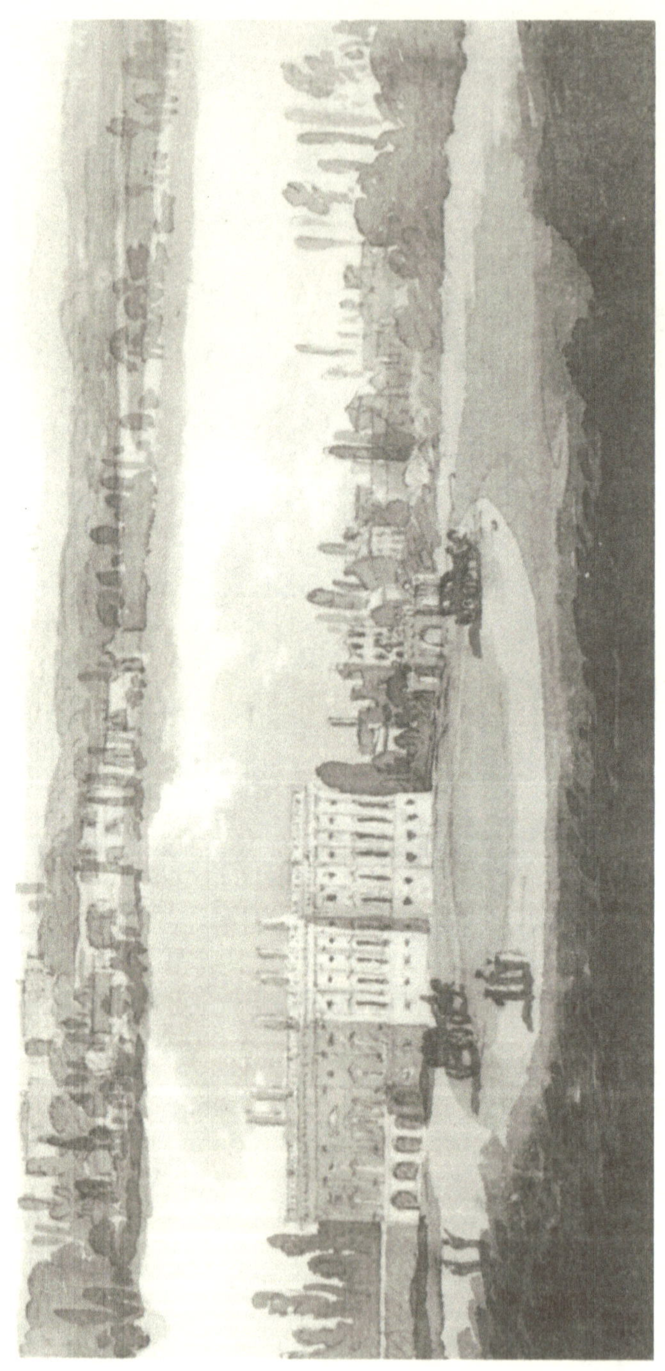

65 / *Palace of the President, Washington*, 1815. Watercolour, 105 × 201 mm. (check-list 335, 231)

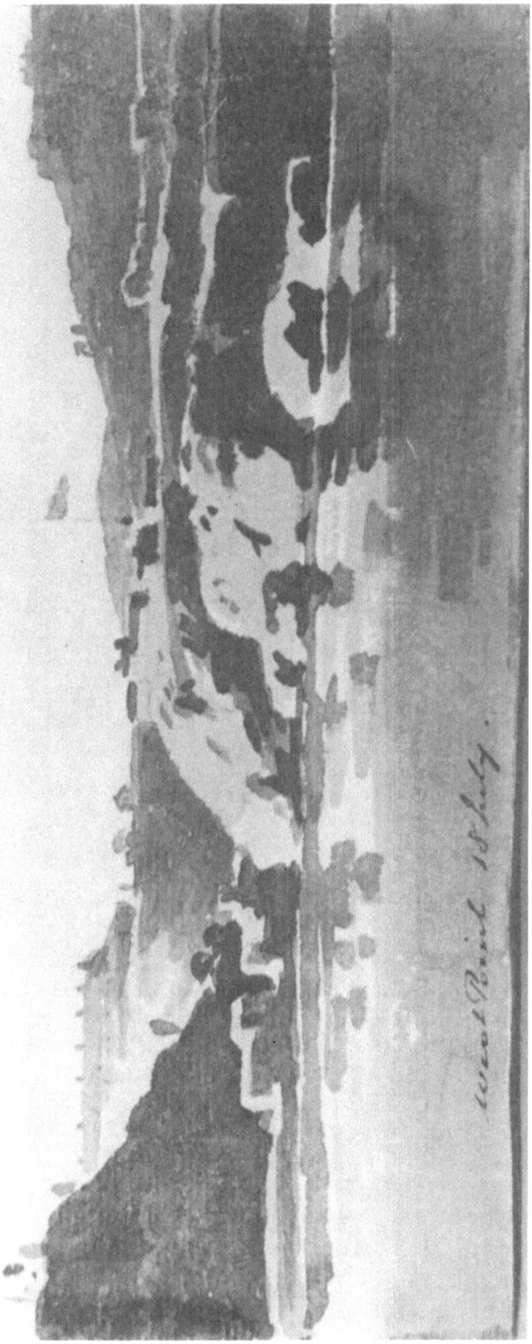

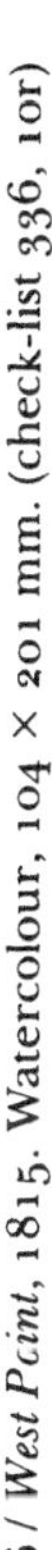

66 / *West Pcint*, 1815. Watercolour, 104 × 201 mm. (check-list 336, 10r)

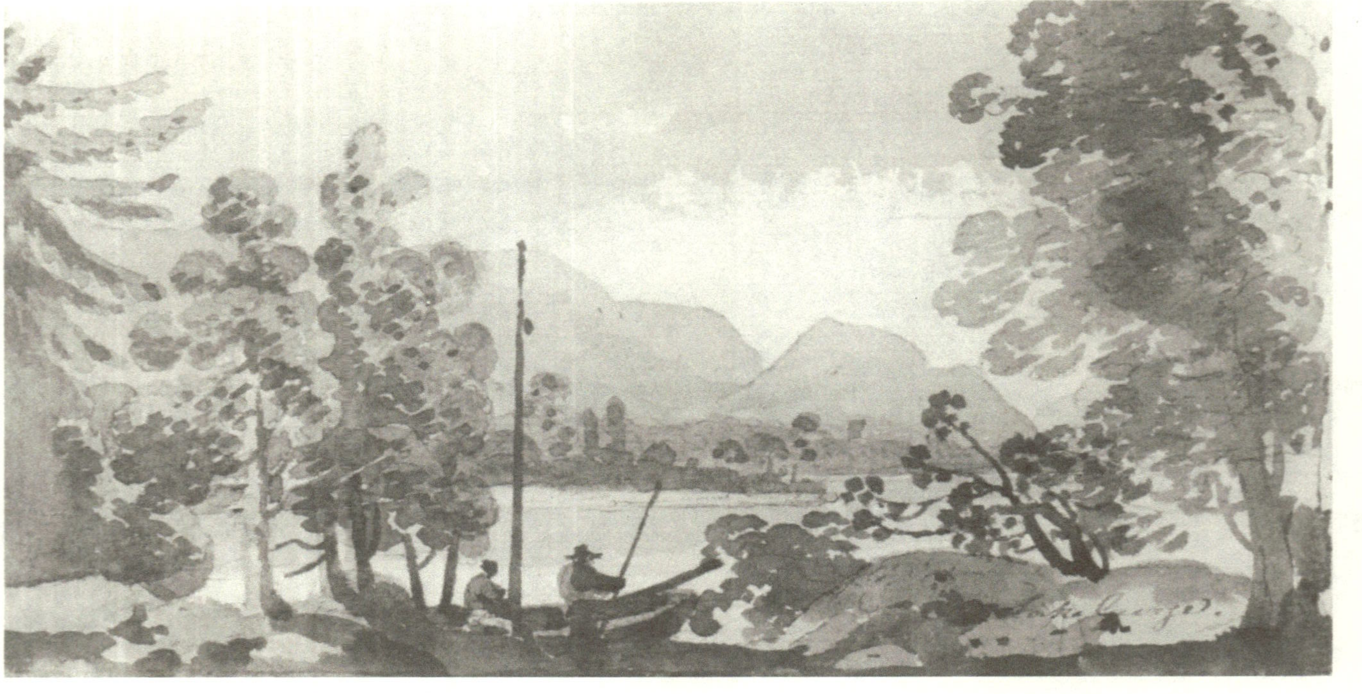

67 / *Lcke George*, 1815. Watercolour, 104 × 201 mm. (check-list 336, 36v)

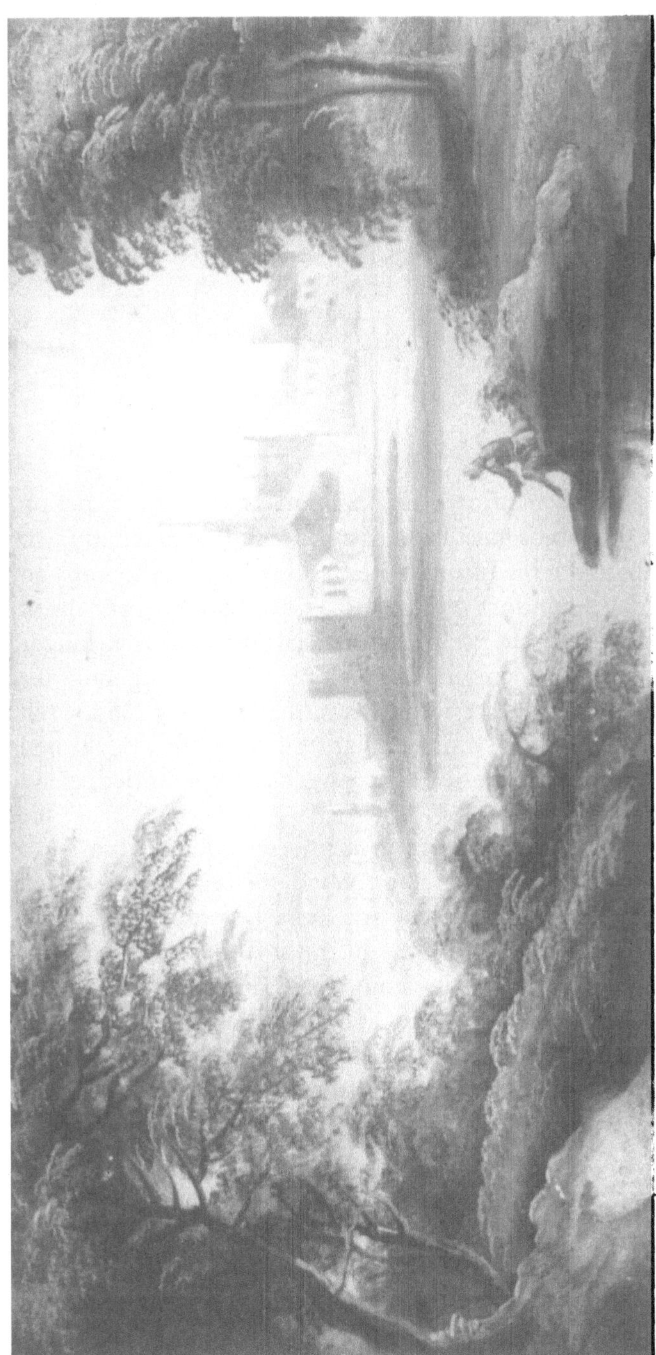

68 / James Norie, *Landscape with a view of Linlithgow*, n.d. Oil on panel, 305 × 610 mm.

9

Last Days in Canada

In view of the possible hazards involved in espionage Heriot's excursion to the United States may not have been easy, but it did give him time to sketch and to contemplate his future. Britain's direction of the war had depressed him and his conduct of the Post Office had for years been criticized and questioned. In addition, his financial position was no longer satisfactory. The cost of living in the colony was soaring and his responsibilities in the Post Office were increasing; by 1815 Heriot felt obliged to ask the Post Office for a rise in salary, but the difficulties he had experienced over the mail deliveries were now common knowledge and his request was refused.[1]

Since March Heriot's stressful situation had been made even harder to bear by the badgering of Sir Gordon Drummond, the recently appointed administrator of Canada, who had been vociferously complaining about the postal service. When he had been administrator in the upper province (1813–15), Drummond had been dissatisfied with Heriot's efforts, and he had resolved to improve the system. But at that time his letters to Heriot went either unheeded or unanswered, and Drummond became infuriated by the deputy postmaster general's apparent disregard of his requests.[2] In his new capacity of administrator of Canada he was now in a stronger position to deal with Heriot, and his opportunity eventually came in October 1815.[3] If Heriot was a strong and determined personality, Drummond was more so, and the administrator also enjoyed the advantages of both a senior political appointment and greater influence. The priorities to which Drummond addressed himself were the removal of Heriot and the improvement of the mails – one, in his opinion, being necessarily contingent on the other.

Towards the end of October Heriot received a letter from Drummond written by his secretary. 'What steps,' Drummond imperiously demanded, had Heriot taken to 'establish the General Post from Montreal to Kingston, from Kingston to York, from York to Niagara and Amherstburg, including intermediate places between these stations?' He also wanted to know 'minutely the period of the departure and arrival of the Post at the several places above mentioned, as also the manner in which it is conveyed, whether in a Carriage, or horseback or by footman.'[4] Drummond threatened that unless Heriot answered these questions and was prepared to establish a regular service without delay, especially between York and Niagara and Amherstburg, he would be forced to lay on 'at vast expense to the Government, a Military Express.' If this proved to be necessary, Drummond believed it would be his duty to report 'without fail' to His Majesty's ministers that the costs were incurred because of Heriot's failure to institute a proper service.[5]

This outburst seems especially to have rankled with Heriot, who, while he kept his temper and coolly and politely replied to Drummond's letter, did not answer his questions:[6] Heriot provided Drummond with only general information about the passage of mails in the upper province, remarking that any increase in the number of deliveries would be 'too exhorbitant ... for the means of the Post Office.'[7] When Drummond received this reply, he was incensed by what he considered to be Heriot's arrogance and evasiveness. Drummond then wrote two important letters – one, immediately, which was addressed to Heriot, informing him in a particularly chilly tone, that his reply 'was by no means of that satisfying nature which ... [I] had it in expectation to receive.'[8] The second letter, written six weeks later, was a fiery missive addressed to the secretary of state in London, in which Drummond bitterly complained of the deputy postmaster general's behaviour; Drummond stated that he was no longer prepared to endure 'the intolerable insolence of ... [this] subordinate officer of Government,' who was totally indifferent to ' the success or good government of the department which it is so much to be lamented has so long been entrusted to his nerveless guidance ... In just consideration to the Public – the Inhabitants of these Provinces, – this indifference alone (manifested I now find, during the administration of my predecessours for a series of time) seems to call for the removal of this gentleman who proves himself every way so unworthy to be employed as a servant of that Public.'[9]

Heriot was forced to defend himself against Drummond's attack and to prepare for the anticipated enquiries from London. Heriot replied to

Drummond that he had made efforts to improve the Upper Canada service in 1812, but, because of the general post office's policy not to initiate routes that would not be self-supporting, and because of the requirement to return all revenues to London, his plan to expend the whole of the 'Revenue produced from the Department in that Province' in order to improve the service had been rejected.[10] If necessary, he informed Drummond, he would return to England to explain the real needs of the upper province to the postmaster general.[11] But Drummond believing that Heriot was shirking his responsibilities, demanded that he should immediately take steps to improve the service between York, Niagara, and Amherstburg. 'With respect to Amherstburg,' he had told Heriot, 'I am commanded to observe that the regular communication with that Post, is of the utmost importance, both on account of the large Naval Establishment forming on Lake Erie, as also from the Military Force now stationed in that part of the Country.'[12] Heriot realized that he had no alternative but to accede to Drummond's demands.[13]

It was probably Drummond's pestering that persuaded Heriot to return to Britain. On 25 October (the day when he received Drummond's letter complaining of the unsatisfactory nature of the information which he had supplied) Heriot, now bruised beyond endurance by these attacks, wrote and delivered for publication in the *Quebec Gazette* a note in which he announced the public sale of his household goods: 'Bedsteads with Curtains, Bedding, Blankets, Window Curtains, two sets of Mahogany Dining Tables, and a Pembroke Table, Chairs, Sopha, Carpets, Looking Glasses, Stoves, Prints, Decanters, China, Books, Plate and Madeira Wine.'[14]

Heriot was determined to return to England to explain the needs of the Canadian postal department to the postmaster general and perhaps to speak of his difficulties with Drummond. Only then would he decide what he should do. If necessary he would resign: he had investments in Britain that would allow him to do so. Although he was now fifty-seven, he remained in excellent health; by resigning he would once more be able to travel, to sketch, and to write. However, by mid-November Heriot had not left Canada,[15] and as he considered it by then too late for an Atlantic crossing, he seems to have taken furnished accommodation in Quebec, planning to remain there until the arrival of spring. During the chilly days of January he decided that the strains caused by his position had become too great to endure, and he made up his mind to resign.[16] Heriot accordingly wrote a letter to the Post Office in London, stating that he would 'no longer be subjected to the indignities & persecutions' that he had undergone, and that 'no motive of interest or advantage' could induce him 'to remain longer in the Service of the Department than until a Successor be appointed.' He would, however, allow the Post Office sufficient time in which to choose his successor, and would therefore remain at his post for another six months.[17] Although Heriot, at his age, was ineligible to receive a pension, he expressed his belief that he was entitled to receive from the Government 'a remuneration for ... [a] long & faithful Service.'[18]

By remaining in his position for this additional period Heriot could further assist the Post Office and simultaneously enjoy some personal benefit: he would have sufficient time both in which to ensure the efficient operation of the recently established extensions of the Upper Canada postal service and, one last time, to travel. Earlier Heriot had inaugurated a weekly postal delivery between Montreal and Niagara; more recently, in response to Drummond's demands, he had extended that service, establishing a fortnightly mail delivery from Dundas to Amherstburg and Sandwich (Windsor). He planned to make a final journey to the upper province in order to assess the success of these services and to carry out any improvements that were deemed necessary. This trip also provided him with a last opportunity to record pictorially the western limits of this land, which he had come to know over the years and whose beauty he had found endlessly satisfying.

In the spring or early summer of 1816, therefore, Heriot undertook what was perhaps one of his most extended western tours, the first lap of which was a jolting ride in the now regular coach from Quebec to Montreal and then to Kingston. At Kingston he boarded a king's ship, which took him to Niagara, from where he travelled by land as far as Sandwich and Amherstburg. It was probably on the land route from Dundas to Amherstburg that Heriot paused to sketch Chief Joseph Brant's Mohawk village on the Ouse (Grand) River. Perhaps it was on his return journey from Sandwich and Amherstburg to Niagara that he stopped to sketch the village of Chippawa – which he had drawn many years before, in 1801. He then continued on to Niagara, where he boarded a ship bound for Kingston. From Kingston he went by coach to Montreal, and from there by stage through to Quebec City.

Heriot's administrative control of the Canadian postal service was relinquished at the end of July, and he prepared to leave. In early August he sailed from Quebec for England; he knew that he had seen Canada for the last time.

The *ad vivum* watercolours which survive from Heriot's 1815 visit to the

United States and from his 1816 trip to Sandwich and Amherstburg are remarkable for their confident, spirited brushwork and for the strength and clarity of their designs. In some respects the watercolours painted on these tours recall the broadly handled views of 1801, drawn during his Canadian classical period. For example, the markedly simplified forms and clearly planned composition of *Chippawas* (1816) (figure 69) are reminiscent of the same characteristics in his view *Whirlpool, Niagara River* (see figure 36) dating from 1801. However, when Heriot chose to draw the village of Chippawa in 1801 (see figure 33), he interpreted the scene in a more self-consciously topographical way then in the later view: that is to say, he adopted a more distant, elevated vantage-point in order to record the village's individual components – its houses, fort, stocks, and bridge. Heriot's 1801 treatment of this scene is essentially 'additive' and does not involve the highly 'synthetic' approach which characterizes the later view, in which the artist carefully subordinates individual landscape elements to the overall composition and thereby achieves an expressiveness lacking in the earlier view. Also, in this later watercolour Heriot more effectively transforms the topographical view into a classical landscape. As we have seen, 'classical' and 'picturesque' are not mutually exclusive terms, and in this late view of Chippawa Heriot's striking silhouettes of landscape forms dramatically focus the viewer's attention on their irregular, picturesque contours.

The decorative quality of the watercolours painted on the 1815 and 1816 trips (especially some of those painted on the 1815 tour, including the views of Lake George) seem to point to a source of influence for Heriot's style previously alluded to (see chapter 2) but never discussed: eighteenth-century Scottish decorative classical landscape painting – especially those works by the Norie family which we may reasonably assume Heriot had seen several times since his youth, in Edinburgh and perhaps elsewhere in Scotland. Thus, while Heriot's watercolours were profoundly affected by the structure of Gilpin's picturesque landscapes (which he came to know through the plates in Gilpin's tour books), by Sandby's landscapes, and by those of other topographical artists influenced by the Picturesque, it seems likely that behind Heriot's classical Canadian style there was also a subconscious reminiscence of the Scottish tradition of decorative landscape painting, to which some of these late Canadian landscapes palpably allude; compare, for example, figures 67 and 68.

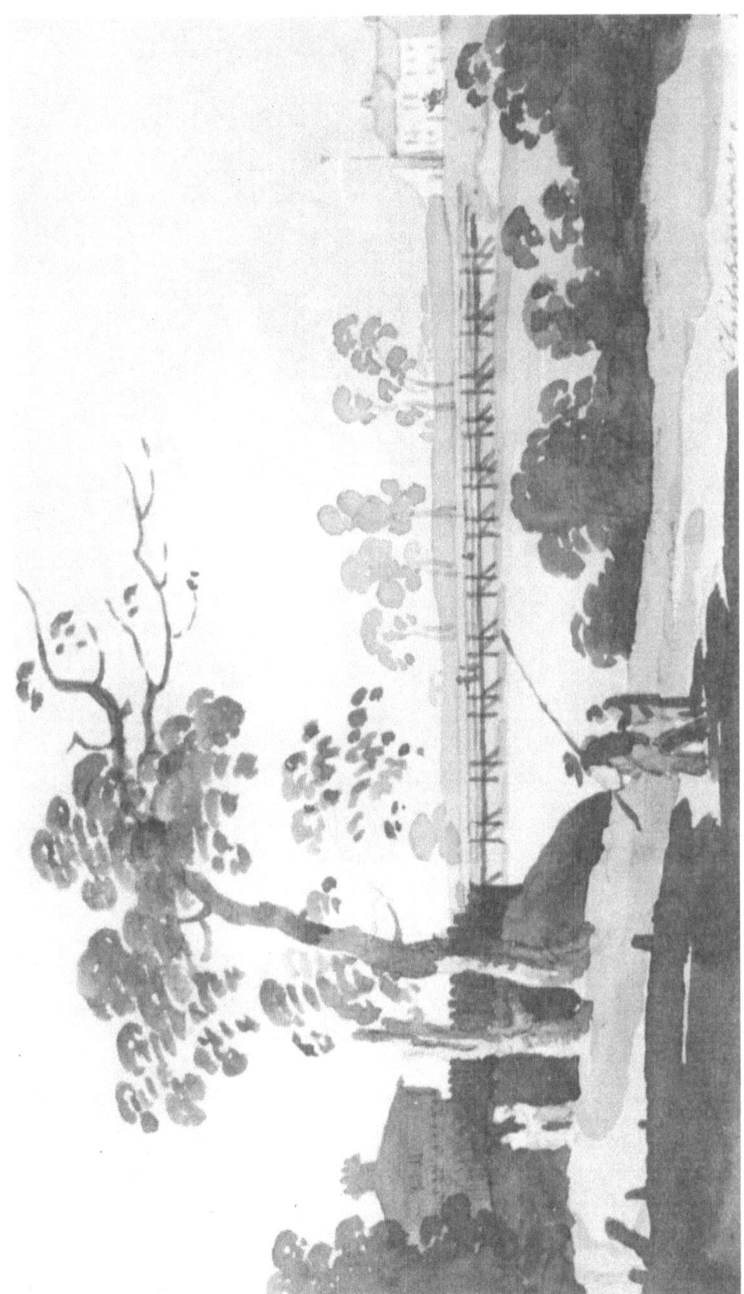

69 / *Chippawa*, c 1816. Watercolour, 113 × 195 mm. (check-list 334, 25r)

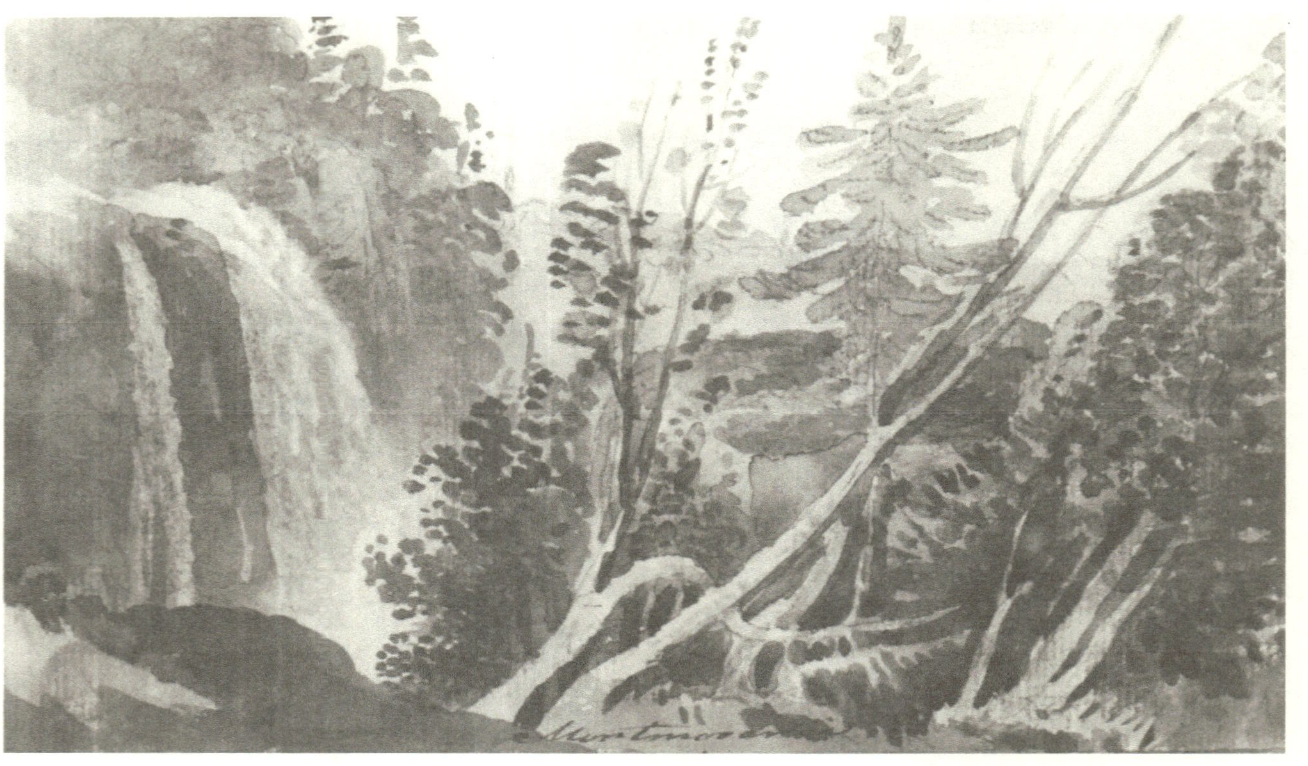

70 / *Fall of Montmorency*, c 1816. Watercolour, 113 × 195 mm. (check-list 334, 63r)

10

Travels in Britain and on the Continent

For Heriot the return to Britain meant retirement only from his Post Office career. He probably remained socially active; he certainly travelled widely in Britain and on the Continent, and almost to the time of his death at the age of eighty he continued to sketch and to paint watercolours. With the exception of the first few years after his return to England Heriot's later life and art are scantily documented. Any reconstruction of this part of his career must therefore be only tentative, and the dating of many of the later works is necessarily provisional. While many dated works survive from the years 1816–20, few are extant for the subsequent period of his life.

We know that, after arriving in England, Heriot settled in London – since his brother John and his sister Sophia lived there, it was natural that he should choose to make his home in the capital. It was not long before he found himself a house, perhaps in Chelsea (he was residing in that district of London in 1822), in which he lived on the investment income derived from the family estate.[1] In the heady days of the Regency London was a centre of fashion and a place of lavish entertainment. Cultural life also flourished: London boasted frequent exhibitions and concerts and many performances both in the opera house and in the theatre. Heriot must certainly have availed himself of at least some of these diversions. He also soon resumed, on a full-time basis, his travelling, sketching, painting, and writing.

Many sketches survive from the year in which Heriot returned to Britain, including a number of views in Kent. Heriot travelled to Woolwich, where many years before he had studied and sketched the countryside in the moments which he could spare from his duties as cadet and clerk. On this return visit he re-examined many of the haunts which he had depicted in those early days. Plumstead, and the landscape in and near Woolwich, attracted his brush once more. The Fox and Hounds Ale House near Woolwich he now redrew from the viewpoint which he had adopted when he was sketching it in 1788 (figures 71, 72). The stylistic changes that had occurred in the interim are significant. The linear skeleton and the pale, harmonious colour washes of the earlier drawing have gone. Now fluid but muscular brushwork, strong chiaroscuro, and saturated pigment provide the necessary landscape structure. This fundamental transformation must be seen as the consequence of Heriot's sojourn in Canada.

It was probably soon after his trip to Kent that Heriot toured Scotland, presumably to visit relatives and friends. Still fresh from his Canadian experience, he sketched the Clyde, its falls near Lanark (figure 73), and, near Ladykirk, Twizel Castle and its bridge on the Till (figure 74). These drawings made on the spot display the liquid washes and strong design so characteristic of Heriot's later years at Quebec, though the forms tend to be more plump and less differentiated in structure.

By visiting Kent Heriot probably wished to revive memories of his early life at Woolwich. It was perhaps for the same reason that he began to copy a number of compositions which were the fruits of his visit to the Channel Islands in about 1786 or 1787 and which he had etched and coloured for sale in 1789 and 1790. Since, however, neither the original sketches nor any finished drawings which may have been made from them have come to light, it is impossible to determine if these copies of 1816 were made from sketches and drawings or from the prints. In any event these copies, like the views which Heriot had recently painted in Kent, express the more dramatic, vital manner associated with Heriot's Canadian years. When one compares the early coloured, etched view *Temple of the Druids* (see figure 13) with the much later watercolour of the same design (figure 76), one is immediately struck by the confidence, the freshness of brushwork, and the strength of chiaroscuro that articulates the latter. Furthermore, all the elements of the composition in the later work have been simplified, and the focus of interest has become more determinate. Indeed, this later watercolour cannot really be called a 'copy': it is rather a revision of the original pictorial idea in which the landscape is presented in a new, aesthetically enhanced light.

This simplification of style, characteristic of some of the immediately post-Canadian views, does not prepare us for the complexity and decorative enrichment which we find in the work of Heriot's next phase. Though some of the late Canadian watercolours provide indications of this trend, it was not until Heriot made his first continental tour in 1817–18 that this stylistic enrichment became his firmly established mode of representation – a mode that may characterize most of his watercolours until at least the late 1820s.

Heriot began his European tour in the spring of 1817. The Napoleonic Wars were over; by this time Europe's physical and emotional wounds seemed to have healed, and travellers from Britain could once more be found patronizing its coffee-houses and inns. Heriot had decided to take the Grand Tour – an experience which, as a result of his family's financial difficulties, he had been deprived of during his youth. One of his main objectives was Italy, for he had long wanted to see its classical art and architecture, to examine its famous paintings, and to enjoy the beauties of its ancient cities, mountains, and shorelines.

Leaving London in February, Heriot crossed the Channel to France and travelled by coach directly to Paris. From there he travelled south to Lyons, where he arrived towards the end of March. The heady excitement of his first continental tour refined his sensitivity to the places that he visited and enhanced his appreciation of the varied countryside which he saw. His finished watercolours of French subjects, composed from on-the-spot sketches, reveal his enthusiasm for the landscape and splendidly inaugurate his new manner (figure 77). The forms of the trees become more attenuated, and the dappled strokes which in his Canadian views suggest foliage structure no longer serve primarily as a space-defining, form-creating element: dappling becomes more uniform, giving the foliage a speckled or spotted appearance, so that these strokes now function more decoratively and no longer fulfil the essentially descriptive purpose that they served before.

How long Heriot remained at Lyons cannot be determined, but he was still there in April. From Lyons he may have gone to Nîmes and then taken the traditional route to Italy over Mont Cenis to Turin, whence he travelled southward to Rome. He was probably in Rome at least as early as June, for there are watercolours of Tivoli dating from this month. Like the French watercolours, these are finished, and reflect the same textural enrichment that the views of Lyons display.

Only one sketch-book which relates to the Italian part of Heriot's tour has come to light. It indicates that he was making drawings south of

Rome: for example, he was sketching at Salerno on 22 July. From there he seems to have continued south to Sicily. The sketch-book documents a return route through Florence and Pisa, where he was in November. Subsequently he travelled up the coast to Genoa, where he sketched the city after Christmas. By early January 1818 Heriot was at Verona; by February he was sketching in Venice. From here he continued north to the Austrian border. He stayed in Salzburg (which is well represented in his watercolours) during May 1818, but his main destination seems to have been Vienna, where he lived for a short while in June and possibly early July.

No sketch-books covering Heriot's sojourn in Austria are extant, though individual sketches and finished watercolours have survived. Heriot's Austrian watercolours are numerous and stylistically unusual – even ambivalent, since they reveal two distinct manners that Heriot seems to have practised almost simultaneously. One style is found in small restrained compositions (many of them views of Salzburg), compact in design and finished in appearance, which foreshadow the drawings which Heriot was to prepare for his *A Picturesque Tour made in the years 1817 and 1820 through the Pyrenean Mountains, Auvergne, The Department of the High and Low Alps and in Part of Spain*, published six years later. The other style, which he subsequently seems to have discarded, is a loose, highly linear manner which he adopted in large sketches. Here, landscape forms are outlined and shaded in sketchy pen-strokes, under which a monochrome wash has usually been laid. Since one of the sketches in this style, a view in the district of Salzburg (figure 79), is compositionally almost identical with one of the smaller, more compact Salzburg landscapes (figure 80), it seems likely that the larger, sketchier drawings provided the inspiration for the smaller ones, or (though this seems less probable) that both types of drawings were developed independently of each other from the same on-the-spot sketches.

Heriot travelled from Vienna to Hungary during July 1818 and then returned, perhaps through Germany, to England. He was in London by 1 August. Though we have no information about the artist's movements during the remainder of 1818, we do have quite a good picture of his activities during the following year, when he made another Scottish tour. In June 1819 he visited Holy Island, on the east coast below Berwick, where he made studies of the ruins of Lindisfarne Priory. By 24 July he was at Dalkeith and by the end of the month he was making sketches of Stirling Castle. Some time in early August he was at least as far north as

Elgin Cathedral, which he sketched; but he did not remain there long, since he was in the vicinity of Edinburgh by the middle of the month, when he made sketches of Roslin Castle (figure 81). We next hear of him visiting Matlock in Derbyshire on 29 September while he was on his way back to London. Little is known of his activities during the last three months of this year.

On his 1818 tour Heriot had made studies such as the smaller views of Salzburg which he hoped to develop as illustrations for a proposed picturesque topographical guide, but he later laid them aside, possibly because he felt that enough such tour guides on this part of Europe had already been published. It may also have been this reason that persuaded him that France and Spain might offer more fruitful material for a new book on picturesque scenery. He therefore decided to publish a series of views consisting of 'scenery in the Pyrenean Mountains, in the low and high Alps, and in Auvergne, as well as ... views of several of the ancient Roman monuments in different parts of France.'[2] With this object in mind he undertook a second continental tour in the spring of 1820.

He crossed the Channel to Le Havre, and from there travelled by coach to Rouen, arriving in early April. After taking views of the city and the cathedral, Heriot journeyed to Caen to see a great fair, 'where numerous assemblage of peasantry from various parts of the country were seen in different costumes.'[3] By 22 April the artist was at Le Mans, where he took views of the city and its monumental cathedral. He did not linger long there, but continued his travel south, often in the slower diligence (public stage-coach) and sometimes by cabriolet, 'in order to have a better view of the country.'[4] He briefly visited Poitiers, where he made a number of concise studies, and then he journeyed south to the cathedral town of Angoulême, which he was sketching at least as early as 28 April. From there he continued to Bordeaux, which he reached in early May and where he took views of the castle and the town.

While staying at Bordeaux Heriot made a point of introducing himself to one of the town's most celebrated artists (whom he does not identify). Fortunately he described this visit in an account which reveals a facet of his personality which is not normally evident in his published writings: his sense of humour. Of the local artist Heriot notes that his landscapes have 'considerable merit,' though his history paintings Heriot regards as outright failures. He mentions being shown one of these histories: 'He had painted from the figure of his wife, a Venus retiring from the Bath, which I took the liberty to criticise; the good-natured artist listened to my remarks with great complacency, and candidly acknowledged their justness.' But the artist's wife was less pleased with the visitor's comments: 'She thought they conveyed either a reflection on the symmetry of her own form, or an impeachment of her husband's skill, and having thus got into a dilemma, I had not the good fortune to gain her entire approbation; *parceque elle aimoit beaucoup la gloire de son mari*.'[5]

From Bordeaux Heriot continued southward to Aire-sur-l'Adour, where he sketched the town on 23 May. He then crossed the Pyrenees, which provided him with an endless number of fascinating compositions, and entered Spain, first visiting several towns near the border and then proceeding to Burgos, which he reached in June. From there he may have gone south to Madrid.[6] He seems to have crossed the Pyrenees again, returning to England, perhaps through France.

The 1820 watercolours have a stylistic affinity with some painted during or after the continental tour of 1817–18. No doubt Heriot was aiming at a homogeneous style for the illustrations that were to embellish his projected picturesque tour book; yet, even after allowance has been made for this, there is an increased compositional and formal tautness. Trees and especially individual foliage forms now begin to mimic the growing regimentation of 'clumping' of the figures. The spottiness of the foliage now seems more ordered; and taut, leafy columns or beaded arcs describe respectively the straight or pendant branches of trees. Heriot's interpretation of nature is now more abstract – yet these landscapes, such as *Burgos Cathedral, Spain* (figure 82), describe a conspicuous, new, formal elegance that seems to provide a sufficiently natural leafy context in which to display the proud, ancient monuments of European civilization.

Documentary evidence for Heriot's life during the 1820s is tantalizingly meagre. There are fewer documents and dated watercolours to inform us either of his activities or of his evolution as an artist. It is therefore impossible to establish an adequate critical context within which to assess the few works that survive from these years. The problem is compounded by the copies of earlier watercolours which he began to make in increasing numbers at this time.

For example, around 1820 Heriot seems to have painted two watercolours of West Indian subjects (whose present whereabouts, unfortunately, are not known): *Grenada, Harbour of St George* (see figure 3) and *Negro Dance, West Indies* (check-list 268). Their styles (especially that of *Grenada, Harbour of St George*) are unusual, and, were it not for our knowledge of Heriot's life and artistic development, their dating would be difficult to determine. However, as we know that Heriot was in the West Indies only during the years 1777–81, we may reasonably assume that both watercolours were based on on-the-spot sketches which he made while there. When painting these works Heriot unconsciously absorbed certain stylistic traits of the original studies and blended them with his post-Canadian manner of about forty years later.

A similar conflation of the styles of two distinctive periods occurs in another pair of contemporary views: this time scenes in Canada. The tree foliage of *Quebec* (figure 83) and *Halifax, Nova Scotia* (figure 84) is datable on stylistic grounds to around 1820. It is built up from a semi-transparent wash, over which fine dots of a darker tone have been applied and seem to float. But if these two watercolours reveal similarities on this level of investigation, on another level they do not. For compositionally they differ considerably. On the one hand, the landscape forms of *Halifax, Nova Scotia* are curvilinear, reflecting the artist's stylistic interests but undoubtedly reflecting, too, the undulations of the topography itself. In *Quebec*, on the other hand, there is a greater angularity and a stress on the horizontal lines of the landscape. Further, the ambience of *Halifax, Nova Scotia* is mainly built up from large simple areas of light and shade, while in *Quebec* space is defined largely by line. Finally, the disposition of figures differs in these watercolours. In *Halifax, Nova Scotia* the figures are set in an immobile sculptural clump, while in *Quebec* they are more active and dispersed throughout the landscape.

The disposition of the landscape and figures differs to such an extent that it would seem that Heriot was copying Canadian views dating from different periods in his career. For example, the linear quality and the scattering of compositional elements in *Quebec* suggest that it might have been copied from a watercolour of the period immediately before 1800. And as we know that Heriot was probably at Halifax only once (in 1807), presumably the original watercolour for *Halifax, Nova Scotia* dates from this time or later. Because of the nature of his treatment of the figures and their arrangement in the copy a suggested date of about 1812 for the original might not be unreasonable. This dating is supported by a comparison between the handling of the figures and their arrangement in this work with the clump of figures in his *Distillery at Beauport, Quebec*, 1812 (see figure 62): the similarity is striking.

The problem of dating copies is a difficult one because of the mixtures of an artist's current and earlier styles which, as we have seen, they necessarily display. In Heriot's case there is no better example of this than

Greenwich from the point (figure 85), which may also date from about 1820. The foliage seems to be of this period, but the handling of the architecture seems to be that of Heriot's earliest topographical style – as indeed it is, for the work is based on a watercolour previously mentioned, *View of the Town of Greenwich* (figure 6), dating perhaps from 1785. In the later copy, then, Heriot has combined his early linear manner with elements from the later, decidedly painterly style which he developed during his Canadian visit, and there are also elements of the decorative phase characteristic of his watercolours of the 1820 period.

But not all Heriot's later watercolours are copies. A solitary drawing, dating from 1821, informs us that he visited and sketched Kenilworth Castle in that year and that the potency of his picturesque viewpoint had not abated. At the same time he must have been writing the text for his *A Picturesque Tour ... through the Pyrenean Mountains.*[7] In 1822 the writing of the *Tour* still occupied him, and doubtless so did the preparation of its illustrations. There is, however, a letter surviving from this year which indicates that the guide could not have been absorbing all of his thoughts and energies. During 1822 he wrote a letter to one of his erstwhile colleagues in Canada, William Hands, the former postmaster at Sandwich, who was later at Amherstburg.[8] In his letter Heriot asks for information about some land near Detroit on behalf of relatives at Charleston who had inherited property there. If it does nothing more, this letter tells us that Heriot was keeping up correspondence with his American relatives and was living in Chelsea, close to his brother John, then comptroller of the Chelsea Hospital.

In 1823 Heriot visited Wales again, and from sketches made on this tour, which lasted at least three months (since he was there during June, July, and August), he developed several compositions in which the now characteristic clumping of figures occurs. Although we know that in 1824 Heriot was living in Dover Street, London, we have little information about either his life or his art for the remainder of the decade. It is certain that he made at least one more continental trip – a precisely dated view of Poitiers, 1828 (check-list 296), has been found – but too few watercolours of this period have come to light to enable us to say more than that Heriot's style appears to have changed little between the early and the later 1820s.

It was perhaps inevitable that, after his return to Britain from Canada, Heriot could not maintain the intensity of expression seen in the Canadian watercolours. The period of excitement and discovery generated by this new country was over, but it had lasted long enough to place Heriot among the most eminent of the topographical artists who worked in Canada during the colonial period. The abatement of his enthusiasm (though not the loss of it) was accompanied in his watercolours by more static, more highly controlled forms. However, he continued to see landscape from a picturesque viewpoint. If his later watercolours are lacking in the spirituality and excitement that the Canadian views express, they nevertheless have the positive qualities of a restrained elegance and a decorative refinement. Heriot's cultivation of these particular qualities in the later watercolours serves once more to suggest his (probably subconscious) allegiance to the ornamental style of the Scottish decorative landscape tradition.

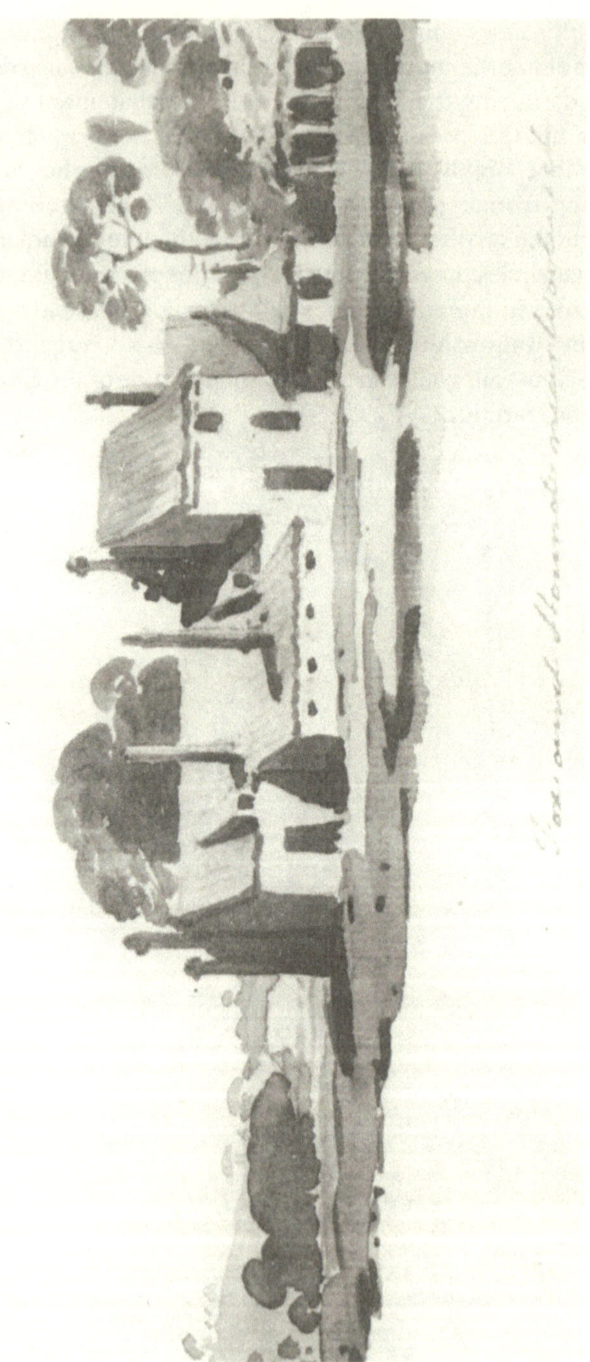

71 / *Fox and Hounds near Woolwich*, c 1816. Watercolour, 113 × 195 mm. (check-list 334, 19v)

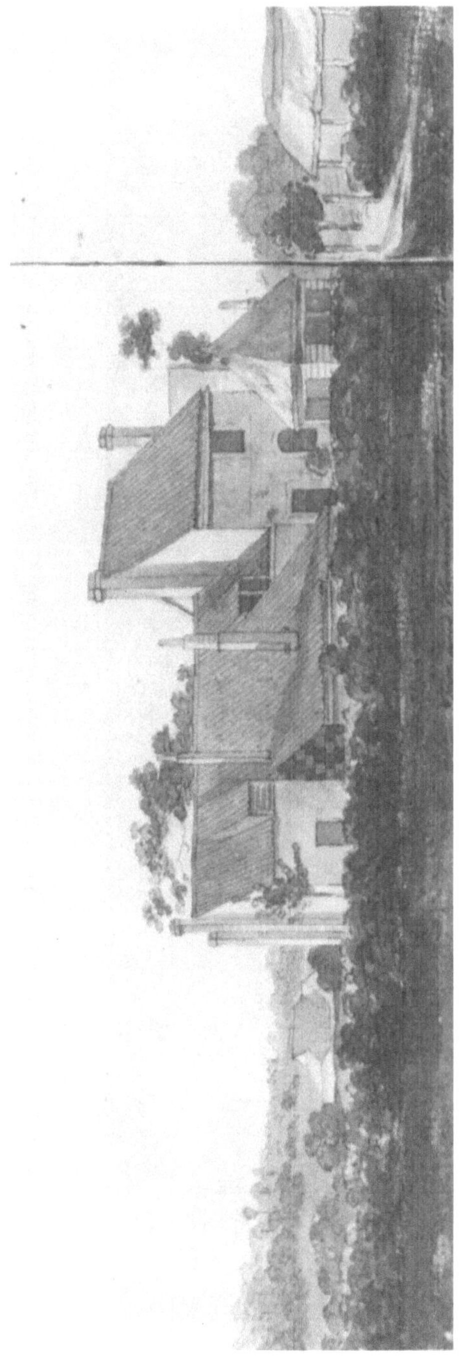

72 / *Fox and Hounds Ale House, Woolwich* (detail), 1788. Watercolour, pen, and ink, 114 × 510 mm. (check-list 333, 30v–31r)

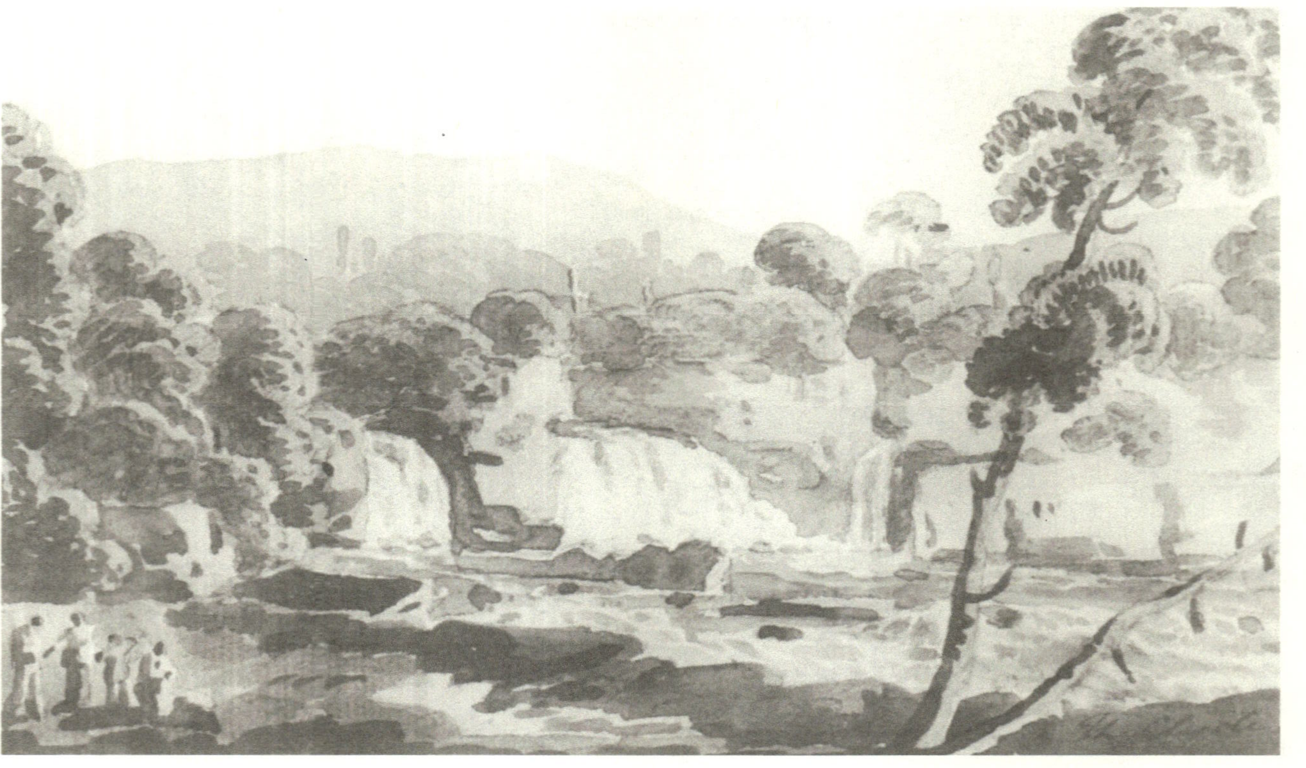

73 / *Falls on the Clyde*, c 1816. Watercolour, 114 × 188 mm. (check-list 192)

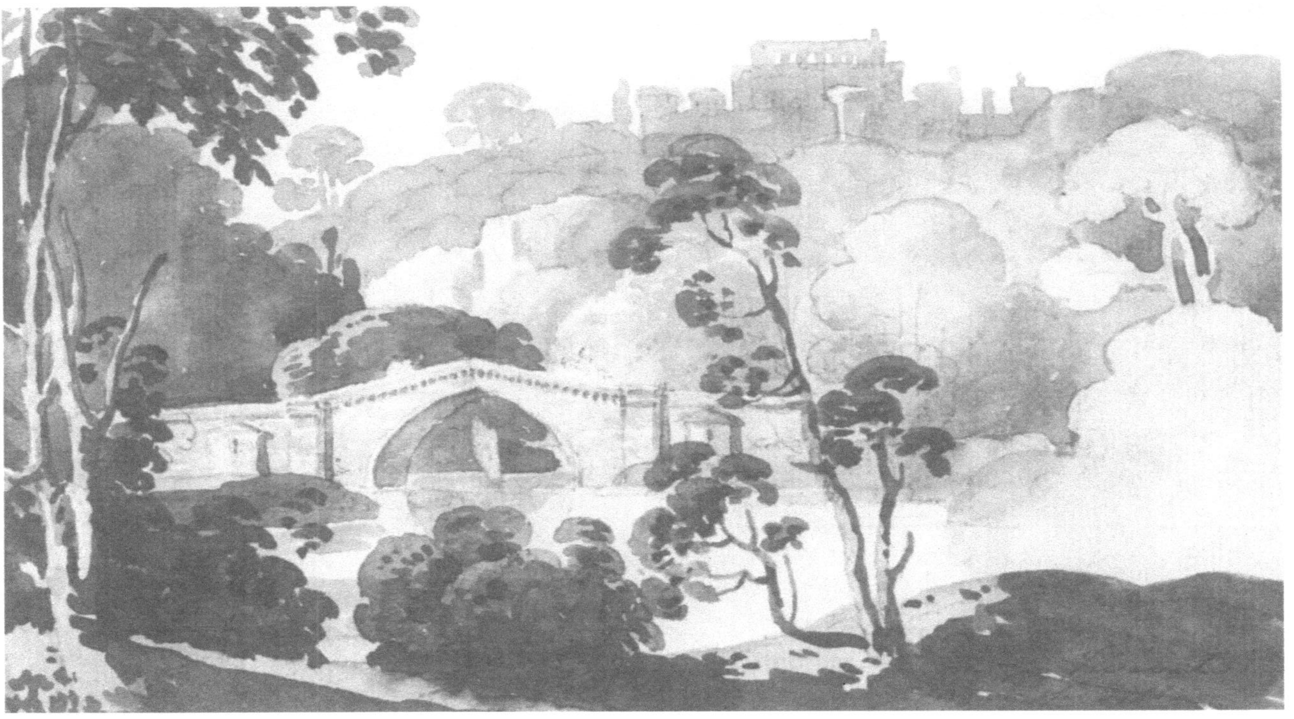

74 / *Twizel Castle and Bridge on the Till*, c 1816. Watercolour, 113 × 195 mm. (check-list 334, 56r)

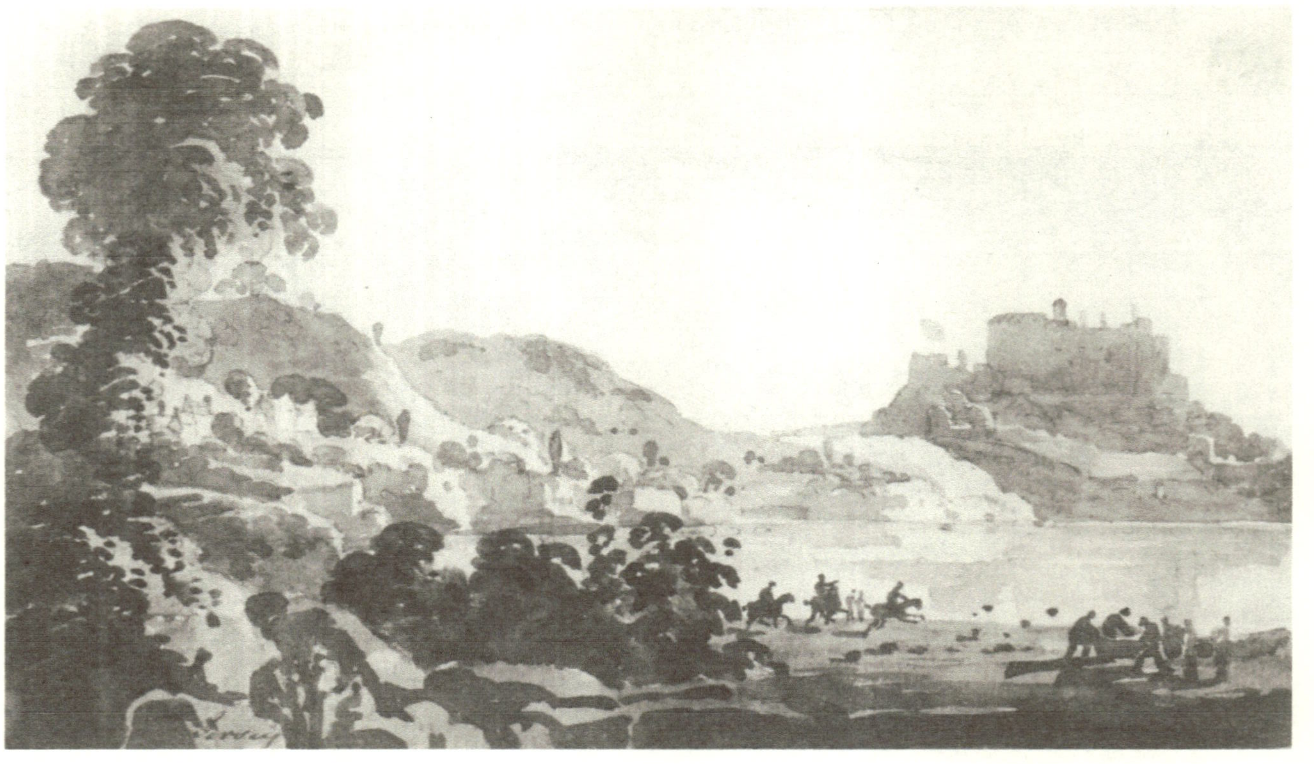

75 / *Mont Orgueil Castle from the sea side near Gouray*, c 1816. Watercolour, 113 × 195 mm. (check-list 334, 60r)

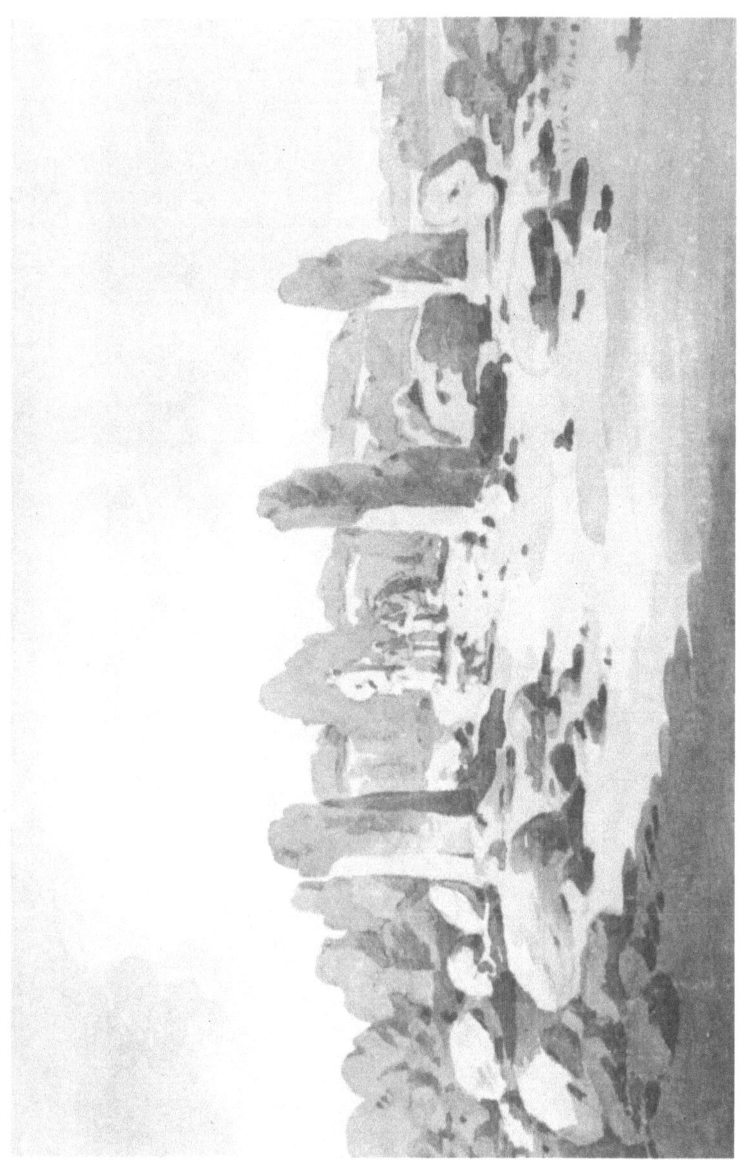

76 / *Druids' Temple, Jersey*, c 1816. Watercolour, 154 × 241 mm. (check-list 196)

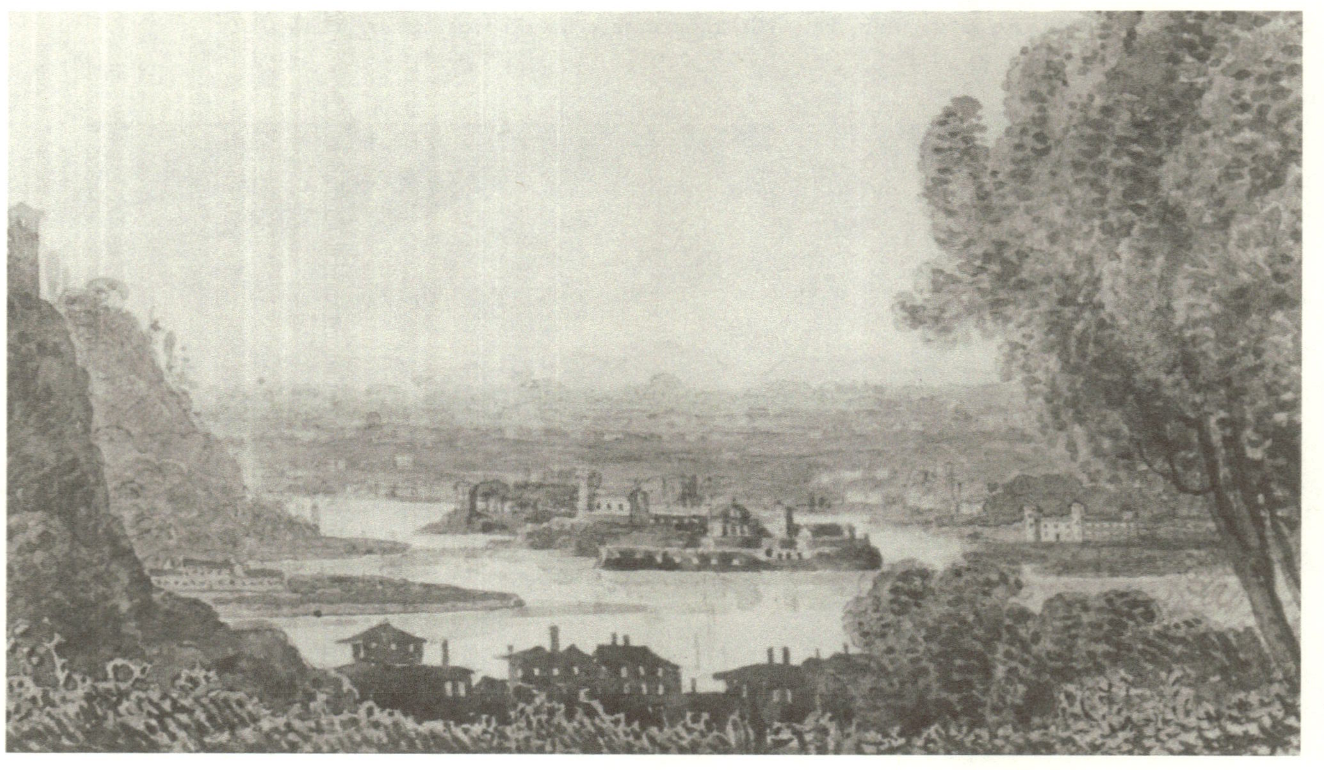

77 / *Isle Barbe near Lyon*, 1817. Watercolour, 102 × 165 mm. (check-list 200)

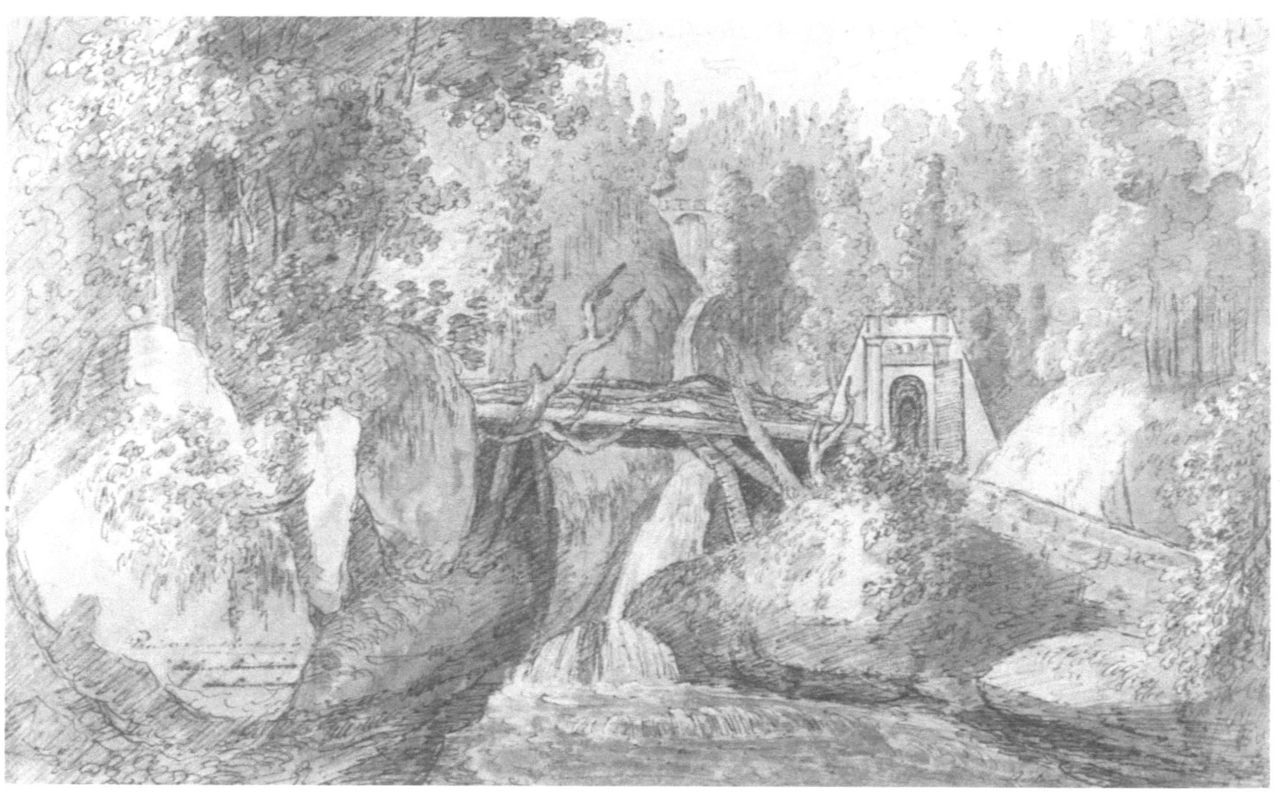

78 / *Prince Schwarzenberg's Egyptian Cemetery*, c 1818. Pen and grey wash, 289 × 464 mm. (check-list 225)

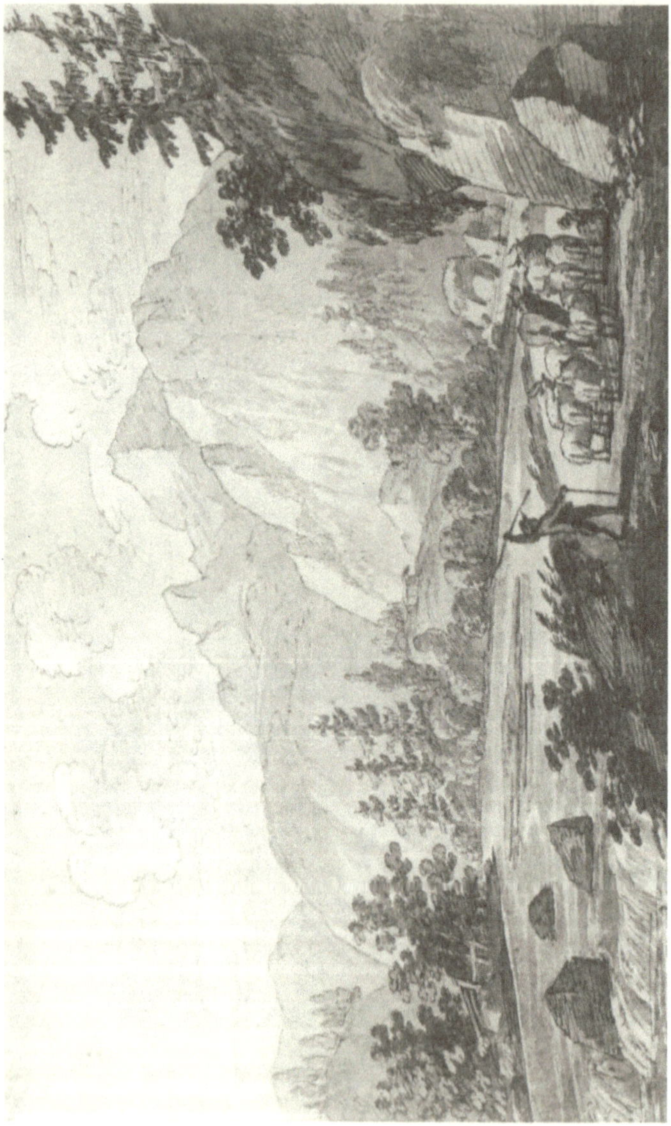

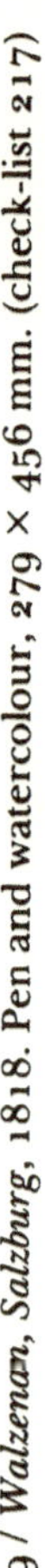

79 / *Walzenan, Salzburg*, 1818. Pen and watercolour, 279 × 456 mm. (check-list 217)

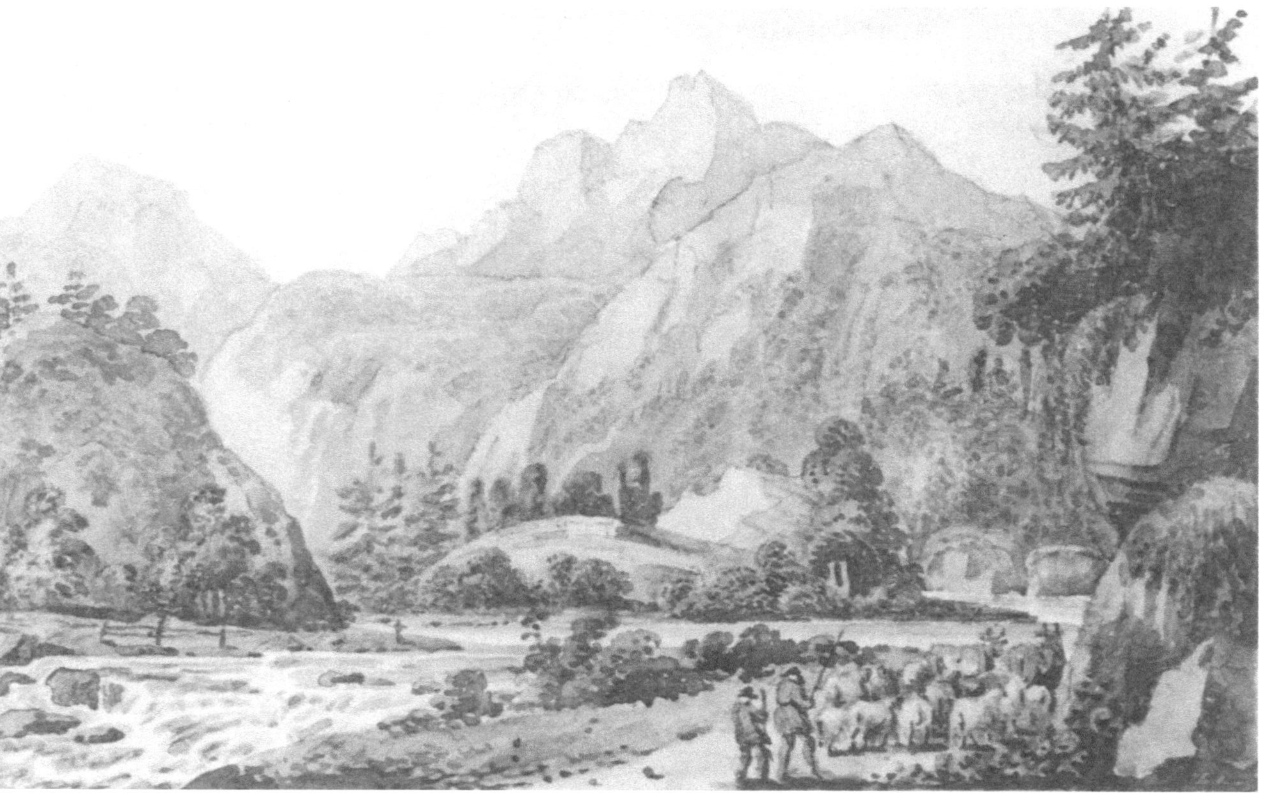

80 / *Salzburg*, 1818. Watercolour, 112 × 175 mm. (check-list 218)

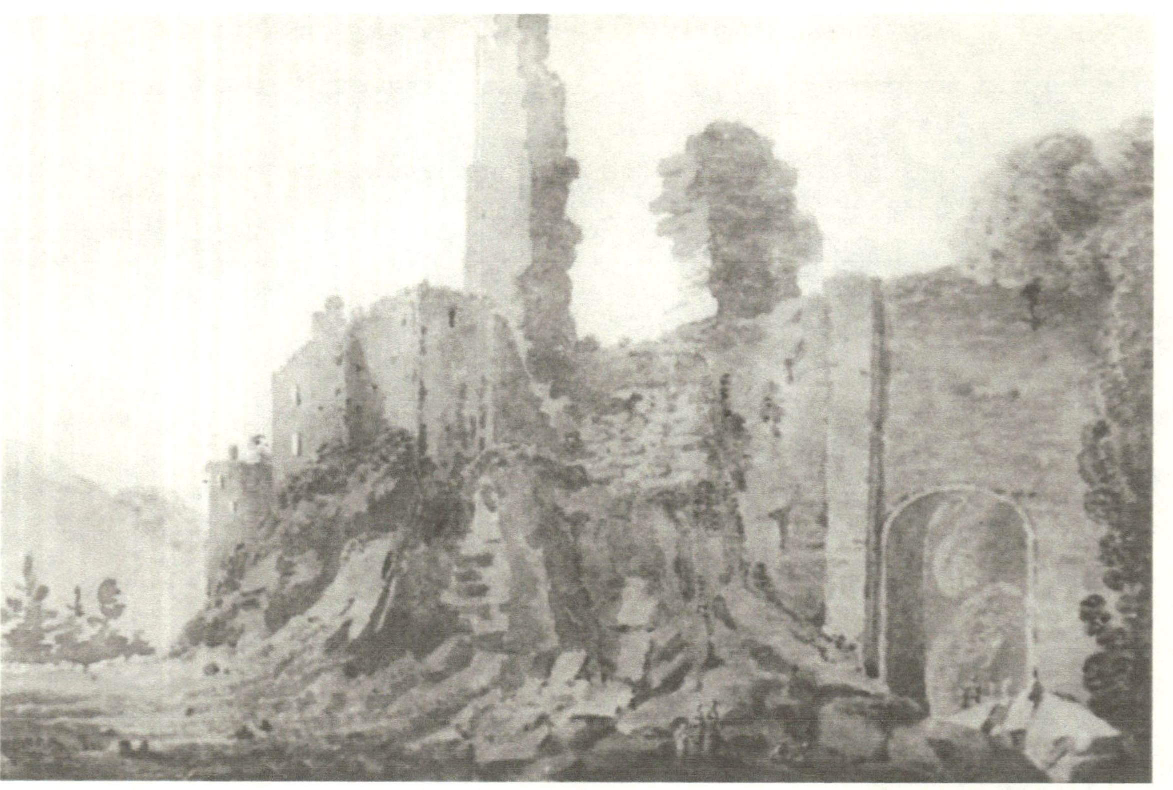

81 / *Roslin Castle, near Edinburgh*, 1819. Watercolour, 182 × 267 mm. (check-list 238)

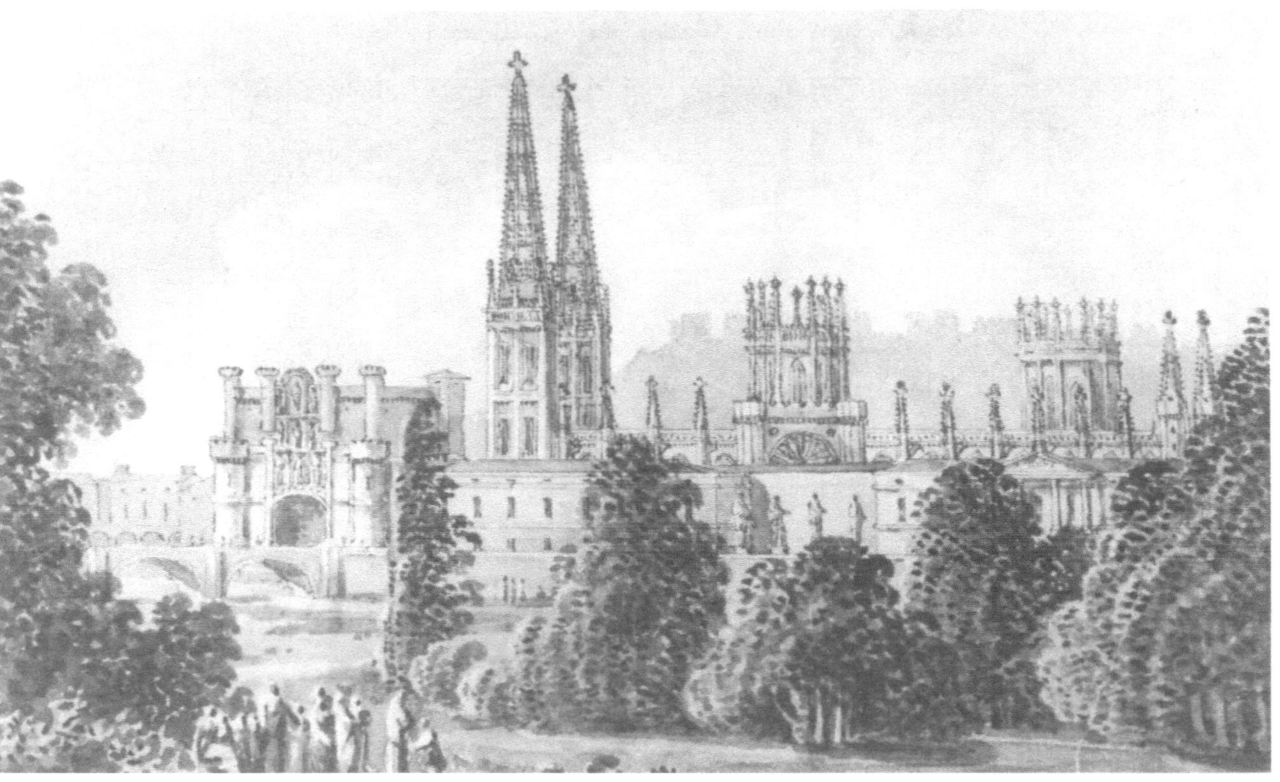

82 / *Burgos Cathedral, Spain*, 1820. Pen and sepia wash, 111 × 171 mm. (check-list 262)

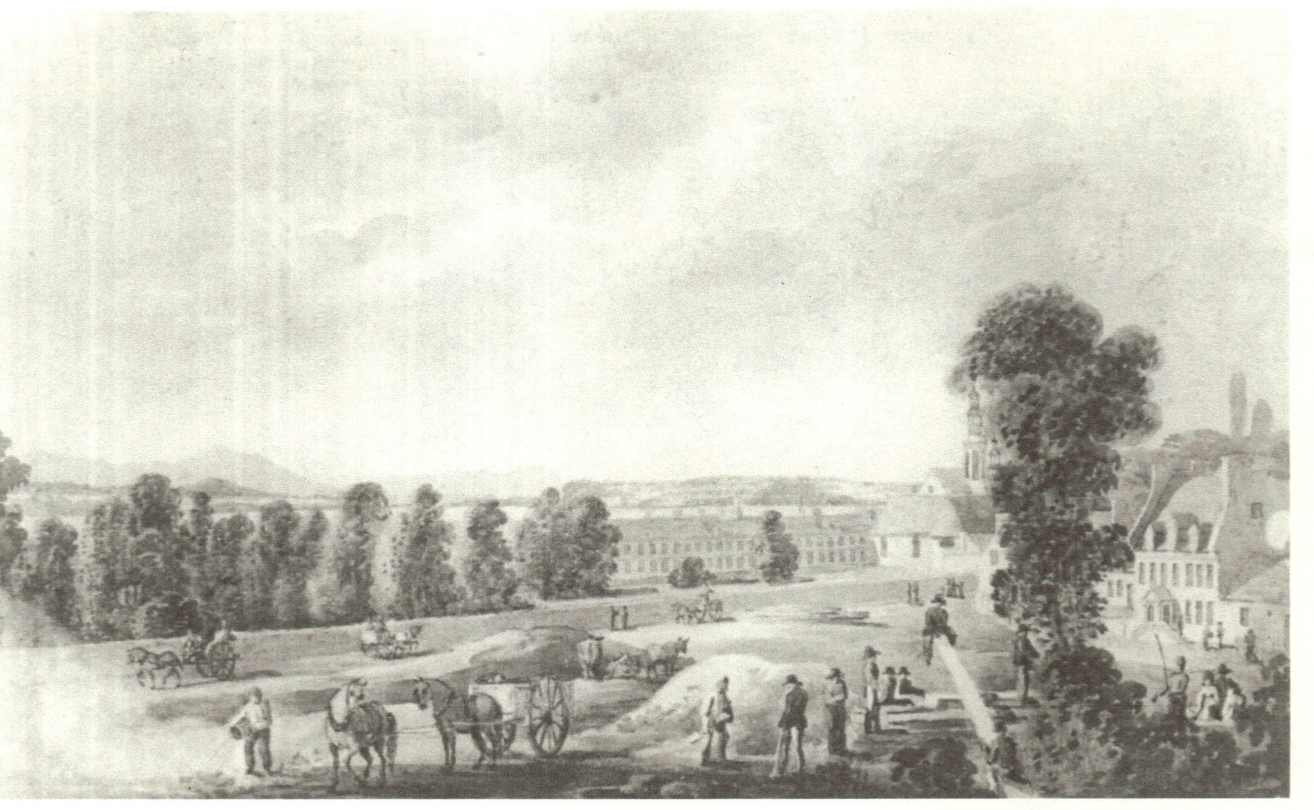

83 / *Quebec*, c 1820. Watercolour, 203 × 318 mm. (check-list 271)

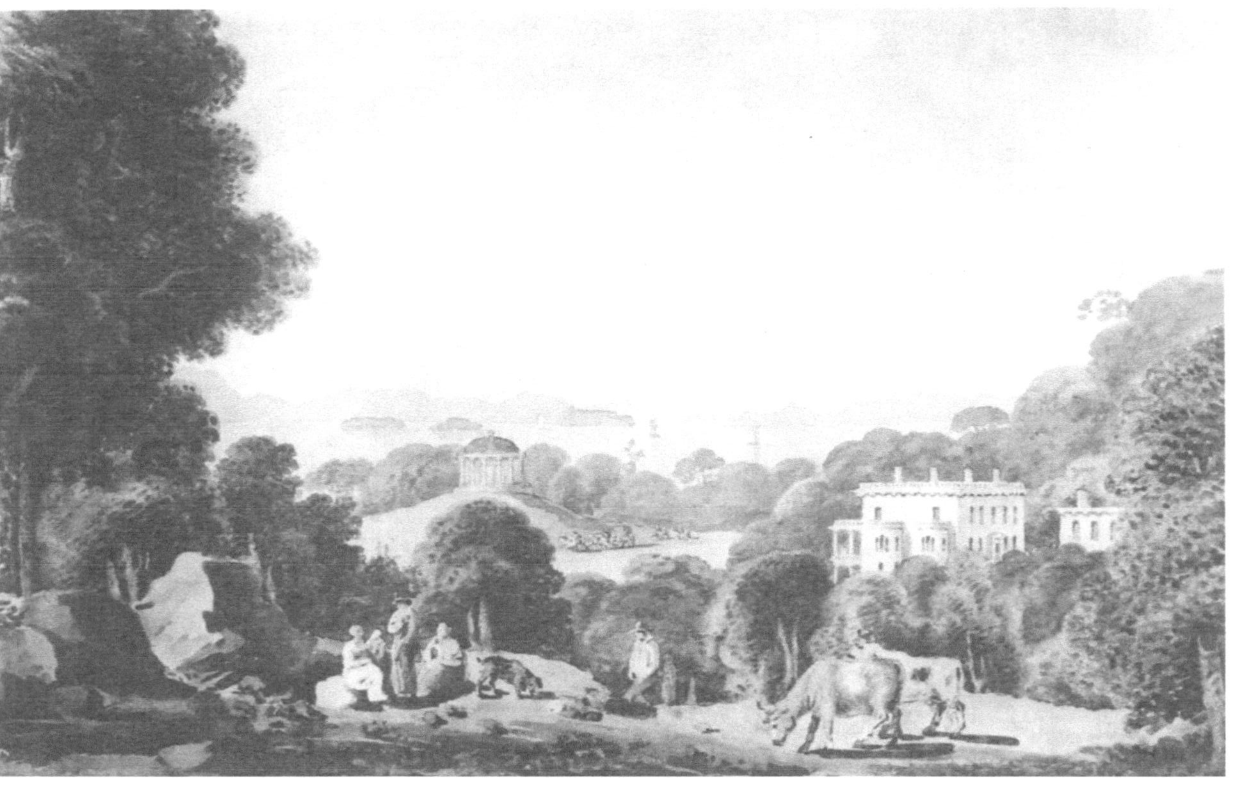

84 / *Halifax, Nova Scotia*, c 1820. Watercolour, 254 × 381 mm. (check-list 270)

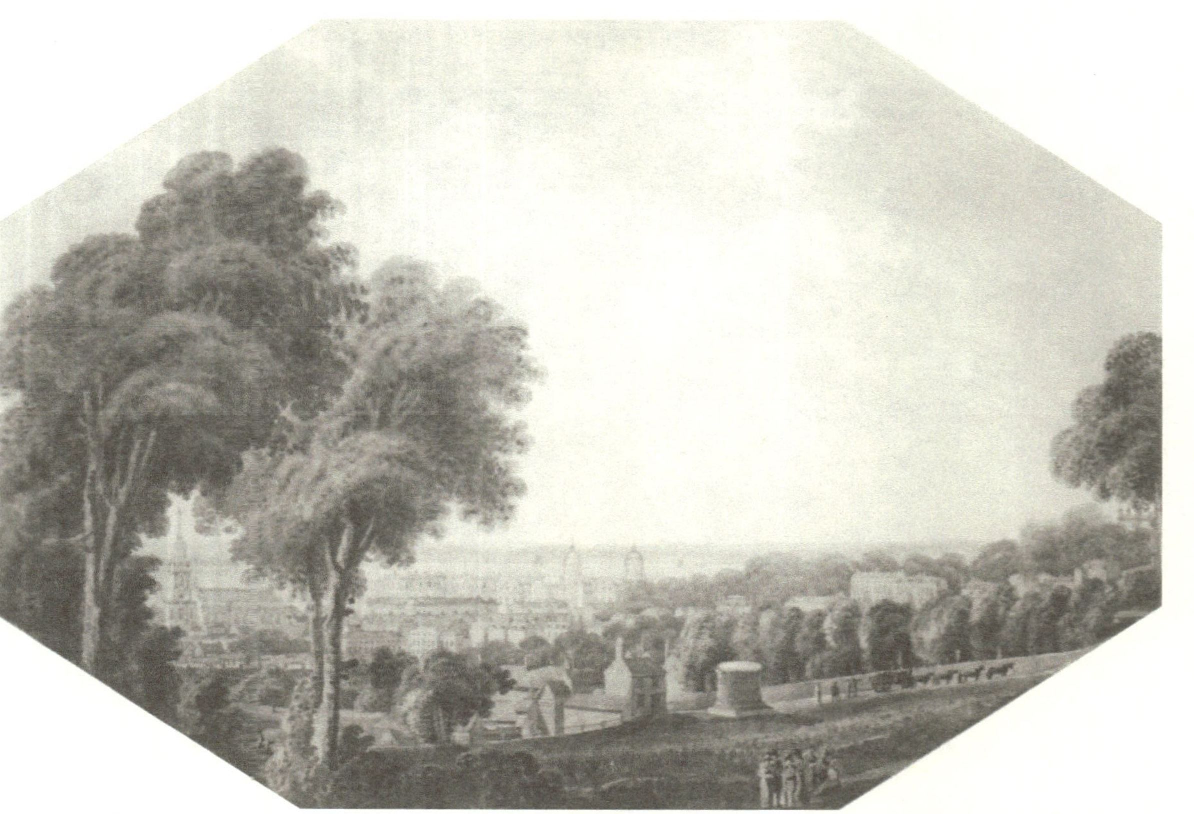

85 / *Greenwich from the point*, c 1820. Watercolour, 305 × 419 mm. (check-list 272)

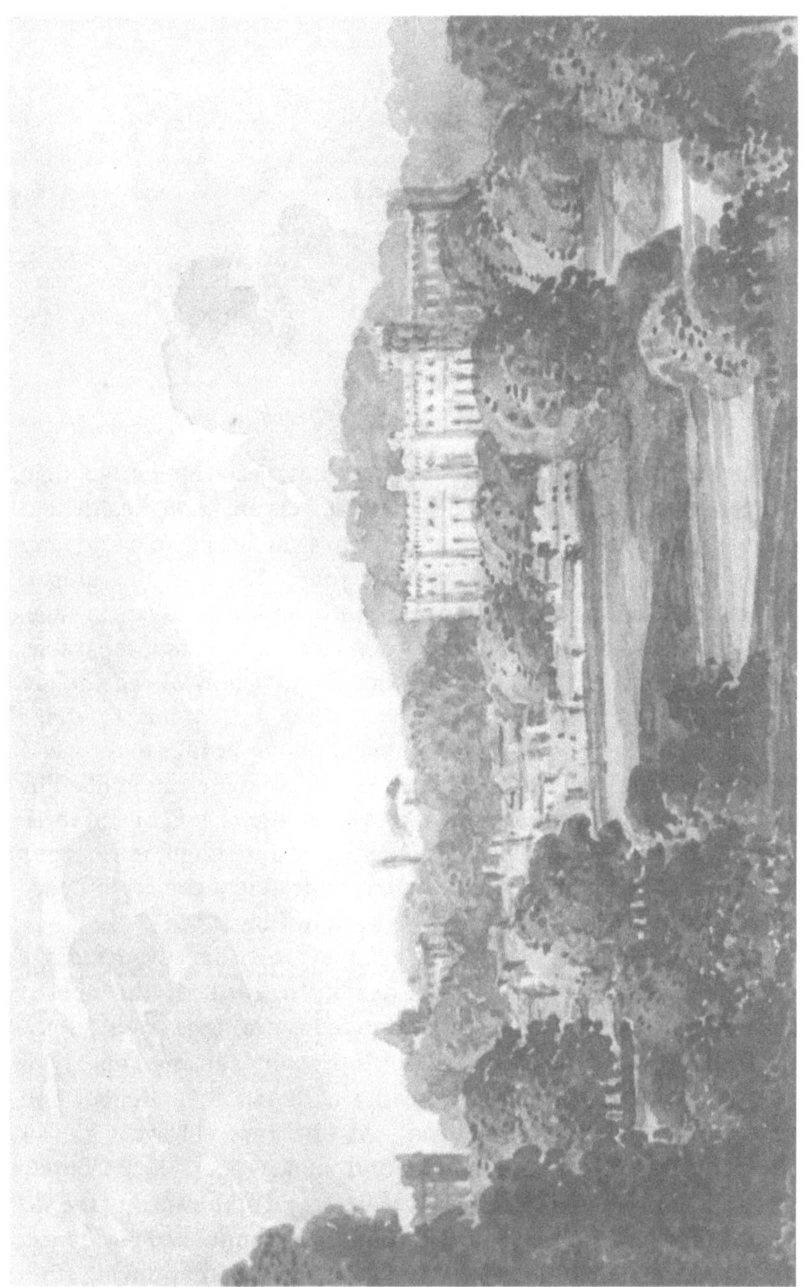

86 / *Arundel Castle, Sussex*, c 1828(?). Watercolour, 117 × 184 mm. (check-list 297)

11

Last Years

We are slightly better informed about Heriot's last years, after 1830, than about the preceding decade of his life. He was in good health and comfortably off, and resided in a Regency house in fashionable Cadogan Place, close to the home of his brother John. There at 7 Cadogan Place Heriot entertained his family and friends, and, with advancing age, he and his brother – who had always been close – became inseparable. However, in 1833 John and his wife both died, victims of the cholera epidemic that swept Britain in that year. The loss of his brother's companionship was a blow from which Heriot was never fully to recover.[1]

The resulting emptiness in the artist's life was to some extent filled by his surviving family. John had a son and two daughters, and one of these daughters, Amelia, seems to have become the brightest light in George's later life. He also began to re-establish a more frequent correspondence with his remaining brother, Roger, who lived in Charleston.

After John's death Heriot became more aware of his advancing age and of the inevitability of his own death. In 1834, at the age of seventy-five, he decided to distribute some of his drawings to his family. He therefore assembled a collection (which probably consisted mainly of views of the North American landscape) and sent it to Roger's son William, who also lived at Charleston.[2] At Christmas that year Heriot wrote to Roger about these drawings and spoke cheerfully of family matters and of himself. One is struck by the zest and optimism that the old artist still conveys: 'I have enjoyed, through the bounty of Providence, good health during a considerable time past. The weather during [the] summer and autumn has been [un]commonly fair & the crops most abundant. I am much gratified by the accounts which you gave me of the welfare and success of your family their good disposition and industrious habits will I doubt not reward them with independence. With kindest regards to you and your family, and the hearty wish of many happy returns of the present season.'[3]

The liveliness of Heriot's mind had obviously not diminished, nor can any serious decline in his artistic abilities be discerned in the majority of his last extant works. As yet no watercolours have come to light which we can unequivocally date to the early 1830s, but there are a considerable number apparently from about the last three years of Heriot's life. Some are remarkably fresh in appearance, such as the view of the *Royal Military Academy* (a late reminiscence of his Woolwich years), which dates from 1836 (figure 89). For a watercolour executed by an artist of seventy-seven years, this work is remarkable for its subtlety of tone, its clarity of colour, and the unusual, controlled austerity of its forms.

Other watercolours which may date from about 1837 are copies of some of Heriot's Canadian scenes; still others are copies of prints after the work of other artists (figures 87, 88). Why he copied prints and his own drawings we cannot say for certain; perhaps he did so for friends. A certain looseness of brushwork and confusion in some passages suggests that some of these copies were made swiftly and in some cases carelessly. Other examples are more successful.

Although ships had long been considered potentially a picturesque subject, there is little evidence that Heriot, apart from his early studies, was particularly attracted to them; indeed, except for his view of Halifax (check-list 169) and his detailed report on the American frigate *Fulton the First*, he did not display any specific interest in shipping. However, to judge from the surviving drawings that may date from about 1838, he must have acquired a knowledge of ships over an extended period of time, for his understanding of rigging and sails in different weather conditions and in time of war is considerable. His watercolours of ships seem to have been conceived as a group (figures 90, 91, 92). They are of similar size, each depicting an individual ship or pair of ships, and each possessing approximately the same proportion of sea to sky. They are not only remarkable as a novel subject in Heriot's œuvre, but they are quite astonishingly strong designs; surely they are evidence of his sustained capacity for development. Even if they are inspired by the paintings and drawings of other marine painters, such as Nicolas Pocock (with whose work some of these watercolours share a marked affinity),[4] they display a vitality and individuality unexpected in the work of an artist in his eightieth year.

Heriot was by then living at 32 Sloane Street, not far from his former house in Cadogan Place, which he had left after his brother's death. Here he lived alone, except, apparently, for his servants. Perhaps among his last letters was one written on 28 December 1838 to his brother Roger. Although this letter has not survived, his brother's reply, written in February 1839, has come down to us, and we can reconstruct from it something of the tenor of what Heriot had written. Heriot had much to say about the family in Scotland and mentioned the sale of the lands at Ladykirk, where their cousins (the Heriots of Ladykirk and Shiels) had been tenants. He may have been reflecting on the sunny days which they passed there in their youth, for Roger remarked: 'my fancy carries me back at times to the Banks of the Tweed & the *Braes* of Ladykirk, the old ruins of Norham Castle &c where ... boyish days were spent. I shall certainly never see them again, but notwithstanding that I live those scenes ... still!' Heriot had also spoken of politics and had mentioned that his eyesight was now very poor, though otherwise he was in good 'general health.'[5]

Though he may not have been able to draw or paint in this his last year, his spirits remained buoyant. It was in the Sloane Street house that he died quietly on a day in July 1839, at the age of eighty. The cause of death was recorded as 'decay of nature.'[6]

Since his death George Heriot has not been accorded the attention he deserves. Twenty years ago – well over a century after Heriot's death – the late Francis St George Spendlove (former curator of Canadiana at the Royal Ontario Museum) implied that justice had yet to be done to the artist when he wrote that 'the next quarter century will probably bring the acceptance of Heriot as being one of the most distinguished artists in watercolour in the history of Canada.'[7] Even today one might consider that Spendlove's prediction was unduly optimistic. I cannot claim to have altered the situation completely by writing this book: there is still too much that we need to discover about Heriot and his art. But I hope that, in the foregoing pages, I have offered a rounded picture of the man, and that I have conveyed both the essence of his attitudes towards Canada as well as fresh insight into the character of his art. Heriot tirelessly compiled notes and made sketches; he published books and painted pictures – all with the object of sharing with other people, both in Canada and in Britain, his passionate response to nature and especially his feelings towards this 'new found land.' Moreover, our knowledge of the artist's record of public service not only adds a further dimension to our understanding of Heriot himself; it also helps us to grasp the essence of the eighteenth-century gentleman's motives and ideals and illuminates the texture of life in the two Canadian provinces during the early years of their settlement.

It was natural that, as a member of the gentry, Heriot should have found his way into public service. He was suited to it both by education and by upbringing. Nevertheless, as we have seen, his public career did not always run smoothly and it ended in frustration and sadness. He did propose wide-ranging reforms of the postal service, though his attempts to implement them were constantly hampered by the obstructions which he found placed in his way. His own difficult personality contributed greatly to his problems. He displayed an uncommon inflexibility and obtuseness, and he treated the local officials with an almost patrician insolence. Yet he rowed valiantly against the tide of these problems, and by the time of his departure from Canada he had managed to improve postal services in both provinces.

As we have seen, through his solitary journeying, his writing, and his painting Heriot found enjoyment and experienced relief from the stresses of his active public life. The contentment which he discovered when investigating and contemplating the beauties of God's creation (which furnished him with the subjects of his writing and art) had first excited him during his youth. It is expressed in the earliest published evidence of his literary ability: *A Descriptive Poem, written in the West Indies* (1781). This poem expresses Heriot's youthful personality and reflects the broadly based culture of an eighteenth-century mind; it reveals his early meditation on nature, his enthusiasm for the new science, and his yearning for an idyllic passive existence – a yearning which throughout his life seems to have remained essentially the same:

Give me, beneath the spreading shade to sit
Of large extensive Fig-tree: there to stretch
My limbs fatigu'd, to catch the gentle breeze
Of grateful *Eurus*, and to eat thy fruit
O generous, juicy Pine! pleasing the taste ...[8]

More significant, however, is Heriot's much later (1807) literary achievement, *Travels through the Canadas*, which gives us a valuable glimpse of early Canada as well as something of his vision of it. Written in a clear style and full of picturesque descriptions, the *Travels* is a fascinating document, greatly enhanced by the many attractive plates with which the artist/writer reinforced and extended the images created in his text. It must be admitted, however, that the style of the *Travels* is somewhat impersonal: while we learn much about the country which Heriot is describing, we are told little of his reactions to it. We can only regret the wall of reserve which interposes itself between us and the writer's deeply felt responses to his adopted land.

But it is as an exponent of the Picturesque in watercolour, and one working in Canada, that Heriot is directly important – and, indeed, exceptional. Not that he was the only artist in this field: he had predecessors and contemporaries as well as successors. As we have observed in chapter 1, two of the more significant of these were Thomas Davies, who left Canada in 1790, and James Pattison Cockburn, who arrived here in 1828. Both artists enjoyed the benefit of an education and cultural background similar to Heriot's, though they differed from him in their approach to the Picturesque as well as in their style of painting and often in their choice of subject-matter. Although Davies and Cockburn were generations apart, they shared Heriot's interest in the Picturesque as a rhetorical device that provided organization and enrichment for a topographical view. Yet for Heriot the Picturesque had a deeper significance, at least as far as his attitude towards Canada was concerned.

During his long residence in Canada Heriot's administrative life became increasingly difficult and demanding but the stresses which it created were relieved by his frequent sketching forays into the countryside. In the sketches he developed an interpretation of landscape that was shaped by his concept of the Picturesque, which, as we have seen, had the *ideal* at its heart. Although Heriot used the Picturesque as a rhetorical, pictorial device, he manipulated it in his views in order to convey his vision of a Canadian Arcadia. He sought to give his vision expression in the watercolours which he painted in the late 1790s, and during and extending beyond the first decade of the nineteenth century. The noble *Lake St Charles*, c 1801 (see figure 37), is a striking example, but even more successful in this respect are the smaller, more spontaneous, and more personal maritime landscapes of 1807, especially the *West View of Partridge Island from Parsborough* (see figure 57), with its felicitous blending of abstract grandeur and ornamental richness. In such works Heriot does, indeed, seem to us to have metamorphosed Canada's landscape into the Arcadia of which he dreamed. The realization of this purpose was the end of Heriot's search for an expression of landscape which should serve both as an aesthetic consolation for the stresses of his career and as a stimulus to inspiration. His *summum bonum* lay in maintaining his Arcadian vision. He would have entirely agreed with the sentiments expressed by William Wycherley:

> But all is quiet, jocund, and serene,
> A Type of Paradise, the Rural Scene!
> Here may he sit, and on the Rocky Shore
> See distant Storms, and hear the Billows roar,
> And count the Wrecks on the tost Ocean spread,
> Safe from each Surge that curls its ridgy Head.
> Here he may laugh, in Privacy and Ease,
> At guilty Grandeur and its Fopperies;
> ...
> More Ease, Peace, Safety to our selves we gain,
> As we from Publick Commerce more abstain.[9]

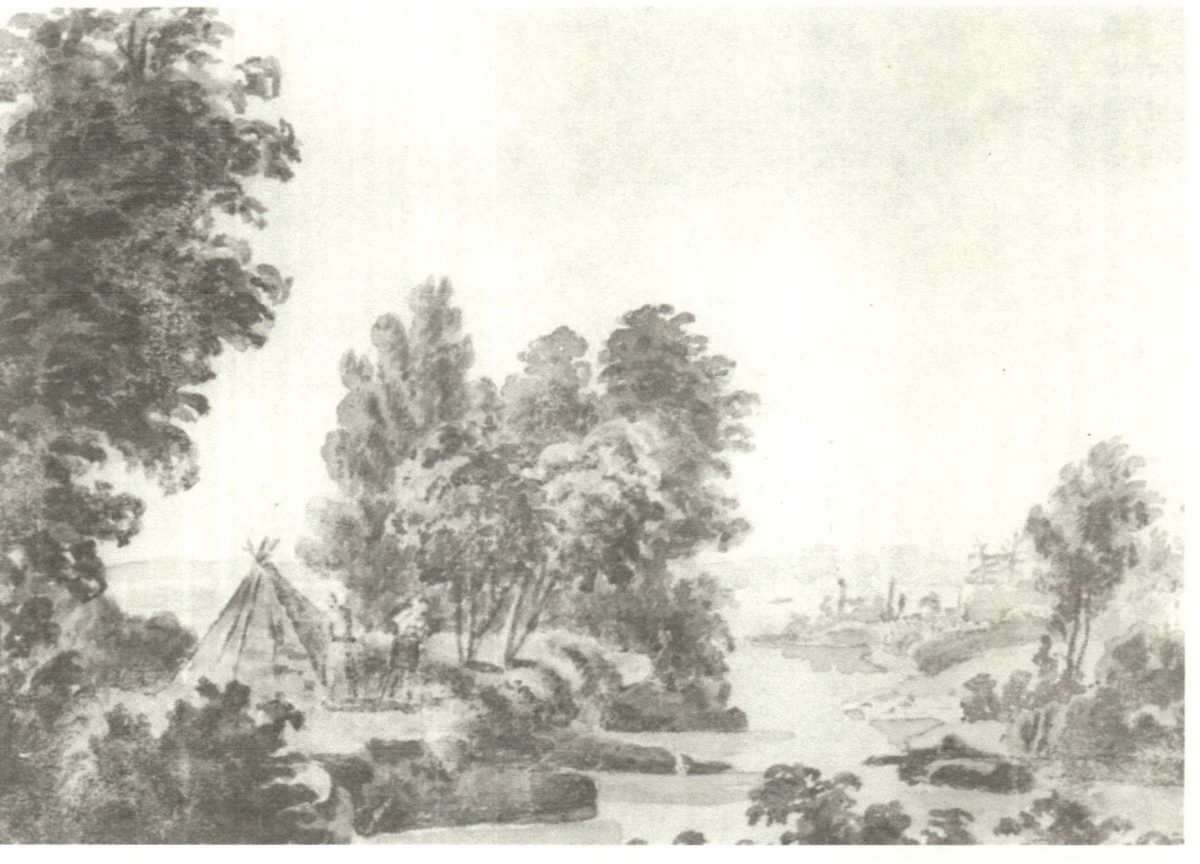

87 / *A View of Lake and Fort Erie from Buffalo Creek*, c 1837(?). Watercolour, 129 × 182 mm. (check-list 308)

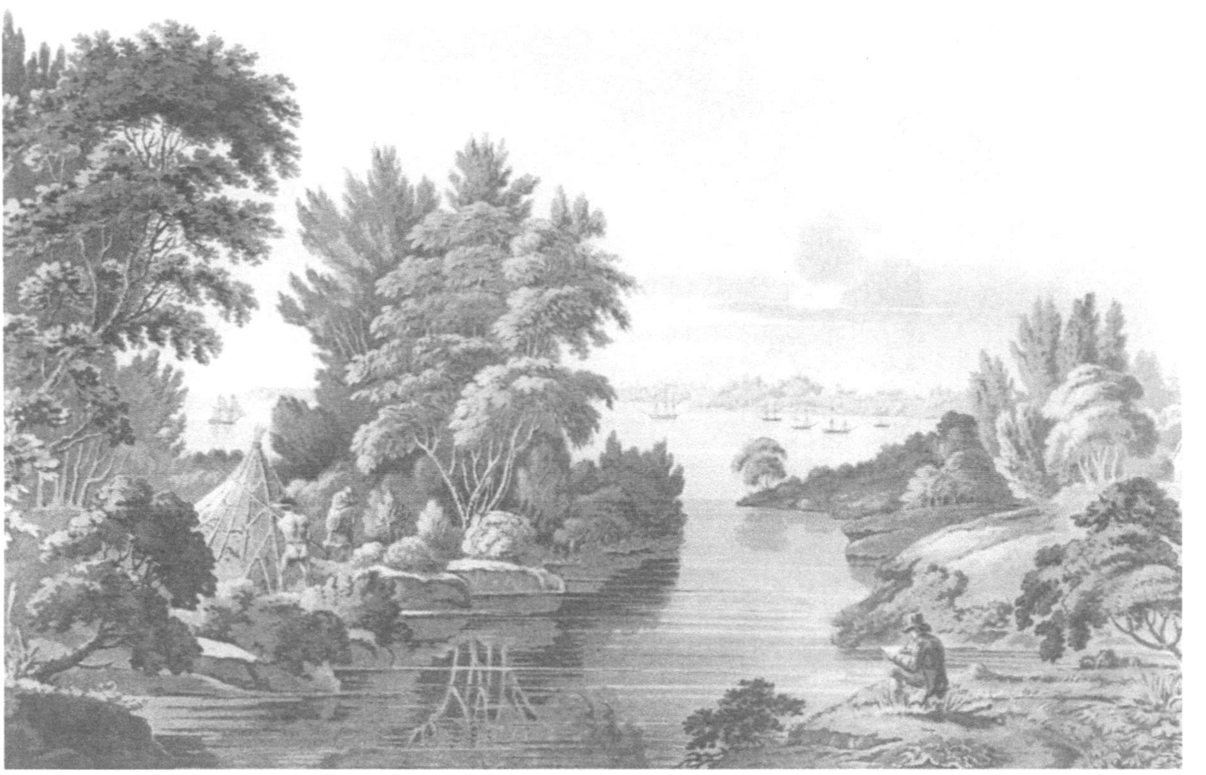

88 / John Bluck, *A View of Lake and Fort Erie from Buffalo Creek*, 1811. Aquatint after E. Walsh, 418 × 544 mm. (image)

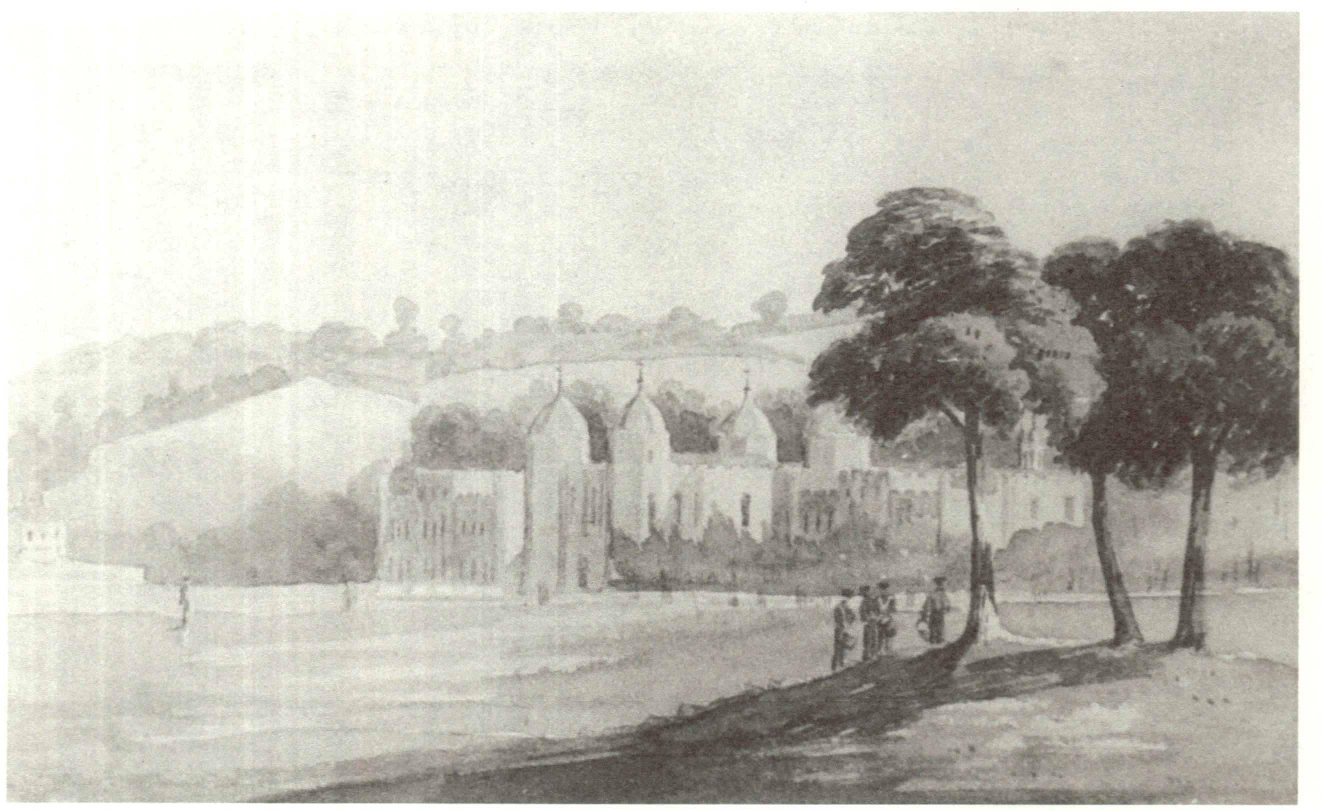

89 / *Royal Military Academy, Woolwich*, 1836. Watercolour, 162 × 254 mm. (sight) (check-list 299)

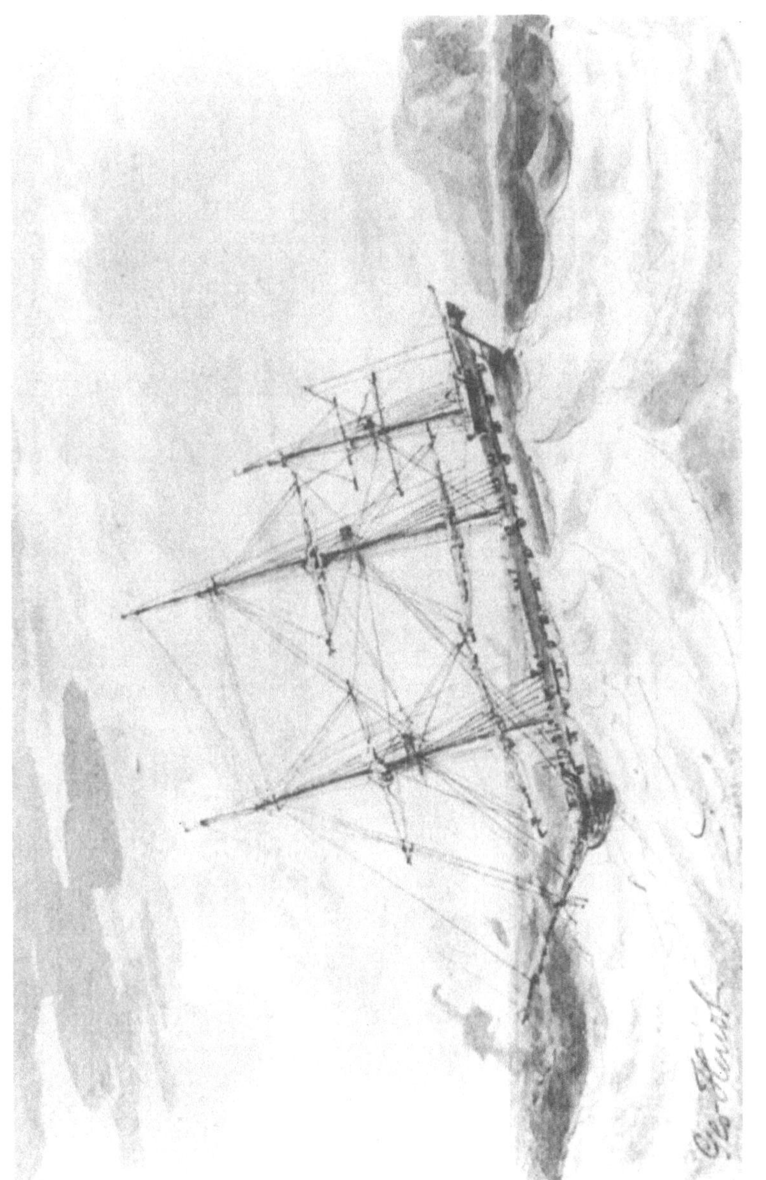

90 / *Strong Gales and Squally reeved out cable*, c 1838. Pen, ink, and watercolour, 81 × 125 mm. (check-list 326)

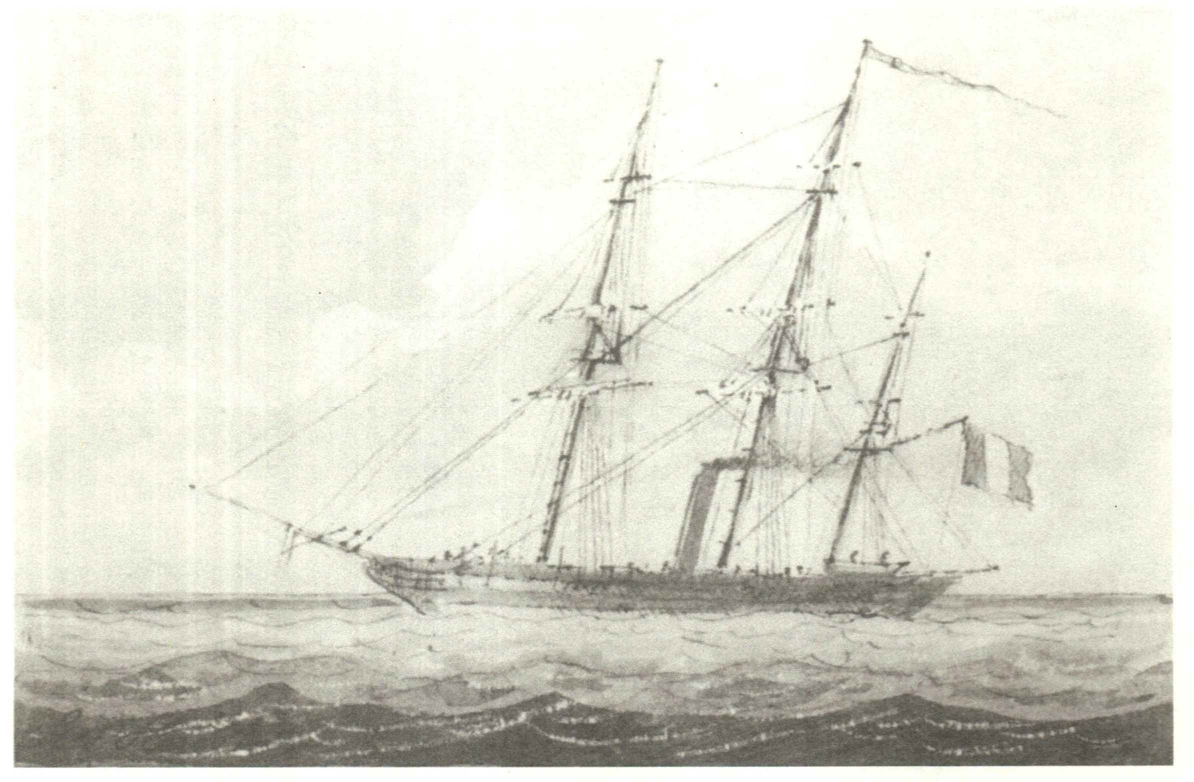

91 / *Compte [sic] D'Eu, King of the French Yachts*, c 1838. Pen, ink, watercolour, and scraping, 83 × 127 mm. (check-list 320)

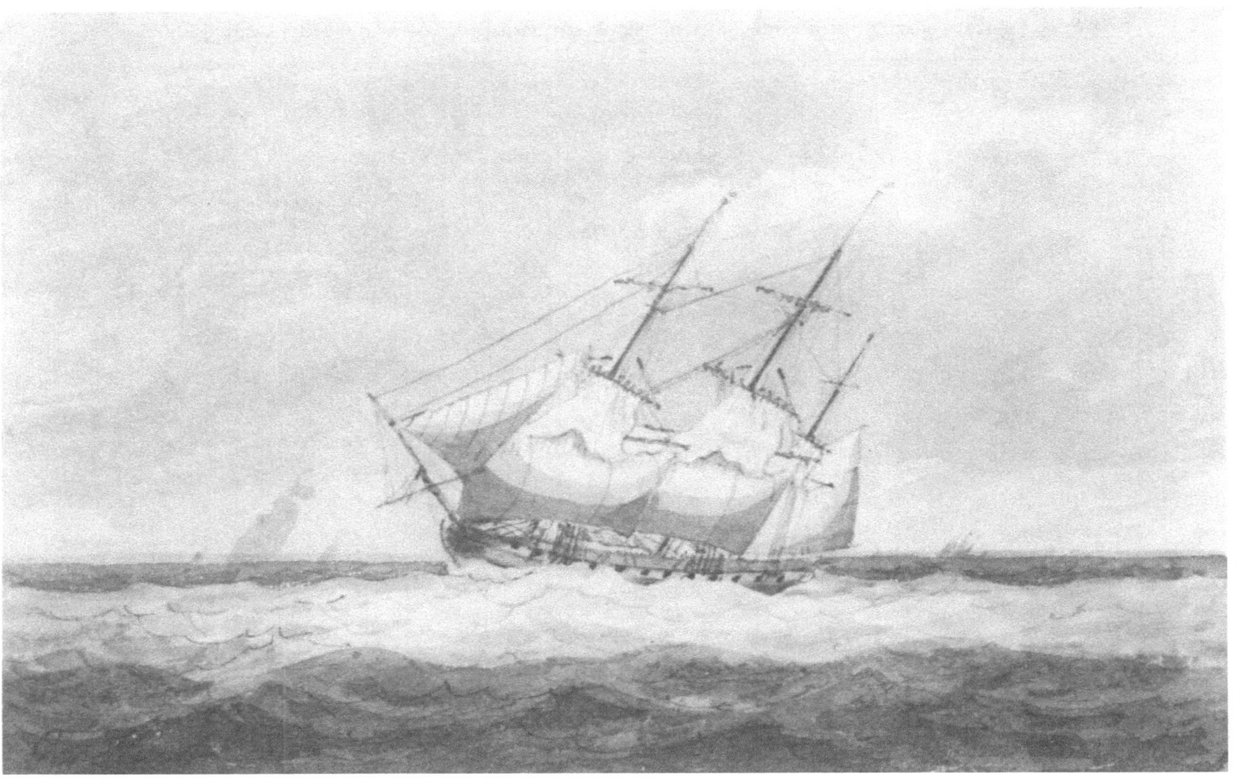

92 / *Reefing Topsails*, c 1838. Pen, ink, and watercolour, 83 × 127 mm. (check-list 323)

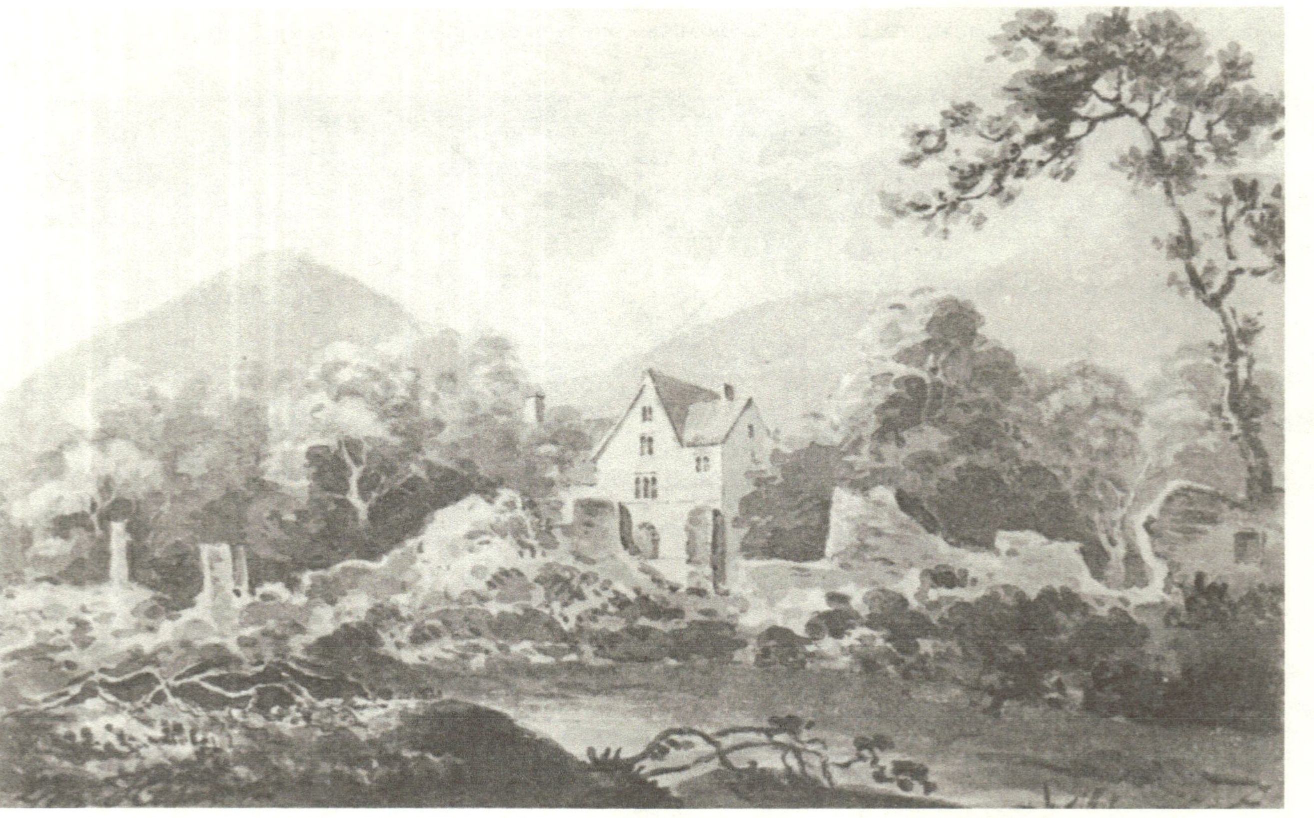

93 / *Abbey Cwm Hir*, c 1838. Monochrome wash, 137 × 202 mm. (check-list 331)

Appendix: The Heriot Family[1]

The name 'Heriot,' which is of Anglo-Saxon derivation, has a long and fascinating history.[2] The earliest eminent member of the Heriot family was George Buchanan (1506–82), the humanist and statesman from whose poetry George Heriot would sometimes quote.[3] Another important ancestor was Heriot's namesake George 'Jingling Geordie' Heriot of Edinburgh (1563–1624), banker, goldsmith, jeweller to James VI of Scotland (James I of England), and benefactor of the Edinburgh school which still bears his name.

The George Heriot who is the subject of this book was descended from a cadet branch of the Heriots of Trabroun. His great-grandfather George (1636–92/8) was a tenant farmer at Dirleton, East Lothian, who served as chamberlain to Sir John Nisbet, advocate to the Crown (of Scotland); on his death an elaborate wall monument was erected at Dirleton Kirk, bearing his arms and those of his wife's family.[4] This marriage produced three children, all sons, one of whom was John Heriot (1664–1725), a tenant farmer of Castlemains (Dirleton). He married Jane Sinclair, a niece of Robert Sinclair, minister of the parish of Dirleton and 'proprietor of Redhouse, with the Manor Place and the east outfield of Longniddry with the tiens.' John was interred beneath his father's wall tomb. In Dirleton Kirk there hangs a wooden plaque, commemorating a gift of £100 by John which was distributed among the poor of the parish.

From John's marriage three sons survived: John, James, and George. John (1698–1744) became a prosperous Edinburgh solicitor. James (1700–62) assumed the tenancy of Castlemains from his father. Two of James's sons began the emigration of one branch of the Heriot family to North America: Robert (1739–92) emigrated to South Carolina in 1759, and his younger brother William (1745–1807) followed in 1769. George (1688–1753), the third of the three brothers, who received the Crown appointment of sheriff clerk of Haddington, is more important to us, since he was the grandfather of George Heriot, the painter. He married one Mary Tannoch, who bore him ten children. Of those who survived to adulthood, John (born in 1738; date of death unknown) was the painter's father. A lawyer and convinced Tory, he, like his father, was given the Crown appointment of sheriff clerk of Haddington. On 2 January 1758, at Norham, he married a distant cousin, Marjory Heriot, who was also a great-grandchild of George (the chamberlain to Sir John Nisbet), and whose branch of the Heriot family held the tenancy of Ladykirk and Sheils, to the south and east of Haddington.[5] The wedding ceremony was performed by Thomas Martindale, curate of the Norham parish church. In the following year George Heriot, the painter, was born to John and Marjory Heriot at Haddington.

Notes

Publications listed in the Bibliography are cited in the notes by author's name and short title only.

CHAPTER 1

1 Rye, *England as Seen by Foreigners*, pp 44–5; see also Whinney and Millar, *English Art*, p 262.
2 Ibid.
3 Reynolds, *Discourses*, XIII (1786), p 238.
4 Waterhouse, *Gainsborough*, p 15.
5 Reynolds, *Discourses*, pp 237–8.
6 Cooper, *Characteristicks*, I, 142–3.
7 Richardson, 'The Theory of Painting,' in *Works*, p 72.
8 Cooper, *Characteristicks*, I, 339–40.
9 Barbier, *Gilpin*, p 98.
10 Burke, *a Philosophical Enquiry*, 'The Sublime and Beautiful Compared,' p 115.
11 Uvedale Price, *Essay on the Picturesque* (London 1794); Richard Payne Knight, *The Landscape, a didactic poem in three books* (London 1794); Uvedale Price, *A Dialogue on the distinct characters of the Picturesque and the Beautiful; in answer to the objections of Mr. K. [in the second edition of 'The Landscape]'* (London 1801).
12 Barbier, *Gilpin*, p 100.
13 Stations are described in such popular guides as John Housman's *A Descriptive Tour and Guide to the Lakes ... in Cumberland, Westmoreland, Lancashire and a Part of the West Riding of Yorkshire*, 3rd ed (Carlisle 1808); James S. Clarke's *A Survey of the Lakes in Cumberland and Westmoreland*, 2nd ed (London 1789); and Thomas West's *A Guide to the Lakes in Cumberland, Westmoreland and Lancashire ...* , 3rd ed (London 1784).
14 Röthlisberger, *Claude Lorrain*, I, 41, 60.

15 Charles Dibdin, *Observations of a Tour through almost the Whole of England and a Considerable Part of Scotland, in a series of letters ...* , 2 vols (London 1801, 1802), II, 128.
16 Arthur Young, *A Six Months' Tour through the North of England ...* , 5 vols, 2nd ed corrected and enlarged (London 1770–1), III, 140.
17 James Denholm, *An Historical Account and Topograhical Description of the City of Glasgow and Suburbs ... To which is added, a sketch of a Tour to the principal Scottish and English Lakes*, 3rd ed (Glasgow 1804), pp 448–9.
18 Henry P. Wyndham, *Tour through Monmouthshire and Wales*, 2nd ed (Salisbury 1781), p 126.
19 Gilpin, *Three Essays*, 'On The Art of Sketching Landscape,' p 69.
20 Gilpin, *Lakes of Cumberland and Westmoreland*, II, 113–7, 154.
21 Dibdin, *Observations*, II, 141.
22 Humphrey Repton, *An Enquiry into the Changes of Taste in Landscape Gardening ...* (London 1806), pp 128, 130.
23 Gilpin, *Lakes of Cumberland and Westmoreland*, II, 10–17.
24 Barbier, *Gilpin*, p 106.
25 Gilpin, *Lakes of Cumberland and Westmoreland*, I, 109.
26 Gilpin, *High-Lands of Scotland*, I, 24.
27 Gilpin considered the rocky hill of Castellet in Borrowdale to be a 'natural ruin' sufficient to dignify 'any scene' (*Lakes of Cumberland and Westmoreland*, I, 195), and at Middleton-dale he encountered rocks 'rearing themselves like the round towers, and buttresses of a ruined castle' (ibid, II, 208). For references to trees as 'natural ruins,' see Gilpin's *Forest Scenery*, I, 14.
28 Ibid.
29 Ibid, I, 9.
30 Brauer, *The Education of a Gentleman*, pp 90–2.
31 Stanhope, *Letters to his Son*, I, 228 (17 Oct. 1747).

CHAPTER 2

1 The school which Heriot attended was built in 1578 and located in Kirk o' Field, Edinburgh. It was demolished in 1777. Today the street name remains a memorial to the location of this building: 'High School Yards.'
2 Luke Fraser's account book (at present in the possession of Edinburgh University) indicates that Heriot joined Mr Fraser's class in 1769, spending four years under his tuition, and subsequently spent one year under the rector's tuition. Heriot's five sessions at the high school were sufficient to allow him to attend the university. I am grateful to the rector, Farquar MacIntosh, for this information.
3 Clark, *Sir Walter Scott*, p 18.
4 Ibid, p 20.
5 Register House, Edinburgh, 'Minute Book,' NG 1/1/20, p 4, 25 Nov. 1772; NG 1/1/25, p 110, 23 Jan. 1786; as quoted in Irwin, *Scottish Painters*, p 91. Unfortunately no class lists survive for this period (1774–7). I am grateful to Barbara H.L. Horn for this information.

6 Register House, Edinburgh, GD 248/54, fol 1v, G. Heriot, London, to Sir James Grant (place not indicated), 18 Aug. 1777.

7 Ibid, GD 248/55, fols 1, 1v, G.H., London, to Sir James Grant (place not indicated), 14 Sept. 1777.

8 Waller, 'Summer Islands,' in *Poems*, pp 52–9. For Heriot's later consideration of the New World, see his poem 'Ode to Columbus' (check-list 334, fol 1r).

9 Stanhope, *Letters*, II, 96–7 (June 1752).

10 At this particular time Britain was struggling, unsuccessfully, to maintain her supremacy in the Caribbean against three nations: France, Spain, and the Netherlands. By 1782 Britain had lost nearly all of its possessions there, with the exception of Barbados, Jamaica, and Antigua.

11 Register House, Edinburgh, GD 248/510/2, fols 1, 1v, G.H., London, to Sir James Grant (place not indicated), 16 July 1781. Heriot's poem was dedicated to the Royal Society, probably because it was concerned largely with the natural sciences and he had probably read of the Society's aims to further their study. He may have hoped that such a dedication would lead to his membership in that august organization. (It is very possible that he knew that Edmund Waller had been a member.)

12 'John Heriot,' Chambers, *A Biographical Dictionary of Eminent Scotsmen*, vol I.

13 Heriot, *A Descriptive Poem*, p 12. In the *Gentleman's Magazine*, 29 July 1833, reference is made to both his *Poem* (1781) and his *Travels* (1807).

14 Heriot must have visited Granada before the French invasion of the island in July 1779.

15 Harper, 'Early Canadian Contrasts,' p 71.

16 Public Record Office, London (henceforth abbreviated as PRO), Ordnance Establishment Register, WO, 54/217 (1783), p 15; Heriot replaced Henry Forman, who had been a £100 per annum clerk; see also Hogg, *The Royal Arsenal*, I, 473. In 1815, while still in Canada, Heriot wrote that (from 1813) his Ordnance pay and allowances had been withheld 'after a service of thirty-two years' (Public Archives of Canada, Ottawa [henceforth abbreviated as PAC], R.G. 8, C-series, vol 284, fol 161, G.H., Quebec, to N. Freer, Quebec, 3 Feb. 1815). Since the original note of appointment is dated 1783, and because Heriot's independent calculation of his years of service (presumably to 1815) coincides with that provided by the Register, 1783 would seem to be the date of his appointment, despite the conflicting evidence furnished by a much later document which states that he was appointed in 1785 (ibid, vol 744, fol 188, 26 Oct. 1811).

17 While it is impossible to establish the precise date of Heriot's visit to Jersey and Guernsey, the Druids' Temple at St Helier, Jersey, which is the subject of one of his prints (see check-list 348), was dismantled in about 1787 and removed to Park Place near Henley-on-Thames in the next year. The 'style' of the coloured prints suggest that the original sketches, or the watercolours developed from them, were made between about 1786 and 1787.

18 *Quebec Gazette*, 27 Sept. 1792: 'Office of Ordnance. Cash wanted for Bills of Exchange on the Honorable Board of Ordnance in London, One Hundred

Eighty-eight Pounds, Two Shillings and Three Pence Stirling, – sealed Proposals to be addressed to the respective Officers of His Majesty's Ordnance, on or before 3d. October, 1792 before 12 o'clock noon. G. Heriot. Clk of Cheque. Quebec, 24th Sept. 1792.' See also PRO, Ordnance Establishment Register, WO 54/217, p 23, where, under 'Quebec,' Heriot's name appears, followed by the year of his assuming the position there: '1792.'

CHAPTER 3

1 Sanson, *Travels*, p 39.
2 Ibid.
3 Heriot, we know, later lived at this address. We cannot determine precisely when he arrived in Quebec, but it was likely in the spring or summer, and he may immediately have rented the house from the owner, John McCord, a merchant. The house was advertised in the *Quebec Gazette* on 19 Apr., 26 Apr., and 3 May 1792. The advertisement stated: 'To be let from 1 May next.'
4 See Mary Allodi, 'Printmaking in Canada: The Earliest Views and Portraits,' Toronto: Royal Ontario Museum 1980). Mrs Allodi discovered an impression of the *Temple of the Druids* in the *Quebec Magazine* (which is certainly from the original plate) and also found the print of the panorama of the city of Quebec which she has attributed to Heriot, and which is undoubtedly by him. Both engraved impressions are reproduced in Mrs Allodi's catalogue. Further, Mrs Allodi has tentatively associated the design of the print of the panorama of the city of Quebec with the watercolour *City of Quebec from Point Levi* (check-list 17).
5 Edinburgh University, *Matriculation Rolls* (1796), II, 568. Matriculation involved signing a *sponsio* to be of good behaviour. The university's term started in October and ended in December. Although joining the university library was not compulsory, Heriot did, paying the customary fee of 2/6d.
6 Graves, *Royal Academy*, IV, 82. Heriot was residing at No. 5 Catherine Street, off the Strand.
7 Ibid. He exhibited a 'View of Swansea in Glamorganshire' and two Canadian views.
8 Heriot, *Travels*, pp 10–11.
9 Ibid, pp 44, 45, 46, 47.
10 Ibid, p 53.
11 Ibid, p 54.
12 Ibid, p 55.
13 Ibid, p 59.
14 Ibid, p 61.
15 One must mention the several volumes by Samuel Ireland, including his *Picturesque Views on the River Thames* (1792), *Picturesque Views on the River Medway* (1793), and *Picturesque Views on the Upper or Warwickshire Avon* (1795); one of the most attractive of these river tour guides was William

Combe's *History of the River Thames* (1794), which was embellished with aquatint plates after drawings by Joseph Farington.

16 A reviewer of Heriot's *Travels* pronounced that the book was 'originally devoted to the service of the Canadian River Gods' (*Edinburgh Review*, Apr. 1808, pp 212–25).

17 Heriot, *Travels*, pp 87, 93.

CHAPTER 4

1 PAC, R.G. 8, C-series, vol 223, fol 157, Duke of Kent, Halifax, to Lieutenant-General Peter Hunter, 20 Oct. 1799.

2 See below, n 5.

3 In October of this year Finlay was dismissed as a defaulter: 'He admitted an indebtedness to the Postmaster General, amounting to £1408' (Smith, *History of the Post Office*, p 94). Finlay's debt was cleared in 1809. At that time Heriot signed a receipt indicating the sum owed was 'received from the Estate of H. Finlay & paid him [Heriot] on account of the Govermt Post Office, being in full of the Judgment debt against the said Hugh Finlay' (G.H., Quebec, to Edward Bowan, Quebec, 22 Feb. 1809). This receipt is now in the collection of the National Postal Museum, Ottawa.

4 PRO, CO 42/140, fol 138, 7 Dec. 1809.

5 General Post Office, London (henceforth abbreviated as GPO), Post 44/1, 'Instructions to Deputies, Packet Captains & Surveyors 1763–1811,' p 196, 18 Oct. 1799; ibid, Post 58/33 (Commission Book), p 212, 'October 18th 1799. Signed a Commission appointing George Heriot Esquire Deputy Post Master Gnl of His Majesty's Provinces of Canada, Nova Scotia & New Brunswick in the Room of Mr Finlay dismissed at a Salary of £400 a year to commence from the Day he takes Charge of the Business.' Heriot actually took charge on 5 April 1800 (PRO, CO 42/144, fol 96v, G.H., Quebec, to F. Freeling, London, 8 Oct. 1810).

6 PAC, R.G. 8, C-series, vol 284, fol 21, General Hunter, York, to Earl Camden, London, Jan. 1805.

7 Ibid, fol 3, G.H., Quebec, to F. Freeling, London, 6 Mar. 1800; ibid, fol 1, G.H., Quebec, to General Hunter, York, 6 Oct. 1800.

8 Ibid, fol 3.

9 National Postal Museum, Ottawa, 'Commissions of Post Masters,' p 12: 'Sketch of a Route proposed for a General Post in the Province of Upper Canada,' 9 Aug. 1800.

10 PAC. R.G. 8, C-series, vol 284, fols 3–4, G.H., Quebec, to F. Freeling, London, 6 Mar. 1800.

11 Ibid, fols 4–5, F. Freeling, London, to G.H., Quebec, 5 July 1800.

12 Ibid, vol 284, fol 15, General Hunter, York, to G.H., Quebec, 24 Oct. 1800; see also ibid, fol 19, J. Green, York, to G.H., Quebec, 11 Dec. 1800; ibid, fol 17, 8 Dec. 1800.

13 *Quebec Gazette*, 29 Nov. 1800.

14 Heriot, *Travels*, p 117.

15 Ibid, pp 131–2.
16 Ibid, pp 150–1.
17 Ibid, p 156.
18 Ibid, p 157.
19 Ibid, p 166.
20 PAC, Executive Council, R.G. 4, A1, s-series, vol 102, p 32410, G.H., Quebec, to W. Allan, York, 6 Mar. 1809.
21 PAC, R.G. 8, C-series, vol 284, fol 22, General Hunter, York, to Earl Camden, London, Jan. 1805; ibid, fol 58, G.H., Quebec, to Major Thornton (military secretary to Sir James Craig), Quebec, 15 Nov. 1807.
22 PAC, Executive Council, R.G. 4, A1, s-series, vol 75, pp 23562–3, G.H., Quebec, to R. Milnes, Quebec, 30 Dec. 1801; PRO, CO 42/120, fols 139, 139v, G.H. Quebec to R. Milnes, 28 Dec. 1801; PAC, R.G. 4, A1, s-series, vol 75, p 23560. Heriot also wrote to the joint postmaster general (the position was held jointly by Lords Auckland and Spencer) in London explaining the necessity of his being appointed superintendent of the *maîtres de poste* (PRO, CO 42/120, fols 137, 137v, G.H., Quebec, to F. Freeling, London, 21 Jan. 1802). The postmaster general in turn, wrote to the secretary of state, supporting Heriot's candidacy (ibid, fols 135–135v, Lords Auckland and Spencer, London, to Lord Hobart, London, 5 May 1802.
23 Ibid, fols 137–137v, G.H., Quebec, to F. Freeling, London, 21 Jan. 1802.
24 Ibid, fol 139v, G.H., Quebec, to R. Milnes, Quebec, 28 Dec. 1801.
25 PRO, CO 42/21, fol 80v, G.H., Quebec, to R. Milnes, Quebec, 21 Mar. 1803. In 1792, the year of Heriot's arrival in Quebec, as clerk of cheque, Board of Ordnance, Taschereau was appointed deputy to Lord Dorchester. Two years later he became 'grand voyer' for the district of Quebec. In 1798 he was appointed to the Legislative Council.
26 Ibid, fol 84, G.H., Quebec, to R. Milnes, Quebec, 25 Mar. 1803.
27 Ibid, fol 81, G.H., Quebec, to R. Milnes, Quebec, 21 Mar. 1803.
28 Ibid, fol 82, G.H., Quebec, to R. Milnes, Quebec, 25 Mar. 1803.
29 PRO, CO 43/19, fol 46, R. Milnes, Quebec, to Lord Hobart, London, 16 Aug. 1802; PRO, CO 42/21, fols 78, 78v, 79, R. Milnes, Quebec, to Lord Hobart, London, 30 Mar. 1803.
30 Ibid, fols 78v, 79; see also PRO, CO 43/19, fol 46, R. Milnes, Quebec, to Lord Hobart, London, 16 Aug. 1802.
31 See also ibid, fol 45v, Lord Hobart, London, to R. Milnes, Quebec, 1 Dec. 1802.
32 PRO, CO 42/128, fol 263, G.H., Quebec, to G. Ryland, Quebec, 4 Aug. 1805.
33 Ibid, fol 255, R. Milnes, Quebec, to Earl Camden, London, 4 Aug. 1805.

CHAPTER 5

1 Heriot, *Travels*, p iv.
2 Ibid, p v.
3 Ibid, pp iv–v.

4 Anonymous review of Heriot's *Travels*, in the *Edinburgh Review*, Apr. 1808, pp 212, 220.
5 Heriot, *Travels*, a reprint of the 1807 edition with an introduction by J.J. Talman.
6 Ibid, pp 69–70.
7 Ibid, p 253.
8 Ibid, pp 151, 152.
9 Ibid, p 35.
10 Ibid.
11 Heriot's first acquaintance with the aquatint medium probably occurred, as we have noted, during his association with Paul Sandby at Woolwich. His own aquatint experiments (which occurred at least as early as 1792) sharpened his awareness of the potential of the medium and increasingly attracted him to the austere yet dramatic landscape effects achieved in the aquatint plates embellishing Gilpin's published tours. It is probable that the classicism of Heriot's watercolours (from about 1800 onward) developed, in part, as a result of his efforts to create effects equivalent to those achieved in Gilpin's plates: he attained the desired effects by subduing or eliminating detail and creating relatively flat, unmodulated areas of light and shade. It is probably not fortuitous that about this time (that is, around 1800) he was already planning a book of Canadian travels (eventually published as *Travels through the Canadas* [1807]), in which he proposed to include plates after his own watercolours, and hence required a watercolour style that would reproduce well in aquatint. (See also my 'The Encapsulated Landscape: An Aspect of Gilpin's Picturesque,' in *City and Society in the 18th Century*, Publications of the McMaster University Association for 18th Century Studies, ed P. Fritz and D. Williams (Toronto 1973), p 206, n 18.)
12 Heriot, *Travels*, pp 95–6.
13 The two watercolour designs (which have not as yet been located) for the large, impressive aquatint views of Quebec *View of the City of Quebec, taken from the Rocks of Point Levi* (check-list 361) and *View of the City of Quebec, taken from the North Banks of the Saint Charles* (check-list 362) were probably painted in 1804. The plates were etched and engraved by J.C. Stadler and published for 'The Proprietor [George Heriot] at Quebec' by F. Walker, No. 7 Cornhill, London, 4 June 1805. These prints were offered for sale in Quebec in the year of publication, according to the evidence of a letter from the Honourable Richard Cartwright to James Cartwright, dated Kingston, 12 Dec. 1805. I am grateful to Mary Stewart for this information.
14 Heriot, *Travels*, pp 159, 161.
15 Ibid, p 81.
16 Ibid, p 82.
17 A previously unknown line engraving of one of Heriot's designs of Indian dances has recently come to light, though the watercolour itself has disappeared. Entitled *Dance Preparatory to War, among the Indians of North America*, it was published in London in 1810 by Sherwood, Neely and Jones. One

impression is in the collection of the Agnes Etherington Art Centre, Queen's University, Kingston (check-list 364). (In the same year Sherwood, Neely and Jones printed another line engraving of a Heriot design, *Costume of Domiciliated Indians of North America*, which had already been published in aquatint [in 1807] in Heriot's *Travels through the Canadas*; see check-list 363).

18 I am indebted to T.J. Brasser of the Canadian Ethnology Service who generously informed me of historical inaccuracies in Heriot's Indian watercolours. This lack of accuracy does seem to contradict Heriot's assertion that his knowledge of Indians, based on the writings of others, had been corrected by information derived 'from living observation, communicated by men on whose veracity a reliance could be placed.' Further, he observed: 'A resident in Canada for a series of years, has afforded to the author opportunities of witnessing the modes of life pursued by several of the Indian nations, and has enabled him to adduce what he has himself observed, as well as to reject what he deemed improbable in the writings he consulted' (*Travels*, pp iv–v).

19 New Brunswick Museum (henceforth abbreviated as NBM), Winslow Papers, vol XIII, fols 2, 2v, G.H., Quebec, to E. Winslow, Kingsclear, 4 Mar. 1811.

20 Heriot, *Travels*, pp 254–5, 257.

21 One could argue that *A London Pieman* is not by Sandby despite A.P. Oppé's belief that it is (*The Drawings of Paul and Thomas Sandby*, cat. 341): the pieman possesses craggy, slightly exaggerated features, and seems more two-dimensional than are Sandby's figures: the style of the drawing is closer to that of Heriot. Still, whether or not this drawing is by Sandby the general comparison which I have drawn between Sandby's figure studies and those by Heriot is essentially valid.

22 Heriot, *A Descriptive Poem*, pp 23, 24.

23 Ibid, pp 27, 28. Compare these lines, for example to lines 225–33 of Alexander Pope's *Essay on Man*, in *Selected Poems of Pope* (London 1740).

CHAPTER 6

1 *Quebec Gazette*, 18 Oct. 1792, 12 Feb. 1807; *Le Bulletin des recherches historiques, Quebec* (1898), IV, 251–2.

2 *Quebec Gazette*, 12 Feb. 1807.

3 Ibid. A few years later, on hearing of King George III's most recent illness, Heriot was to express his deep feeling toward the monarchy: 'Every well wisher to his Country must feel particularly concerned at His Majesty's Indisposition. From the bulletins of the physicians, I would hope that it is not very dangerous – if it be his former disorder, he will in all probability recover, which will be a great consolation to every friend of virtue and morality, as it prolongs for a time the inestimable benefits which have been derived from the high respectability of his character, and from his public and private virtues' (NBM, Winslow Papers, vol XIII, fol 2v, G.H., Quebec, to E. Winslow, Kingsclear, 11 Jan. 1811).

4 *Quebec Gazette*, 12 Feb. 1807.
5 Wrong, *A Canadian Manor*, p 107.
6 Ibid, p 53.
7 Heriot, *Travels*, p 53.
8 The militia was the subject of discussion between Winslow and Heriot on at least one occasion (see Raymond, *Winslow Papers*, p 609, G.H., Quebec, to E. Winslow, Kingsclear, 11 Mar. 1808).
9 Fenety, *Joseph Howe*, pp 80–92.
10 Raymond, *Winslow Papers*, p 586, E. Winslow, Kingsclear, to Sir J. Wentworth, Halifax, June 1807.
11 'I frequently reflect with pleasure on the agreeable days I passed with you in travelling from Halifax to Fredericton' (NBM, Winslow Papers, vol x, fol 1v, G.H., Quebec, to E. Winslow, Kingsclear, 19 Mar. 1810.)
12 Raymond, *Winslow Papers*, p 586, E. Winslow, Kingsclear, to Sir J. Wentworth, Halifax, June 1807.
13 Ibid.
14 Ibid, p 584 (in the hand of Edward Winslow). Raymond notes that this information was probably prepared for George Heriot.
15 Ibid, p 585.
16 NBM, Winslow Papers, vol XIII, fol 2, G.H., Quebec, to E. Winslow, Kingsclear, 14 Jan. 1811.
17 Ibid, fols 1v, 2, G.H., Quebec, to E. Winslow, Kingsclear, 4 Mar. 1811.
18 Ibid, vol x, fol 1v, G.H., Quebec, to E. Winslow, Kingsclear, 4 Mar. 1811.
19 Raymond, *Winslow Papers*, pp 584–6, G.H., Quebec, to E. Winslow, Kingsclear, 11 Mar. 1808.
20 NBM, Winslow Papers, vol x, fol 2, G.H., Quebec, to E. Winslow, Kingsclear, 13 June 1810.
21 'I have lately entertained an idea of printing ... [the sketches] with a description of the Country, as the whole of the British Colonies have now become interesting. If you could favor me from your observation and recollection with some account of the original number of settlers, of their names and characters, such as General Arnold, with anecdotes of the most eminent persons who have resided among you, such as, Gov. Carleton, General Hunter, Chief Justice Ludlow and his brother, &c., &c., &c., you will much oblige me, and should I be enabled to accomplish something of this kind, it might perhaps be of service to the Colony' (Raymond, *Winslow Papers*, p 681, G.H., Quebec, to E. Winslow, Kingsclear, 23 June 1813).

CHAPTER 7

1 PAC, R.G. 8, C-series, vol 284, fol 61, G.H., Quebec, to military secretary, Major Thornton, Quebec, 15 Feb. 1808.
2 However, Heriot had taken positive steps to improve the service. In Jan. 1810 he established a fortnightly post between Montreal and Kingston, and before the end of this year the service had been extended to York (*Quebec Gazette*, 6 Dec. 1810).

3 PRO, CO 42/144, fols 99–102, 'Memorial of the Committee of British Merchants interested in the Trade and Fisheries of His Majesty's North American Colonies,' 26 Jan. 1811.

4 Ibid, fols 56–56v, 57, G.H., Quebec, to joint postmaster general, London, 8 Oct. 1810; see also PRO, CO 42/142, fols 79–81v, J.H. Craig, Quebec, to Lord Liverpool, London, 19 Nov. 1810; see also below n 16.

5 PRO, CO 42/144, fols 97, 97v, G.H., Quebec, to F. Freeling, London, 8 Oct. 1810.

6 Ibid, fol 97.

7 Ibid, fols 94, 94v, 95, 97v.

8 Ibid, fol 95v.

9 Ibid.

10 Ibid, fol 96.

11 That Heriot did improve the service may have been partly because of the intervention of the lieutenant governor of Upper Canada in 1809. The latter directed William Allan, the provincial postmaster, to write to Heriot to inform him of the immediate need for improved service. In response to Allan's letter to him Heriot stated that he had not acted because the lieutenant governor had not notified him of any deficiencies in the service. Still, he was prepared to correct the existing inadequacies. He declared that as long as the cost of improving the service could be financed through revenue received, he had 'no objection to establishing a Post once a fortnight, between Montreal & Kingston, both in Summer & Winter' (PAC, R.G. 4, A1, S-series, vol 102, pp 32409–10, G.H., Quebec, to William Allan, York, 6 Mar. 1809.)

12 GPO, Post 44/2, fol 1, G.H., Quebec, to F. Freeling, London ('extract from a letter from Major Gen[l] Brock, President administering the government of Upper Canada, to an Officer in Quebec,' 13 Apr. 1812).

13 See PRO, CO 42/146, fols 62–6, G. Prevost, Quebec, to Lord Liverpool, London, 16 Mar. 1812. Prevost mentioned the plan submitted to Heriot (see below, n 15) in which he laid out a route for 'transportation of the Mails between Quebec & Halifax, as afford reasonable ground for believing that the evil complained of with regard to that establishment will soon be effectively remedied' (ibid, fols 62–62v.)

14 Ibid, fol 62v.

15 Ibid. A detailed draft of a letter from Prevost (presumably to Heriot) survives, dated 14 Dec. 1811 (PAC, R.G. 4, A1, S-series, vol 116, pp 36997–10), in which the former proposes an elaborate plan and schedule for improving the deliveries of post between Halifax and Quebec.

16 PRO, CO 42/146, fols 62v, G. Prevost, Quebec, to Lord Liverpool, London, 16 Mar. 1812. In 1810 Heriot had made similar proposals to improve the postal service: '[I have] finished a Report on that Subject consisting of about twelve pages, which I was enjoined to do by Their Lordships, The Postmaster General, that it might be laid before The Lords of the privy Council for Trade &c. I am not very sanguine in my Expectations, but still I think it will produce some good, especially for the province of Lower

Canada. The above communication is 'entre nous' (NBM, Winslow Papers, vol x, fols 1v, 2, G.H., Quebec, to E. Winslow, Kingsclear, 18 Oct. 1810).

17 PRO, CO 42/146, fols 65–65v, G. Prevost, Quebec, to Lord Liverpool, London, 16 Mar. 1812.

18 NBM, Winslow Papers, vol x, fol 2, G.H., Quebec, to E. Winslow, Kingsclear, 25 July 1810.

19 Ibid. During this visit Heriot sketched at least two views of the Jacques Cartier River, in which, perhaps, he represents himself and his friends. See 334, fols 22r, 24r; for his poem on the beauties of the river see also fol 21v. An English translation of the poem is given below:

TO THE JACQUES CARTIER RIVER
Confined between narrow crags, it
pours churning waters along its
rough stream and licks gloomy
caves with rushing billows.

Through rocks, through fields
it pursues its twisting course
with crashing din, and the shady
woods echo as it seeks the
St Lawrence with its foaming mouth.

20 NBM, Winslow Papers, vol x, fol 1, G.H., Quebec, to E. Winslow, Kingsclear, 18 Oct. 1810.

CHAPTER 8

1 NBM, Winslow Papers, vol x, fol 2, G.H., Quebec, to E. Winslow, Kingsclear, 11 Mar. 1808.

2 Ibid, vol XIII, fol 2, G.H., Quebec, to E. Winslow, Kingsclear, 3 July 1811.

3 Heriot considered the American troops to be 'mere rabble' because of their lack of adequate leadership: 'There is not in the States one officer,' he maintained, 'who is fit to command a regiment, nor have they any school for forming Officers. The case is very different now from what it was during the revolution, where the principal part of their Officers had been formed in the School of the British Army. But these are all dead or superannuated' (ibid, fol 1v, G.H., Quebec, to E. Winslow, Kingsclear, 13 Apr. 1813). Heriot was also persuaded that 'Americans are easily led, and duped by their Government. The firing off of a few proclamations on the part of the President [Madison], is sufficient to disperse an army. Their present Government has ludicrously been termed a *Logocracy* – a dynasty of words without meaning, and of schemes without energy' (ibid, fol 2, G.H., Quebec, to E. Winslow, Kingsclear, 23 July 1813). Although Winslow was American by birth, he had little sympathy for his former countrymen: '[they] have been accused of hypocrisy – duplicity and deceit – all of 'em – pretty names for Lying. From the time of their landing at Cape Cod in 1620 (when the Devil's Adjutant – General Cromwel[l] first began to parade & discipline

them) they were atrocious & ungrateful rebels – but *Jolly* has never been their characteristic. Yet a set of Orangotangs – could not have comitted such gross acts of stupidity & absurdity. Their Trade – their wealth and their comfort have all been sacrified on the altars of envy & spite' (ibid, vol x, fol 2, E. Winslow, Kingsclear, to G.H., Quebec, Sept. 1810 [draft]).

4 Raymond, *Winslow Papers*, p 671, G.H., Quebec, to E. Winslow, Kingsclear, 3 July 1811.

5 See PAC, R.G. 8, C-series, vol 284, fols 95–6, G.H., Quebec, to N. Freer, military secretary, Quebec, 1 Aug. 1812; ibid, fol 105, 20 May 1813; ibid, fol 152, D. Sutherland, Quebec, to N. Freer, Quebec, 24 Oct. 1814; ibid, vol 1218, fol 426, N. Freer, Quebec, to G.H., Quebec, 13 Nov. 1813; ibid, vol 1220, fol 343, N. Freer, Quebec, to G.H., Quebec, 27 Apr. 1813.

6 PAC, R.G. 8, C-series, vol 1220, fol 343, N. Freer, military secretary, Quebec, to G.H., Quebec, 27 Apr. 1813.

7 Ibid, vol 284, fol 156, G.H., Quebec, to joint postmaster general, London, 3 Feb. 1815; a view of Monkville (Monklands) near Montreal is dated 16 May 1813; see check-list 180.

8 GPO, Post 44/2, fols 1, 2, 2v, G.H., Quebec, to F. Freeling, London, 13 July 1813.

9 PAC, R.G. 8, C-series, vol 1219, fol 102, G. Prevost, Kingston, to Earl Bathurst, London, 12 Aug. 1813.

10 NBM, Winslow Papers, vol XIII, fol 2v, G.H., Quebec, to E. Winslow, Kingsclear, 13 Apr. 1813. The apparent failure of the British to prosecute the blockade, to which Heriot refers, was, in part at least, a matter of policy early in the war. The reason was that the New England merchants, knowing the likely losses they would suffer in any conflict, opposed it; as this agreed with British thinking, the British navy did not immediately put on the pressure.

11 Ibid, fol 2, G.H., Quebec, to E. Winslow, Kingsclear, 23 July 1813.

12 PAC, R.G. 8, C-series, vol 680, fols 362–3, G.H., Quebec, probably to military secretary, Quebec, Oct. [1814].

13 Ibid, fol 364.

14 Ibid.

15 Ibid. As a consequence of his disgraceful military conduct Prevost was recalled to England to face a court-martial; but he died before it began.

16 PAC, R.G. 8, C-series, vol 405, fol 191, 'Extract of a Report from the Honourable Board of Ordnance,' 20 July 1805.

17 He was appointed to this position on 12 Mar. 1804 (ibid, vol 744, fol 188).

18 Ibid, vol 387, fol 74, G. Glasgow, Quebec, to Lieutenant Colonel E. Brenton, Quebec, 19 June 1813.

19 Ibid, fol 77, G.H., Quebec, to Lieutenant Colonel E. Brenton, Quebec, 21 June 1813.

20 Ibid, vol 284, fol 161, G.H., Quebec, to joint postmaster general, London, 3 Feb. 1815.

21 *Quebec Gazette*, 23 Oct. 1815.

22 Post Office personnel were often enlisted to transmit and collect intelligence. See Ellis, *The Post Office in the Eighteenth Century*, pp 60–77.

23 PAC, R.G. 8, C-series, vol 680, fol 366, G.H., Quebec, probably to military secretary, Quebec, Aug. [1815].
24 Ibid, fol 367.
25 New York Historical Society, American Sketch-Book I (see check-list 335, fol 34v).
26 NBM, Winslow Papers, vol XIII, fol 2, G.H., Quebec, to E. Winslow, Kingsclear, 14 Jan. 1811.
27 Ibid. Similar comments have been attributed to the Duke of Gloucester who, when he met the celebrated historian, remarked, 'Another damned thick, square book! Always scribble, scribble, scribble! Eh! Mr Gibbon?'

CHAPTER 9

1 At least as early as 1810 Heriot was complaining of the rising cost of living in Quebec: 'I believe I formerly observed to you that provisions had become very scarce in Quebec and Montreal, and that the Articles of life had mounted up to a price that is almost incredible, when compared with that of former times' (NBM, Winslow Papers, vol X, fols 1v–2, G.H., Quebec, to E. Winslow, Kingsclear, 13 June 1810). By the next year Heriot observed: 'this country has become almost as extravagant as England and the *habitants* are the only people who enrich themselves; as all the silver passes ultimately into their coffers, where it will be hidden for years from the face of day. This causes a great scarcity of money as there is no possibility, under our government, [of] again drawing the coin from its dark recesses (NBM, Winslow Papers, vol XIII, fol 3. G.H., Quebec, to E. Winslow, Kingsclear, 4 Mar. 1811).
2 GPO, Post 44/2, fols 1–2v, G. Drummond, Kingston, to Earl Bathurst, London, 25 Mar. 1815.
3 When Heriot returned to Quebec in August, Drummond renewed his demands for an improved postal service (PAC, R.G. 8, C-series, vol 284, fols 170–1, G.H., Quebec, to Major Foster, military secretary, Quebec, 28 Aug. 1815). At the end of the first week of September Drummond, through his military secretary, wrote to Heriot of the urgent need for better communication between Montreal and Kingston and York. On the Montreal-to-Kingston route Heriot had already established a fortnightly post and was planning a more frequent, weekly service. Heriot believed that the revenue from such a service could pay for itself. However, Drummond was not satisfied with Heriot's proposal; he insisted that there should be a twice-weekly service between these points (ibid, fol 172, G.H., Quebec, to Major Foster, Quebec, 9 Sept. 1815).
4 PRO, CO 42/163, fols 170–170v, Major R. Loring, military secretary, Quebec, to G.H., Quebec, 23 Oct. 1815.
5 Ibid, fols 170v–171.
6 Ibid, fols 172–173v, G.H., Quebec, to Major R. Loring, Quebec, 24 Oct. 1815.
7 Ibid, fol 172.
8 Ibid, fol 174, Major R. Loring, Quebec, to G.H., Quebec, 25 Oct. 1815.

9 Ibid.

10 Ibid, fol 176v, G.H., Quebec, to Major R. Loring, Quebec, 27 Oct. 1815; see Smith, *History of the Post Office*, p 111; GPO, Post 44/2, fols 1, 1v, G.H., Quebec, to provincial postmaster W. Allan, York, 19 Mar. 1812.

11 Ibid, fol 224v, G. Drummond, Quebec, to Earl Bathurst, London, 10 Dec. 1815.

12 Ibid, fol 175, Major R. Loring, Quebec, to G.H., Quebec, 25 Oct. 1815.

13 Ibid, fols 230–230v, G.H., Quebec, to Major R. Loring, Quebec, 8 Dec. 1815.

14 *Quebec Gazette*, 26 Oct. 1815.

15 'As I have found it necessary to postpone my voyage to England until Spring, Mr Lindsay will not take charge of the Office until my departure' (PAC, R.G. 8, C-series, vol 284, fol 183, G.H., Quebec, to Major Foster, Quebec, 15 Nov. 1815). Drummond wrote to Earl Bathurst: 'To my surprise ... [in November] Mr Heriot ... relinquished the idea ... of proceeding to England' (PRO, CO 42/163, fols 224v–225, 10 Dec. 1815).

16 GPO, Post 44/2, fol 1, D. Sutherland, Montreal, to Baron F. de Rottenburg, Quebec, 12 Jan. 1816: '[I] received a letter from Mr Heriot to inform me of his intention of resigning his situation.' Heriot probably submitted his resignation in Jan., though it did not reach London for some time. In consequence of Heriot's 'disrespectful conduct,' the joint postmaster general issued a severe reprimand (PRO, CO 43/23, fols 212, 212v, Earl Bathurst, London, to G. Drummond, Quebec, 10 Feb. 1816).

17 GPO, Post 41/2, fol 456, F. Freeling, London, to joint postmaster general, London, 30 Mar. 1816.

18 Ibid. The joint postmaster general were not inclined to deter Heriot from his intended course of action: 'Considering all the Circumstances of the Case, Mr Heriots temper ye footing upon which he is with the Governor &c. I think that the Service will suffer by his remaining & that his Claims to consideration will not be affected by accepting his Resignation & it may be stated to him that it is not intended by accepting his Resignation to preclude him from stating every thing he may think necessary for his Credit or Interest' (ibid, fol 455). Whether Heriot received a sum of money cannot be determined, but it seems likely that he did. He was reimbursed for travel expenditures (£423.19.0) incurred during his tenure as deputy postmaster general (ibid). Although he resigned from the Post Office, according to the Ordnance Office Register Heriot did not give up his position on the Board of Ordnance – he was dismissed from it in 1817 (PRO, WO 54/218, fol 29).

CHAPTER 10

1 At his death Heriot held mortgages on several London properties including a dwelling in Gloucester Place near Portman Square. He also possessed a considerable number of bank annuities (PRO, prob. 11, 1915, sec. 512 [13]).

2 Heriot, *A Picturesque Tour ... through the Pyrenean Mountains*, 'Preface.'

3 Heriot, *A Picturesque Tour*, p 5.
4 Ibid, p 7.
5 Ibid, p 31.
6 There exists at least one large panoramic view of Madrid (watercolour with etched outline), which is probably based on sketches made on this tour (check-list 358).
7 Two parts of this work were published, in 1824. Heriot had originally proposed eight parts, each of which was to contain six prints after his watercolours. Possibly the appearance of Joseph Hardy's *A Picturesque and Descriptive Tour in the Mountains of the High Pyrenees*, published in London in 1825 and illustrated with twenty-four coloured plates, contributed to Heriot's decision to abandon the project.
8 Detroit Public Library, Burton Historical Collection, G.H., London, to W. Hands, Sandwich, 2 Apr. 1822.

CHAPTER 11

1 Heriot was also shocked to learn that John's poor business sense had resulted in 'six or seven thousand pounds of bad debts' (G.H., London, to R. Heriot, Charleston, 22 Dec. 1834; this letter is in a private collection).
2 Ibid. That many were North American views seems to be borne out by references made to drawings owned by his family's American descendants, one of whom noted that she possessed 'sketches of his Canadian scenery Falls of Montmorenci Views of St Lawrence etc.' (excerpt from a letter written by Emma Heriot to Julia Sherwood, n.d., owned by Mrs L.H. Sternau). The watercolour *Chambly Castle* (check-list 182) seems to have belonged to this group of North American views.
3 Ibid.
4 I am grateful to Peter Fraser who kindly pointed out specific similarities between the work of Heriot and that of Pocock.
5 R. Heriot, Charleston, to G. Heriot, London, 23 Feb. 1839; the letter is in the possession of Mrs L.H. Sternau.
6 Death certificate, General Register Office, Somerset House, London, N. 445. DX 193243; date of death 22 July 1839; see also, *the Gentleman's Magazine*, XII (1839), 211.
7 See Spendlove, *The Face of Early Canada*, p 26.
8 Heriot, *A Descriptive Poem*, p 29.
9 William Wycherley, 'For Solitude and Retirement against the Publick, Active Life,' from *The Complete Works of William Wycherley*, ed M. Summers, 4 vols (London 1924), IV, 205–13.

APPENDIX

1 Material for this appendix derives largely from typescript histories of the family which have been deposited with the Library of Congress, Washington, DC. See 'Selective Bibliography.'
2 The word 'heriot' seems to have described the tribute that the lord of the

manor was to receive from a tenant after the latter's death. The lord provided his tenant, either as a gift or as a loan, with arms and a horse, which were to be used by him for military service. On the death of the tenant the lord claimed the equipment. By the tenth century land rather than equipment was given. It is perhaps for this reason that 'heriot' is a term that was employed to describe places or lands. A parish and river southeast of Edinburgh possess the name 'Heriot' and there is a stream in the parish of Cockburnspath, Berwickshire, with that name.

3 See chapter 3.

4 The coat of arms includes the motto: FORTEM POSE ANIMUM.

5 Marjory was the daughter of John Heriot (1701–78) and Marjory Johnson (dates unknown). Marjory, the daughter, had a brother, Roger (born in 1748; date of death unknown), who became a surgeon in the British Army, 13th Foot Regiment. During the period of his services he was stationed on the island of Jersey, and while there he married Anne Nugent (daughter of Major Walter Nugent, a member of an old Irish family). There were five sons from this marriage, three of whom entered the military or naval services. One of these, the third son, was Frederick George Heriot, who was born on Jersey in 1786. It was he whom George Heriot, the subject of this study, came to know quite well at Quebec (see chapter 6).

Selective Bibliography

MANUSCRIPT SOURCES

Detroit Public Library (Burton Historical Collection)
Edinburgh University (Matriculation Rolls)
General Post Office, London (abbreviated throughout as GPO)
General Register Office, Somerset House, London
Library of Congress, Washington, DC. Possesses typescript histories of the Heriot family: Caldwell Woodruff's 'Family of Heriot of Castlemains, Dirleton, Haddington, Scotland' (Baltimore 1918). A later edition of this work in the Library of Congress is entitled 'Heriots of Scotland and South Carolina' (Linthicum Heights, Maryland 1939); it includes material from another work by the same author: 'Roger Heriot of South Carolina and his descendants with a record of the Heriots of Ladykirk and Shiels, Berwickshire, Scotland' (Linthicum Heights, Maryland 1937), also in the Library of Congress. The account which it contains on the Scottish Heriots was prepared for Woodruff by J.C.A. Heriot of Montreal. A further typescript history by Odille Dodge Stewart, 'Heriot Genealogy: Additional Manuscript Containing the Roger Heriot Branch' (1931), also deposited in the Library of Congress, depends heavily on Woodruff's earliest work.
National Postal Museum, Ottawa
New Brunswick Museum, Saint John (abbreviated throughout as NBM), Winslow Papers
Public Archives of Canada, Ottawa (abbreviated in text and notes as PAC)
Public Record Office, London (abbreviated throughout as PRO)
Scottish Record Office, Register House, Edinburgh

PRINTED MATERIAL

Allodi, Mary. *Canadian Watercolours and Drawings in the Royal Ontario Museum*. Toronto 1974

– 'Printmaking in Canada: The Earliest Views and Portraits.' Royal Ontario Museum, exhibition catalogue. Toronto 1980

Anonymous. Review of George Heriot's *Travels through the Canadas* (1807), in the *Edinburgh Review* (April 1808), 212–25

Anonymous. Some analysis of, but largely excerpts from, George Heriot's *Travels through the Canadas* (1807), in *A Collection of Modern and Contemporary Voyages and Travels*, 10 volumes. London: R. Phillips 1805–9. Volume 7

Barbier, Carl Paul. *William Gilpin, His Drawings, Teaching and Theory of the Picturesque*. Oxford: Clarendon Press 1963

Brauer, George C. *The Education of a Gentleman: Theories of Gentlemanly Education in England, 1660–1775*. New York: Bookman Associates 1959

Bruchési, Jean. 'George Heriot, peintre, historien, et maître de poste,' *Les Cahiers des Dix*, 10 (1945), 191–206. Also appears in *Evocations*. Montreal: Les Editions Lumen 1947). Pages 56–74

Burke, Edmund. *A Philosophical Enquiry into the Origins of our Ideas of the Sublime and Beautiful*. Edited by J.T. Boulton. London: Routledge and Kegan Paul 1958

Clark, A.M. *Sir Walter Scott: The Formative Years*. Edinburgh/London: Blackwood 1969

Cooper, Anthony Ashley, third Earl of Shaftesbury. *Characteristicks of Men, Manners, Opinions, Times* ... 6th edition. 3 volumes. London: James Purser 1737

Ellis, Kenneth. *The Post Office in the Eighteenth Century: A Study in Administrative History*. London: Oxford University Press 1958

Fenety, George E. *Life and Times of the Honorable Joseph Howe*. Saint John, New Brunswick 1896

Finley, Gerald. 'The Genesis of Turner's "Landscape Sublime,"' *Zeitschrift für Kunstgeschichte*, 12 (1979), 141–65

– 'George Heriot: Painter of the Canadas.' Agnes Etherington Art Centre, exhibition catalogue. Kingston 1978

– *George Heriot, 1759–1839*. Edited by Dennis Reid. Canadian Artists Series. National Gallery of Canada 1979

Gilpin, William. *Observations on the River Wye, and Several Parts of South Wales, & c. relative chiefly to Picturesque Beauty* ... London: R. Blamire 1782

– *Observations relative chiefly to Picturesque Beauty, made in the Year 1772, On Several Parts of England; particularly the Mountains, and Lakes of Cumberland and Westmoreland* ... 2 volumes. London 1786

– *Observations relative to Picturesque Beauty, Made in the Year 1776, on Several Parts of Great Britain; particularly the High-Lands of Scotland*. 2 volumes. London: R. Blamire 1789

– *Remarks on Forest Scenery and other Woodland Views (relative chiefly to Picturesque Beauty), illustrated by the Scenes of New Forest in Hampshire* ... 2 volumes; London: R. Blamire 1791

– *Three Essays: on Picturesque Beauty; on Picturesque Travel; and on Sketching Landscape, to which is added a poem, On Landscape Painting* ... London 1792

Graves, Algernon. *The Royal Academy of Arts: A Complete Dictionary of Contributors and Their Work from Its Foundation in 1769 to 1904*. New York: B. Franklin 1972. Reprint of the 1905–6 edition

Harper, J. Russell. 'European Tradition and Pioneer Vernacular: Early Canadian Painting Contrast,' *Canadian Collector*, 9:1 (January–February 1974)

Heriot, George. *A Descriptive Poem, written in the West Indies, 1781, Humbly inscribed to the Royal Society*. London: J. Dodsley 1781

– *The History of Canada from its first discovery*. Volume 1. London: Longman and Rees 1804

– *A Picturesque Tour made in the years 1817 and 1820, through the Pyrenean Mountains, Auvergne, The Departments of the High and Low Alps and in Part of Spain*. 2 parts. London: R. Ackermann 1824

– *Travels through the Canadas, containing a description of the picturesque scenery on some of the rivers and lakes; with an account of the productions, commerce and inhabitants of those provinces. To which is subjoined a comparative view of the manners and customs of several of the Indian nations of North and South America*. London: Richard Phillips 1807. Illustrated with a folding map and twenty-seven plates after watercolours by Heriot

– *Travels through the Canadas* ... Philadelphia 1813. A reprint of the first part of the 1807 edition

– *Travels through the Canadas* ... Edmonton: M.G. Hurtig 1971. A reprint of the 1807 edition with an introduction by J.J. Talman

Heriot, J.C.A. 'George Heriot, Author-Artist,' *The Canadian Antiquarian and Numismatic Journal*, 7 (July 1910), 101–5. Also in *Americana*, 5 (September–October 1910), 888–92

Hogg, O.F.G. *The Royal Arsenal: Its Background, Origin and Subsequent History*. 2 volumes. London: Oxford University Press 1963

Horseman, Reginald. *The War of 1812*. New York: Alfred A. Knopf 1969

Hussey, Christopher. *The Picturesque: Studies in a Point of View*. London/New York: Putnam 1927

Irwin, D. and F. *Scottish Painters at Home and Abroad, 1700–1900*. London: Faber 1975

Jouvancourt, Hughes de. *George Heriot (1766–1844)*. Montreal. Editions la Frégate 1973

Oppé, A.P., *The Drawings of Paul and Thomas Sandby in the Collection of His Majesty the King at Windsor Castle. Oxford/London: Phaidon 1947*

Perkins, Bradford. *Prologue to War – England and the United States 1805–1812*. Berkeley/Los Angeles: University of California Press 1961

Raymond, William O. *Winslow Papers,* A.D. *1776–1826. Printed under the Auspices of the New Brunswick Historical Society*. Edited by W.O. Raymond. Saint John, New Brunswick: Sun Printing Company 1901

Reynolds, Sir Joshua. *Discourses on Art*. Edited by Robert R. Wark. San Marino, California: Huntington Library 1959

Richardson, Jonathan. 'The Theory of Painting,' in *The Works of Jonathan Richardson*. London: White and Son 1792

Roestvig, M.S. *The Happy Man: Studies in the Metamorphosis of a Classical Ideal.* Oslo Studies in English, number 2. 2 volumes. Bergen: University of Oslo 1962–71

Röthlisberger, Marcel. *Claude Lorrain.* Yale Publications in the History of Art, number 13. 2 volumes. New Haven: Yale University Press 1961

Rye, William Brenchley. *England as seen by Foreigners in the Days of Elizabeth and James the First. Comprising Translations of the Journals of the two Dukes of Wirtemberg in 1592 and 1610; both illustrative of Shakespeare.* London: John Russell Smith 1865

Sanson, Joseph. *Travels in Lower Canada.* London 1820

Smith, William. *The History of the Post Office in British North America 1639–1870.* Cambridge: Cambridge University Press 1920

Spendlove, F. St George. *The Face of Early Canada: Pictures of Canada Which Have Helped to Make History.* Toronto: Ryerson Press 1958

Sprat, Thomas, Bishop of Rochester. *History of the Royal Society of London for the improving of natural knowledge by Tho. Sprat ...* 4th edition. London 1734

Stanhope, Philip Dormer, fourth Earl of Chesterfield. *Letters to his Son.* Edited by Oliver H. Leigh. 2 volumes. New York: Tudor Publishing Co. 1937

Steven, William. *The History of the High School of Edinburgh.* Edinburgh 1849

Thornbury, Walter. *Old and New London: A Narrative of its History.* 6 volumes. London n.d.

Waller, Edmund. *Poems 1645.* London: Scolar Press 1971. Reprint

Waterhouse, Ellis K. *Gainsborough.* 2nd edition. London: Spring Books 1966

Whinney, M., and O. Millar. *English Art: 1625–1714.* Edited by T.R. Boase. Oxford History of Art, number 8. Oxford: Clarendon Press 1957

Wrong, George M. *A Canadian Manor and Its Seigneurs: The Story of a Hundred Years, 1761–1861.* Toronto: Macmillan of Canada 1908

Wycherley, William. *The Complete Works of William Wycherley.* Edited by Montague Summers. 4 volumes. London: Nonesuch Press 1924

Check-List of the Works of George Heriot

This is a check-list of the oil paintings, watercolours, sketch-books, and prints by George Heriot, and of plates based on his works, which I have examined, or seen photographs of, or found references to during my researches for this book. Works included are mainly, though not entirely, those that I have examined, or of which I have seen photographs. I wish to thank the owners and the custodians of works by Heriot who kindly sent me measurements of, and information concerning inscriptions on, the drawings, paintings, and prints that I have not been able to examine. To this check-list I have added a few watercolours which I have not examined and of which I have not seen reproductions; this is because the unillustrated references to them which I have read in sales catalogues contain inscriptions which persuade me that the works are by Heriot. In one or two instances it seems likely that a drawing I have not examined, and of which I have not seen photographs, could appear more than once in the check-list. This situation would exist if the published sales-catalogue measurements and inscriptions of a particular drawing, sold at different auction sales, happened to differ. Still, as Heriot sometimes made a number of drawings of the same location at the same time, all possessing similar inscriptions, it is possible that these separate sales-catalogue entries describe different drawings. Because an element of doubt exists in these cases, and because I have encountered relatively few problems of this kind, I have decided to consider these different auction-catalogue entries as describing different drawings.

I have excluded from this list watercolours which I have seen and which, while possessing some similarities in style, do differ fundamentally from authenticated examples of Heriot's works; as there are many years of his artistic output for which we have few or no firmly dated examples of his work, we must wait until these gaps are filled before the authenticity of these watercolours can be reassessed. It is reasonable to assume that watercolours by Heriot are bound to appear on the market, thus filling the existing gaps, for, on the basis of our present knowledge of his considerable output, we can calculate that his œuvre must include hundreds of watercolours which have not yet come to light.

Of the watercolours, oil paintings, and prints which we know, documentation of their histories is vexingly limited. One compelling reason for this is that until relatively recently Heriot's art has not been widely admired. Even Heriot himself did not place a particularly high value on his art, and he made no mention of it in his will. Still, from inscriptions on the backs of his watercolours and paintings, and from suggestions and statements made in his own correspondence and in that of his acquaintances and his descendants, we can learn something of the histories of his work. For example, we can infer from this material that Heriot sometimes gave away his drawings to his acquaintances and friends. Further, we can establish that in Britain, in 1834 (when he was seventy-five), Heriot decided to distribute at least some of his art works to his family. He assembled a watercolour collection (which seems to have consisted mainly of his North American landscapes) and sent it to the son of his brother Roger, in Charleston, South Carolina. A number of drawings in this collection were of places in Canada; almost certainly one was a view of Fort Chambly in Lower Canada which he had sketched in 1815 (**182**) a year before he left Canada to return to Britain for the last time.

However, Heriot probably left the bulk of his artistic estate to his family in Britain. Some of it went to his brother John's family. John's grandson, John Charles Alison Heriot, inherited some of the oil paintings and watercolours (he is said to have had five hundred sketches, but this estimate may include the contents of two inherited sketch-books). And another descendant, the Reverend C.A. Mackonochie, possessed two volumes of Heriot's watercolours which he sold at auction on 21 July 1943 (Sotheby, London). Each volume comprised one of the two lots of watercolours by Heriot in the sale. The first lot contained watercolour views of Switzerland, Austria, Spain, and France (several of these were dated 1817–20); this lot was sold to the Bournemouth dealer Alister Mathew; see also **200**. The second lot of drawings contained views in Scotland, Wales, and Cornwall (dating from 1798 onwards), views in Canada and the West Indies, and scenes of North American Indian ceremonies. (The watercolours of this lot were purchased by B. Barnett.)

Still, it has been relatively difficult to trace Heriot's watercolours and paintings through auction and exhibition sales catalogues because, as I have noted, until recently little interest has been shown in his art. He has often been considered merely a topographical artist and thus his work has been thought to be of relatively minor artistic importance. For this reason, until the 1950s Heriot's art did not frequently appear in auction and exhibition sales catalogues; when it did, it was inadequately described, and often no former ownership was given. However, in recent years this situation has changed: the widening search for works of art to satisfy a clamorous art market, fuelled by the recent surge of Canadian nationalism and the consequent search for this country's cultural roots, has brought about Heriot's rediscovery. There is yet another and equally important reason why Heriot's work has been difficult to trace through the sales catalogues. Because Heriot did not sign many works and because little has been known about his art (and therefore about its wide stylistic diversity), many of his works have passed unattributed, or incorrectly attributed, through the auctioneers' and dealers' hands.

This check-list of oil paintings, watercolours, and prints is chronologically arranged. Establishing the chronology of Heriot's work has not, however, been an easy task. For example, only three oil paintings (and these unsigned and undated) can at present be attributed to Heriot. Fortunately at the beginning of this century J.C.A. Heriot, the descendant of the artist mentioned above, assigned dates to two of the three pictures, presumably having determined them on the basis of external evidence that has since disappeared. Because these dates provide at least a starting-point, one can tentatively assign an approximate date to the third painting.

The dating of Heriot's watercolours is no easier, nor can it be done with greater precision, even though he inscribed many of them with dates. The difficulties that confront the cataloguer are fourfold: first, Heriot sometimes revived earlier drawing styles or practised more than one style concurrently. Second, from about the middle of the first decade of the nineteenth century the distinction between his original, on-the-spot sketches and the finished watercolours made from them becomes, in some instances, difficult to establish, not only because the sketches appear to be more composed than they were earlier, but because they are more 'finished' (sometimes they were completed a considerable time after they were drawn on the spot). Furthermore, when Heriot painted watercolours from his sketches, these watercolours are often little larger in size than the on-the-spot studies from which they were developed. The third difficulty facing the cataloguer of the watercolours is that on many of them Heriot inscribed dates which do not establish when he painted them, for if he copied an earlier watercolour, or developed a new composition from it, he sometimes transcribed the date that was given on the original. Also since his memory was not always reliable, he occasionally inscribed inaccurate dates on watercolours that he had painted years before. Therefore the date given to a watercolour in this check-list has sometimes been determined by Heriot's apparent stylistic development rather than by the date that he actually inscribed on it. A fourth vexing difficulty, related to the first three, has been created by the absence of securely dated watercolours from a number of important periods of Heriot's artistic career – a situation which compounds the problems created by his stylistic idiosyncracies and unreliable inscriptions. As a result of finding, or being presented with, fresh evidence I have changed my mind about the dating of a number of watercolours which were included in the exhibition 'George Heriot: Painter of the Canadas' (1978) and which appear in my published essay *George Heriot* (1979).

Heriot's prints have created fewer difficulties that have his watercolours, partly because there are fewer of them. I have included in this part of the check-list only prints which Heriot etched himself; thus the two large plates published for him in England, *View of the City of Quebec, taken from the Rocks of Point Levi* and *View of the City of Quebec, taken from the North Banks of the Saint Charles*, the plates in *Travels through the Canadas* and *A Picturesque Tour ... through the Pyrenean Mountains*, and the impressions of four additional plates have been listed with the image size of the plates and the engravers' names in the section on plates at the end of the check-list.

The entries in the check-list are normally brief and contain only the most essential information. In a number of cases the names of private collectors have not been given. Nor have I noted every publication in which a work has been reproduced; often I have included only the most recent or most accessible works. Where possible I have used abbreviations:

autogr.	autograph
exh	exhibition
ill.	illustrated
inscr.	inscribed *or* inscription
lit	literature
r	recto
sign.	signed *or* signature
v	verso

In referring to the placing of an inscription on a work (inscriptions on watercolours and prints are in ink unless otherwise specified) the following abbreviations are used:

l.c.	lower centre
l.l.	lower left
l.r.	lower right
u.c.	upper centre
u.l.	upper left
u.r.	upper right

The three catalogues of Heriot's works most frequently used in the check-list are referred to in abbreviated form:

ROM cat.	Mary Allodi, *Canadian Watercolours and Drawings in the Royal Ontario Museum* (Toronto 1974)
G.H. cat.	Gerald Finley, 'George Heriot: Painter of the Canadas,' Agnes Etherington Art Centre, Queen's University, Kingston 1978
G. Heriot	Gerald Finley, *George Heriot (1759–1839)*, ed Dennis Reid, Canadian Artists Series (Ottawa: National Gallery of Canada 1979)

OIL PAINTINGS

*1 *The North West Part of the City of Quebec taken from the St Charles River*, c 1804–c 1810. Figure 16
Oil on canvas, 737 × 1105 mm.
Old Print Shop, New York; Royal Ontario Museum, Toronto, 1955, 955.227
Exh: G.H. cat. 92 (ill.)
Lit: J. Russell Harper, *Painting in Canada: A History* (Toronto 1966), p. 49 (40). The attribution of this picture to Heriot was first suggested by Mary Allodi. The subject-matter can be associated with that of pre-1800 watercolours. For example, the theme is that found in *View of Quebec taken from the*

Pont near Point Levi of 1798 (**53**), but the small dog standing on its hind legs was taken from *La Danse Ronde*, c 1799 (**65**). In addition, this painting embodies certain stylistic elements that occur in the unusual watercolour *An Encounter, Canada*, which has been tentatively dated c 1799 (**64**). Yet the oil painting cannot have been finished before 1804, since the Anglican cathedral, in the right background, was not completed until that year.

2 *Loch Dochart, Perthshire*, c 1811
Oil on canvas, 637 × 820 mm. V: inscr. u.l. in hand of J.C.A. Heriot: *Loch Dockhart, Perthshire, Scotland painted in 1811 by George Heriot Deputy Postmaster General of British North America from 1799 to 1816*
J.C.A. Heriot, Esq.; W.L. Day, Esq.; Sotheby (Toronto), 5–7 Nov. 1979 (294); Galerie Bernard Desroches, Montreal
This and the painting of **3** seem to have been developed from watercolour sketches made on Heriot's 1806 visit to Scotland, when the artist visited Perthshire (see **138**). It is impossible to be certain about the dating of these pictures, since no dated oil painting has yet come to light. However, there is no reason at this time to question the dates assigned to these paintings by J.C.A. Heriot, who may have possessed external evidence, since lost, to support his dating. Certainly George Heriot had been painting in oil at least as early as 1810 (NBM, Winslow Papers, vol x, fol 2r, G. Heriot, Quebec, to E. Winslow, Kingsclear, 25 July 1810). This picture and that of **3** have been over-cleaned in parts, and these parts have been ineptly repainted by an unknown hand.

***3** *View of Taymouth or Kenmore Bridge, Perthshire*, c 1812. Figure 59
Oil on canvas, 640 × 822 mm. V: inscr. u.l. in hand of J.C.A. Heriot: *View of Thymouth or Kenmore Bridge Perthshire, Scotland painted in 1812 by George Heriot Deputy Postmaster General of British North America from 1799 to 1816 J.C.A. Heriot, Montreal, March, 1910*
J.C.A. Heriot, Esq.; W.L. Day, Esq.; Sotheby (Toronto), 5–7 Nov. 1979 (293); Galerie Bernard Desroches, Montreal
See **2**.

WATERCOLOURS

***4** *White River – S^t. Mary's – Jamaica*, c 1780. Figure 1
Pen, ink, and watercolour, 387 × 324 mm. R: inscr. l.l as title
Dudley Snelgrove, Esq.
Exh: G.H. cat. 20

***5** *Greenwich with tower of the Hospital*, c 1783. Figure 4
Pen, ink, and watercolour, 125 × 279 mm.
Colnaghi, London; Ingram family collection, 1952
Exh: G.H. cat. 21
Purchased as by J. Glover but correctly attributed to Heriot by Mr M.W. Ingram

***6** *Greenwich with Hospital towers*, c 1783. Figure 5
Pen, ink, and watercolour, laid down, 125 × 275 mm.

Christopher Powney, London; Ingram family collection, 1960
Exh: G.H. cat. 22
Purchased as by 'unattributed English c 1820'; correctly attributed to Heriot by Mr M.W. Ingram

***7** *View of the Town of Greenwich*, c 1785. Figure 6
Pen, ink, and coloured washes, 108 × 521 mm. R: autogr. inscr. u.c.: *Greenwich. 178[?]*; v: another landscape study
Sir Bruce Ingram: Sotheby (London), 17 Feb. 1965 (628); Collection John H. Appleby, Esq., Jersey
Exh: G.H. cat. 23 (ill.)
Two leaves of a sketch-book glued together; see **272**.

8 *Greenwich Park*, c 1786
Pen, ink, and watercolour, 95 × 192 mm. V: inscr. *c1795* in a modern hand
L.G. Duke, Esq.; Sir Bruce Ingram; Sotheby (London), 9 Dec. 1964 (272); anonymous donor; Museum of Art, Rhode Island School of Design, Providence, 1972, 72.171.19
Exh: Colnaghi, *Watercolour Drawings of Three Centuries* (Ingram Collection), Feb. 1956 (75); G.H. cat. 24
Lit: *G. Heriot*, p 25 (ill.)
Collector's mark (Sir Bruce Ingram, Lugt. Suppl. 1405a)

***9** *Greenwich Park and the River*, c 1786. Figure 7
Pen, ink, and watercolour, 91 × 192 mm.
L.G. Duke, Esq.; Sir Bruce Ingram; N.A.C.F.; Ashmolean Museum, Oxford, 1963
Exh: Colnaghi, *Watercolour Drawings of Three Centuries* (Ingram Collection), Feb. 1956 (71); Ashmolean Museum, *English Drawings purchased from the Collection of the Late Sir Bruce Ingram*, 1963 (41); G.H. cat. 25

10 *Conduit Vale Blackheath*, c 1787
Pen, ink, and watercolour, 111 × 254 mm. R: autogr. inscr. u.r. as title
Sir Bruce Ingram; present whereabouts unknown
Lit: Iolo Williams, *Early English Watercolours* (London 1952), pp 59, 60 (105)
See **332**.

***11** *Path through a forest*, c 1788. Figure 10
Pen, black ink with grey wash, and pencil, 276 × 430 mm. R: sign. l.l: *G. Heriot.* v: inscr. in pencil: *H.R.D.*
Jacoby, 16 Dec. 1970 (1820); Sotheby (Toronto), 14 June 1972 (171); University of Guelph, 72.15
Exh: G.H. cat. 26 (ill.)
Lit: *G. Heriot*, p 26 (ill.)

12 *Wycombe [?Wickham] Church &c 1788*, 1788
Pen, ink, and watercolour, 114 × 254 mm. R: autogr. inscr. l.c. as title
J.C.A. Heriot, Esq.; McCord Museum, McGill University, Montreal, 1928, M 6354
This watercolour appears to be fol 14v, **333**.

13 *View on the road descending from [L ... ?] Heath 1788*, 1788
Pen, ink, and watercolour, laid down, 113 × 254 mm. R: autogr. inscr. l.c. as title

J.C.A. Heriot, Esq.; McCord Museum, McGill University, Montreal, 1928, M 671
Exh: G.H. cat. 28 (ill.)
This watercolour appears to be fol 15v, **333**.

14 *Unidentified view with river and cliffs*, c 1792
Watercolour, 254 × 355 mm.
Private collection
Later reworking of foreground by an unknown hand

***15** *West View of Chateau Riché [Château Richer]*, c 1792. Figure 18
Watercolour, graphite, brown ink, 214 × 324 mm. R: autogr. inscr. l.c. mount as title; sign. l.r. mount: *GH*.
Maggs Bros., London; Grand Central Galleries, New York; The W.H. Coverdale Collection of Canadiana; Manoir Richelieu; National Gallery of Canada, Ottawa, 1970, 16674
Lit: Maggs Bros. cat. 514 (1929), 16 (ill.); Grand Central Galleries, *Canadiana* (1942), (60); G.H. cat. 54

16 *St Lawrence River (?)*, c 1792
Watercolour over pencil, laid down, 131 × 188 mm. R: inscr. l.c. margin of mount in later hand: *ST Lawrence 1791*
Public Archives of Canada (at this time lacking accession number)
Correctly attributed to Heriot by J. Burant, Chief, Collections Management Section, Picture Division, Public Archives of Canada. The vessel in the left foreground is that found in **169** – this was noted by Mr Burant. The foreground of this drawing was reworked by the artist in about 1809. The style and subject-matter of the middle- and background portions of the watercolour are reminiscent of Heriot's watercolour sketches made in 1787 on the south coast of England (see, for instance, **333**, fols 17v–18r).

***17** *City of Quebec from Point Levi [Pointe Lévis]*, c 1792. Figure 17
Watercolour, brown ink, 214 × 324 mm. R: sign. l.r. mount: *GH*.; autogr. inscr. l.c. mount as title
The W.H. Coverdale Collection of Canadiana; Manoir Richelieu; National Gallery of Canada, Ottawa, 1970, 16677
Exh: G.H. cat. 55
Heriot prepared an etched view of Quebec based on this watercolour; see **357**.

18 *Quebec from Point Levis*, c 1792 (?)
Watercolour over graphite, 385 × 515 mm.
National Gallery of Canada, Ottawa, 1982; not yet accessioned
Probably based on the design of **17**; it is possible that this drawing was executed as late as 1793 or 1794.

19 *Quebec from Point Levi [Pointe Lévis]. S.E. View. 1793.*, 1793
Watercolour, 113 × 243 mm. R: autogr. inscr. l.c. as title; v: 20
Public Archives of Canada, Ottawa, 1922?, 1-33
Lit: *G. Heriot*, p 28 (ill.)

20 *View from P^{t}. Levi [Pointe Lévis].*, 1793
Watercolour, 113 × 243 mm.; V: 19
Public Archives of Canada, Ottawa, 1922?, 1-34

***21** *Quebec. from Point Levi [Pointe Lévis]. S.W. Sept. 1793.*, 1793. Figure 19
Watercolour, 113 × 407 mm. R: autogr. inscr. l.l. of right sheet, as title; v: 28, 29
Public Archives of Canada, Ottawa, 1922?, I-37
Two leaves of sketch-book glued together

22 *View of Cape Diamond from the River S. Lawrence*, c 1793
Watercolour, 113 × 235 mm. R: autogr. inscr. l.r. as title; v: 23
Public Archives of Canada, Ottawa, 1922?, I-61

23 *Grant's Wharf [Quebec]*, c 1793
Watercolour, 113 × 235 mm. R: autogr. inscr. l.l: *[Gra]nt's Wharf*; l.c. in pencil in another hand: *Grant's Wharf*; v: 22
Public Archives of Canada, Ottawa, 1922?, I-60

24 *View of Quebec from Grant's Wharf.*, c 1793
Pen, ink, and watercolour, 112 × 463 mm. R: autogr. inscr. l.l. at title; v: 34, 25
Public Archives of Canada, Ottawa, 1922?, I-31
Exh: G.H. cat. 47
Lit: Michael Bell, *Painters in a New Land* (Toronto 1973), pp 56–7 (ill.)
Two leaves of sketch-book glued together

25 *View of Point Levi [Pointe Lévis] from Grant's Wharf. continued*, c 1793
Watercolour, 112 × 237 mm. R: autogr. inscr. l.l. as title; v: 24
Public Archives of Canada, Ottawa, 1922?, I-32
Lit: *G. Heriot*, p 27 (ill.)
Glued to 34

26 *Cap Santé Church*, c 1793
Watercolour, 113 × 240 mm. R: inscr. in pencil on mount: *Cape Sante Church*; v: 27
Public Archives of Canada, Ottawa, 1922?, I-35

27 *View of Quebec from the N. Side of the River S^t^. Charles.*, c 1793
Watercolour, 113 × 240 mm. R: autogr. inscr. l.c. as title; inscr. in pencil on l.r. mount: *G. Heriot*; v: 26
Public Archives of Canada, Ottawa, 1922?, I-36

28 *Wooded bank*, c 1793
Watercolour, 113 × 239 mm.; V: 21
Public Archives of Canada, Ottawa, 1922?, I-38

29 *Block House on Cape Diamond*, c 1793
Watercolour, 113 × 168 mm. R: autogr. inscr. l.l. as title; v: 21
Public Archives of Canada, Ottawa, 1922?, I-39

30 *Plains of Abraham & Cape Diamond &c.*, c 1793
Watercolour, 113 × 239 mm. R: autogr. inscr. l.l. as title; v: 31
Public Archives of Canada, Ottawa, 1922?, I-50

31 *Scene on bank of a river or lake. Building on right*, c 1793
Watercolour, 113 × 239 mm.; V: 30
Public Archives of Canada, Ottawa, 1922?, I-51

32 *Dorchester Bridge near Quebec with a View of the General Hospital.*, c 1793
Watercolour, 168 × 266 mm. R: autogr. inscr. l.c. as title; v: 33

Old Print Shop, New York; Royal Ontario Museum, Toronto, 1953, 953.132.32A
Exh: Willistead Art Gallery of Windsor, 1967 (22)
Lit: ROM cat. 828 (ill.)

33 *View from the North Bank which extends from Quebec to Cape [Cap] Rouge, showing the General Hospital, River St. Charles &c Mountains of Beauport.*, c 1793
Watercolour, 168 × 536 mm. R: autogr. inscr. l.c. as title; v: 32
Old Print Shop, New York; Royal Ontario Museum, Toronto, 1953, 953.132.32B
Lit: ROM cat. 829
Sketch on two sketch-book leaves; **32** is on reverse of one leaf

34 *View of the Suburbs of St. Roque [St Roch] from ... [remainder of inscription missing]*, c 1793
Watercolour, 112 × 226 mm. R: autogr. inscr. l.r. as title; v: 24
Public Archives of Canada, Ottawa, 1922?, I-30
Glued to 25

35 *Montreal from Isle de St. Helen*, c 1793
Watercolour, 113 × 467 mm. R: autogr. inscr. l.r. as title; v: 36
Public Archives of Canada, Ottawa, 1922?. I-67(a)
Lit: Michael Bell, *Painters in a New Land* (Toronto 1973), pp 78–9 (ill.)
Two leaves of a sketch-book glued together
The landscape to the right has been cut and the remaining part is on the left of **36**.

36 *Montreal and St. Helen's Island*, c 1793
Watercolour, 113 × 467 mm. R: left leaf: 113 × 253 mm.; autogr. inscr. l.l: *Montreal continued.*; right leaf: 113 × 214 mm.: autogr. inscr. l.l: *Island of St. Helen*; v: 35
Two leaves of a sketch-book glued together

37 *N. View of Montreal taken from Mr. Frobisher's Country Seat*, c 1793
Watercolour, 113 × 418 mm. R: autogr. inscr. l.r. as title; v: 38, 39
Public Archives of Canada, Ottawa, 1922?, I-41
Lit: Jean Bruchési, 'George Heriot,' *Cahiers des Dix*, 10 (Montreal 1945), opp. p 192 (ill.)
Exh. G.H. cat. 48
Two leaves of a sketch-book glued together

38 *View of Montreal from a Wind Mill on the Banks*, c 1793
Watercolour, 113 × 200 mm. R: autogr. inscr. l.r. as title; v: 37
Public Archives of Canada, Ottawa, 1922?, I-40
Glued to 39

39 *View of Montreal from the side of the Mountain.*, c 1793
Watercolour, 113 × 218 mm. R: autogr. inscr. l.l, as title; v: 37
Public Archives of Canada, Ottawa, 1922?, I-42
Glued to 38

40 *Montreal. Quebec Gate*, c 1793
Watercolour and pencil, 239 × 351 mm. R: autogr. inscr. l.c. as title
The W.H. Coverdale Collection of Canadiana; Manoir Richelieu; National Gallery of Canada, Ottawa, 1970, 16676

***41** *Fall of Montmorenci [Montmorency] in Winter.*, c 1794. Figure 20
Watercolour, pen and brown ink, and graphite, 216 × 325 mm. R: autogr. inscr. l.c. mount as title; sign. mount l.r.: *GH.*
Maggs Bros., London; Grand Central Galleries, New York; The W.H. Coverdale Collection of Canadiana; Manoir Richelieu; National Gallery of Canada, Ottawa, 1970, 16675
Exh: G.H. cat. 50 (ill.)
Lit: Maggs Bros. cat. 514 (1929), (15); Grand Central Galleries, *Canadiana* (1942), (61)
Probably of the same date as the watercolour for the engraving found in Heriot's *Travels through the Canadas* (1807); see **359** (7).

***42** *North View of Lake St. Charles, Quebec*, 1795. Figure 21
Watercolour, laid down, 216 × 324 mm. R: sign. l.r. mount: *G. Heriot 1795*; v: inscr. as title
C.J. Hegan, Esq.; Harrow School, London, 1935
Exh: G.H. cat. 49

***43** *Neath Abbey – Glamorganshire/1796.*, 1796. Figure 22
Watercolour, 267 × 368 mm. R: autogr. inscr. as title l.c. mount
Sir Leonard Twiston-Davies; National Museum of Wales, Cardiff, 1934, 34.173
Exh: G.H. cat. 51
Another view was exhibited by Frank T. Sabin, London, Autumn Exhibition 1950 (127).

44 *View of Swansea in Glamorganshire*, c 1796
Watercolour, size unknown; present whereabouts unknown
Lit: Algernon Graves, *The Royal Academy of Arts*, (London 1906), IV, 82

45 *Oystermouth Castle, Glamorganshire*, c 1796
Watercolour, 362 × 533 mm. R: autogr. inscr. l.c. mount as title
Sotheby (London), 24 Nov. 1977 (166) ill.; Mrs. R.F. Hull

***46** *Penrice Castle, Glamorganshire*, c 1796. Figure 23
Watercolour, 241 × 381 mm. V: inscr. as title, on paper cut presumably from original mount
Frank T. Sabin, London; National Museum of Wales, Cardiff, 1949, 49.195
Exh: G.H. cat. 52

47 *South View of Lake St. Charles 1797*, 1797
Watercolour, 216 × 324 mm. V: inscr. as title
A.E. Anderson; Williamson Art Gallery and Museum, Birkenhead, 1933

***48** *Island of Orleans with Quebec in the Distance*, c 1797. Figure 40
Watercolour over pencil, laid down, 214 × 322 mm. R: autogr. inscr. l.c. mount: *Isle of Orleans, &c.*; sign. l.r. mount: *GH.*
Old Print Shop, New York; Royal Ontario Museum, Toronto, 1954, 954.102.3
Exh: G.H. cat. 79
Lit: ROM cat. 810; *G. Heriot*, p 29 (ill.)

***49** *Oystermouth Castle, Glamorganshire*, c. 1797. Figure 27

Watercolour, 214 × 325 mm. V: inscr. in pencil as title; also: *George Heriot*; similar inscr. in pencil inside mount
Frank T. Sabin, London, Autumn Exhibition 1950 (128); National Library of Wales, Aberystwyth, 1954, PB 2615

50 *Neath Abbey with Gnoll Castle*, c 1797
Watercolour, 167 × 260 mm. V: inscr. in pencil as title; pencil inscr. inside mount: *George Heriot, Neath Abbey & Gnoll Castle across the river*
Frank T. Sabin, London, Autumn Exhibition 1950 (127); National Library of Wales, Aberystwyth, 1960, PB 3902
Exh: G.H. cat. 53

51 *Ruins of the Intendant's Palace-Quebec./1798.*, 1798
Watercolour over pencil, 265 × 375 mm. V: autogr. inscr. as title, on paper cut from old mount
Old Print Shop, New York; Royal Ontario Museum, Toronto, 1953, 953.132.25
Exh: G.H. cat. 56
Lit: ROM cat. 820

52 *Ruins of the Intendant's Palace./1798.*, 1798
Watercolour, pen and ink over pencil, 260 × 376 mm. V: autogr. inscr. as title, on paper cut from old mount
Old Print Shop, New York; Royal Ontario Museum, Toronto, 1953, 953.132.26
Exh: G.H. cat. 57
Lit: ROM cat. 823; *G. Heriot*, p. 28 (ill.)

*53 *View of Quebec taken from the Pont near Point Levi [Pointe Lévis]*, 1798. Figure 24
Pen, ink, and watercolour, 254 × 356 mm. R: autogr. inscr. as title, l.c. mount; sign. l.r. mount: *Geo Heriot delineavit et Pinxit March 1798*
Mrs John Spencer; Sotheby (London), 21 Dec. 1964 (249); Mme Hughes Lapointe, 1964
Exh: G.H. cat. 80
Lit: *G. Heriot*, p. 30 (ill.)

*54 *Col^l. Nairne's Settlement at Mal Bay [La Malbaie]*, 1798. Figure 28
Watercolour, 264 × 378 mm. R: autogr. inscr. as title, l.c. mount; sign. l.l. mount: *Geo Heriot 1798*
Mrs J.A. Gray; W.E. Duggan Gray, Esq.; Vancouver Art Gallery, 1971, 71.8
Exh: G.H. cat. 58
Traditionally thought to have been given by Heriot to Colonel Nairne and his family

55 *N:W: View of the City & Fortification/of Quebec taken from the banks of/the St Charles.*, c 1798
Watercolour, laid down, 510 × 897 mm. R: autogr. inscr. l.r. as title; sign. l.r.: *Geo: Heriot.*
Mary Helen Beaton; presented by her to the Royal Ontario Museum, Toronto, 1981, 981.208
Badly faded and discoloured

56 *View on the river Chaudiere./1799.*, 1799
Watercolour, laid down, 254 × 368 mm. R: autogr. inscr. l.c. mount, as title
W.H. Coverdale, Esq.; Edgar Sittig, Delaware Water Gap; Kennedy Galleries, New York; Galerie Bernard Desroches, Montreal; Montreal Museum of Fine Art, 1980
This drawing seems to have been reworked in parts in about 1804; there is evidence of still later reworking

57 *View on the River Montmorenci [Montmorency], Canada/1799*, 1799
Watercolour, 213 × 330 mm. V: inscr. as title
W.H. Coverdale, Esq., Edgar Sittig, Delaware Water Gap; Kennedy Galleries, New York
Lit: *The Kennedy Quarterly*, 12:4 (Dec. 1973), 200 (ill.)

58 *View of the Ruins of the Monastery of the Recollects taken from the Garden, 1799*, 1799
Watercolour, 248 × 362 mm. V: autogr. inscr. as title on paper cut from old mount
Private collection
Exh: G.H. cat. 62 (ill.); *A Pageant of Canada* (Ottawa 1967), cat. 222 (ill.)

59 *La Jeune Lorette, Taken in March 1799*, 1799
Watercolour, laid down, 255 × 369 mm. R: autogr. inscr. as title, l.c. mount
Private collection
Exh: G.H. cat. 83 (ill.)

***60** *Ruins of the Intendant's Palace./1799.*, 1799. Figure 31
Watercolour, pen and ink over pencil, 268 × 379 mm. V: autogr. inscr. as title, cut from old mount
Old Print Shop, New York; Royal Ontario Museum, Toronto, 1953, 953.132.24
Exh: G.H. cat. 63
Lit: ROM cat. 821

61 *Ruins of the Intendant's Palace/1799.*, 1799
Watercolour, pen and ink over pencil, 267 × 375 mm. R: autogr. inscr. as title, l.c. mount, cut from old mount
Old Print Shop, New York; Royal Ontario Museum, Toronto, 1953, 953.132.27
Lit: ROM cat. 822 (ill.)

62 *Chateau Richer Formerly a Monastery, 1799*, 1799
Watercolour, 232 × 375 mm. R: autogr. inscr. as title, l.c. mount, cut from old mount
Private collection
Exh: G.H. cat. 61; *A Pageant of Canada* (Ottawa 1967), cat 223 (ill.)

***63** *Calumet Dance.*, c 1799. Figure 41
Pen, ink, and watercolour, 213 × 330 mm. R: autogr. inscr. l.c. mount as title; sign. l.r. mount: *GH.*
Joseph Pariseau; Henry Pariseau; Mrs E.K. Burnett; Kennedy Galleries, New York; Art Gallery of Windsor, 1967, 67.43, purchased with funds provided by a small group of members and a special grant from the Can-

ada Council in 1967. This statement also applies to **95**, **99**, **102**, **105**, **108**, **109**, **111**, **120**.
Exh. Windsor, *Nine Watercolour Paintings*, 1967 (ill.)
Lit: *The Kennedy Quarterly*, 7:2 (June 1967), 81–7 (ill.); Art Gallery of Windsor, *Checklist of the Permanent Collection to Dec. 31, 1971*, p 10; J.R. Harper, 'Early Canadian Painting Contrasts,' *Canadian Antiques Collector* (Jan.–Feb. 1974), p. 72 (ill.)
This watercolour and eight others by Heriot depicting Indians and their dances (see **95**, **99**, **102**, **105**, **108**, **109**, **111**, **120**) were in the collection of Mrs E.K. Burnett, who inherited them from her uncle, Henry Pariseau, who lived in St Paul, Minnesota. He had owned a farm in Centerville, Minnesota, where Mrs Burnett was born. These watercolours were originally in the possession of Mrs Burnett's grandfather, Joseph Pariseau, who had come to the United States from Canada. There is evidence that Heriot may have painted many more watercolours of Indian subjects than are in this check-list. For example, the Reverend C.A. Mackonochie sale, Sotheby (London), 21 July 1943 (for reference to the Mackonochie family, see **200**), contained, in lot 3210, 'some Red Indian ceremonies.' Also, in Canada, W.H. Coverdale's personal art collection included forty of Heriot's 'pencil, pen and ink and watercolour drawings' 'of scenes in Canada, Indians etc.,' some of which were inscribed with dates between 1797 and 1810. (These were sold to a New York book dealer 1949–50; I am grateful to Peter and Mary Winnett Fraser for this information.) At least some of the watercolours from the Coverdale collection were directly acquired by the American dealer Edgar Sittig, Delaware Water Gap, Pennsylvania, though none of those which have been identified as belonging to him depicts an Indian subject (see **56**, **57**, **64**, **103**, **144**, **270**). An Indian dance design in addition to those included in the group of watercolours of Indian subjects listed above has been preserved through an engraving: see **364**.

***64** *An Encounter, Canada*, c 1799. Figure 48
Watercolour with scraping, 203 × 292 mm. V: inscr. in a later hand: *Canada*
W.H. Coverdale, Esq.; Edgar Sittig, Delaware Water Gap; Kennedy Galleries, New York; National Gallery of Canada, Ottawa, 1981, 26730
Exh: G.H. cat. 82
Lit: *The Kennedy Quarterly*, 12:4 (Dec. 1973), 201 (ill.)
This watercolour with its unusual winter subject is the only one of its kind by Heriot that has come to light.

***65** *La Danse Ronde*, c 1799. Figure 46
Watercolour, (oval) 216 × 298 mm. R: sign. l.c. mount: *GH*.
Hugh Johnson, Esq., London; Christie (Montreal), 30 Apr. 1970, cat. 11 (2); Louis Melzack, Esq.
Exh: G.H. cat. 81
Elements of this design were apparently borrowed both for *La Danse Ronde, Circular Dance of the Canadians* in Heriot's *Travels through the Canadas*

(1807) – see **359**(23) – and the oil painting *The North West Part of the City of Quebec*; see **1**.

***66** *Double Fall of the River La Puce*, c 1799. Figure 30
Watercolour, 216 × 324 mm. R: autogr. inscr. as title, l.c. mount, cut from old mount
Private collection
Exh: G.H. cat. 59 (ill.)

***67** *Cataract of the River La Puce, Canada*, c 1799. Figure 29
Watercolour, 213 × 318 mm. R: autogr. inscr. as title, l.c. mount, cut from old mount
Private collection
Exh: G.H. cat. 60

68 *Chaudière Falls, Quebec*, c 1799
Watercolour over pencil, 208 × 320 mm.
Royal Ontario Museum, Toronto, 1960, 960.276.13
Lit: ROM cat. 2150
Catalogued as by an 'anonymous artist,' but the cataloguer has noted that the style is similar to that of Heriot; possibly parts of this drawing were later reworked by the artist.

69 *The Falls of Chaudière*, c 1799
Watercolour, 260 × 373 mm. V: inscr. modern hand: *1797 The Falls of Chaudiere*
Private collection

70 *North Aspect of Furness Abbey [Lancashire]*, c 1799
Grey wash over pencil, 331 × 494 mm. V: inscr. as title
Joseph McCrindle, Esq., on indefinite loan to The William Benton Museum of Art, The University of Connecticut, Storrs
Lit: *British Drawings and Watercolours: A Selection from the J.F. McCrindle Collection*, The William Benton Museum of Art, The University of Connecticut, Storrs (Spring 1974), p 19, no 13
Perhaps developed from sketches that Heriot may have made in England in 1796–7

71 *Quebec from Point Levi [Pointe Lévis].*, 1800
Watercolour, 250 × 363 mm. R: autogr. inscr. as title, l.c. mount; sign. l.r. mount: *Geo. Heriot 1800.*; v: slight pencil sketch of ruin
Sotheby (Toronto), 15, 16 May 1978, 109 (ill.); withdrawn from sale

72 *View [of Quebec] from Cape Diamond*, c 1800
Watercolour, pen and ink over pencil, 301 × 474 mm. R: autogr. inscr. l.r. as title; v: inscr.: *Quebec.*
Frank T. Sabin, London; Royal Ontario Museum, Toronto, 1953, 953.163.1
Exh: G.H. cat. 85
Lit: ROM cat. 826 (ill.)

73 *Quebec seen from Outside the Walls Near St. Louis Gate*, c 1800
Watercolour over pencil, 247 × 360 mm. V: inscr.: *Quebec.*
Old Print Shop, New York; Royal Ontario Museum, Toronto, 1953, 953.132.31
Lit: ROM cat. 825 (ill.)

***74** *Powel[l] Place ... ; Sir Robert L. [?S.] & Lady Milnes, Family and the Bishop of Quebec*, c 1800. Figure 34
Watercolour, 260 × 368 mm. R: autogr. inscr. l.r. mount: *George Heriot del. et pinxit 1802*; inscr. as title; dedicated and dated 19 Aug. 1858 by Charlotte Milnes
Waddington's Toronto, 14, 16 June 1978, 554 (ill.); Mr and Mrs J. Wallace Beaton
Exh: G.H. cat. 91
The dimensions and verso inscriptions indicated here are those that appear in the sale catalogue. Badly faded. See **166**.

75 *North View of Chateau Riché [Château Richer]*, c 1800
Watercolour over pencil, 222 × 324 mm. R: autogr. inscr. as title, l.c. mount; sign. l.r. mount: *GH*.
Francis Edwards, London; F.G. Ketchison, Esq., Montreal; Louis Melzack, Esq., Montreal; Sotheby (Toronto), 28–30 Oct. 1968 (28); W.P. Wolfe, Montreal; Christie (Montreal), 25 Sept. 1969 (2); Christie (Montreal), 19 Oct. 1973, 6 (ill.); present whereabouts unknown

76 *Encampment of Domiciliated Indians*, c 1800
Watercolour and gouache over pencil, 254 × 374 mm. V: autogr. inscr. as title
Frank T. Sabin, London; Royal Ontario Museum, Toronto, 1950, 950.224.27
Exh: Willistead Art Gallery of Windsor, 1967 (19); G.H. cat. 96
Lit: Engraved in Heriot's *Travels through the Canadas* (1807); see **359** (25); ROM cat. 843 (ill.); *G. Heriot*, p 41 (ill.)

77 *Indian Lorette*, c 1800
Watercolour and graphite, 254 × 375 mm.
W.D. Lighthall, K.C.; National Gallery of Canada, Ottawa, 1937, 4300
Exh: Willistead Art Gallery of Windsor, 1967, 1 (ill.); G.H. cat. 84
Lit: National Gallery of Canada *Catalogue of Paintings* (Ottawa 1948), p 176; *G. Heriot*, p 32 (ill.)

78 *Indians at a Waterfall [?Montmorency River]*, c 1800
Watercolour over pencil, 270 × 373 mm.
Miss Emily Driscoll; Royal Ontario Museum, Toronto, 1960, 960.176.5
Exh: G.H. cat. 64 (ill.)
Lit: ROM cat. 2161; *G. Heriot*, p 31 (ill.)
Watermark: Lily on shield, surmounted by crown, finial of initials. Catalogued in ROM cat. as by an 'anonymous artist'

79 *Southampton*, c 1800
Watercolour, 135 × 345 mm. R: later inscr. in pencil u.r.: *[... ?] 88*; v: inscr. as title
Hampshire Gallery, Bournemouth; private collection

80 *Gabriel[le] Espagnole.*, c 1800–c 1816
Watercolour, laid down at corners, 137 × 107 mm. R: autogr. insc. u.c. as title; sign. l.l.: *G. Heriot*
Sotheby (Toronto) 25–7 May 1970 (195); Warda Drummond, Montreal
Exh: G.H. cat. 87 (ill.)

Mary Allodi of the Royal Ontario Museum has kindly informed me of two drawings of habitants that she has recently discovered in a private collection. One of these drawings represents two habitants, the other a habitant with a wooden leg. Unfortunately I have not as yet been able to see them.

***81** *Old Woman*, c 1800–c 1816. Figure 50
Watercolour, 241 × 152 mm. R: sign. l.l.: *G. Heriot.*
Laing Galleries, Toronto; present whereabouts unknown
Lit: Paul Duval, *Canadian Water Colour Painting* (Toronto 1953), pl. 4

82 *Habitant Figure Studies*, c 1800–c 1816
Watercolour, 210 × 235 mm. R: sign. l.l.: *G. Heriot.*
L.G. Duke, Esq.; Sotheby (London), 22 Oct. 1970 (98); P. Mellon, Esq.; Yale Center for British Art, Paul Mellon Collection
Exh: G.H. cat. 88

***83** *Insects*, c 1800–c 1805. Figure 49
Pen, ink, and watercolour, individual studies laid down: l.l: 42 × 64 mm.; u.c.: 91 × 160 mm.; l.r.: 53 × 86 mm.; mount size: 137 × 255 mm. (sight).
R: sign. beneath each study: l.l.: *GH.*; u.c.: *G. Heriot.* l.r.: *G.H.*
Laing Galleries, Toronto
Exh: G.H. cat. 86 (ill.)
Large moth in centre; family *Sphingidae* (sphinx or hawk moth)

84 *Bull preparing to Charge*, c 1800–c 1816
Watercolour, 203 × 254 mm. R: sign. l.l.: *G. Heriot.*
Kennedy Galleries, New York
Lit: *G. Heriot*, p 36 (ill.)
Probably copied from a print

85 *Buffalo [?] Female*, c 1800–c 1816
Watercolour, 203 × 254 mm.
Kennedy Galleries, New York

86 *Falls of St Nicholas*, 1801
Watercolour, 248 × 356 mm. Dated: *1801*
Lord Thomson of Fleet

87 *Rapids of the Coteau du Lac, Saint Francois, St Lawrence*, 1801
Watercolour, 137 × 185 mm. V: inscr. as title, dated 1801; sign.
Sotheby (Toronto), 14, 15 May 1973 (196); Laing Galleries, Toronto; Lord Thomson of Fleet

88 *Falls of Niagara.*, 1801
Watercolour, 132 × 185 mm. R: on album page in pencil: *Niagara 1801*; v: autogr. inscr. as title; sign.: *G. Heriot 1801.*
Walter T. Spencer, London; Public Archives of Canada, Ottawa, 1910, 1-2
From the 'George Heriot Album'

89 *Niagara River 1801/June 6th.*, 1801
Pencil and watercolour, 141 × 187 mm. V: autogr. inscr. as title
Old Print Shop, New York; Royal Ontario Museum, Toronto, 1953, 953.132.22
Lit: ROM cat. 838

***90** *Whirlpool[,] Niagara River./1801*, 1801. Figure 36
Watercolour over pencil, 143 × 187 mm. V: autogr. inscr. as title
Old Print Shop, New York; Royal Ontario Museum, Toronto, 1953, 953.132.23
Exh: Willistead Art Gallery of Windsor, 1967 (15)
Lit: ROM cat. 839; *G. Heriot* p 33 (ill.)

91 *Dance in the Château St. Louis*, 1801
Watercolour, 249 × 368 mm. R: sign. l.l.: *Geo Heriot* v: prob. late autogr. inscr.: *Chateau St Louis/G.H. 1801*
Walter T. Spencer, London; Public Archives of Canada, Ottawa, 1922, 1-68
Exh: G.H. cat. 89
Lit: Michael Bell, *Painters in a New Land* (Toronto 1973), p. 53 (ill.); *G. Heriot*, p 35 (ill.)

***92** *Village of Chippawa near the Falls of Niagara*, c 1801. Figure 33
Watercolour, 140 × 181 mm. V: inscr. as title; sign.(?): *[Pai]nted by Geo Heriot Esq.*
Kennedy Galleries, New York
Lit: *The Kennedy Quarterly*, 12:4 (Dec. 1973), 202 (ill.)
Later copy in possession of Public Archives of Canada; see **311**.

***93** *Lake St Charles near Quebec*, c 1801. Figure 37
Watercolour, 271 × 445 mm. R: inscr. l.r. mount: *Lake St Charles, near Quebec/G. Heriot/1766–1844*
Walker's Galleries, London; National Gallery of Canada, Ottawa, 1954, 6320
Exh: G.H. cat. 65
Lit: *Annual Report* (Ottawa: National Gallery of Canada 1954–5), (ill.); Patricia Godsell, *Enjoying Canadian Painting* (Don Mills 1976), p 38 (ill.); *G. Heriot*, p 34 (ill.)

94 *Falls of Montmorenci [Montmorency] from Point Levy [Pointe Lévis] near Quebec.*, c 1801
Watercolour over pencil, 114 × 165 mm. V: autogr. inscr. as title; sign.: *Geo. Heriot*
Old Print Shop, New York; Royal Ontario Museum, Toronto, 1953, 953.132.10
Lit: ROM cat. 817

95 *Ceremonial Scalp Dance*, c 1801
Watercolour, 210 × 324 mm. R: sign. l.r. mount: *GH.*
Joseph Pariseau; Henry Pariseau; Mrs E.K. Burnett; Kennedy Galleries, New York; Art Gallery of Windsor, 1967, 67.40
Exh: Windsor, *Nine Watercolour Paintings*, 1967
Lit: *Burlington Magazine* (June 1967), (advertisement); *Connoisseur* (June 1967), (advertisement); *The Kennedy Quarterly*, 7:2 (June 1967) 81–7 (ill.); The Art Gallery of Windsor, *A Checklist of the Permanent Collection to Dec. 31, 1971*, p 9; J.R. Harper, 'Early Canadian Painting Contrasts,' *Canadian Antiques Collector* (Jan.–Feb. 1974). 72 (ill.)
The Jeune Lorette church can be seen on the extreme right. See **63**.

***96** *La danse ronde à l'Intérieur*, c 1801. Figure 47
214 × 321 mm. R: autogr. inscr. l.r. mount: *GH*.
Hugh Johnson, Esq.; Christie (Montreal), cat. 11, 30 Apr. 1970 (1); Art Gallery of Windsor, 70.18
Lit: Art Gallery of Windsor, *A Checklist of the Permanent Collection to Dec. 31, 1971*, p 10
Figures are similar to those in **91**

***97** *Minuets des Canadiens*, c 1801. Figure 15
Watercolour, 214 × 328 mm. R: autogr. inscr. l.r. mount: *GH*.
Hugh Johnson, Esq.; Christie (Montreal), cat. 11, 30 Apr. 1970 (3); Louis Melzack, Esq.
Related in composition to the aquatint in Heriot's *Travels through the Canadas* (1807); see **359** (24).

98 *Montreal (?)*, c 1802
Watercolour over pencil, 254 × 349 mm.
Frank T. Sabin, London; Royal Ontario Museum, Toronto, 1956, 956.54
Lit: ROM cat. 851
Watermark: *J. Whatman 1801*
This watercolour was possibly developed from sketches made on a visit to Montreal in the previous year.

***99** *Dance of Indian Women.*, c 1802. Figure 42
Pen, ink, and watercolour, 219 × 324 mm. R: autogr. inscr. as title l.c. mount; sign. l.l. mount: *Geo Heriot Esq pinxit*; l.r. mount: *GH*.
Joseph Pariseau; Henry Pariseau; Mrs E.K. Burnett; Kennedy Galleries, New York; Art Gallery of Windsor, 1967, 67.44
Exh: Windsor, *Nine Watercolour Paintings*, 1967; G.H. cat. 90 (ill.)
Lit: *The Kennedy Quarterly*, 7:2 (June 1967), 81–7 (ill.) (cover); Art Gallery of Windsor, *A Checklist of the Permanent Collection to Dec. 31, 1971*, p 10
See **63**.

100 *Quebec [from Lévis]*, c 1803
Watercolour over pencil, 160 × 396 mm. V: inscr. as title
Old Print Shop, New York; Royal Ontario Museum, Toronto, 1953, 953.132.30
Lit: ROM cat. 827; *G. Heriot*, p. 35 (ill.)
Watermark: *J. Whatman 1801*

101 *Pointe au Baptheme [Baptême]. Pictaonaic [Ottawa] River.*, c 1803
Watercolour over pencil, 184 × 285 mm. R: autogr. inscr. l.r. as title
Old Print Shop, New York; Royal Ontario Museum, Toronto, 1953, 953.132.28
Exh: Willistead Art Gallery of Windsor, 1967 (23)
Lit: ROM cat. 837
Watermark: Lily on shield with finial

102 *War Dance*, c 1803
Watercolour, 270 × 289 mm.
Joseph Pariseau; Henry Pariseau; Mrs E.K. Burnett; Kennedy Galleries, New York; Art Gallery of Windsor, 1967, 67.38

Exh: Windsor, *Nine Watercolour Paintings*, 1967
Lit: *The Kennedy Quarterly*, 7:2 (June 1967), 81–7 (ill.); Art Gallery of Windsor, *A Checklist of the Permanent Collection to Dec. 31, 1971*, p 9
See **63**.

***103** *View at Cape [Cap] Rouge*, 1804. Figure 38
Watercolour, 133 × 181 mm. V: inscr. as title; sign. (?): *Geo Heriot 1804*
W.H. Coverdale, Esq.; Edgar Sittig, Delaware Water Gap; Kennedy Galleries, New York

104 *Falls of Niagara – 1804*, 1804
Watercolour, laid down, 133 × 186 mm. R: autogr. inscr. as title l.c. mount to which is added sign.: *– Geo: Heriot –*
Frank T. Sabin, London; Royal Ontario Museum, Toronto, 1951, 951.67.1
Lit: ROM cat. 840; *Globe and Mail*, Toronto, 25 June 1954 (ill.); *G. Heriot*, p 37 (ill.)

105 *Group of Warriors, with a view of Indian Wigwams composed of Bark.*, 1804
Watercolour, 175 × 295 mm. R: autogr. inscr. as title l.c. mount; sign. l.l. mount: *Painted by Geo Heriot Esq 1804*
Joseph Pariseau; Henry Pariseau; Mrs E.K. Burnett; Kennedy Galleries, New York; Art Gallery of Windsor, 1967, 67.46
Exh: Windsor, *Nine Watercolour Paintings*, 1967 (ill.)
Lit: *The Kennedy Quarterly*, 7:2 (June 1967) 81–7 (ill.); Art Gallery of Windsor, *A Checklist of the Permanent Collection to Dec. 31, 1971*, p 10; *G. Heriot*, p 38 (ill.)
See **63**.

106 *View at Saint Augustin/on the S^t. Lawrence*, c 1804
Watercolour, laid down, 133 × 184 mm. R: inscr. as title on mount in pencil
Sotheby (London), 24 June 1971 (113); Sotheby (Toronto), 14, 15 May 1973 (195) (ill.); Lord Thomson of Fleet
A later copy of this can be found in the Public Archives of Canada, I-56; see **305**.

107 *Falls of Montmorenci [Montmorency] – 1806*, c 1804
Watercolour over pencil, laid down, 133 × 184 mm. R: autogr. inscr. as title l.c. mount to which is added: sign.: *–Geo: Heriot–*
Old Print Shop, New York; Royal Ontario Museum, Toronto, 1954, 954.102.1
Lit: ROM cat. 813
This view shows General Haldimand's small summer house.
This design is similar to that found in Heriot's *Travels through the Canadas* (1807); see **359** (6).

108 *Dance of Warriors previous to going on an Expedition.*, c 1804
Watercolour, 184 × 286 mm. R: autogr. inscr. as title l.c. mount; sign. l.l. mount: *Painted by Geo Heriot Esqr*
Joseph Pariseau; Henry Pariseau; Mrs E.K. Burnett; Kennedy Galleries, New York; Art Gallery of Windsor, 1967, 67.41
Exh: Windsor, *Nine Watercolour Paintings*, 1967 (ill.); G.H. cat. 93
Lit: *Apollo* (June 1967), (advertisement); *The Kennedy Quarterly*, 7:2 (June

1967), 81–7 (ill.); Art Gallery of Windsor, *A Checklist of the Permanent Collection to Dec. 31, 1971*, p 10
The disposition and stance of the figures in the watercolour were adapted from an illustration in P. Lafitau's *Mœurs des sauvages ameriquains* (Paris 1724), II, 194. The author describes the scene under the heading 'Depart des Guerriers,' noting that 'Le jour du depart, tous les Guerriers dans leurs plus beaux atours, & armés de toutes pieces, s'assemblent dans la Cabane du Chef du parti, lequel est toûjours noirci & armé à son ordinaire. Pendant ce temps – là les femmes chargées de leur provisions prennent les devants, & vont les attendre à une certaine distance hors du Village. Lors qu'ils sont assemblés, le Chef les harangue courtement, & sort le premier chantant seul sa chanson de mort au nom de tous les autres qui le suivent à la file un à un sans dire mot. Hors de la palissade, ils font une décharge de leur fusils, s'ils en ont, on décochent une fleche, en l'air, & le Chef continuë à chanter en marchant jusqu' à ce qu'il soit hors de la veüe du Village.'
See **63**.

109 *War Dance, performed by one, or two persons, who are afterwards joined in it by the party of warriors surrounding them.*, c 1804
Watercolour, 171 × 295 mm. R: autogr. inscr. as title l.c. mount; sign. l.l. mount: *Painted by Geo Heriot Esq*[r]
Joseph Pariseau; Henry Pariseau; Mrs. E.K. Burnett; Kennedy Galleries, New York; Art Gallery of Windsor, 1967, 67.42
Exh: Windsor, *Nine Watercolour Paintings*, 1967 (ill.)
Lit: *Burlington Magazine* (June 1967), (advertisement); *The Kennedy Quarterly*, 7:2 (June 1967), 81–7 (ill.); Art Gallery of Windsor, *A Checklist of the Permanent Collection to Dec. 31, 1971*, p 9; *G. Heriot*, p 39 (ill.)
See **63**.

110 *View on the Jacques Quartier [Cartier].*, 1805
Watercolour, 123 × 180 mm. (corners are cropped). R: inscr. l.r. old mount in pencil: *Jacques Cartier*; v: autogr. inscr. as title; sign.: *Geo Heriot 1805*
Walter T. Spencer, London; Public Archives of Canada, Ottawa, 1910, 1-3
From the 'George Heriot Album'

***111** *Dance for recovery of the Sick.*, 1805. Figure 43
Watercolour, 175 × 298 mm. R: autogr. inscr. as title l.c. mount; sign. l.l. mount: *Painted by George Heriot Esq*[r]*. 1805.*
Joseph Pariseau; Henry Pariseau; Mrs E.K. Burnett; Kennedy Galleries, New York; Art Gallery of Windsor, 1967, 67.39
Exh: Windsor, *Nine Watercolour Paintings*, 1967; G.H. cat. 95
Lit: *The Kennedy Quarterly*, 7:2 (June 1967) 81–7 (ill.); Art Gallery of Windsor, *A Checklist of the Permanent Collection to Dec. 31, 1971*, p 9; *G. Heriot*, p 42 (ill.)
The dancing figure fourth from the right may have been derived directly from 'The Conjurer,' an illustration for Thomas Harriot's *A briefe and true report of the new found land of Virginia* (1590). (See Dover facsimile ed, New

York: 1972, p 54.) This was kindly brought to my attention by T.J. Brasser.
See **63**.

112 *Quebec Point Levi [Pointe Lévis] from Ange Gardien 12 miles from Quebec*, 1805
Watercolour, 127 × 191 mm. V: autogr. inscr. as title; sign.: *Geo. Heriot 1805*
Private collection
See **317**.

113 *Ruins of a Monastery at Chateau Richer./15 miles N.E of Quebec.*, 1805
Watercolour over pencil, 135 × 187 mm. V: autogr. inscr. as title; sign.: *Geo. Heriot 1805.*
Old Print Shop, New York; Royal Ontario Museum, Toronto, 1953, 953.132.4
Lit: ROM cat. 811; *G. Heriot*, p 43 (ill.)
Similar in design to that in *Travels through the Canadas* (1807); see **359** (12).

114 *View of the banks of the S^t. Lawrence/below Cape [Cap] Rouge.*, 1805
Watercolour over pencil, 133 × 186 mm. V: autogr. inscr. as title; sign.: *Geo. Heriot 1805*
Old Print Shop, New York; Royal Ontario Museum, Toronto, 1953, 953.132.18
Lit: ROM cat. 830

115 *View under Cape [Cap] Rouge.*, 1805
Watercolour over pencil, 131 × 185 mm. V: autogr. inscr. as title; sign.: *Geo Heriot 1805.*
Old Print Shop, New York; Royal Ontario Museum, Toronto, 1953, 953.132.34
Lit: ROM cat. 831

116 *Rapids at the Pitch of the Fall of Montmorenci [Montmorency]*, 1805
Watercolour over pencil, 130 × 183 mm. V: autogr. inscr. as title; sign.: *Geo. Heriot 1805*
Old Print Shop, New York; Royal Ontario Museum, Toronto, 1953, 953.132.11
Lit: ROM cat. 812

***117** *[Falls of] Niagara*, 1805. Figure 39
Watercolour, 311 × 705 mm. R: autogr. inscr. l.l. as title; sign.: *Geo: Heriot pinxit 1805.*
Canon R.V. Potts; Victoria and Albert Museum, London, 1949, P.11-1949
Exh: Corcoran Gallery, Washington, '*American Processional*,' 1950 (92); G.H. cat. 66

118 *Citadel of Quebec [seen from the Plains of Abraham]*, c. 1805
Watercolour over pencil, 136 × 187 mm. V: autogr. inscr. as title; sign.: *[...] Heriot*
Old Print Shop, New York; Royal Ontario Museum, Toronto, 1953, 953.132.1
Lit: ROM cat. 824

119 *Landscape with Figures and River*, c 1805
Watercolour over pencil, laid down, 238 × 332 mm. R: sign. l.l.: *G. Heriot*
Frank T. Sabin, London; Royal Ontario Museum, Toronto, 1951, 951.67.2
Exh: Willistead Art Gallery of Windsor, 1967 (21)
Lit: ROM cat. 844
Watermark: *E & P 1804* (Edmunds & Pine)
Possibly a view on the St Lawrence River

***120** *Dance, on the reception of Strangers previous to their introduction into the Village.*, c 1805. Figure 44
Watercolour, 175 × 298 mm. R: autogr. inscr. as title l.c. mount; sign. l.l. mount: *Painted by Geo Heriot Esq*[r]
Joseph Pariseau; Henry Pariseau; Mrs E.K. Burnett; Kennedy Galleries, New York; Art Gallery of Windsor, 1967, 67.45
Exh: Windsor, *Nine Watercolour Paintings*, 1967; G.H. cat. 94 (ill.)
Lit: *The Kennedy Quarterly*, 7:2 (June 1967), 81–7 (ill.); Art Gallery of Windsor, *A Checklist of the Permanent Collection to Dec. 31, 1971*, p 10; *G. Heriot*, p 40 (ill.)
Two of the figure groups are derived directly from an illustration in P. Lafitau's *Mœurs des Sauvages Ameriquains* (Paris 1724), II, pl. 18, under 'Explication': 'Le Malade entre les mains de deux Devins, est promené lentement sur un long brazier de charbons ardents [not indicated in Heriot's watercolour], tandis que le Choeur est occupé à une danse de Religion.' See **63**.

121 *Lake St Charles*, c 1805
Watercolour, 260 × 368 mm. R: autogr. inscr. l.r. as title
The Hon. John Hale (1765–1838) to descendants; Sotheby (Toronto), 20 Oct. 1975 (124); Sotheby (Toronto), 18, 19 Oct. 1976 (255); private collection
Paper watermarked *1799*
The Honourable John Hale came to Canada in 1793 as military secretary to the Duke of Kent. In 1799 he was appointed paymaster-general of the British forces. He was a member of the Legislative Council of Lower Canada in 1808, and of the Executive Council in 1820.

122 *View on the St Lawrence (?)*, c 1805
Watercolour over pencil, 238 × 317 mm. R: sign. l.l.: *G. Heriot*
Old Print Shop, New York; Royal Ontario Museum, Toronto, 1954, 954.102.5
Lit: ROM cat. 799; *G. Heriot*, p 44 (ill.)

123 *River Landscape*, c 1805
Watercolour over pencil, 235 × 336 mm. R: sign. l.l.: *G. Heriot.*
Old Print Shop, New York; Royal Ontario Museum, Toronto, 1954, 954.102.4
Lit: ROM cat. 845
Watermark: *E & P 1804* (Edmunds & Pine)
Possibly a view of the St Lawrence River

124 *View of St. Paul's Bay [Baie St Paul], River St. Lawrence*, c 1805
Watercolour over pencil, 133 × 184 mm. V: inscr. in pencil as title
Old Print Shop, New York; Royal Ontario Museum, Toronto, 1953, 953.132.8
Lit: ROM cat. 809
Watermark: Seated woman with spear, shield, and flower in medallion surmounted by crown

125 *West View of Fall of Montmorenci [Montmorency].*, c 1805
Watercolour over pencil, 124 × 181 mm. V: inscr. in pencil as title; sign.: *Geo. Heriot*
Old Print Shop, New York; Royal Ontario Museum, Toronto, 1953, 943.132.3
Lit: ROM cat. 815

126 *Falls of Montmorenci [Montmorency]*, c 1805
Watercolour over pencil, laid down, 130 × 189 mm. R: autogr. inscr. as title l.c. mount; sign. l.l. mount: *G. Heriot delin*
Laing Galleries, Toronto; Royal Ontario Museum, Toronto, 1955, 955.157.1
Exh: Willistead Art Gallery of Windsor 1967 (20)
Lit: ROM cat. 818

127 *Quebec, from the St Charles River*, c 1805
Watercolour, size unknown
J.C.A. Heriot, Esq.; present whereabouts unknown
Lit: J.C.A. Heriot, 'George Heriot, Author-Artist,' *Americana*, 5 (Sept.–Oct. 1910), 888–92 (ill.), 'as it appeared in 1805.'

128 *Falls of Niagara taken from beneath the Western Bank.*, c 1805
Watercolour, 133 × 184 mm. v: autogr. inscr. as title; sign.: *Drawn by Geo Heriot Esq*; inscr. (in another hand) on paper strip pasted on v: *Saut du Niagara dessiné d'apres nature par Mr. le Colonel Scott.*
Private collection
See later version: **312**.

129 *View of Quebec from Mr Caldwell's Mills/at Point Levi [Pointe Lévis] ... /The distance shews the heights of Abraham and the Citadel*, 1806
Watercolour, 134 × 187 mm. R: inscr. in pencil l.r. on mount: *Quebec etc.*; v: autogr. inscr. as title; sign.: *Geo Heriot. July 1806.*
Walter T. Spencer, London; Public Archives of Canada, Ottawa, 1910, 1-5
Probably Henry Caldwell (1738–1810), lessee of the seigneury of Lauzon
From the 'George Heriot Album'

130 *Fall of Saint Ann[e]'s/30 Miles N.East from Quebec*, 1806
Watercolour, 133 × 184 mm. V: autogr. inscr. as title; sign.: *Geo Heriot 1806*
Dr P.A. Forman
Exh: G.H. cat. 112
A copy of this was made in c 1837 (?). See **304**.

131 *N. View of Twisle [Twizel] Castle Northumberland./taken from Kersfield.*, 1806

Watercolour, 137 × 191 mm. V: autogr. inscr. as title; sign.: *Geo Heriot delin*[t].; also: *31*[st] *Octob. 1806.*
Walter T. Spencer, London; Public Archives of Canada, Ottawa, 1910, I-18
From the 'George Heriot Album'

132 *Sketch Loch Tay with ... [word obscured] in the Distance*, 1806
Watercolour, 125 × 193 mm. V: autogr. inscr. as title; also: *Loch Tay*; sign.: *Geo. Heriot 1806.*
Walter T. Spencer, London; Public Archives of Canada, Ottawa, 1910, I-23
From the 'George Heriot Album'
Reworked c 1820

133 *Loch Lomond Octob 1806 Geo Heriot*, 1806
Watercolour, 137 × 197 mm. V: autogr. inscr. as title; also autogr. inscr. in pencil: *NE View of Loch Lomond*
Victoria and Albert Museum, London, 1921, P.11-1921

134 *View of Loch Lomond*, 1806
Watercolour, 133 × 184 mm. V: inscr. as title with date: *14th October 1806*; also inscr.: *View of Ben Lomond & Lake*
Squire Gallery, London; Gilbert Davis, Esq.; Henry E. Huntington Library and Art Gallery, San Marino, California, 1959, 59.55.670

135 *Corra Rocks on the Clyde Oct 1806*, 1806
India ink and wash, 137 × 187 mm. V: inscr. as title
Squire Gallery, London; private collection, 1949

136 *Greenock, Renfrewshire*, 1806
Watercolour, size unknown, inscr.: *1806*
Walker's Galleries, London, Exhibition, June–July 1956 (50); present whereabouts unknown

137 *Ardgowan, near Inner Kipp. on the estuary of the Clyde.*, c 1806
Watercolour, 210 × 340 mm. R: autogr. inscr. as title l.c. mount; sign. l.r. mount: *Geo Heriot Octob 1807*
Walker's Galleries, London; Northampton Museum, 1933–4, P.12.1933-34
The artist was in the vicinity of this location in Oct. 1806.

***138** *South View of Perth*, c 1806. Figure 52
Watercolour, 119 × 189 mm.
Frank T. Sabin, London; Glasgow Art Gallery, 1956, 56-11 (1)

139 *Chief Justice Blower's Seat near Windsor N. Scotia.*, 1807
Watercolour, 132 × 185 mm. R: in pencil, l.c. mount: *Chief Justice Blower's Seat near Windsor N.S./1807*; v: autogr. inscr. as title; also sign.: *Drawn on the spot by Geo Heriot. 22*[d] *June 1807.*
Walter T. Spencer, London; Public Archives of Canada, Ottawa, 1910, I-14
Exh: G.H. cat. 71 (ill.)
Lit: Michael Bell, *Painters in a New Land* (Toronto 1973), p 39 (ill.)
From the 'George Heriot Album'; King's College can be seen on the extreme right.

140 *View in the Basin of Mines [Minas Basin]. near Windsor. N.Scotia.*, 1807
Watercolour over pencil, 136 × 186 mm. V: autogr. inscr. as title; sign.: *Drawn on the spot by Geo Heriot. 22*[d] *June, 1807*

Old Print Shop, New York; Royal Ontario Museum, Toronto, 1953, 953.132.17
Lit: ROM cat. 798

141 *View in the Basin of Mines [Minas Basin]. N. Scotia.*, 1807
Watercolour, 137 × 185 mm. R: inscr. in pencil, l.r. album page: *Basin of Mines*; v: autogr. inscr. as title; sign.: *Drawn on the spot by Geo Heriot. 22[d] June 1807*
Walter T. Spencer, London; Public Archives of Canada, Ottawa, 1910, I-15
From the 'George Heriot Album'

142 *Parsboro' [Parrsboro] Bay of Fundy.*, 1807
Blue-grey wash, 180 × 252 mm. R: autogr. inscr. l.r.: *Presqu' Isle S[t]. Johns River [struck]*; below, autogr. inscr. as title; v: autogr. inscr.: *Parsborough – Bay of Fundy. June 1807.*
Walter T. Spencer, London; Public Archives of Canada, Ottawa, 1910, I-9
From the 'George Heriot Album'

*143 *View from Partridge island in the Bay of Fundy.* I, 1807. Figure 56
Watercolour over pencil, 124 × 184 mm. V: autogr. inscr. as title; sign.: *Drawn on the spot by Geo Heriot. 24th June 1807.*
Old Print Shop, New York; Royal Ontario Museum, Toronto, 1953, 953.132.21
Lit: ROM cat. 801

144 *View from Partridge Island in the Bay of Fundy.* II, 1807
Watercolour, 135 × 186 mm. V: autogr. inscr. as title; sign.: *Drawn on the spot by Geo Heriot. 24th June 1807.*
W.H. Coverdale, Esq.; Edgar Sittig, Delaware Water Gap; Kennedy Galleries, New York; Galerie Bernard Desroches, Montreal; Agnes Etherington Art Centre, Queen's University, Kingston, 1979, A13860

*145 *West view of Partridge island from Parsborough [Parrsboro], Bay of Fundy.*, 1807. Figure 57
Watercolour over pencil, 135 × 186 mm. V: autogr. inscr. as title; sign.: *Drawn on the spot by Geo. Heriot, 24th June 1807*
Old Print Shop, New York; Royal Ontario Museum, Toronto, 1953, 953.132.19
Exh: G.H. cat. 69
Lit: ROM cat. 802 (ill.); *G. Heriot*, p 53 (ill.)

*146 *View on Partridge Island – Bay of Fundy.*, 1807. Figure 58
Watercolour and pencil, 127 × 184 mm. V: autogr. inscr. as title; sign.: *Drawn on the spot by Geo. Heriot, 24th June 1807.*
Old Print Shop, New York; Royal Ontario Museum, Toronto, 1953, 943.132.20
Exh: Willistead Art Gallery of Windsor, 1967 (13); G.H. cat. 68
Lit: ROM cat. 800

*147 *Chief Justice Ludlow's on the river/S[t]. John New Brunswick.*, 1807. Figure 54
Watercolour over pencil, 336 × 489 mm. R: inscr. l.r.: *1807*; v: autogr. inscr. as title

Kennedy Galleries, New York; Royal Ontario Museum, Toronto, 1950, 950.31
Exh: G.H. cat. 70
Lit: ROM cat. 807 (ill.); *G. Heriot*, p 51 (ill.)
Watermark: *J. Whatman*
George Duncan Ludlow (1734–1808), first chief justice of New Brunswick 1784–1808, lived at 'Spring Hill' in the parish of Kingsclear, five miles above Fredericton.

***148** *Belle Isle Bay S^t. John's River.*, 1807. Figure 55
Grey-brown wash over pencil, 133 × 184 mm. V: autogr. inscr. as title; sign.: *Drawn on the spot by Geo. Heriot, 29th June 1807*
Old Print Shop, New York; Royal Ontario Museum, Toronto, 1953, 953.132.9
Lit: ROM cat. 805

149 *View on the river Saint John near the Poquioq [Pokiok].*, 1807
Brown wash over pencil, 135 × 184 mm. V: autogr. inscr. as title; sign.: *Drawn on the Spot by Geo. Heriot, 23^d. [July 1807]*
Old Print Shop, New York; Royal Ontario Museum, Toronto, 1953, 953.132.2
Exh: Willistead Art Gallery of Windsor, 1967 (14)
Lit: ROM cat. 804

150 *Falls of the Poquisque [Pokiok] on the River St John, New Brunswick*, 1807
Monochrome grey wash, 130 × 191 mm.; signed and dated 23 July 1807
Sotheby (Toronto), May 1968 (253)
The above information appears in the sale catalogue.

151 *Falls of Poquisquod [Pokiok] on St. John River, New Brunswick, July 23, 1807*, 1807
Sepia wash, 125 × 188 mm.; inscr. as title on mount
Sotheby (Toronto), 27–8 May 1980 (147)
The above information appears in the sale catalogue.
See **160**.

152 *Presqu'Isle [Presque Isle], S^t. John's River*, 1807
Blue-grey wash, 181 × 254 mm. R: autogr. inscr. l.r. as title; v: autogr. inscr.: *Presque Isle – St John's River July 1807*
Walter T. Spencer, London; Public Archives of Canada, Ottawa, 1910, I-8
From the 'George Heriot Album'

153 *View of the Great Falls of the Saint John.*, 1807
Grey wash, 134 × 187 mm. V: autogr. inscr. as title; below is sign.: *Drawn on the spot by Geo Heriot/ July 29th. 1807.*
Walter T. Spencer, London; Public Archives of Canada, Ottawa, 1910, I-28
Reworked c 1820

154 *Narrows of S^t. John's River – /N Brunswick 1807*, 1807
Grey-brown wash over pencil on light-pink paper, 125 × 188 mm.
V: autogr. inscr. as title
Old Print Shop, New York; Royal Ontario Museum, Toronto, 1953, 953.132.5
Lit: ROM cat 806

155 *Saint John River*, 1807
India ink wash, 130 × 171 mm. V: inscr.: *Settlement of Madawaska on the River St. John*; sign.: *Drawn on the spot by Geo. Heriot 29 July 1807*
Frank Jewett Mather; Art Museum, Princeton University, 1949, 49.10
Exh: G.H. cat. 67
Lit: *G. Heriot*, p 50 (ill.)

156 *Ferry on the Jacques Quartier [Cartier]/20th September 1807.*, 1807
Dark brown wash over pencil, 127 × 187 mm. V: autogr. inscr. as title
Old Print Shop, New York; Royal Ontario Museum, Toronto, 1953, 953.132.7
Exh: Willistead Art Gallery of Windsor 1967 (17)
Lit: ROM cat. 835 (ill.)

157 *Repentigny*, 1807
Grey wash, 127 × 183 mm. V: autogr. inscr.: *[... ?] and Replentini. 22d Septem 1807/River St. Lawrence.*
Walter T. Spencer, London; Public Archives of Canada, Ottawa, 1910, I-6
From the 'George Heriot Album'; see **307** for a later copy.

158 *St. Anne's Church[,] Ottawa River[,] Montreal*, 1807
Grey wash, 125 × 186 mm. R: inscr. on old mount l.c.: *Passage of N.W. Voyagers*; below: autogr. inscr. as title; below in another hand: *Sept 30. 1807*; l.r. on mount also in another hand: *Geo Heriot*; v: autogr. inscr.: *[... ?]/of the N.W. Voyagers. 30th. Sept 1807/St. Anne's Church. Ottawa River/Montreal.*
A.H. O'Brien, Esq.(?); Public Archives of Canada, Ottawa, 1918?, I-66

159 *[... ?] Lake of the/Two Mountains, 1st October, 1807.*, 1807
Brown wash over pencil, 127 × 186 mm. V: autogr. inscr. as title
Old Print Shop, New York; Royal Ontario Museum, Toronto, 1953, 953.132.16
Exh: Willistead Art Gallery of Windsor, 1967 (16)
Lit: ROM cat. 836 (ill.); *G. Heriot*, p 52 (ill.)
The view shows the Indian village and the Catholic mission.

160 *Fall of the Poquioc [Pokiok], St John's River./New Brunswick*, c 1807
Brown wash with scraping, 241 × 344 mm. V: autogr. inscr. as title
Old Print Shop, New York; Royal Ontario Museum, Toronto, 1953, 953.132.29
Lit: ROM cat. 803 (ill.); Paul Duval, *Canadian Water Colour Painting* (Toronto 1953), pl.2
Copy (?) of **151**

161 *Grand Isle. Settlement of Madawaska./River St John. America*, c 1807
Black and grey washes, 111 × 184 mm. V: inscr. as title
Old Print Shop, New York; Royal Ontario Museum, Toronto, 1953, 953.132.14
Lit: ROM cat. 808

162 *The Three Falls of the Montmorency*, 1808
Grey brown wash, pencil on stained yellow paper, 130 × 190 mm. V: autogr. inscr.: *Les Trois Saults de Montmorenci./12 miles from Quebec.*; sign.: *Heriot. 12th Augt. 1808.*

Old Print Shop, New York; Royal Ontario Museum, Toronto, 1953, 953.132.15
Exh: Willistead Art Gallery of Windsor, 1967 (18)
Lit: ROM cat. 814; G. Heriot, p 54 (ill.)

163 *Part of the Fort Slausser Fall at Niagara*, 1808
Watercolour, 133 × 184 mm. V: autogr. inscr. as title; sign.: *Geo Heriot May 1808.*
Dr P.A. Forman
Exh: G.H. cat. 72
Copies of this drawing were made in c 1837 (?); see **313**, **314**.

164 *Part of the Fort Slausser Fall of Niagara.*, 1808
Watercolour, 133 × 184 mm. V: autogr. inscr. as title; sign.: *Geo Heriot 1808.*
Waddington's (Toronto), 15–17 Feb. 1978 (479); National Postal Museum, Ottawa

165 *View of a Waterfal[l] at/Wolf's [Wolfe's] Cove.*, c 1808
Grey wash, 129 × 182 mm. R: in pencil, l.r. album page: *Wolfe's Cove*; v: autogr. inscr. as title; sign.: *Geo Heriot.*
Walter T. Spencer, London; Public Archives of Canada, Ottawa, 1910, 1-7
From the 'George Heriot Album'

***166** *Fête given by/Sir James Craig at Spencer Wood*, 1809. Figure 53
Watercolour over pencil, 247 × 365 mm. R: sign. l.r.: *Geo Heriot/1809*; v: autogr. inscr. as title; also: *General Brock/Sir James Kempt/General Thornton/ Bishop of Quebec Dr Mountain/Chief Justice Sewell*
Purchased in Hamburg; Walter A. Brandt (formerly)
Exh: G.H. cat. 97
Lit: Derek Clifford, *Collecting English Water Colours* (London 1970), (108); *G. Heriot*, p 55 (ill.)
Spencer Wood was an estate overlooking the St Lawrence about two miles west of the city walls of Quebec. First named Powell Place after its owner Sir Henry Watson Powell, who resided there from 1780 to 1795, it was later renamed Spencer Wood after Spencer Percival, prime minister of Great Britain from 1809 to 1812; it was used by various governors as a centre of social entertainment from the time of Sir James Craig (1748–1812), governor-general of Canada from 1807 to 1811. The members of the band in the foreground are wearing the tunics of the 100th Foot Regiment, which was serving in Quebec at this time. It later became the Leinster Regiment (Royal Canadians), which name it held until its disbandment in 1922.

167 *Natural Steps, Montmorency, 21 June 1809*, 1809
Grey wash, 137 × 178 mm.
Reford Sale, Sotheby (Toronto), 27–9 May 1968 (254)
The above information appears in the sale catalogue.

168 *Naturel Steps, Montmorency, June 21, 1809*, 1809
Sepia wash, 138 × 175 mm.
Sotheby (Toronto), 27–8 May 1980 (146)
The above information appears in the sale catalogue.

169 *Halifax from St George's [George's] Island, Nova Scotia*, c 1809
Watercolour over pencil, 130 × 185 mm. V: autogr. inscr.: *G[... ?] Saint George's Island*
Anthony Reed, London; Sotheby (London), 22 Oct. 1980, 152 (ill.)
See **16**.

170 *L'Assomption.*, 1810
Watercolour over pencil, 196 × 285 mm. V: autogr. inscr. as title; sign. below: *Geo Heriot 26 Octob 1810*
Old Print Shop, New York; Royal Ontario Museum, Toronto, 1953, 953.132.13
Lit: ROM cat. 834 (ill.); *G. Heriot*, p 56 (ill.)
'I visited two places where I had never before been, and was charmed with both – L'Assomption, and Terrebonne' (NBM, Winslow Papers, vol X, G.H., Quebec, to E. Winslow, Kingsclear, 18 Oct. 1810).

***171** *Terrebonne*, 1810. Figure 60
Watercolour, 192 × 292 mm. V: autogr. inscr. as title; sign.: *Geo Heriot 26 Octob 1810*
Private collection
See **170**.

172 *Chateau Richer*, 1810
Watercolour, 133 × 178 mm. V: autogr. inscr. as title; sign.: *Geo Heriot 1810*
Private collection

173 *River St Charles, 1810*, 1810
Watercolour, 124 × 178 mm.
Private collection
Exh: *A Pageant of Canada* (Ottawa 1967), cat. 224 (ill.)
See **303**.

174 *Beauport*, c 1810
Watercolour, 124 × 178 mm.
Private collection
Exh: *A Pageant of Canada* (Ottawa 1967), cat. 225
Lit: *G. Heriot*, p 56 (ill.)

175 *Falls of La Puce*, 1812
Watercolour, 130 × 195 mm. R: on album page, l.r.: *La Puce 1812*; v: autogr. inscr. as title to which is added: *Feb. 1812*
Walter T. Spencer, London; Public Archives of Canada, Ottawa, 1910, I-4
Lit: Jean Bruchési, 'George Heriot,' *Cahiers des Dix*, 10 (Montreal 1945), opp. p 193; *G. Heriot*, p 58 (ill.)
From the 'George Heriot Album'

176 *Part of Upper Lake St Charles.*, 1812
Watercolour, 134 × 174 mm. V: autogr. inscr. as title; below sign.: *Geo Heriot. March 1812.*
Walter T. Spencer, London; Public Archives of Canada, Ottawa, 1910, I-11
From the 'George Heriot Album'

***177** *Distillery at Beauport near Quebec.*, 1812. Figure 62
Watercolour over pencil, 121 × 174 mm. R: sign. l.l.: *G. Heriot*; v: autogr. inscr. as title; sign.: *Geo Heriot March 1812*
Old Print Shop, New York; Royal Ontario Museum, Toronto, 1954, 954.102.2
Lit: ROM cat. 819 (ill.)

***178** *Falls of the Chaudiere. Quebec.*, c 1812. Figure 61
Watercolour over pencil, laid down, 138 × 209 mm. R: autogr. inscr. l.c. mount as title; sign. l.r. mount: *Geo Heriot.*; v: inscr.: *J & A.H. Mackonochie*
Laing Galleries, Toronto; Royal Ontario Museum, Toronto, 1955, 955.157.10
Lit: ROM cat. 832; *G. Heriot*, p 57 (ill.)
Probably from the Mackonochie Sale, Sotheby (London), 21 July 1943
For a reference to the Mackonochie family, see **200**.

179 *Cottages in Canada*, c 1812
Watercolour, 124 × 189 mm.
Squire Gallery, London; Ingram family collection, 1954

180 *Monkville [Monklands] near Montreal*, 1813
Watercolour on pencil, 138 × 189 mm. V: autogr. inscr.: *Monkville near Montreal/Geo Heriot 16 May 1813.*; r: autogr. inscr. l.c. old mount as title; inscr. l.l. old mount: *16 May 1813*; inscr. l.r. old mount: *Geo Heriot*; v: inscr. old mount: *Matlock, Derbyshire, 1819* (date in pencil)
A.H. O'Brien, Esq.; Public Archives of Canada, Ottawa, 1918, I-65
The colour of the drawing has faded. Heriot was in Montreal this year to arrange a daily post between Montreal and Quebec (GPO, London, Post 44/2, fol 1, G.H., Quebec, to F. Freeling, London, 8 June 1814.) Monklands, built by the Monk family, was situated at Côte St Antoine.

***181** *Providence, Rhode Island, 18 June/1815*, 1815. Figure 64
Watercolour, 154 × 584 mm. V: inscr. as title
Maxim Karolik, Esq.; presented by him to Boston Museum of Fine Arts, 1959, 59.106

182 *Chambly Castle. Canada.*, c 1815
Watercolour, laid down, 121 × 184 mm. R: inscr. l.c. mount as title; l.r.: *G. Heriot.*
William Basil Heriot; Mrs L.H. Sternau; Art Gallery of Windsor, 1968, 68–20
Lit: *G. Heriot*, p 59 (ill.)
Possibly related to visit of 5, 6 June 1815; see **335**, fols 2r, 3r. A letter written by William B. Heriot to Dr Caldwell Woodruff in response to a letter from the latter includes the following information: 'We have ... one original pen picture of Chambly Castle Canada done by George Heriot the P.M. General.' This letter, dated 31 Dec. 1932, is in the possession of Mrs Lillian Heriot Sternau.

183 *Middlebury, Vermont*, c 1815
Watercolour, 162 × 229 mm.
Old Watercolour Society, New York (1949); present whereabouts unknown

Lit: *Panorama* (Feb. 1949), (ill.)
Developed from sketches dated 10 June 1815; see **335**, fol 9r.

184 *Panoramic view from Salem Neck around Salem from Beverly to Marblehead*, c 1815
Watercolour, 133 × 2286 mm. V: inscr.: *Marble Head near Boston N. America* and *Marblehead* and *Salem 17 June*
Old Print Shop, New York; Mrs Augustus P. Loring, Jr; Peabody Museum, Salem, Mass., 1947, 11,864
Lit: M.V. and D. Brewington, *Marine Paintings and Drawings at the Peabody Museum* (Salem 1968), (640)

185 *West Point on the Hudson or North River*, c 1816
Watercolour, 211 × 356 mm. V: inscr. as title
Maxim Karolik, Esq.; presented by him to Boston Museum of Fine Arts, 1959, 59.105
Probably based on sketches of this location dated 18 July 1815; see **336**.
Watermark: Fleur-de-lys in shield ending in trefoil; *1811* below

186 *Distant View of Washington from Georgetown June, 1815*, c 1816
Grey wash, 194 × 319 mm. V: inscr. as title
Maxim Karolik, Esq.; presented by him to Boston Museum of Fine Arts, 1959, 59.104

187 *The Government Buildings at Washington D.C.*, c 1816
Watercolour, size unknown
J.C.A. Heriot, Esq.; Ernest C. Dodge, Esq.; present whereabouts unknown
Lit: J.C.A. Heriot, 'George Heriot, Author-Artist,' *Americana*, 5 (Sept.–Oct. 1910), 888–92 (ill.)
Based on sketch, fol 19r, **335**

188 *Lake [St] Charles near Quebec 1815.*, c 1816
Watercolour, 163 × 247 mm. R: inscr. on old mount in pencil, l.c.: *Lake Saint Charles Near Quebec/1807*; v: inscr. as title
Walter T. Spencer, London; Public Archives of Canada, Ottawa, 1910, I-13
From the 'George Heriot Album'

189 *Montreal*, c 1816
Watercolour, laid down, 113 × 195 mm. R: autogr. inscr. l.c. as title; also *1810* (in a later hand?)
J.C.A. Heriot, Esq. (?); Miss A. Lighthall; McCord Museum, McGill University, Montreal, 1973, M 973.152.1
Paper yellowed by exposure to light; his watercolour is possibly on fol 17, **334**.

190 *View from the Warren, Woolwich.*, c 1816
Watercolour, 136 × 186 mm.
Public Archives of Canada, Ottawa, 1922?, I-64
Exh: G.H. cat. 113

191 *Rochester Abbey, Canterbury*, c 1816
Watercolour, 112 × 195 mm. (sight). R: autogr. inscr. l.c. as title; inscr. on mount: *Leaf from Sketch Book of George Heriot 1766–1844*; v: watercolour; autogr. inscr. l.c.: *Netley Abbey nr Southampton*

J.C.A. Heriot, Esq.; W.L. Day, Esq.; Sotheby (Toronto), 5–7 Nov. 1979 (292)
Possibly fol 68, **334**.

***192** *Falls on the Clyde*, c 1816. Figure 73
Watercolour, 114 × 188 mm. R: autogr. inscr. l.r.: *The Clyde*; v: pen sketch of trees
Walter T. Spencer, London; Public Archives of Canada, Ottawa, 1910, I-12
From the 'George Heriot Album'
See **193**.

193 *Falls on the Clyde*, c 1816
Watercolour, size unknown
Present whereabouts unknown
This watercolour was illustrated in *The Times* (London), 17 June 1961.
It appears to have been developed from **192**.

194 *Bonnington Fall – Clyde*, c 1816
Watercolour, 114 × 189 mm. (corners cropped). R: autogr. inscr. l.l. as title; v: pen sketch of three trees
Public Archives of Canada, Ottawa, 1922?, I-19
Lit: *G. Heriot*, p 65 (ill.)
From the 'George Heriot Album'; this sketch provided the design for **195**.

195 *Bonnington Falls of the Clyde*, c 1816
Watercolour, 137 × 187 mm.
Iolo A. Williams, Esq.; Dudley Snelgrove, Esq.
See **194**.

***196** *[Po...lax?] or Druid's Temple which was found/on the Town Hill – Isle of Jersey – Transferred to Park Place, seat of Gen. Conway*, c 1816.
Figure 76
Watercolour over pencil, 154 × 241 mm. R: autogr. inscr. l.c. mount as title
Colnaghi, London; anonymous donor; Museum of Art, Rhode Island School of Design, Providence, 1969, 69.154.23
Exh: G.H. cat. 114 (ill.)
This may have been developed from a watercolour of c 1786–7, or may have been based on the etching of c 1789 (**348**). About 1787 the 'Temple of the Druids' was removed from its location on St Helier's Hill to make way for military improvements on the site. It was presented by the 'Vingtaine de la Ville' to the then-governor, Marshall Seymour Conway, who had it removed from the hill to his estate at Park Place, near Henley-on-Thames, where it still stands.

197 *Mont Orgueil Castle, Jersey – Channel Islands*, c 1816
Watercolour, 127 × 191 mm. V: autogr. inscr. as title; sign.: *Geo. Heriot*
Billingshurst, Sussex; Brigadier Willis Moogk, OBE, 1942
Exh: G.H. cat. 115
Perhaps based on a watercolour, c 1786–7, or the etching of c 1789 (**351**).
A watercolour of the same subject appeared in Sotheby (Toronto) sale, 24 Apr. 1969 (369).

198 *St[e] Geneviève, or the Pantheon at Paris – February 1817*, 1817
Watercolour, 187 × 268 mm. V: autogr. inscr. as title
Richard Ivor, London; private collection, 1976

199 *La Tour Magne a Nismes [Nîmes]*, 1817
Watercolour, size unknown; 'signed and dated 1817'
Present whereabouts unknown
Lit: *The Times* (London), 17 June 1961 (ill.)

***200** *Isle Barbe near Lyon. March 1817.*, 1817. Figure 77
Watercolour, 102 × 165 mm. R: autogr. inscr. as title, on mount
Family descent from John Heriot (1760–1833) to present owner, Miss Mary Alison Emma Mackonochie
One of the three watercolours on a page from a Heriot album which was sold at the Mackonochie Sale, Sotheby, 21 July 1943. This album is believed to have been signed on the flyleaf and had a description indicating that this and other watercolours contained were intended to be part of a 'Picturesque tour' (perhaps originally intended for the publication later entitled *A Picturesque Tour ... through the Pyrenean Mountains* [1824]). Although the majority of the watercolours in the album were placed three to a page, there were instances when only two appeared and sometimes only one. See the other two watercolours: **201**, **202**.

201 *Lyon. March 1817.*, 1817
Watercolour, 102 × 165 mm. R: autogr. inscr. as title l.c. mount
Family descent from John Heriot (1760–1833) to present owner, Miss Mary Alison Emma Mackonochie

202 *View from the Old Castle at Lyon Apr. 1817*, 1817
Watercolour, 102 × 165 mm. R: autogr. inscr. as title l.c. mount
Family descent from John Heriot (1760–1833) to present owner, Miss Mary Alison Emma Mackonochie

203 *Superga near Turin 1817*, 1817
Sepia wash, pen and ink on pencil, 110 × 174 mm. V: inscr. in pencil as title
Walter T. Spencer, London; Public Archives of Canada, Ottawa, 1910, I-26
From the 'George Heriot Album'

204 *Tivoli, June 1817.* I, 1817
Watercolour, 111 × 176 mm. R: autogr. inscr. as title on paper strip pasted on l.c. mount
Trustees of Miss Kathleen Fenwick Estate
Exh: Willistead Art Gallery of Windsor, 1967 (10); G.H. cat. 116
Lit: *G. Heriot*, p 71 (ill.)

205 *Tivoli, June 1817.* II, 1817
Watercolour, 111 × 176 mm. R: autogr. inscr. as title on paper strip pasted on l.c. mount
Trustees of Miss Kathleen Fenwick Estate
Exh: Willistead Art Gallery of Windsor, 1967 (11); G.H. cat. 117

206 *Tivoli : June 1817.*, 1817

Watercolour, laid down, 111 × 178 mm. R: autogr. inscr. as title on paper strip pasted on l.c. mount
Richard Ivor, London; Mrs F.K. Smith, 1976
A watercolour 'from his [Heriot's] Italian Tour of 1817' of this subject, and of similar dimensions, was offered for sale in 1954 by Alister Mathews, Bournemouth, cat. 45 (Autumn 1954), 907 (12).

207 *A View of Sicily*, c 1817
Watercolour, laid down, 151 × 217 mm. R: inscr. as title l.c. mount with date: *1817*
A. Mathews, Hampshire; Richard Ivor, London; Professor D.F. Crawley, 1976
Lit: Alister Mathews, Bournemouth, cat. 45 (Autumn 1954) 907 (5)

208 *Distant view of Turin*, c 1817
Watercolour, size unknown
Present whereabouts unknown
This watercolour was illustrated in *The Times* (London), 17 June 1961.

209 *Florence from the Gardens of Boboli.*, c 1817
Pencil and watercolour, laid down, 118 × 185 mm. R: autogr. inscr. l.l. mount; sign. attached to l.r. mount: *Geo Heriot*
J.F. McCrindle, Esq., on indefinite loan to The William Benton Museum of Art, The University of Connecticut, Storrs
Lit: *British Drawings and Watercolours: A Selection from the J.F. McCrindle Collection, The William Benton Museum of Art, the University of Connecticut* (Storrs 1974), p 20 (14)

210 *View in Italy – Vents of the airy caverns*, c 1817
Black chalk, pencil, and watercolour, laid down, 171 × 248 mm. R: inscr. l.c. mount as title; also;*G. Heriot 1766–1844*; v: *Mount Rolius [?] in Italy with the vents of the airy caverns* and another notation: *Bridge at Stirling*
Miss Margaret Pilkington; Whitworth Art Gallery, Manchester, 1950, D.3.1950

211 *Bonnington Falls*, c 1817
Watercolour, 111 × 175 mm.
de Vooght Galleries Ltd., Vancouver

212 *Side View of the Falls of Montmorenci [Montmorency]./from the West.*, c 1817
Brown, grey, and green washes, scraping, 189 × 136 mm. V: autogr. inscr. as title; sign.: *Geo Heriot*
Old Print Shop, New York; Royal Ontario Museum, Toronto, 1953, 953.132.12
Lit: ROM cat. 816

213 *Landscape with Waterfall [Montmorency Falls]*, c 1817
Watercolour, laid down, 117 × 184 mm.
Sir Harry F. Wilson, KCMG , KBE; Victoria and Albert Museum, London, 1927, P.50-1927
Lit: *G. Heriot*, p 72 (ill.)
This watercolour may have been developed from a sketch of c 1816 (possibly reworked in 1817): fol 62r, **334**.

214 *Lintz [Linz]. Upper Austria. May 1818*, 1818

Watercolour, 117 × 195 mm. R: autogr. inscr. as title l.c. mount
Ven. F.H.D. Smythe; British Museum, London, 1949, 1949.10.4
Date incorrectly transcribed '1808' by British Museum

215 *Salveln[,] Saltzburg [Salzburg]. 1818*, 1818
Pen and grey wash, 279 × 460 mm. R: autogr. inscr. l.r. as title; sign.: *G Heriot*
Mr Macpherson; British Museum, London, 1867, LB 4 1867-12-14-85
Exh: G.H. cat. 119
Lit: L. Binyon, *Catalogue of English Drawings* (London 1900), p 307 (4)

216 *Mill in the Principality of Saltzburg [Salzburg] 1818*, 1818
Pen and grey wash, 314 × 464 mm. R: autogr. inscr. l.c. as title
Mr Macpherson; British Museum, London, 1867, LB 1 1867-1-12-773
Lit: L. Binyon, *Catalogue of English Drawings* (London 1900), p 307 (1)

***217** *Walzenan [? Watzmann][,] Saltzburg [Salzburg] 1818.*, 1818. Figure 79
Pen and watercolour, 279 × 456 mm. R: autogr. inscr. l.r. as title
Mr Macpherson; British Museum, London, 1867, LB 3 1867-12-14-86
Lit: L. Binyon, *Catalogue of English Drawings* (London 1900), p 307 (3)
See **218**.

***218** *Salzburg*, 1818. Figure 80
Watercolour, 112 × 175 mm. R: autogr. inscr. l.c. mount: *Saltzburg.1818.*
Miss K. Fenwick; Dr R.H. Hubbard, 1974, acquired from the Kathleen Fenwick Estate
The view is the same as that of **217**.

219 *View near Salzburg*, 1818
Watercolour, 111 × 187 mm. R: autogr. inscr. l.c. mount: *Saltzburg.1818*
Witt Collection, Courtauld Institute, London, 4231
Exh: G.H. cat. 121

220 *View near Salzburg*, 1818
Watercolour, 150 × 228 mm.; inscr. and dated: *23 May 1818*
Sotheby (New York), 19 Jan. 1980 (95) (ill.)
The above information has been taken from the sale catalogue.

221 *Roman Temple at Holbroun [? Hellbrunn] near Saltzburg [Salzburg]./24 May 1818.*, 1818
Grey wash over pencil, 169 × 242 mm. R: autogr. inscr. l.c. old mount: *Temple in the Rock at Holbrün Saltzburg 24 May 1818*; v: autogr. inscr. as title
Sotheby (Toronto), 1–3 Nov. 1971; Public Archives of Canada, Ottawa, 1971.88.6

222 *Rustic figures in a country lane*, 1818
Watercolour over pencil, 132 × 181 mm. R: inscr.: *Finchley August 1 1818*
Private collection

223 *A Ruin in Britain (?)*, c 1818
Watercolour over pencil on blue-grey paper, laid down, 216 × 335 mm. R: autogr. inscr. l.c. mount: *Cataract of the Chaudiere.*; sign. l.r. mount: *G.H.*; in pencil l.r. mount: *G Heriot/Engraved*
Sotheby, London; Royal Ontario Museum, Toronto, 1951, 951.41.23
Lit: ROM cat. 842

224 *Landscape in France*, c 1818
Sepia wash, 165 × 229 mm. R: inscr. l.c. (in elderly hand): *somewhere in France 1818*
A. Beese; Ingram family collection, 1963

***225** *Prince Schwarzenberg's Egyptian Cemetery*, c 1818. Figure 78
Pen and grey wash, 289 × 464 mm. R: autogr. inscr. l.l.: *Prince Schwarzenberg's Aegin – [Cemetière des Romains]*; (the words in square brackets have been struck) and l.r.: *Aiden*
Mr Macpherson; British Museum, London, 1867, LB 2 1867-10-12-774
Exh: G.H. cat. 120 (ill.)
Lit: L. Binyon, *Catalogue of English Drawings* (London 1900), p 307 (2)

226 *Mäusethurm on the Rhine*, c 1818
Watercolour, 140 × 191 mm. R: inscr. on paper attached to l.c. mount: *Mauseturm*
Alister Mathews, Bournemouth; Gerald C. Paget, Esq., 1960; Dr Helmut Tenner, Heidelberg, sale cat., 1975 (3274)

227 *Pfalz on the Rhine*, c 1818
Watercolour, 140 × 191 mm. R: inscr. on paper attached to l.c. mount: *Phalz*
Alister Mathews, Bournemouth; Gerald C. Paget, Esq., 1960; Dr Helmut Tenner, Heidelberg, sale cat., 1975 (3274)

228 *Hammerstein*, c 1818
Watercolour, 140 × 191 mm. R: inscr. on paper attached to l.c. mount: *Hammerstern*
Alister Mathews, Bournemouth; Gerald C. Paget, Esq., 1960; Dr Helmut Tenner, Heidelberg, sale cat., 1975 (3274)

229 *Heidelberg*, c 1818
Watercolour, 140 × 191 mm. R: inscr. as title on paper attached to l.c. mount
Alister Mathews, Bournemouth; private collection, 1960

230 *Ehrenbreitstein*, c 1818
Watercolour, 140 × 191 mm.
Alister Mathews, Bournemouth; Gerald C. Paget, Esq., 1960; Dr Helmut Tenner, Heidelberg, sale cat., 1975 (3274)

231 *Castle ruin on the Rhine*, c 1818
Watercolour, 140 × 191 mm.
Alister Mathews, Bournemouth; Gerald C. Paget, Esq., 1960; Dr Helmut Tenner, Heidelberg, sale cat., 1975 (3274)

232 *Rheinfels*, c 1818
Watercolour, 140 × 191 mm.
AlisterMathews, Bournemouth; Gerald C. Paget, Esq., 1960; Dr Helmut Tenner, Heidelberg, sale cat., 1975 (3274)

233 *Near Bingen*, c 1818
Watercolour, 140 × 191 mm. R: inscr. as title on paper attached to l.c. mount as title
Alister Mathews, Bournemouth; Gerald C. Paget, Esq., 1960; Dr Helmut Tenner, Heidelberg, sale cat., 1975 (3274)

234 *View on the Danube near Lintz [Linz]*, c 1818
Sepia wash, laid down, 108 × 173 mm. R: autogr. inscr. l.c. mount as title
Private collection

235 *St Cuthbert's [Lindisfarne Priory], Holy Island, Durham*, 1819
Watercolour, 127 × 216 mm. V: inscr. as title and dated: *30 June 1819*
Billingshurst, Sussex; Brigadier Willis Moogk, OBE, 1942
Exh: G.H. cat. 122
The sketch for the finished watercolour **247**

236 *View of a Bridge, Dalkeith*, 1819
Bistre ink, pen, and wash, 117 × 184 mm. V: autogr. inscr.: *Dalkeith 24th July 1819*
P. Mellon, Esq.; Yale Center for British Art, Paul Mellon Collection

237 *Stirling Castle 31 July 1819*, 1819
Grey wash with white gouache on grey paper, 126 × 192 mm. V: autogr. inscr. as title
Walter T. Spencer, London; Public Archives of Canada, Ottawa, 1910, I-21
From the 'George Heriot Album'

***238** *Roslin Castle. Edinburgh.*, 1819. Figure 81
Watercolour, laid down, 182 × 267 mm. R: autogr. inscr. as title l.c. mount; sign. l.l. mount: *Geo Heriot 19 Augt. 1819.*
Richard Ivor, London; Mr. and Mrs Donald Good, 1976
Exh: G.H. cat. 124 (ill.)

239 *View of Bowder Stone [Cumberland]*, 1819
Watercolour, 150 × 229 mm. V: autogr. inscr. as title; also: *Rust White Carn, [?] and Gladdermore. 14th Septem 1819/Stone 62 feet, height 36 do, Circumference 89 do Weight 1971 Tons-13 Cwt.*
Alex Gibson, Toronto

240 *Matlock*, 1819
Watercolour, 120 × 185 mm. V: autogr. inscr. as title, cut from original mount with date: *28th September 1819*
Warda Drummond, Montreal
A view of cottages at Matlock was exhibited at the Walker's Galleries, London, Christmas Exhibition, Nov. 1957 (50).
A view of Matlock appeared in the Sotheby (London) sale, 2 Mar. 1966.

241 *View near Crumpford [Cromford] Bridge. Matlock. 29 Sept 1819*, 1819
Watercolour over pencil, 120 × 185 mm. V: autogr. inscr. as title on paper cut from old mount
Frank T. Sabin, London; Royal Ontario Museum, Toronto, 1962, 962.58.6
Lit: ROM cat. 850

242 *Elgin Cathedral, 1819*, 1819
Watercolour, 127 × 178 mm. V: inscr. as title
Wren Gallery, London; Art Gallery of Windsor, 1968, 68.19
Exh: G.H. cat. 125
Lit: *G. Heriot*, p 74 (ill.)

243 *Barton House[,] Dawlish[,] Admiral Shanks*, 1819
Watercolour, 184 × 267 mm. V: inscr. as title; sign.: *Geo Heriot 1819*
S. Sabin, London; private collection, 1965

244 *Gruffenstein [Greifenstein] on the Danube/1818*, c 1819
Sepia wash on pencil, 118 × 175 mm. V: autogr.(?) inscr. in pencil as title
Walter T. Spencer, London; Public Archives of Canada, Ottawa, 1910, I-22
Lit: *G. Heriot*, p 73 (ill.)
From the 'George Heriot Album'; probably based on sketch(es) made in the previous year
A view of Griffenstein (sic) Castle attributed to Heriot appeared in the Christie (London) sale, Dec. 1961 (53)

245 *Caernarvon Castle./N Wales.*, c 1819
Grey wash on pencil, 132 × 270 mm. V: autogr. inscr. as title
Walter T. Spencer; Public Archives of Canada, Ottawa, 1910, I-24
From the 'George Heriot Album'

246 *View on the Hudson [River].*, c 1819
Grey-brown wash over pencil, 140 × 217 mm. V: autogr. inscr. as title
Old Print Shop, New York; Royal Ontario Museum, Toronto, 1953, 953.132.33
Lit: ROM cat. 848

247 *Lindisfarne Priory*, c 1819
Watercolour, 150 × 220 mm. V: inscr. in pencil: *Lindisfarne*; pencil sketch of Farnese Bull
Warda Drummond, Montreal
Exh: G.H. cat. 123
Based on a sketch dated 1819; see **235**.
A watercolour entitled *Lindisfarne Abbey, Holy Island, Northumberland – 1819* was exhibited at The Fine Arts Society, London, Apr. 1967 (65). Another entitled *Lindisfarne Abbey Ruins, Holy Island*, dated July 1819, was exhibited at Frank T. Sabin, London, Autumn Exhibition, 1950 (125).

248 *St Cuthbert's Abbey [Lindisfarne Priory], Durham*, c 1819
Watercolour, 146 × 229 mm.
George Robert Minkoff, Mass., USA
Lit: Rare Book Catalogue, no. 27 (1975), (52)
A watercolour attributed to Heriot entitled *St Cuthbert's Holy Island Durham* appeared in Sotheby (Toronto) sale, 24 Apr. 1969 (371).

249 *Wade's Bridge, Aberfeldy*, c 1819
Watercolour, 111 × 184 mm.
Christie (London), 14 Jan. 1975 (34); Richard Ivor, London
Formerly entitled 'A View in the West Highlands'

250 *Bridge and Castle Stirling*, c 1819
Watercolour, 151 × 186 mm. V: inscr. as title
Frank T. Sabin, London; Autumn Exhibition, 1950 (131); Glasgow Art Gallery, 1956, 56-11 (k)

251 *Culzean Castle*, c 1819
Watercolour, 105 × 430 mm. V: inscr. as title
Frank T. Sabin, London; Glasgow Art Gallery, 1956, 56-11 (m)

252 *Rouen April 1820*, 1820
Sepia wash, laid down, 108 × 171 mm. V: autogr. inscr. as title

R.H. Stephenson, Esq.; Victoria & Albert Museum, London, 1929, E.547-1929
Engr. Heriot's *A Picturesque Tour ... through the Pyrenean Mountains* (1824); see **360** (1).

253 *Le Mans Cathedral and part of the Town*, 1820
Watercolour, 124 × 200 mm. R: inscr. l.c. attached to mount: *Le Mans, 22 April 1820*
Alister Mathews, Bournemouth; private collection, 1957

254 *Cathedral at Le Mans 1820*, 1820
Sepia wash on pencil, 108 × 172 mm. V: inscr. in pencil, as title
Walter T. Spencer, London; Public Archives of Canada, Ottawa, 1910, I-27
Engr. Heriot's *A Picturesque Tour ... through the Pyrenean Mountains* (1824); see **360** (3).
From the 'George Heriot Album'

255 *Cathedral of Angouleme, April 28, 1820*, 1820
Watercolour, 140 × 216 mm. V: inscr. as title
Vincent Price Collection, Washington, DC; private collection, 1966

256 *La Pierre Levée. Poitiers 30th Apr. 1820*, 1820
Watercolour, 121 × 196 mm. R: autogr. inscr. as title cut from old mount l.c. mount; V: autogr. inscr.: *La Pierre Levée, on the field where the battle of Poitiers/ was fought; under which several English officers of rank lay./27th. April 1820.*
Helene-Arthur Galleries (Toronto); Waddington's (Toronto), 7 May 1981 (885); Dr and Mrs Bernard Greisman
Possibly this finished composition was based on **280**.

257 *South East View of the Cathedral at Bordeaux*, 1820
Watercolour, 184 × 273 mm. R: inscr. l.c. attached to mount: *South East View of the Cathedral at Bordeaux, begun by the English, carried on by the French and finished by the former in the Reign of Henry IV of England, 8, May, 1820*
Alister Mathews, Bournemouth; private collection, 1957
Page from a sketch-book; a view of Langon, 30 miles from Bordeaux, dated 18 May 1820, appeared in the exhibition of the Fine Arts Society, London, Mar. 1971 (76).

258 *Cathedral at Bourdeaux [Bordeaux]*, 1820
Sepia wash on pencil, 113 × 174 mm. V: inscr. in pencil as title and: *G. Heriot/1820*
Walter T. Spencer, London; Public Archives of Canada, Ottawa, 1910, I-25
Lit: *G. Heriot*, p 76 (ill.)
Engr. Heriot's *A Picturesque Tour ... through the Pyrenean Mountains* (1824); see **360** (6).
From the 'George Heriot Album'

259 *Aire on the Adour [Aire-sur-l'Adour]*, 1820
Watercolour, laid down, 127 × 203 mm. R: autogr. inscr. as title pasted on l.c. mount with date: *23d. May 1820.*
Vincent Price Collection, Washington, DC; Simpson Sears, Calgary; Glenbow-Alberta Institute, 1965, H.65.61

Exh: G.H. cat. 127
Lit: *G. Heriot*, p 75 (ill.)

260 *Château of Henri IV [... ?] [Pau]*, 1820
Watercolour, 118 × 216 mm. V: autogr. inscr. as title; also: *29 May 1820*
Martyn Gregory, London, 1980

261 *Citadel of Bayonne from the Town Walls*, 1820
Watercolour, 121 × 152 mm. R: inscr. as title on old mount and dated: *24 June 1820*
Christie (London), 17 June 1975 (12)
Information from sale catalogue

***262** *Burgos in Spain, June 1820*, 1820. Figure 82
Pen and sepia wash, laid down, 111 × 171 mm. V: inscr. as title
R.H. Stephenson, Esq.; Victoria and Albert Museum, London, 1929, E.550-1929
A watercolour attributed to Heriot entitled 'A Wooded Mountain Valley in Spain' was exhibited at Thos. Agnew and Sons, London, 15 Jan.–16 Feb. 1973 (287).

263 *Panoramic View of the Pyrenees*, 1820
Watercolour, partly laid down, 98 × 1270 mm. R: autogr. inscr. u.c.: *High Pyrenées*; v: autogr. inscr.: *Panoramic View of the Pyrénees, taken from Bagneres de Bigorre 1. Tourmalet 2. Pic du Midi 3. Mont Aigue 4. Montagnes de Pierfille 5. Montagnes de Edacterets [?] 6. Caesar's Camp*; also: *Geo. Heriot – 16 Augt 1820*
Private collection

264 *Bridge at Stirling*, c 1820
Watercolour, 127 × 217 mm. V: inscr. as title
Frank T. Sabin, London; Glasgow Art Gallery, 1956, 56-11 (j)
Probably based on a sketch of 1819

265 *Chepstow Castle*, c 1820
Watercolour, 116 × 182 mm. (sight)
Dr R.H. Hubbard, 1965
Exh: Willistead Art Gallery of Windsor, 1967 (12)

266 *Pittville near Cheltenham*, c 1820
Watercolour, 113 × 210 mm. (sight). V: autogr. inscr. (cut from original mount, taped on card backing framed drawing): *Pitt: Ville near Cheltenham*; sign.: *Drawn by G. Heriot Esqr.*
Christie (London), 13 Nov. 73 (106); Richard Ivor, London; W.F.E. Morley, Esq., 1980

***267** *Grenada, Harbour of St George*, c 1820. Figure 3
Watercolour, 191 × 298 mm.
Old Watercolour Society, New York, 1949; present whereabouts unknown
Lit: *Panorama* (Feb. 1949), (4) (ill.)
Probably based on sketches of 1778–81; see **268**.
The Rev. C.A. Mackonochie sale, Sotheby (London), 21 July 1943, contained, in lot 3210, views in the 'West Indies.' (For information on the Mackonochie family, see **200**.)

268 *Negro Dance, West Indies*, c 1820
Watercolour, 216 × 324 mm.
Old Watercolour Society, New York, 1949; present whereabouts unknown
Lit: *Panorama* (Feb. 1949), (5) (ill.)
Probably based on sketches of 1778–81; see **267**.

269 *Falls of La Puce near Quebec*, c 1820
Watercolour, touches of gouache on grey paper, 117 × 181 mm. V: faint pencil sketch
Old Print Shop, New York; Royal Ontario Museum, Toronto, 1953, 953.132.6
Lit: ROM cat. 833

***270** *Halifax, Nova Scotia*, c 1820. Figure 84
Watercolour, 254 × 381 mm.
W.H. Coverdale, Esq.; Edgar Sittig, Delaware Water Gap; Kennedy Galleries, New York; National Museums of Canada, 1974
Lit: *The Kennedy Quarterly*, 12:4 (Dec. 1973), 162 (ill.)
Probably based on a watercolour of c 1812

***271** *Quebec*, c 1820. Figure 83
Watercolour, 203 × 318 mm.
Private collection
Probably based on a sketch of the late 1790s

***272** *Greenwich from the point*, c 1820. Figure 85
Watercolour and gouache, 305 × 419 mm. V: inscr.: *J. & A. H. Mackonochie*
Colnaghi, London; National Maritime Museum, London, 1956, PR 56/61
Probably from the Mackonochie Sale, Sotheby (London), 21 July 1943. Based on **7**. For information on the Mackonochie family, see **200**.

273 *Caen*, c 1820
Sepia wash, laid down, 105 × 175 mm.
R.H. Stephenson, Esq.; Victoria & Albert Museum, London, 1929, E.548-1929
Engr. Heriot's *A Picturesque Tour ... through the Pyrenean Mountains* (1824); see **360** (2).

274 *Waterfalls in a Canyon [in the Pyrenees?]*, c 1820
Watercolour over pencil, 165 × 243 mm.
Laing Galleries, Toronto; Royal Ontario Museum, Toronto, 1955, 955.157.2
Lit: ROM cat. 846
Possibly a representation of the French Pyrenees, where torrents (called *gaves*) often fall in cascades such as are shown here

275 *Lauruns – Pyrenees*, c 1820
Sepia wash, laid down, 113 × 173 mm. R: autogr. inscr. l.c. mount as title
Private collection

276 *Cailnets[,] Pyrenees*, c 1820
Sepia wash, laid down, 108 × 171 mm. R: autogr. inscr. l.c. mount as title
Private collection

277 *Chateau de Lourde; in the Pyrenees*, c 1820
Sepia wash, laid down, 110 × 174 mm. R: inscr. l.c. mount as title
Phillips (Toronto), 26, 27 Jan. 1982 (20); private collection
A sepia wash drawing *View in the Pyranees [Pyrenees]* was sold 17 June 1982 by D. and J. Ritchie Ltd (Toronto); it is laid down with autogr. inscr. l.c. mount as title; it measures 102 × 175 mm.

278 *Pyrenees*, c 1820
Sepia wash, 116 × 178 mm.
Private collection

279 *Poitiers*, c 1820
Sepia wash, laid down, 108 × 175 mm.
R. H. Stephenson, Esq.; Victoria and Albert Museum, London, 1929, E.549-1929
Lit: *G. Heriot*, p 77 (ill.)
Engr. Heriot's *A Picturesque Tour ... through the Pyrenean Mountains* (1824); see **360** (5).

280 *Pierre Levée Poictiers [Poitiers]*, c 1820
Sepia wash over pencil, 106 × 173 mm. R: autogr. inscr. l.c. old mount as title
Sotheby (Toronto), 1–3 Nov. 1971 (161); Public Archives of Canada, Ottawa, 1971.88.4
See **256**.

281 *Angoulême*, c 1820
Sepia wash, 108 × 175 mm.
Squire Gallery London; Ingram family collection, 1954

282 *Bagnères-de-Bigorre*, c 1820
Sephia wash over pencil, 110 × 170 mm.
Christie (London), 21 May 1974 (65); Professor E. Aunger

283 *Panoramic View of Salzburg with the surrounding mountains and countryside*, c 1820
Watercolour, 298 × 794 mm. V: inscr.: *Geo. Heriot 22 May 1818*; autogr. inscr.: *View of Saltzburg*
The Venerable F.H.D. Smythe; Victoria and Albert Museum, London, 1949, E.871-1949
Exh: G.H. cat. 126
Probably based on sketches made in 1818

284 *Lindeau [Lindau], in Bavaria – an Island – in Lake Constance —*, c 1820
Sepia wash over pencil, laid down, 115 × 178 mm. R: autogr. inscr. as title l.c. old mount
Sotheby (Toronto), 1–3 Nov. 1971 (161); Public Archives of Canada, Ottawa, 1971.88.3

285 *View of Salerno*, c 1820
Watercolour, 318 × 775 mm.
Christopher Powney, London; Wren Gallery, London; Art Gallery of Windsor, 1970, 70.19
Exh: G.H. cat. 128

286 *Lake of Killarney.* I, c 1820
Watercolour, 137 × 192 mm. V: autogr. inscr. as title
Walter T. Spencer, London; Public Archives of Canada, Ottawa, 1910, I-1
From the 'George Heriot Album'

287 *Lake of Killarney.* II, c 1820
Watercolour, 137 × 197 mm. R: inscr. in pencil, l.r. album page: *Killarney*; v: autogr. inscr. as title
Walter T. Spencer, London; Public Archives of Canada, Ottawa, 1910, I-10
From the 'George Heriot Album'

288 *Château de Henri IV, Pau,* c 1820
Watercolour, 108 × 172 mm.
Wren Gallery, London; Art Gallery of Windsor, Gift of the Director's Fund, 1968, 68.42
Exh: G.H. cat. 129
Lit: *G. Heriot*, p 78 (ill.)

289 *Plymouth, England,* 1820–30
Watercolour and pencil, 116 × 183 mm. V: inscr. in pencil: *Plymouth George Heriot 1826*
Frank T. Sabin, London; Royal Ontario Museum, Toronto, 1962, 962,58.7
Lit: ROM cat. 849
A view of Ilfracombe, Devon, dated 18 May 1826, was shown at the exhibition of the Fine Arts Society, London, Mar. 1971 (75).

290 *North [Hudson] River, New York,* 1820–30(?)
Neutral washes, 129 × 187 mm. V: inscr.: *wash drawing of river with high banks*; inscr. in pencil as title
Maxim Karolik, Esq.; presented by him to Boston Museum of Fine Arts, 1962, 62.108

291 *Kenilworth Castle, 17th September 1821,* 1821
Watercolour, laid down, 127 × 241 mm. (sight). V: inscr. as title on mount
Walker Galleries, London; Herbert Art Gallery, Coventry, 1959, 79.59
Lit: *G. Heriot*, p 79 (ill.)

292 *Pembroke Castle,* 1823
Watercolour, 105 × 175 mm. V: autogr. inscr. on cut card as title; also: *3 June 1823*
Private collection

293 *E. View inner square of Pembroke Castle 4th June 1823,* 1823
Watercolour, 125 × 207 mm. V: inscr. as title; sign.(?): *Geo Heriot Esq.*; similar inscr. inside mount; also pencil sketch Pembroke Castle
Frank T. Sabin, London, Autumn Exhibition, 1950 (129); National Library of Wales, Aberystwyth, 1957, PB 3400
Lit: *G. Heriot*, p 80 (ill.)

294 *View of Aberystwyth Castle from the N.E. 31 July 1823,* 1823
Watercolour, 128 × 215 mm. V: inscr. as title; sign.(?): *Geo: Heriot Esq.*; similar inscr. as title in pencil inside mount

Frank T. Sabin, London, Autumn Exhibition, 1950 (123); National Library of Wales, Aberystwyth, 1970, PB 3399
Very faint pencil sketches on back of drawing

295 *Llanbadarn Church, Wales, near Aberystwyth. Augt 1823*, 1823
Watercolour, 105 × 175 mm. V: inscr. as title; similar inscr. in pencil inside mount
Frank T. Sabin, London; National Library of Wales, Aberystwyth, 1960, PB 3901

296 *S.W. View of Poitiers*, 1828
Watercolour, 124 × 197 mm. R: autogr. inscr. as title; also: *27th Apr. 1828*, on paper attached to mount Private collection

***297** *Arundel Castle, Sussex*, c 1828(?). Figure 86
Watercolour, 117 × 184 mm. V: inscr. as title
Billingshurst, Sussex; Brigadier Willis Moogk, OBE, 1942
Exh: G.H. cat. 130 (ill.)
Watermark: *1828*

298 *Castle of Vaucluse [near Avignon]*, c 1835 (?)
Grey wash over pencil, 122 × 178 mm. R: autogr. inscr. l.c. old mount as title; beneath in pencil: *near Avignon*
Sotheby (Toronto), 1–3 Nov. 1971 (161); Public Archives of Canada, Ottawa, 1971.88.5
Watermark: *G Wilmot 1835*

***299** *Royal Military Academy, Woolwich 1836*, 1836. Figure 89
Watercolour, 162 × 254 mm. (sight). V: inscr. as title
Richard Ivor, London; Woolwich Garrison Officers' Mess, 1974
Exh: G.H. cat. 131

300 *River S[t] John's/Canada*, c 1837(?)
Watercolour, 134 × 185 mm. V: inscr. as title; also: *James Scripps*
Public Archives of Canada, Ottawa, 1922?, I-58
Exh: Willistead Art Gallery of Windsor, 1967 (2)
A copy; the original, which has not yet come to light, must date from 1807 when Heriot was in the Maritimes.

301 *Reversing Falls of St John*, c 1837(?)
Watercolour, 183 × 246 mm. (sight). V: inscr.: *Mr Harriott – believed to have been made by George Heriot who travelled in New Brunswick ca. 1807*
Dr J. Clarence Webster; New Brunswick Museum, Saint John, 6633
Lit: *Webster Collection of Pictorial Canadiana Catalogue*, no. 4
A copy; whereabouts of original unknown

302 *Cape Diamond*, c 1837(?)
Watercolour, 128 × 183 mm. R: inscr. u.r. in pencil: *JS*; v: autogr. inscr. as title
Public Archives of Canada, Ottawa 1922?, I-57
Possibly 'JS' refers to 'James Scripps'; for example, see **300**, **303**, **312**, **316**.

303 *View on the River St Charles 1810*, c 1837(?)
Watercolour, 128 × 174 mm. R: inscr. on old mount: *View on the River Hill 1810*; v: inscr.: *James Scripps Mar 1810 View on the River S[t][... ?]/G.H. 18 [... ?]*

Public Archives of Canada, Ottawa, 1922?, I-44
A copy of **173**

304 *Fall of S[t] Ann[e]'s 30 Miles/N.E. from Quebec taken 1806*, c 1837(?)
Watercolour, 132 × 180 mm. R: inscr. on old mount: *Fall of St. Anne's 30 Miles/N.E. from Quebec. taken 1806*; v: autogr. inscr. as title
Public Archives of Canada, Ottawa, 1922?, I-53
Exh: G.H. cat. 132
A copy of **130**

305 *View at St. Augustin/on the St. Lawrence*, c 1837(?)
Watercolour, laid down, 125 × 181 mm. R: inscr. in pencil l.r. mount as title
Public Archives of Canada, Ottawa, 1922?, I-56
A copy; see original watercolour, **106.**

306 *Montmorency Falls*, c 1837(?)
Watercolour, 134 × 176 mm.
Public Archives of Canada, Ottawa, 1922?, I-43
A copy; present whereabouts of original unknown

307 *Repentigny*, c 1837(?)
Grey wash, laid down, 115 × 182 mm. R: inscr. l.r. mount: *James Scripps*; v: on mount in recent hand: *Copy of this picture in Album of Heriot pictures bears title Repentini 22d Septr. 1807 River St Lawrence*
Public Archives of Canada, 1922?, I-52
This is a copy of **157**.

***308** *A View of Lake and Fort Erie from Buffalo Creek*, c 1837(?). Figure 87
Watercolour, laid down, 129 × 182 mm.
Public Archives of Canada, Ottawa, 1922?, I-49
Exh: G.H. cat. 133
Copy of *A View of Lake and Ft Erie from Buffalo Creek* (aquatint by John Bluck after E Walsh 49th Regt.; dated 1811)

309 *Queens Town [Queenston]. Upper Canada/Landing place near which/Sir Gen. Brock/was killed*, c 1837(?)
Watercolour, 129 × 171 mm. V: autogr. inscr.: *Where the [... ?] the British is/near which [... ?] Brock was killed*; in another hand in pencil as title
Public Archives of Canada, Ottawa, 1922?, I-46
A copy; present whereabouts of original unknown

310 *Queen's Town [Queenston] Upper Canada/taken 1805*, c 1837(?)
Watercolour, 133 × 183 mm. V. autogr. inscr. as title
Public Archives of Canada, Ottawa, 1922?, I-59
Lit: Michael Bell, *Painters in a New Land* (Toronto 1973), p 146 (ill.)
A copy; present whereabouts of original unknown

311 *Village of Chippawa near the Falls of Niagara*, c 1837(?)
Watercolour, 133 × 180 mm.
Public Archives of Canada, Ottawa, 1922?, I-55
A copy; for the original watercolour, see **92**.

312 *Niagara Falls*, c 1837(?)
Grey wash on pencil, 130 × 179 mm. V: inscr. in pencil: *James Scripps Sep 1817*

Public Archives of Canada, Ottawa, 1922?, I-45
A version of **128**

313 *Part of Fort Hausser [Slausser] Fall Niagara 1804./J. Scrippes.*, c 1837(?)
Watercolour, 132 × 182 mm. R: inscr. in pencil on old mount as title; v: inscr. in pencil: *Part of Fort Slausser Fall/ Niagara 1804*; also in pencil: *W.W. Scripps*; *J. Scripps*
Public Archives of Canada, 1922?, I-47
A copy of **163**; despite the mount inscription the original watercolour seems to date from 1808; see also **314.**

314 *Part of the Fort Slausser Fall at Niagara*, c 1837(?)
Watercolour, 128 × 173 mm. R: inscr. in pencil on mount: *Part of the Fort Slausser Fall/at Montreal taken June 1804*; v: autogr. inscr.: *Part of the Fort Slausser Fall Niagara/taken [... ?]*
Public Archives of Canada, Ottawa, 1922?, I-48
A copy of **163**; see also **313**.

315 *View of a Shoreline*, c 1837(?)
Watercolour, 125 × 180 mm. V: inscr. in pencil: *W.W. Scripps 1817*
Public Archives of Canada, Ottawa, 1922?, I-63
This is a copy of an earlier drawing that has not yet come to light. Heriot mentioned a William A. Scripps of South Molton Street, London, in his will [prob. 11 195, sec. 512 (13)].

316 *View of River with Vessels*, c 1837(?)
Watercolour, 128 × 183 mm. V: inscr.: *James Scripps*
Public Archives of Canada, Ottawa, 1922?, I-62
This is another copy of the design of **315.**

317 *Pointe Lévis from Ange Gardien*, c 1837(?)
Watercolour, 131 × 186 mm.
Public Archives of Canada, Ottawa, 1922?, I-54
A copy of **112**.

318 *The Capture*, c 1838
Brown ink and watercolour, laid down, 85 × 128 mm. R: inscr. l.c. mount as title; sign. l.l.: *Geo Heriot*
Wren Gallery, London; Art Gallery of Windsor, 1970, 70 104b
Exh: G.H. cat. 135 (ill.)

319 *Virginia Pilot Boat*, c 1838
Watercolour, laid down, 83 × 127 mm. R: inscr. as title l.c. mount; sign. l.l.: *Geo Heriot*
R.F. Appleby, London; National Maritime Museum, London, 1954, PR 54/174 (5)
Exh: G.H. cat. 140

***320** *Compte [sic] D'Eu, King of the French Yachts*, c 1838. Figure 91
Pen, ink, watercolour, and scraping, laid down, 83 × 127 mm. R: inscr. as title l.c. mount; sign. l.l.: *Geo Heriot*
R.F. Appleby, London; National Maritime Museum, London, 1954, PR 54/174 (1)
Exh: G.H. cat. 138

321 *Lugger beating to Windward*, c 1838

Watercolour, laid down, 83 × 127 mm. R: inscr. as title l.c. mount; sign. l.l.: *Geo Heriot*
R.F. Appleby, London; National Maritime Museum, London, 1954, PR 54/174 (2)
Exh: G.H. cat. 139

322 *A Yacht Close-Hauled*, c 1838
Watercolour, laid down, 83 × 127 mm. R: sign. l.l.: *Geo Heriot*
R.F. Appleby, London; National Maritime Museum, London, 1954, PR 54/174 (3)

***323** *Reefing Topsails*, c 1838. Figure 92
Pen, ink, and watercolour, laid down, 83 × 127 mm. R: inscr. as title l.c. mount; sign. l.l.: *Geo Heriot*
R.F. Appleby, London; National Maritime Museum, London, 1954, PR 54/174 (6)
Exh: G.H. cat. 141

324 *H M Ship St George in the Hurricane of 1805, in the West Indies. Commanded by Honble Mic^{l} De Courcy*, c 1838
Watercolour, laid down, 83 × 127 mm. R: inscr. as title l.c. mount; sign. l.l.: *Geo Heriot*
R.F. Appleby, London; National Maritime Museum, London, 1954, PR 54/174 (4)

325 *Beating to Windward*, c 1838
Brown ink and watercolour, laid down, 92 × 130 mm. R: inscr. as title l.c. mount; sign. l.l.: *Geo Heriot*
Wren Gallery, London; Art Gallery of Windsor, 1970, 70.104a
Exh: G.H. cat. 136

***326** *Strong Gales and Squally reeved out cable*, c 1838. Figure 90
Pen, ink, and watercolour, 81 × 125 mm. R: sign. l.l.: *Geo Heriot*; v: inscr. as title W.P. Wolfe, Montreal; Musée du Québec, 1966, A 66 185 D
Exh: G.H. cat. 137 (ill.)

327 *Scudding in a Gale Wind*, c 1838
Sepia wash with pen and ink, laid down, 102 × 162 mm. R: inscr. as title l.c. mount; sign. l.l.: *Geo Heriot*
Morris Galleries, Toronto, 1976; private collection
Lit: *Canadian Classics* (1976), (28) (ill.)

328 *Carring [sic] Sail in Chase*, c 1838
Watercolour, pen and ink, laid down, 79 × 121 mm. R: inscr. as title l.c. mount; sign. l.l.: *Geo Heriot*
Morris Galleries, Toronto, 1976; private collection; Manuge Galleries, Halifax, 1979
Lit: *Canadian Classics* (1976), (27)

329 *Lugger close to the Wind*, c 1838
Sepia wash with pen and ink, laid down, 83 × 124 mm. R: inscr. as title l.c. mount; sign. l.l.: *Geo Heriot*
Morris Galleries, Toronto, 1976; private collection
Lit: *Canadian Classics* (1976), (26)

330 *Ullswater, Lake District*, c 1838

Watercolour, 162 × 241 mm. V: inscr. as title
Billingshurst, Sussex; Brigadier Willis Moogk, OBE, 1942

*331 *Abbey Cwn Hir*, c 1838. Figure 93
Monochrome wash, 137 × 202 mm. R: sign. l.l.: *Geo. Heriot*; v: inscr. in pencil: *1766–1844 George Heriot was Deputy Postmaster of Canada. Much travelled publisher Travel through the Canadas Abbey Cwn Hir, near Rhaidr or Rhayader*
R.G. Thornton, Esq.; National Library of Wales, Aberystwyth, 1963, PB 4916
Exh: G.H. cat. 134
Lit: *G. Heriot*, p 81 (ill.)

SKETCH-BOOKS

Many watercolours of long, narrow format (such as are included among the earliest works by Heriot in this check-list) are from sketch-books. During the period of research for this study I discovered the existence of six sketch-books. Five of them I have examined; the sixth (*Woolwich Sketch-Book* I) went missing from the Sotheby (London) sale of 17 March 1965, and has never, to my knowledge, reappeared. Of the five sketch-books that I have examined, I have had access to four of them over an extended period, and because of this, and because three of them illustrate North American landscapes, I have decided to list their contents. All descriptions and notes in the sketch-books in Heriot's handwriting are indicated within double quotation marks.

332 *Woolwich Sketch-Book* I, 1780s (probably)
Pencil, and watercolour, 111 × 254 mm.
W. Wheeler, Esq., Colnaghi (London); Sir Bruce Ingram; Sotheby (London) 17 Mar. 1965 (801A), missing from sale, present whereabouts unknown
In the entry in the sale catalogue the sketch-book is described as containing views in 'Southern England, including Woolwich, Blackheath, Box Hill, Dorking, Greenwich, Purfleet, Margate and Kingsgate, some inscribed, and contains autograph on the inside cover.' While the catalogue indicates that the sketch-book was from the collection of a 'Mr Guy,' research has indicated that it was actually owned by a 'Mr Wheeler.' Perhaps Guy was the previous owner, and possibly a descendant of George Heriot's sister Sophia, who married a Guy. The sale-catalogue entry also refers to a watercolour, *Conduit Vale Blackheath*, (pl 105 in Iolo Williams's *Early English Watercolours*), which seems to suggest that it is on a leaf from this particular sketch-book (see **10**).

333 *Woolwich Sketch-Book* II, 1787–89
Pencil, pen, and watercolour, approximate page size, 114 × 255 mm.
J.C.A. Heriot, Esq.; McCord Museum, Montreal (1928), M 6356; G.H. cat. 27
A grey cardboard-covered book
inner cover "G. Heriot"; also a book-plate inscribed 'John Charles

	Alison Heriot' and a modern label on which is inscribed: 'Water Colour Sketches By George Heriot, Deputy Postmaster-General of British North America From 1799 to 1816'
1r	"containing 43 different drawings"
1v	blank
2r	blank
*2v	study of trees. Figure 9
3r	study of trees
3v–4r	"View from the N.E. summit of Shooter's Hill. 1787."
4v–5r	"View of Belvidere &c: from the River. 1787."
5v–6r	"View of Woolwich from Mr. Bowater's Fields." "1787"
6v–7r	"View of House in Vanburgh Fields with the Observatory. 1789"
7v	"Sir Gregory Page Turner's House on Blackheath. 1787"
8r–8v	missing
9r	blank
9v–10r	"View of Plumstead Church &c. 1787."
10v–11r	shipping
11v–12r	"View from the Warren at Woolwich. 1787."
12v–13r	shipping
13v	"Wycomb Valley. 1788."
14r–15v	missing
16r	"View of Peeveley Point &c from the Channel. 1787."
16v–17r	"Isle of Wight./1787."
17v–18r	"View of S. Yarmouth, the Needles/&c. from the Straits between Hampshire & the Isle of Wight. 1787."
18v–19r	"View of Cowes in the Isle of Wight, from the Straits. 1787."
19v–20r	"View of Luttrells Folly, and Calshot Castle from the Straits. 1787."
20v–21r	"View of Erith, Belvidere &c. from the River. 1788"
21v–22r	"View of Purfleet from the River. 1788."
22v–23r	"View of Purfleet, Erith, Belvidere &c. from the Top of the Chalky Cliffs. 1788"
23v–24r	"Battersea Bridge. 1787."
24v–25r	"Greenwich Observatory. 1787."
25v	"Greenwich Park. 1787."
26r–26v	missing
27r	View at Greenwich (?)
27v	"Farmer Davey"
28r	"Ale House in Plumstead. 1788."
28v–29r	"Sand Pits near Woolwich. 1788."
29v–30r	"Part of Woolwich 1788."
*30v–31r	"Fox and Hounds, Ale House Woolwich 1788." Figure 72

31v	blank
32r	"View on the Road near Greenwich. 1788."
*32v–33r	"View from one of Bowater's Fields. 1788." Figure 8
33v–34r	"View from Plumstead-Common. 1788."
34v–35r	"View from Martin's Sand Pits near Woolwich. 1788."
35v–36r	"View of Shooter's Hill from Blackheath. 1788./View on Blackheath 1788."
36v	"Windmill &c from near the New Barracks at Woolwich. 1788."
37r	"Publick House on Blackheath. 1788."
37v–38r	"View from the Gravel Pit near Dartmouth Row. Blackheath. 1788."
38v	blank
39r	blank
39v	faint outline of shoreline with cliffs
inside back cover	faint outline of shoreline with cliffs

334 *England and Canada Sketch-Book*, c 1797, 1810, 1816
Pencil, pen, and watercolour, approximate page size 113 × 195 mm.
J.C.A. Heriot, Esq.: McCord Museum, Montreal, 1928, M 6357; G.H. cat. 29
A brown leather-bound book

inside cover — "136 English and American Sketches"; stencilled silhouette of G. Heriot; book-plate inscribed 'John Charles Alison Heriot'

1r — "CARMEN. COLUMB.

1
Virum quae causa impulit audacem,
Rate transire fines Atlanticos
Et viam persequere intentatam, in
Mare patenti?

2
An desiderium tentare novas
Res inquietum quod regit spiritum?
An amor Gloria ardens? aut sordidus
Auri Cupido?

3
Hunc nec venti truces nec furiosae
Flexerunt aquae, non indignantes
Socii, speratam, neque dira fames
Linquere metam.

4
Cum per incertam nebulam erupi[t]
Tellus, et novam patefecit formam
Quo tibi gaudio calebat pectus,
Magne Columbe!

GH. 1810"

[ODE TO COLUMBUS
What purpose drove the daring man
to cross the bounds of the Atlantic
in his ship and follow an untried
road to its end on the open sea?

Was it longing for new experiences
that ruled his restless soul? Or burning
love of Glory? Or sordid
passion for gold?

Neither fierce winds nor raging
waters bent him, nor
grumbling comrades, nor dire
hunger, to abandon his hoped-
for goal.

When the land burst out
through concealing mist
and revealed its new
outline, what joy warmed your
heart, Great Columbus!]

1v	"Peverel Point/Yarmouth"; "Isle of Wight"
2r	"Christ Church/Isle of Wight./Calshot Castle"
2v–3r	"Curvas, Isle of Wight/Luttrell's folly &c./Erith, Kent."
3v–4r	"Margate, [... ?] &c/King's Gate &c./Dover Castle &c."
4v–5r	"Borry Head, Torbay"; "Isle of Wight/Isle of Portland./ Brixham"
5v–6r	"Torbay &c./coast near Plymouth./Dartmouth/coast near Plymouth"
6v–7r	"South west view of St Miguel, Azores." "NE. View of St Miguel, Azores"
7v–8r	"Pico Azores./St. Miguel continued [from 7r]"
8v–9r	"Cape Raye N.E. &c by E. 8 leagues/Cape Gaspé looking down./Cape Chatte"; "Cape Gaspé. N.W. 2 leagues./ Cape Rosier./Tortuga [Turtiggo River]."
9v–10r	"Mont Camille; looking up/Cape Orignal." "Mont Camille & St Barnaby's Island./Green Island"
10v–11r	"Mountains near Camouraska./Crane Island." "Hare Island & Brandy Pots/L'Islette./Crane Island."
11v–12r	"Cape Tourment"; "Cape Tourment Isle Madame/Cape Tourment/Island of Orleans &c. from the S. Shore"
12v–13r	"View from S. Shore of St Lawrence./Les Eboulements."
13v–14r	"General Hospital, Quebec &c./Cape Diamond &c."
14v–15r	"St Augustin &c from Cape Rouge/Cape Diamond &c."
15v	"Cape Diamond."

16r	"View of the St Charles/& Charlesburgh &c from Quebec"
16v	"Cape Santé"
17r–17v	missing
18r	"Montreal from St Helens"
18v	"Plumstead – Kent"
19r	"Plumstead – Kent" Ale House
*19v	"Fox and Hounds near Woolwich". Figure 71
20r	"Greenwich"
20v	blank
21r	oak tree with house
21v	"Fluv. Jacart. Descrip."

"AD FLUVIUM IACARTINUM

1.

Angustos inter scopulos repressus
Rivum vexatas fundit per asperum
Undas, et atras fluctibus proruptis
Lambit speluncas.

2.

Per Saxa, per agros, strepitu fremente
Tortilem agit cursum, et umbrosa
Nemora sonant, dum Laurentem petit
Ore spumante.
Geo Heriot 1810"

[TO THE JACQUES CARTIER RIVER
Confined between narrow crags, it
pours churning waters along its
rough stream and licks gloomy
caves with rushing billows.

Through rocks, through fields
it pursues its twisting course
with crashing din, and the shady
woods echo as it seeks the
St Lawrence with its foaming mouth.]

"Jacques Quartier bridge"

22r	view of the remains of a bridge on the Jacques Cartier River
22v	blank
23r	"Montmorenci"
23v	"Near Quebec"
24r	"Jacques Cartier"

24v	"Upper Canada."
*25r	"Chippawas." Figure 69
25v	"The Clyde"
26r	"The Clyde 1816"
26v	"Estuary of the Clyde."
27r	"The Clyde"
27v	"Greenwich Park"
28r	"Powick [?] Castle Glamorgan. Built by Sir Reece [?] M[... ?]"
28v	three men and trees
29r	landscape with windmill
29v	"Greenwich"
30r	"Battersea"
30v	"Chelsea."
31r	"Plumstead."
31v	"Black Heath"
32r	"Woolwich"
32v	"Black Heath"
33r	"Purfleet"
33v	trees, three cattle, and cottage
34r	trees with ruin
34v	trees with two cattle
35r	trees with three cattle and ruin
35v	trees with three cattle
36r	two tree clumps
36v	trees with building to left and three cattle to right
37r	trees and seven cattle
37v	trees
38r	trees with two figures to right
38v	trees with ruin
39r	two trees
39v	tree with farm buildings
40r	tree
40v	trees with ruin
41r	"The Clyde"
41v	tree
42r	"The Clyde"
42v	tree
43r	tree
43v	tree
44r	"The Clyde"
44v	trees
45r	"The Clyde."
45v	two trees
46r	tree clumps with two figures

46v	two tree clumps
47r	two tree clumps
47v	two tree clumps
48r	two tree clumps with six figures
48v	trees
49r	trees
49v	trees
50r	trees
50v	trees
51r	trees
51v	trees
52r	trees
52v	trees
53r	"Joseph Brandt's on the Ouse"
53v	trees
54r	trees
54v	landscape with figures and tower to right
55r	"Teignmouth Castle."
55v	"River des Loups Canada"
*56r	"Twisel on the Till." Figure 74
56v–57r	"River S[t] Charles/Quebec"
57v	waterfall
58r	trees
58v	trees
59r	trees
59v	landscape with fir trees and figures to right
*60r	"Jersey"; Mont Orgueil Castle from the seaside near Gouray; see **350**. Figure 75
60v	landscape with distant ruin and setting sun
61r	landscape with ruin and setting sun
61v	landscape
62r	"Montmorenci"
62v	another, similar view of the falls of Montmorency
*63r	"Montmorenci." Figure 70
63v–64r	"Montmorenci 1816"
64v	English landscape
65r	"Dover Castle. 1816"
65v	"Castle of Canterbury"
66r	"Canterbury"
66v	"Canterbury 1816."
67r	"Canterbury. 1816"
67v	"Canterbury."
68r–68v	missing
69r	"Powderham Castle"
69v	"Mr Angerstein's Villa – Blackheath"
70r	"Chastleton."

70v "Lee[... ?] Blackheath"

71r landscape with cottage and cows

71v London from Greenwich (?)

inside back cover 'McCord – No. 3B' (in pencil in recent hand)

335 *American Sketch-Book* I, 1815

Pencil and watercolour, approximate page size, 105 × 201 mm.

Stiles Stevens, Esq.; New York Historical Society, New York 1944, 1944.430 B

A brown leather-covered book

inner cover "46 Sketches in America, by George Heriot Esq D Postmaster General Brit. America/Taken in 1815.' Stencilled silhouette of G. Heriot in brown-grey wash

1r "Montmorenci"

1v blank

2r "St Charles river Chambly. 5 June 1815"

2v blank

3r "Chambly Castle 6 June 1815."

3v blank

4r "Bellieul [? Beloeil] 6 June 1815 1350 french feet in height."

4v blank

5r "Ile and Noire [? Isle-aux-Noix] 7 June 1815"

5v blank

6r "McNeals/Lake Champlain 1815. 8 June"

6v blank

7r "View near McNeal's – Vermont 9 June 1815"

7v landscape with cabins

8r "Burlington 9th June."

8v blank

9r "Middlebury. Vermont 10 June 1815"

9v "Sutherland's Falls./10 June 1815."

*10r sketch of location indicated on fol 9v. Figure 63

10v "Sutherland Falls/11th June 1815"

11r sketch of location indicated on fol 10v

11v "Sutherland's falls–/11 June 1815"

12r sketch of location indicated on fol 11v

12v "Fall near Rutland on/the Otter Creek or River 11 June"

13r sketch of location indicated on fol 12v

13v "From the Battery, New York/22^{d}. June 1815"

14r four views of New York indicated on fol 13v

14v "View from the Permanent Bridge/on the Schuilkill 25 June 1815"

15r sketch of location indicated on fol 14v

15v "View of Philadelphia from Camden on the/opposite side of the Delaware 27 June 1815./Wind Mill Island."

16r view described on fol 15v

16v "Philadelphia from Camden 27 June 1815."

17r	three views of location indicated on fol 16v
17v	"Camden 27th June 1815"
18r	views of location indicated on fol 17v
18v	"375 feet long./123 feet wide. 99 ft long each wing./Capitol at Washington/30th June 1815."
19r	sketch of location indicated on fol 18v
19v	architectural detail; "Capitol at Washington 30th. June 1815"
20r	sketch of location indicated on fol 19v
20v	"Mount Vernon 2 July"
21r	sketch of location indicated on fol 20v
21v	"Bridge at George Town 2d July 1815."
22r	sketch of location indicated on fol 21v
22v	"Palace of the President 1st. July 1815/150 feet long./80 ft wide"
*23r	sketch of location indicated on fol 22v; another view of Washington. Figure 65
23v	"Treasury Chambers, Washington 1st July 1815"
24r	view of location indicated on fol 23v; the building is shown in ruin
24v	"View from the Banks of the Schuylkill 7 July 1815"
25r	sketch of location indicated on fol 24v
25v	"View up the Schuylkill about two miles/higher than the wire Manufactory at Bridge of/chains. 7th. July 1815."
26r	sketch of location indicated on fol 25v
26v	"View of the Wire manufactory and Chain Bridge on the Schuykill. 7 July 1815"
27r	sketch of location indicated on fol 26v
27v	"Waterworks at the Schuylkill 7 July 1815"
28r	sketch of location indicated on fol 27v
28v	"View up the Schuylkill from the Waterworks./7th July 1815."
29r	sketch of location indicated on fol 28v
29v	"View of Woodlands the seat of Mr Hamilton/3 miles from Philadelphia 9th. July 1815"
30r	sketch of location indicated on fol 29v
30v	"View from Woodlands. 9 July 1815."
31r	sketch of location indicated on fol 30v
31v	"View of New Brunswick in Jersey. 11th July 1815."
32r	sketch of location indicated on fol 31v
32v	"View of New York from Brooklyn – Long Island/14th. July 1815."
33r	sketch of location indicated on fol 32v
33v	"View of New York from Brooklyn–/Long Island 14 July 1815"
34r	sketch of location indicated on fol 33v
34v	"Passaic Falls – 16th. July 1815/O'er rugged cliffs his rapid current pours,/Throwing through gloomy chasms his silver

	showers;/Like a coy fair, whose beauties, half conceal'd,/ Impart a lustre to the charms reveal'd./G.H."
35r	view of location indicated on fol 34v
35v	"Passaic Falls. 16 July 1815"
36r	sketch of location indicated on fol 35v
36v	"Passaic Falls – 16th July 1815."
37r	sketch of location indicated on fol 36v
37v	"View down the Passaic from the Cliff/near the Falls. 16 July 1815. New Jersey, with/part of Patterson N.J. on the Passaic river. In this village are 13 Cotton spinning esta/ blishments with about 17,000 spindles, employing between 160 and 70 men, 50 to/60 women, and 600 children in the spinning departments; also a great/number occupied in weaving. There are about 5 Tons of yarn spun/weekly, and in capital supposed to amount to 1,000,000 dollars engaged/ in the manufacturing branch at this place. The above, with the addition/of two or three other establishments, gives employment and support to about/two thousand inhabitants; a great number of them are poor, and dependent/on the prosperity of the establishment for support. Many families are en- [continued on fol 38v]"
38r	sketch of location indicated on fol 37v
38v	"[continued from 37v]-tirely supported through the medium of their children's wages./Top of the Passaic Falls – 16th July 1815."
39r	sketch of location indicated on fol 38v
39v	"Vendidiky Hook. Pallisade Rocks. 18 July 1815"
40r	"New York from the North River."
40v	"New York – 18 July 1815/View of the City of New Jersey 17 July."
41r	sketches of locations indicated on fol 40v
41v–42r	"Pallisade Rocks – 18 July 1815."
42v	"Tappeau [?Tappan] Hook the Village where Major [John] André was executed."
43r	"Opposite to Dobb's Ferry. 18 July./Territon [?Tarrytown] where Major André was taken. 18 July."
43v	pencil sketch of a mammoth's skull
44r	pen sketch of a reading chair
44v	inscribed in pencil in a later hand: 'Henry Stevens Son T Stiles'
outside cover	blank

336 *American Sketch-Book* II, 1815
Pencil and watercolour, approximate page size, 104 × 201 mm.
Stiles Stevens, Esq.; New York Historical Society, New York, 1944, 1944.430 A
A brown leather-covered book

inner cover	"55 Sketches (by George Heriot Esq[r] D. Postmaster General. Brit. America/in the United States 1815 [)]."; stencilled silhouette of G. Heriot in brown wash; inscr. in a later hand in pencil: 'These are mostly very rough.'
1r	"Hudson's River N. York July, 18th"
1v	"61 Sketches in the United States of America./Taken in 1815./Hudson's river./Looking down the river towards/West Point. 19 July 1815"
2r	view of location indicated on fol 1v
2v	"Verplank's./Stony Point 18 July. 1815."
3r	sketches of places indicated on fol 2v
3v	"Stony Point looking down./Caldwell's Ferry 18 July/Pease Kiln [?Peekskill]
4r	sketches of locations indicated on fol 3v
4v	"Anthony's Nose. up the riv[er]"
5r	"Anthony's Nose 18 July 1815/looking down."
5v	"looking up towards West Point."
6r	"Fort Montgomery 18 July 1815"
6v	on the Hudson River
7r	"Anthony's Nose 18 July 1815. Looking up."
7v	"Looking up the River near Buttermilk Falls/18 July"
8r	"Buttermilk Falls. 18 July"
8v	"Looking down the river 18th. July 1815"
9r	"West Point/Fort Putnam"; "Fort Clinton"
9v	"Capt. Phillips W. Point 18 July."
*10r	"West Point 18 July." Figure 66
10v–11r	"Looking up the River 18 July"
11v–12r	"West Point looking down the river. 18 July."
12v–13r	"Looking down the river to W. Point 18 July"
13v–14r	"Looking down to West Point."
14v–15r	"Part of Newbing [?Newburg]. 18 July 1815 down."; "Poughkepsie, looking down."
15v–16r	"Poughkepsie 19 July."
16v –17r	"Poughkepsie 19 July."
17v–18r	"Poughkepsie/19 July."
18v–19r	"Landing at [... ?]/Hudson. 20 July 1815"; "Town of Hudson, from 2 miles above it."
19v	"Looking down the North river 20 July"
20r	"Mr Livingston's"; "Red [?] Hook – looking down/Catskill 20 July. looking down."
20v	"View from the Bridge at the Cohoe falls. Mt Ida./21st July 1815 Mowhawk River."
21r	"Mowhawk River. Cohoe falls 21st July 1815"
21v	blank
22r	"Cohoe falls from the Bridge/21st July 1815."
22v	study of trees "22 July"

23r	"22 July/Albany./Buttermilk Falls/22^d July"
23v–24r	"View near Albany 22 July 1815." "View near Albany 22^d July 1815"
24v	"Ballston 24 July. [... ?] of the Hotel 157 feet long. 150 Bed Chambers."
25r	"Palmerston Lake, Saratoga/25 July"
25v–26r	"Lake Palmerston, Saratoga. 25 July."
26v	[... ?] Glens Falls
27r	Glens Falls
27v–28r	"Glens Falls./25 July 1815"
28v	"Lake Champlain 29 July./Lake George 26 July"
29r	Lake George
29v	"Lake George 26 July"
30r	view of location indicated on fol 29v
30v–31r	"Lake George 26 July"
31v–32r	"Fort George/Fort George 26 July"; "Panorama Lake George/26 July"
32v–33r	"Panorama View of Lake George 26 July 1815."
33v–34r	"Caldwell – Lake George/26 July 1815."
34v–35r	"27 July. Lake George"; "Lake George 27 July."
35v–36r	"[... ?] 27 July"
*36v–37r	"Lake George." "Lake George 27 July." Figure 67
37v–38r	"Lake George. 27 July 1815"
38v–39r	"Lake George"
39v–40r	"Buck Mountain/[?&] Sabbatic Point [Lake George]"; "27 July 1815."
40v–41r	"View from Sabbatic Pt/27 July 1815"
41v–42r	"Sabbatic Point &c. looking up Lake George. 27 July." "Monirice [?] Point. L. Champlain. 28 July."
42v	"Falls half mile from Ticonderoga 28 July"
43r	"Crown Point 29 July/Lake Champlain 29th July 1815."
43v–44r	"South West View of Lake Champlain 29 July 1815"
44v	inscr. in pencil in a later hand: 'Henry Stevens' Son T Stiles'
back cover	blank

337 *Italian Journey Sketch-Book*, 1817–18
Pencil and watercolour, approximate page size, 108 × 197 mm.
Private collection; G.H. cat. 118
A green leather-bound book inscribed on cover with "Nr 7." Inside cover contains autogr. inscr.: "89 Foreign Sketches drawn in 1817 and beginning of 1818." The sketch-book includes views of Naples, Salerno, Florence, Pisa, Venice, Genoa, Padua; it also contains views in Austria.

PRINTS

Because plate lines are often missing, only the image measurements are provided.

Picturesque views on Guernsey and Jersey, Channel Islands

These newly discovered prints of Guernsey and Jersey (the first is of Guernsey, the remainder of Jersey) are the first indication of Heriot's personal experiments in print-making. Fortunately a number of these etchings (for that is what they are) have been signed and dated by him, either 1789 or 1790. They are not 'etchings' in the full sense of the term, but etched outlines to which watercolour has been added (Heriot followed a practice fairly common among artists of his day). Paul Sandby, Heriot's mentor at Woolwich, may have taught him etching, since Sandby had perfected several etching processes, particularly aquatint, a method that was subsequently to be widely used in Britain. Indeed we now have evidence that Heriot practised the process of aquatint when he came to Canada, and he used the method for the reproduction of his watercolours for his two travel books, *Travels through the Canadas* (1807) and *Picturesque Tour ... through the Pyrenean Mountains* (1824), though the plates for these books were not etched by Heriot himself. I am grateful to the members of the Société Jersiaise, who sent me the measurements of the prints of Channel Island subjects in the collection of the Société, and to Mrs P. James of the Société, who informed me that its 'Book of Dons' records a gift from Mlle A.H. de Ste Croix in 1916 of 'Dessins coloriés de vues de Jersey exécutés par George Heriot.'

338 *Castle Cornet, taken from the Road at Guernsey.*
Etched outline with watercolour, 176 × 257 mm. R: autogr. inscr. l.c. margin as title
Société Jersiaise, 120/65/12

339 *East View of St Brelade's Church*
Etched outline with watercolour, 168 × 246 mm. R: autogr. inscr. l.c. margin as title
Société Jersiaise, 1916, 120/66/5
Water damaged

340 A *South West View of the Hermitage, the Town of St Helier. &c. Jersey*
Etched outline with watercolour, 168 × 248 mm. R: autogr. inscr. l.c. margin as title; sign. l.l margin: *G. Heriot delin[t]. et fecit.*
Société Jersiaise, 1916, 120/55/9

340 B *S:W: View of the Hermitage with the Town of S[t]. Helier*
R: autogr. inscr. l.c. margin as title
Société Jersiaise, 1916, 120/79/4

340 C *South West View of the Hermitage with the Town of S[t]. Helier in the Distance*
R: autogr. inscr. l.c. margin as title; sign. l.l. margin: *G. Heriot delin[t] et fecit.*; l.r. margin: *Published as the Act directs Jany 1790*
Private collection

341 A *View in S^{t}. Peter's Valley, Jersey.*
Etched outline with watercolour, 167 × 243 mm. R: autogr. inscr. l.c. margin as title; sign. l.l. margin: *G. Heriot delin^{t} et fecit.*
Société Jersiaise, 1916, 120/66/3

341 B *View in S^{t}. Peter's Valley.*
R: autogr. inscr. l.c. margin as title
Société Jersiaise, 1916, 120/67/2

342 *North View of the Town of S^{t}. Aubin.*
Etched outline with watercolour, 181 × 257 mm. R: autogr. inscr. l.c. margin as title
Société Jersiaise, 1916, 120/65/13

*343 A *View near the Town Mills. Jersey.* Figure 12
Etched outline with watercolour, 179 × 260 mm. R: autogr. inscr. l.c. margin as title; sign. l.l. margin: *Geo: Heriot delin^{t}. et fecit.*
Société Jersiaise, 1916, 120/65/7
Exh: G.H. cat. 36

343 B *View near the Town Mills, Jersey*
R: autogr. inscr. l.c. margin as title
Société Jersiaise, 1916, 120/68/1

343 C Title as above
R: autogr. inscr. l.c. mount as title; sign. l.l. margin; *Geo: Heriot delint et fecit*; autogr. inscr. l.r. margin: *Published as the Act directs 1st April 1790*
Private collection

344 A *North East View of the Town of St Helier, Jersey, taken from near St Saviour's Church, Jersey*
Etched outline with watercolour, 170 × 246 mm. R: autogr. inscr. l.c. margin as title; sign. l.l.: *G. Heriot delint et fecit*
Société Jersiaise, 1916, 120/57/3

344 B *N.E. View of the Town of St. Helier from near S^{t}. Saviour's Church*
R: autogr. inscr. l.c. margin as title
Société Jersiaise, 1916, 120/79/2

345 A *South West View of Elizabeth Castle and S^{t}. Helier's Bay, from les Rochés fendues. Jersey.*
Etched outline with watercolour, 168 × 243 mm. R: autogr. inscr. l.c. margin as title; sign. l.l. margin: *Geo: Heriot delin^{t}. et fecit*
Société Jersiaise, 1916, 120/68/4

345 B *S:W: View of Elizabeth Castle and S^{t}. Helier's Bay, from Les Roches fendues*
R: autogr. inscr. l.c. margin as title
Société Jersiaise, 1916, 120/79/5

346 A *North West View of Elizabeth Castle, Jersey.*
Etched outline with watercolour, 167 × 241 mm. R: autogr. inscr. l.c. margin as title; sign. l.l. margin: *G. Heriot delin^{t}. et fecit.*
Société Jersiaise, 1916, 120/65/6

346 B *North West View of Elizabeth Castle, Jersey.*
R: autogr. inscr. l.c. margin as title; sign. l.r.: *Geo: Heriot fecit. 1789*
Société Jersiaise, 1916 120/66/8

The Witt Library, Courtauld Institute of Art, London, possesses a magazine cutting illustrating this print with the inscription: 'Elizabeth Castle (G. Heriot) 1789.'

347 A *View of the Chapel at Havre des Pas [Jersey] 1789.*
Etched outline with watercolour, 178 × 256 mm. R: autogr. inscr. l.r. margin as title
Société Jersiaise, 1916, 120/68/5
Exh: G.H. Cat. 35
Dark border added to bottom of impression

347 B *View of the Chapel and Havre de Pas.*
R: autogr. inscr. l.c. margin as title (to which has been added: *Jersey.* in the artist's hand); sign. l.l. margin: *Geo: Heriot delint et fecit.*
Société Jersiaise, 1916, 120/68/7

347 C Title as above
R: autogr. inscr. l.c. as title; l.l. margin: *Geo Heriot delint. et fecit*; l.r. margin: *Published as the Act directs 1st April 1790*
Private collection

347 D Title as above
Without colour; R: autogr. inscr. as title (to which has been added: *Jersey.* in the artist's hand); l.l. margin: *Geo Heriot delint. et fecit.*
Société Jersiaise, 1916, 35/80/1

***348** A *North East View of the Temple of the Druids on St. Helier's Hill, Jersey.* Figure 13
Etched outline with watercolour, 170 × 245 mm. R: autogr. inscr. l.c. margin as title
Société Jersiaise, 1916, 120/68/8
See **196**.

348 B *N:E: View of the Druid's Temple in the summit of the Town Hill.*
R: autogr. inscr. l.c. margin as title
Société Jersiaise, 1916, 120/67/1

348 C *North East View of the Temple of the Druids on the Town Hill Jersey*
R: autogr. inscr. l.c. margin as title; sign. l.l. margin: *Geo Heriot delint. et fecit*; autogr. inscr. l.r. margin: *Published as the Act directs 1st Decr 1789*
Private collection

348 D *View of a Druid's Temple in the Island of Jersey*
R: etched title in capitals as above, by Heriot; plate reworked with additional etched lines and with aquatint; printed in sepia ink
McCord Museum, Montreal
Lit: M. Allodi, *Printmaking in Canada* (1980), no. 3
This reworked plate was published in the *Quebec Magazine* (Nov. 1792), and was described as 'an elegant and correct representation, taken upon the spot by a Gentleman at present in this City.'

349 A *View in the Valley near St. Saviour's Church.*
Etched outline with watercolour, 168 × 246 mm. R: autogr. inscr. l.c. margin as title; sign. l.r. margin: *Geo: Heriot fecit 1789.*
Société Jersiaise, 1916, 120/66/10

349 B *View in the Valley near S[t]. Saviour's Church, Jersey.*
R: autogr. inscr. l.c. margin as title; sign. l.l. margin: *G. Heriot delin[t]. et fecit.*
Société Jersiaise, 1916, 120/66/1
Exh: G.H. cat. 30 (ill.)

***350** A *S.W. View of Mont Orgueil Castle, from the sea side near Gouray.* Figure 11
Etched outline with watercolour, 176 × 252 mm. R: autogr. inscr. l.c. margin as title
Société Jersiaise, 1916, 120/66/11
See **334**, 60r.

350 B *South West View of Mont Orgueil Castle from the Side of Grouville Bay, Jersey.*
R: autogr. inscr. l.c. margin as title; sign. l.l. margin: *G. Heriot delin[t]. et fecit.*
Société Jersiaise, 1916, 120/65/8

351 A *North View of Mont Orgueil Castle, Jersey.*
Etched outline with watercolour, 167 × 246 mm. R: autogr. inscr. l.c. margin as title; sign. l.l. margin: *G. Heriot delint. et fecit.*
Société Jersiaise, 1916, 120/65/10
Exh: G.H. cat. 32
See **197**.

351 B *North View of Mont Orgueil Castle.*
R: autogr. inscr. l.c. margin as title
Société Jersiaise, 1916, 120/66/4

352 *West View of Mont Orgueil Castle, Seymour Tower &c.*
Etched outline with watercolour, 170 × 244 mm. R: autogr. inscr. l.c. margin as title
Société Jersiaise, 1916, 120/65/11
Exh: G.H. cat. 34

353 A *East View of Mont Orgueil Castle, from the Rocks beneath it, Jersey.*
Etched outline with watercolour, 170 × 243 mm. R: autogr. inscr. l.c. margin as title; sign. l.l. margin: *G. Heriot delin[t]. et fecit.*
Société Jersiaise, 1916, 120/65/9
Exh: G.H. cat. 33

353 B *East View of Mount Orgueil Castle.*
R: autogr. inscr. l.c. margin as title
Société Jersiaise, 1916, 120/66/6

354 A *West View of the Town of St Helier, the Hill & Harbour, Jersey.*
Etched outlined with watercolour, 170 × 243 mm. R: autogr. inscr. l.c. margin as title; sign. l.l. margin: *G. Heriot delint. et fecit.*
Société Jersiaise, 1916, 120/51/1

354 B *West View of the Town of St Helier with the Hill & part of the Harbour.*
R: autogr. inscr. l.c. margin as title; sign. l.r.: *G: Heriot*
Société Jersiaise, 1916, 120/79/1

355 A *E: View of the Bay of S[t]. Helier, Elizabeth Castle & the Town Hill from Samarez.*
Etched outline with watercolour, 178 × 255 mm. R: autogr. inscr. l.c. margin as title; sign. l.r. margin: *Geo: Heriot fecit 1789*; l.r. on impression: *G:H:*
Société Jersiaise, 1916, 120/66/12

355 B *East View of the Bay of St Helier, Elizabeth Castle &c. from the Heights near Samarez, Jersey.*
R: autogr. inscr. l.c. margin as title; sign. l.l. margin: *G. Heriot delin^t. et fecit.*
Société Jersiaise, 1916, 120/65/4

356 A *View taken from the Moulin de Pot, Jersey*
Etched outline with watercolour, 170 × 249 mm. R: autogr. inscr. l.c. margin as title
Société Jersiaise, 1916, 120/66/7
Exh: G.H. cat. 31
Black surround

356 B *View taken from the Moulins Pois, Jersey.*
R: autogr. inscr. l.c. margin as title; sign. l.l. margin: *G. Heriot delint. et fecit*
Société Jersiaise, 1916, 120/66/2

Additional prints

357 *City of Quebec taken from Point Levi*
Etching and aquatint, 157 × 236 mm.
Public Archives of Canada, Ottawa
Lit: Allodi, *Printmaking in Canada* (1980), 4 (ill.)
This print, which is based on the watercolour of this title (**17**), probably dates from c 1793.

358 *View of Madrid*
Etched outline with watercolour, 114 × 813 mm.
Private collection
This print is probably datable to c 1820.

PLATES

In this section are listed engravings after Heriot's watercolours published in *Travels through the Canadas* (1807) and *A Picturesque Tour ... through the Pyrenean Mountains* (1824), plus impressions of four additional plates. None of the following plates was etched or engraved by Heriot. Each entry includes the title, the image size of the plate, and the name of the engraver of the plate.

359 *Travels through the Canadas* (1807)
The technique used on the plates is aquatint except where otherwise described.
These are perhaps the most familiar prints after Heriot's work. However, it is not generally known that some volumes of the *Travels* lack plates altogether, that plates were sometimes bound separately, and that complete sets of unfolded plates were printed on large sheets (mainly two impressions to a page) and issued in a folio. Beautifully coloured by hand, these latter impressions undoubtedly reflect the colour schemes established for the prints by Heriot; indeed, at least some of these sets may have

been coloured by the artist himself. (A set of impressions of these plates printed on large (495 × 330 mm.) sheets is in the colleciton of the Public Archives of Canada, Ottawa (1932), IIB). After examining engraved impressions in the original (1807) edition of the *Travels* I noted some discrepancies in sizes between the same design printed in two different copies of the work, indicating that fresh plates were prepared during the production of the book. The following image measurements were taken from one copy of the *Travels*.

1 *View of Quebec (taken from Point Levi).* 230 × 498 mm. J.C. Stadler
2 *S.W. View of St. Michael, One of the Azores/ E. End of the Island of St. Michael/ S.W. View of Pico.* 182 × 306 mm. F.C. Lewis
3 *View at St Paul's Bay on the River St Lawrence.* 134 × 187 mm. F.C. Lewis
4 *Quebec from Cape Diamond.* 136 × 183 mm. F.C. Lewis
5 *View of Quebec, from the Distillery at Beauport.* 134 × 185 mm. F.C. Lewis
6 *Fall of Montmorenci (246 Feet High).* 133 × 182 mm. F.C. Lewis
7 *Fall of Montmorenci in Winter.* 145 × 207 mm. F.C. Lewis
8 *View of Jeune Lorette, the Village of the Huron's, nine Miles North of Quebec.* 135 × 181 mm. F.C. Lewis
9 *View of the Falls of Chaudiere, nine Miles West of Quebec.* 133 × 181 mm. F.C. Lewis
10 *View of the Lower Fall of La Puce.* 133 × 188 mm. Hassel [? J. Hassell]
11 *Fall of La Puce (taken from the Eastern Bank).* 135 × 178 mm. F.C. Lewis
12 *Ruins of the Chateau Richer, with Cape Tourment.* 132 × 185 mm. F.C. Lewis
13 *View on the Upper Lake St Charles near Quebec.* 131 × 186 mm. [W.] Cartwright
14 *View on the River Etchemin, near Quebec.* 131 × 182 mm. F.C. Lewis
15 *New Bridge, on the River Jacques Cartier.* 132 × 182 mm. F.C. Lewis
16 *City of Montreal (taken from the Mountain).* 135 × 186 mm. [W.] Cartwright
17 *Cascades of the St. Lawrence.* 134 × 182 mm. F.C. Lewis
18 *British Fort at Niagara (taken from the East Bank of the St Lawrence).* 133 × 181 mm. F.C. Lewis
19 *The Whirlpool, of the St Lawrence.* 136 × 182 mm. F.C. Lewis
20 *View of the Falls of Niagara, from the bank near Birche's Mills.* 134 × 182 mm. F.C. Lewis
21 *View of the Falls of Niagara, from beneath the bank of the Fort Slausser side.* 131 × 184 mm. F.C. Lewis
22 *Fall of the Grande Chaudiere, on the Outaouais River.* 135 × 188 mm.
23 *La Danse Ronde, Circular Dance of the Canadians.* 228 × 366 mm. J.C. Stadler
24 *Minuets of the Canadians.* 226 × 360 mm. J.C. Stadler
25 *Encampment of Domiciliated Indians.* 225 × 374 mm. F.C. Lewis
26 *Costume of Domiciliated Indians of North America.* 172 × 299 mm. J.C. Stadler

27 *Moose Deer of North America (17 Hands High).* Line engraving, 190 × 250 mm. Warner

360 *A Picturesque Tour ... through the Pyrenean Mountains* (1824)
The technique used on the plates is aquatint. The (image) measurements were taken from one copy of this work.
Only two numbers of this work were issued.
1 *Rouen.* 107 × 173 mm. F.C. Lewis
2 *Caen.* 109 × 172 mm. F.C. Lewis
3 *Le Mans.* 105 × 169 mm. W. Read
4 *Tours.* 105 × 166 mm. W. Read
5 *Poitiers.* 106 × 172 mm. W. Read
6 *Bordeaux.* 107 × 174 mm. F.C. Lewis
7 *L'Eglise Cathedrale de Bordeaux.* 114 × 175 mm. W. Read
8 *Le Palais Galien.* 120 × 179 mm. F.C. Lewis
9 *Chateau de Henri IV.* 110 × 190 mm. F.C. Lewis
10 *Montagnes des Eaux Bonnes.* 122 × 171 mm. W. Read
11 *Bergers et Bergères de Pyrénées.* 129 × 177 mm. W. Read
12 *Costume de Pau.* 117 × 174 mm. W. Read

361 *View of the City of Quebec, taken from the Rocks of Point Levi.*
312 × 496 mm. 'J.C. Stadler sculp^{t}.' (aquatint)
Published by E. Walker, no. 7 Cornhill, London, 'for the Proprietor at Quebec' (George Heriot), 'June 4th. 1805'
Public Archives of Canada, Ottawa, II-1d
See also chapter 5, n 13.

362 *View of the City of Quebec, taken from the North Banks of the Saint Charles.*
312 × 497 mm. 'J.C. Stadler sculp^{t}.' (aquatint)
Published by E. Walker, no. 7 Cornhill, London, 'for the Proprietor at Quebec' (George Heriot), 'June 4th. 1805'
Public Archives of Canada, Ottawa, II-28a
See also chapter 5, n 13

363 *Costume of Domiciliated Indians of North America*
178 × 293 mm. Busby (line engraving)
Published by Sherwood, Neely and Jones, 1810, London
Public Archives of Canada, Ottawa, 1975-1-1
Same design as **359** (26); see also chapter 5, n 17.

364 *Dance Preparatory to War, among the Indians of North America*
Line engraving, 155 × 233 mm.
Published by Sherwood, Neely and Jones, 1810, London
Agnes Etherington Art Centre, Queen's University, Kingston, CR 16-41
See also chapter 5, n 17.

Places Illustrated in Heriot's Works

This index refers the reader to entries in the check-list, not to text pages.

ENGLAND, IRELAND, SCOTLAND, AND WALES

EUROPE

UNITED STATES OF AMERICA

Subjects Illustrated in Heriot's Works

This index of subjects other than landscape in Heriot's works refers the reader to entries in the check-list, not to text pages.

Collections and Collectors of Heriot's Works

The index refers the reader to entries in the check-list, not to text pages.

CANADA

UNITED KINGDOM AND DEPENDENCIES

UNITED STATES OF AMERICA

General Index

In the entry for George Heriot in this index the check-list numbers of oil paintings, prints, and watercolours by Heriot, and of prints after his work, are shown in bold type.

This book

was designed by

ANTJE LINGNER

and was printed by

University of

Toronto

Press

www.ingramcontent.com/pod-product-compliance
Lightning Source LLC
LaVergne TN
LVHW090804070826
844660LV00022B/1078

* 9 7 8 1 4 8 7 5 9 8 5 4 9 *